WELSH AND SCOTTISH
NATIONALISM
A STUDY

WELSH AND SCOTTISH NATIONALISM

A STUDY

By

SIR REGINALD COUPLAND

K.C.M.G., C.I.E., M.A., F.B.A.

*Formerly Beit Professor of the History
of the British Empire and Fellow of
All Souls College, Oxford*

Foreword by
JACK SIMMONS

COLLINS
ST JAMES'S PLACE, LONDON
1954

PRINTED IN GREAT BRITAIN
COLLINS CLEAR-TYPE PRESS: LONDON AND GLASGOW

Contents

Contents

Foreword

Sir Reginald Coupland died on November 6, 1952. On the previous day he had left the typescript of this book with his publishers. A preliminary note is necessary to fix it in the sequence of his works and to explain some points that have arisen in preparing the text for the press.

This is not the place to attempt a biographical sketch of Coupland or a critical account of his work.[1] He was sixty-seven when he died, and he had published twelve substantial books—all of them in the last thirty years of his life—together with a number of minor studies. (A list of his works appears on p. xiii.) With the sole exception of *The War Speeches of William Pitt*, a selection edited by him in 1915, his books were all concerned with the history or the current politics of the British Empire and Commonwealth. His most important historical work dealt with Tropical Africa: above all, the two large volumes, published in 1938 and 1939, in which he related the history of East Africa and its contacts with Britain from the earliest times down to 1890. But history was never separated, in Coupland's mind, from the politics of the world he lived in; and he made important contributions to the discussion of contemporary problems, first as a member of the Royal Commission on Palestine in 1937 (for whose report he was largely responsible)

[1] Cf. *The Times*, November 7, 1952, and *Britain To-day*, February 1953, pp. 6-10.

and second by his war-time *Report on the Constitutional Problem in India.*

In view of his preoccupation with the British Empire overseas, it may seem strange that his last book should deal with nationalism in Wales and Scotland. But, placed in its proper setting, this book is really an outcome of much of his earlier work. His studies of the past, and of current problems, had been much concerned with nationalism: not the nationalisms that are most familiar to students of history in this country, those of Germany and Italy, of Eastern and South-Eastern Europe, but the nationalisms that have developed within the British Commonwealth itself.

He became interested first in the nationalism of British North America: the feelings and ideas of the conquered French Canadians, their attitude to the British government and to their new British neighbours after 1763. He discussed this topic at length in *The Quebec Act* (1925) and again in *The American Revolution and the British Empire* (1930). It led him on to a close study of the work of Lord Durham. The only direct consequence of that study was his abridged edition of the Durham Report; but he intended to return to it later with a book on the Radical Imperialists, which unhappily he did not live to undertake. His study of French-Canadian nationalism was not pursued in isolation. He was deeply interested also in the parallel problem presented by the Dutch South Africans. And then, in the 1930s, his attention came to be fixed on the nationalisms newly emerging within the Commonwealth: especially in Palestine, when it was under British mandate, and in India, but also in Ceylon and West Africa and the West Indies. What interested him most of all was the political problem of the multi-communal state, which he began to study some time before the sociologists had agreed to name it the ' plural society.'

In 1941-1945 his mind was entirely filled by the problems of government in the vast plural society of India. He was the first English writer to give full and serious attention to the idea of 'Pakistan,' which up to 1939 had been little more than an academic notion and was regarded even in 1943 as an unlikely and most undesirable method of solving the communal antagonism between Muslims and Hindus. When he had made his final contribution to the problem in *India: a Re-statement* (1945), he turned back again to the study of history. Looking at the swift changes coming over the position of Britain in the mid-1940s, and considering that he was now sixty and approaching the time of retirement from his Oxford chair, he determined to devote the remaining years of his life to a great *History of British Imperialism*, which should sum up the accumulated reading and experience and reflection of the past thirty years.

He made a start on this book, writing some chapters on the expansion of England under the Tudors and Stuarts. But they did not satisfy him—partly because in them he was working at second hand, his own close knowledge being of the nineteenth and twentieth centuries, partly perhaps because the subject seemed to him so remote from the modern world. He therefore laid them aside, in favour of an immediate discussion of one or two topics that appeared to him to need particularly full attention, out of scale with the rest, to be followed ultimately by the regular history of the whole subject, treated in due chronological order. The first and the greatest of these topics was nationalism.

At first he thought of devoting a single large volume to the subject. He might have achieved that feat of condensation if he had been dealing solely with Irish, Canadian, South African, and Indian nationalism; for he knew those subjects intimately, and he had thoroughly digested them. But before he could embark even upon the story of Ireland, he had to consider nationalism in Great Britain itself, the relations of Wales and Scotland with England. No adequate study of that subject had ever been written: he must therefore provide one for himself, as a necessary preliminary to the rest. Books always tended to grow under his hand as he worked. The more deeply he investigated this new subject, the more interesting and important it seemed to him. It soon became clear that nationalism in the British Commonwealth could not be treated satisfactorily in a single volume: a series of studies would be required, of which the first, devoted to Wales and Scotland, would make a book on its own.

While he was being pressed to this conclusion, Coupland's health was breaking down. His work went ahead more and more slowly and for a time, during a very serious illness, it had to be put by altogether. Though his recovery was never complete, he returned to the book again, and with a splendid tenacity of purpose he completed it. He was able to correct the typescript, leaving only some details to be filled in and minor adjustments to be made. But his death prevented him from putting the finishing touches to the book that would have been applied, according to his custom, in proof.

It has fallen to me, as his literary executor, to pass the book through the press. Beyond correcting a few trifling slips, and some errors in the spelling of place-names, I have not thought it right to alter anything that Coupland wrote. I have done my best to supply the references that were missing, or left incomplete. But I have not been able to go further. If he had lived, Coupland would certainly have asked a number of friends to read the proofs, wholly or in part, especially the friends he had made during his visits to Wales and Scotland, while the book was being prepared; and there is no doubt that he would have made some changes in it, as a result of his discussions with them. If Coupland had written a preface to the book, he would have specified in it the help he received from these friends. Unfortunately, it was his usual practice to destroy every letter he received immediately it was answered. I cannot therefore now trace their names. But I hope that those of them who read the book will recognise the contribution they made to it, and that they will feel assured that the kindness he received— at Harlech and Aberystwyth and Cardiff, for instance, at Edinburgh and Glasgow—was remembered and valued highly by him.

One further point needs explaining. The story is taken in detail down to the end of the second World War. Coupland was writing at a time when the situation was changing very rapidly, in Wales and still more in Scotland. He therefore added a four-page 'Post War Postscript' (pp. 407-411), in which he sketched the further course of events down to the appointment of the Scottish Royal Commission in July 1952. On the principle of adding nothing to Coupland's text, I have not attempted to bring this 'Postscript' up to date. It seemed best to leave the book exactly as its author left it. One day somebody will take up the story again, from a different point of view no doubt, and carry it on. Meanwhile, this account must be read in its context: as the first volume in a projected series of ' Studies of Nationalism in the British Commonwealth,' and as the last completed work of one of the most distinguished of British imperial historians.

J. S.

University College
Leicester
August 8, 1954

BIBLIOGRAPHY

The following is a list of Sir Reginald Coupland's published books:

The War Speeches of William Pitt the Younger. Oxford: Clarendon Press. 1915. 2nd edition, 1916. 3rd edition, 1940.

Wilberforce: a Narrative. Oxford: Clarendon Press. 1923. 2nd edition, Collins, 1945.

The Quebec Act: a Study in Statesmanship. Oxford: Clarendon Press. 1925.

Raffles: 1781-1826. Oxford University Press. 1926. 2nd edition, 1934. 3rd edition (as *Raffles of Singapore*), Collins, 1946.

Kirk on the Zambesi: a Chapter of African History. Oxford: Clarendon Press. 1928.

The American Revolution and the British Empire. Longmans. 1930.

The British Anti-Slavery Movement. Thornton Butterworth (Home University Library). 1933.

The Empire in these Days: an Interpretation. Macmillan. 1935.

East Africa and its Invaders. Oxford: Clarendon Press. 1938.

The Exploitation of East Africa. Faber & Faber. 1939.

Britain and India. Longmans. 1941.

Report on the Constitutional Problem in India. Oxford University Press. Published in three parts: *The Indian Problem: 1833-1935*, 1942; *Indian Politics: 1936-1942*, 1943; *The Future of India*, 1943.

The Cripps Mission. Oxford University Press. 1942.

India: a Re-statement. Oxford University Press. 1945.

The Durham Report. Abridged Edition, with Introduction and Notes. Oxford: Clarendon Press. 1945.

Livingstone's Last Journey. Collins. 1945.

Zulu Battle Piece: Isandhlwana. Collins. 1948.

Introduction
Nation and State

THE TRENDS of race-migration in the dawn of European history determined that the inhabitants of the British Isles should be of more than one stock and culture, so that in course of time four different nations grew up within their narrow bounds, the English, Scottish, Welsh and Irish. Three of them, though not, unfortunately, the fourth, have long learned to live happily together; and, though this process was facilitated by the fact that their national homes lay side by side within one small island, nevertheless the unity of modern Britain represents a great political and psychological achievement. Britain was once a Balkans. The age-long strife between the stronger nation and its weaker neighbours was a constant factor in British history—wars of conquest and wars of liberation, rebellions and repressions, a stubborn tradition of border-fighting, and from generation to generation a legacy of hate as bitter as any that vexed the peace of continental Europe. Yet to-day those warring nations have been harmoniously combined, two of them for over 400 years, all three for nearly 150, in one close-knit multi-national state.

This achievement is the more remarkable in view of the inequality in size and strength of the three partner nations. Scotland is roughly three-fifths the size of England: its population to-day one-seventh of the English. Wales is roughly one-seventh the size of England, its population to-day one-sixteenth.

Yet the political combination of the three nations does not mean, as might be supposed, that the bigger nation has swallowed the smaller ones. Scottish and Welsh nationality have survived. The price of unity has not been uniformity.

In these brief opening statements can already be discerned the problem which will haunt the pages of this book and stand over for discussion at the end of it—the problem of the relationship between the nation and the state. And already the basic fact, without which there could be no such problem, has been disclosed. Though in present-day speech the two words are often used as if they were interchangeable, their meaning is not the same. A nation is not a state. There is a Welsh and a Scottish nation. There is no Welsh or Scottish state.

Certainly the association of nationhood with statehood has usually been very close. Often, indeed, the one was no more than a potentiality without the other. Lacking at least some rudimentary form of state, the primitive elements of nationality were not strong enough to foster the sense of community and so make possible the slow growth of conscious nationhood. How greatly that growth was aided by the state in England will be manifest in the next chapter. Yet it cannot be said that a nation can only come to birth in the cradle of a state and cannot live without its aid. Political combination on a slighter scale has sometimes been enough. The Welsh nation has maintained its existence despite the fact it acquired statehood only in a very loose form and only for transient periods. The Irish nation survived for centuries after losing such flimsy statehood as it once possessed. The Scottish nation was embodied at an early stage in a national state, which grew steadily in strength as time went on; but at the outset of the eighteenth century the Scottish state disappeared.[a]

Thus the problem of nation-state relationship had already been

[a] The Poles retained an ardent nationalism for generations after their state had been torn into subject fragments.

recognised and discussed in the British Isles when the course of the French Revolution brought it to the front of European politics; and the saying that nationalism[a] and democracy were the twin-children of the Revolution is only true of the British Isles in so far as it gave a new stimulus to nationalism in Ireland. But it is true enough that in continental Europe the Revolution changed the character of nationalism where it existed and brought it to active life where it did not. First in France itself the 'sovereignty of the people' extended the scope of national sentiment from the circle of the court and aristocracy to the nation as a whole. The nation was now embodied in a truly national state and inspired with a sense of a national mission. Next, the reaction to that mission, when Napoleon had converted it into an attempt to make his France the mistress of a multi-national European empire, engendered a new birth of nationalism in the subjected countries, particularly Spain and Germany. Last the spread of democratic doctrine after 1815 awakened a dormant nationalism within the Austrian, Russian and Turkish Empires. For those survivals of the *ancien régime* were not only absolutist states: they were also multi-national states in which the smaller or weaker nations were dominated by the one imperial nation. So the struggle for popular freedom was also a struggle for national freedom. Democracy and nationalism were allies, fighting the same foe.

The fortunes of this dual cause are a familiar story—on the one hand the unification of Italy and the liberation of most of the Balkans from the decaying Turkish Empire; on the other hand, the persistence of Austrian and Russian imperialism throughout the nineteenth century and on into the twentieth, and the creation of a new German Empire which sought to revive Napoleon's dream of dominating Europe. Hence, when Europe was caught

---

[a] The word 'nationalism' has acquired in our time a sinister implication; but in this book it will be used to mean no more than an active consciousness of nationality and a devotion to the national interest. Nationalism in this sense is virtually identical with patriotism. Its morality depends on whether the national interest is rightly or wrongly understood.

in a second crisis of war and revolution a hundred years after the first, the cause of freedom was again twofold; and this time the claims of nationalism were more widely understood and stated in more explicit terms. Hitherto, the still subject nations had striven mainly to preserve or to recover their cultural freedom—their language above all—but the first German war gave them the chance of winning political independence too. So on the banners of the Allied and Associated Powers two watchwords were inscribed: to ' making the world safe for democracy ' was added, somewhat hastily, ' national self-determination '; and one of the fruits of victory was a political pattern of Europe which registered, as far as seemed practicable, the achievement of both aims. Nearly all the states of Europe were now democratic states and all of them were either uni-national states or multi-national by agreement between their component nations. In Western Europe this pattern has survived the second German war; but eastwards it has been modified by Soviet Russia. Though Finland has retained the independence won in 1919, the other Baltic nations have reverted to centralised Russian control, while Poland, Czechoslovakia, Hungary, Roumania and Bulgaria are only nominally independent. But the long crisis of our time is not yet over, and only when it is finally resolved in a new age of stability and peace will the interwoven fate of democracy and nationalism be determined.

The cardinal importance of nationalism in the politics of Europe forced men to think more about it than they had thought before; and the discussion thus raised gave it a theoretical content it had previously lacked.[a] It was no longer a matter of mere sentiment: it became a philosophy. The concept of a nation, its

---

[a] There is now a considerable literature, mostly written since 1914, on the origin and meaning of nationality and nationalism. Students should consult C. A. Macartney, *National States and National Minorities* (Oxford, 1934); F. Hertz, *Nationality in History and Politics* (London, 1944); E. Barker, *National Character* (London, 3rd ed., 1939); Royal Institute of International Affairs, *Nationalism* (London, 1939); A. Cobban, *National Self-Determination* (London, 1945).

function, its rights and duties, and, not least, its connection with the state were analysed and formulated. The outcome may be baldly summarised as follows:

(1) While certain primary elements—a common homeland, a common stock[a] and, less invariably, a common language—are to be found in the composition of most nations, the word defies a precise all-inclusive academic definition. But it is generally agreed that in its essence nationhood is always a matter of the spirit. As Renan put it in his famous essay *Qu'est ce qu'une nation*?[1] a nation is a 'spiritual principle,' sustained by the continuing force of a tradition from one generation to another and inspired by the memory of 'great things done together' and the desire to do more of them. It is chiefly this spiritual character that differentiates a nation from a state. The nation is incorporated in the state as the soul in the body.[b]

(2) There is also a consensus of opinion that a nation, great of small, should be free to maintain and develop its distinctive character, and that a strong nation is not entitled to suppress a weak one or to try to impose its own nationality on it.[c]

(3) As to the function or duty which justifies this claim to life and freedom, Mazzini's doctrine still holds the field in western thought. Selfishness, he preached, is as wicked in a nation as in an individual. A nation's *raison d'être* is the contribution it can make to the welfare of the international community. 'A nation is a living task; her life is not her own.'[2] It is clearer in our day

[a] A 'common stock' does not, of course, imply a single or pure race. There is no such thing. The racial composition of every nation is, to a greater or less extent, a mixture.

[b] There are other differences, of course. The nation, for example, is natural, the state artificial. A man is the child of his fatherland and can no more choose it than a child can choose its father. Nor is there identity of function. There are aspects of national life with which the state (unless it is totalitarian) is not directly concerned.

[c] The contrary doctrine, now (it may be hoped) discredited by defeat in two wars, was well stated by von Bülow, Chancellor of the German Empire, in 1914. 'Nations of military ability and economic skill and of superior culture . . . will expend their energy on making the national conquest follow the political. . . . There is no third course. In the struggle between nationalities one nation is the hammer and the other the anvil; one is the victor, the other the vanquished.' *Imperial Germany* (English translation, London, 1914), 239-40.

Introduction

than it was in Mazzini's that the future of our civilisation depends on the extent to which fallible humanity can rise to that ideal.

(4) There remains the final question which *must* be but has not yet been answered. A nation's will to do its duty is one thing, the way to do it is another. What kind of political instrument is needed?

One school of thought says 'none.'[a] In a democratic age, it is argued, a nation needs no politics. Its nature is spiritual, its function cultural. Assured of its cultural freedom, its duty is to preserve and augment its cultural tradition as its distinctive contribution to the common treasury of civilisation. For that no political agency is wanted. The members of all nations are also members of states; but, provided it is democratic, the state's frontiers need not correspond with the nation's. May it not be said, indeed, that a multi-national state is a more advanced, a more civilised polity than a uni-national? In the modern democratic world a man's nationality is no more the state's affair than his religion, and to make it the basis of the state is something like a reversion to the days of *cuius regio, eius religio.*

To most students of nationalism this simple solution of the nation-state problem seems too simple. For the traditions which inspire the lives of nations have always been political as well as cultural. The two threads, indeed, are inseparable. Every nation's literature would be the poorer if it were robbed of all the poetry of patriotism, and no nation can reserve its national pantheon for the men of letters, art and science and turn the men of action out. Can Shakespeare, Milton, Wordsworth be denied the company of Elizabeth, Cromwell, Nelson? Clearly the political problem cannot be evaded. Somehow or other it must be determined what kind of political agency, what form of polity, is needed to enable a nation to maintain its political tradition and perform its 'task' in international politics.

[a] This thesis was first expounded in Acton's well-known essay on 'Nationality' in 1862 (*History of Freedom*, London, 1908). It was revived in a new form in Zimmern's memorable study of *Nationality and Government* (London, 1918).

Nineteenth-century Liberalism had its answer—an answer dictated by the alliance of nationalism with democracy. Democracy in itself meant that the nation controlled the state. Linked with nationalism, democracy implied a uni-national state. For the operative principle of democracy is majority rule, and majority rule can only work successfully in a society which is so homogeneous, which shares the same traditions and standards and purposes to such an extent, that a minority can acquiesce in the decisions of the majority. In a state in which more than one nation is embodied national differences may be so relatively slight as not to obstruct the working of majority rule; but, if the differences go deep, an intractable problem is created. For a nation is not like a party: it cannot enhance its voting power by winning converts: if it is weaker than the other nation or nations which compose the multi-national state, its position will be that of a permanent minority subjected to the rule of a permanent majority. How intractable that problem may be has been illustrated in our own times within the British Commonwealth, on a small scale by the partition of Ireland, on a vast scale by the partition of India. But it did not need the force of those unhappy examples of a later day to convince the Aristotle of nineteenth-century Liberalism, keenly concerned as he was with minority rights in a democracy, that in theory democratic states should all be uni-national. In his classic exposition of representative government (1861) Mill went so far as to say that ' free institutions are next to impossible in a country made up of different nationalities,' and that ' the boundaries of governments should coincide in the main with those of nationalities.'[3] This doctrine was challenged by Acton. Alarmed at its possible effects on the stability of the Hapsburg Empire, he pleaded in an essay on Nationality (1862), which has been more closely read in our day than in his, that ' the combination of different nations in one state is as necessary a condition of civilised life as the combination of men in society.'[4] But Acton did not grapple with the crux of majority rule and

Mill prevailed. Fifty years later it was still prevailing against new ideas of multi-national federalism; and, stimulated by German aggression in 1914, it hardened into the ultimate dogma of national self-determination, endowing every nation with an absolute right to sovereign statehood.[a]

That dogma and the doctrine from which it grew are in question now. The current of opinion in the democratic world has begun to run the other way. Civilisation, it is now at last agreed, cannot survive the continuance of international anarchy; and the problem of the relationship between nation and state is being probed more deeply than it has ever been before. Some seek to solve it by denying any use or worth to nationalism and demanding its absorption into a less ' parochial ' allegiance. To more realistic minds it seems that national traditions have a moral value, that at this stage of human history they cannot and will not be forgotten or discarded, and that the only practical question now is whether they need a political framework to make the best of what is in them. If so, must it always be a state? Need it ever be a sovereign state?

[a] See A. Cobban's masterly treatise, cited page xviii, note, above.

[1] *Discours et Conferences* (Paris, 1887), 277.

[2] *Mazzini's Letters to an English Family*, ed. E. F. Richards (London, 1920-22), iii. 63.

[3] *Representative Government* (Everyman, London, 1910), 361-3.

[4] *History of Freedom* (London, 1907), 290.

PART ONE

England

I. THE NATION

THIS BOOK is mainly concerned with Welsh and Scottish nationalism; but, since in each case its development and character have been shaped to a greater or less extent by reaction to English policy, some preliminary account must be given, however brief and slender, of the growth of English nationhood.

Britain was one of those geographical compartments or countries, separated by frontiers of sea or mountain, which emerged from the prehistoric age in Europe already differentiated by their physical features, their climate and the nature of their inhabitants. Broadly speaking, the people of each country belonged to the same race, spoke the same or a kindred language, worshipped the same or similar gods and maintained the same kind of primitive social system. The main elements of nationality were thus present from the outset—a common homeland, a common stock, a common culture.

The people who lived in Britain in that dawn of history may be conveniently called ' Celts ' and their culture ' Celtic.' And the same terms may be applied to the people of Ireland. For Ireland, so close to Britain and cut off from the rest of the world by the Atlantic, inevitably shared Britain's prehistoric fate. The lesser island became Celtic like the greater. The British Isles might be said, indeed, to have formed a single geographical compartment, and they might have developed a more or less uniform culture and ultimately acquired a single nationhood if they had not been subjected to further invasions from without, the course of which, so far from bringing the islands closer together, thrust them farther apart.

The Romans conquered all England and Wales and, for a time, the Scottish Lowlands, but never Ireland; and in England itself the rough belt of hills and mountains to which the country rises northwards and westwards, though garrisoned by Roman legions, was little affected by Roman civilisation. Nor in the more settled areas in the east and south were the effects of the long occupation enduring. When Roman rule was withdrawn the Britons quickly relapsed into their Celtic way of life. With the decay of the Roman towns the Romanised culture of the upper classes faded out. The Latin they had spoken succumbed to the old Celtic dialects of the countryside. The religions which the Romans had brought with them from the Mediterranean suffered the same fate, with one exception. Though mainly rooted in the towns, Christianity had also spread widely over the non-Romanised highland zone. It had survived the years of persecution, made memorable by St. Alban's martyrdom. British bishops had attended some of the great continental Councils in the fourth century; and even in the fifth, when other ties were breaking, the Church in Britain never lost contact with Rome. It was the age of such famous British theologians as Pelagius and Fastidius and of such famous missionaries as Ninian in Galloway and Cumberland and Patrick in Ireland. Yet the Celtic Church could not supply the unifying force which Celtic tribalism so desperately needed when the next invasion came from over the North Sea. Roman rule had imposed a kind of unity, but it had not been such as to foster the growth of an indigenous nationality. That was never the function of Roman imperialism; and, when the legions departed, the Roman administrative system soon fell to pieces, and the Britons reverted to the jealous clannish separatism, the inability to combine for a common interest, that has always been ' the bane of the Celts.' On occasion all outstanding warriors could gather a formidable army, win battles and stay the tide of conquest for a time. The legend of Arthur is not pure myth. But on the whole, the Britons' resistance to the fierce Nordic invaders was sporadic and unorganised and its ultimate result inevitable.

The Anglo-Saxon conquest was very different from the Roman. The conquerors this time were barbarians and, over a steadily widening area from landing-places on the east and south-east coasts, they wiped the country clean of such civilisation as it possessed. All that survived of Rome in crumbling town or neglected villa disappeared. Christianity and the pagan Celtic gods were ousted by Woden and Thor. The Celtic language died out. Only the Celtic stock survived. Many Britons were massacred and some were driven west and north-west—into the ' Celtic fringe ' of Cornwall, Wales and Cumberland—but most of them probably remained on their native soil, the men as slaves, the women as handmaids or concubines, to contribute a rich strain of Celtic blood to the making of the people who gave England its name and brought to birth the English nation.

It was, of course, a gradual process. For a long time the new-comers, who were farmers as well as warriors and had been tempted oversea by hearsay of land to be had much better than their own, were mainly occupied with clearing the forest, draining the marshy flats and valleys, and cultivating the soil. But fighting was also their profession, and presently out of the conflict of rival war-bands emerged a regional division of the country between the more powerful warrior-chiefs or kings. In Northumbria, Mercia, Wessex there was peace within, if not without; local crafts developed side by side with agriculture, trade expanded, towns grew up. Thus it was in the favouring conditions of a relatively stable community-life that the foundations of an

English polity and an English culture were laid together. It began with the return of Christianity. The old contact with Rome, which had been snapped by the invasions, was renewed when at the end of the sixth century and early in the seventh the missionary saints invaded England in south and north. Landing in 597 in Kent, Augustine established his base at Canterbury. Entering Northumbria from Scotland in 635, Aidan recreated Iona at Lindisfarne. Thence the two streams, one obeying the Celtic rule, the other the Roman, spread out over all England, converting the heathen kinglets and their peoples. At the Synod of Whitby in 664, the conflict between the rival rules was resolved, and the decision that the English Church should follow the Roman, not the Celtic, practice was a far-reaching step towards English nationhood. For this new kind of Roman conquest brought back the old Roman gift of organisation. The country was divided into sees administered by bishops and the sees into parishes, with their little ' Saxon ' parish churches under episcopal control; and the creation of this unified ecclesiastical system confirmed the trend towards political unity. It helped to widen such regional patriotism as had already developed into something nearer to a consciousness of nationhood. Hence, when England had to face the next wave of Nordic invasion, English resistance to Danes and Norsemen was more nearly national than the Britons' resistance to the Anglo-Saxons. The invaders succeeded in occupying the eastern half of England—and so making a valuable Scandinavian contribution to the English stock—but the rest of the country rallied to the leadership of Alfred. He was King of Wessex only, but his sons became Kings of all England. It could hardly be said, however, that the English nation had thus become embodied in an English state. The political structure, indeed, was so loose-knit that it could not survive the impact of the last Danish invasion. When the Normans came, in England as in Ireland, the door was opened to them by civil war.

In this same period, side by side with the birth of an English polity, an English culture was born. Northumbria took the lead. The writing of English history began with Bede's famous book. The Lindisfarne gospels were the first triumph of English monastic art. But this brilliant beginning in Northumbria was only, so to speak, half-English. It was a Latinised culture, spun from Roman threads; and when the lead passed to Alfred's Wessex, it took on a more native hue. Alfred's own translation of Bede's Latin book began the writing of English prose; and the Anglo-Saxon Chronicle he promoted was the first English history of England. Thus an English cultural tradition had been established before the Norman Conquest; and, since it was impossible for the Normans, even had they wished, to blot out English life as the Anglo-Saxons had blotted out British life in England, English culture—the English language, English song, English crafts—were able to survive the long period of political subjection.

II. THE STATE

THE NORMAN CONQUEST forced on the free-spirited English the unity they needed for the growth of their nationhood. It imposed on them a genuine, powerful, well-organised state. Now at last, in secular affairs as well as in religious, they were well and firmly governed; and this by itself made for a closer coherence in the community at large and a clearer consciousness of its common interest and character. Trade and other forms of intercourse between one locality and another steadily increased as the government became more efficient and more centralised, suppressing civil strife and banditry, improving communications for administrative purposes. And the effects of closer intercourse were confirmed by the growing uniformity of the social and administrative system. The unity of the Church was strengthened by prelates who were also statesmen. The feudalism already rooted in the country before the conquest was now fully developed. Local custom survived only if it were not in conflict with one overriding law.

But the state was not yet a national, an English state. For three centuries it was ruled by kings who were more French in blood and sentiment than English and administered by a mainly foreign governing class who spoke French and wrote in Latin. Yet the sturdy young plant of English nationality was not stifled. Perhaps because the invaders were few in number and held their subjects at arm's length or because, being tied to their estates in France and often residing there, they long remained half-strangers or because of some strain of native pride or obstinacy in the English temper—for whatever reason the English, through all those generations of subjection, were not Normanised. So far from becoming blurred and overborne, their distinctive character was confirmed and strengthened. As a rule, but not quite always, the best proof of the survival of a subject nationality is the preservation of its language; and throughout those formative years English not only continued to be, in its various dialects, the only speech of the common people: it gradually spread into the higher orders of society until at last it ousted French even in the field of government and law. It was a memorable event in English history when in 1362 a statute was enacted in the young English Parliament requiring judges and lawyers in the courts to use their *mother tongue*. The process was completed by the restoration of English, a standard English overruling local dialects and enriched by French infusion, as the language of education. Thus the ground was prepared for the coming of Chaucer and Wycliffe.

The triumph of the English language was facilitated by the fact that its rival was the language of the ' French dogs ' with whom Englishmen were fighting for a hundred years. French nationhood was growing side by side with English at that time, and in both countries the growth was greatly stimulated by their conflict. Most of the men who fought in the ranks of the little armies at Agincourt or Orleans may have had small sense of allegiance to a national cause, but the Englishmen and Frenchmen of Shakespeare's day were right in glorifying Henry V and Joan of Arc as personifications of a nascent nationalism. For, though for England the Hundred Years' War was a useless, costly, distracting and, in the end, an unsuccessful war, it did something to awaken national self-consciousness and, despite the ultimate defeat, to kindle national pride. Conflict with another nation inevitably inflates the good opinion of itself which every nation holds, and that long-sustained hostility to France and the hatred and contempt it bred must have helped to inspire the insular arrogance which was presently—and often afterwards—remarked by foreign critics. Not long after the end of the war, an Italian envoy to the English court observed that Englishmen ' think that there are no other men than themselves; and, whenever they see a handsome foreigner they say " he looks like an Englishman." '[1]

The age of the Tudors brought the processes which had been at work in England since the Norman Conquest to their climax. England became in the full sense a national state, and the English nation became fully conscious of its nationhood.

By 1603 the whole of England had acquired a more closely organised, more firmly centralised government than it had ever had before, and with it a political and social unity which had emerged unbroken from the critical period of religious strife. Under the impact of danger from without, the insularity of this compact society had become intensified. Love of the island home, the ' precious stone set in the silver sea,' was now combined with the knowledge that it could be kept aloof and secure from a ' whole world in arms ' as long as English sea-power, so triumphantly exhibited in the war with Spain, continued to control the ' moat defensive.' But in another sense Englishmen had ceased to be insular. Sea-power was not confined to the ' narrow seas,' and the oceanic exploits of the great Tudor seamen had not only excited in English minds an eager and imaginative interest in the

New World; it had evoked the instinct of expansion. Providence, it seemed, had intended the little island to be the inviolable base of English enterprise and achievement far beyond its bounds.

III. THE POLITICAL TRADITION

THE CULTURAL tradition may be left to speak for itself, but for the purposes of this book something must be said about the political tradition. It was an interweaving of two main threads. The first was the maintenance of a constitutional monarchy. Since its inception in the fourteenth century representative government had proved a powerful factor in promoting the growth of nationhood. The English parliament and the English nation, it has been said, were born together. And, great as was their personal authority, both Henry VIII and Elizabeth recognised that Parliament was the authentic mouthpiece of the nation or at least of its governing class, and were careful to pursue their policies, if not always with Parliament's ' advice,' at least with its ' consent.' Thus sustained at a time when the parliaments of continental Europe were withering into impotence under absolutist rule, the tradition of parliamentary partnership with the Crown was strong enough to resist and finally, at the cost of civil war and revolution, to defeat the Stuart reaction. It has often been remarked how temperate a war it was despite the tragic sequel in Whitehall, how mild, how almost legal a revolution, and how significant the swing of national sentiment against Cromwell's dictatorship on the one hand and James II's absolutism on the other. It was this instinctive English moderation, this hatred of extremes, this deep-rooted desire to keep the changes required by changing circumstances in line with past tradition, that enabled constitutional monarchy to emerge from its ordeal into the placid and tolerant eighteenth century, all the more assured of the nation's allegiance now that Parliament was

8

recognised to be the predominant partner. Thenceforth the way was open for the English form of government to develop gradually and peacefully till, weathering the storms that shook the Continent, it grew in the Victorian age into the parliamentary government on which the English nation prides itself to-day.

Nor was the tradition confined to England. It was spread not only over all Britain but also oversea. While English merchants were invading the East, English colonists were settling in the West and transplanting in New Englands the traditions of the old. In an unhappy day nearly all the fine young colonies in North America were lost precisely because those English traditions were ignored by an obstinate king and his second-rate advisers. But the harsh lesson was learnt, and in the colonies which survived or were subsequently founded in Canada and the southern seas, the practice of parliamentary government was assimilated, stage by stage, to that of England, so that in course of time they acquired their own free nationhood without a rupture with the country in which, for the most part, the forefathers of their people had been born. So English pride in the English Parliament extended its range. She was now a mother of parliaments, each clinging as steadfastly as herself to what had become a family tradition. And it has grown in our own day beyond the family. In India, Pakistan, Ceylon, parliamentary government has been in operation for some years and a beginning has been made of it in West Africa.

The second major thread in the English political tradition is the defence of English liberty. The occasion of the conflict with the Spanish Empire was England's refusal to acquiesce in the claim of Spain and Portugal, backed by the Pope, to maintain an exclusive monopoly of all the new world. But its basic cause lay deeper. The Spanish war, like the Dutch revolt, was a war of national independence. Though the open rupture was long delayed, the conflict began with resistance to foreign authority over the English Church, and it ended with resistance to foreign conquest of English soil. It was, in fact, unlike the old wars with France, a war for the survival of an independent England, free to shape her own domestic life, free to play her own part in the politics of Europe, free to trade and settle overseas. And, unlike Agincourt, the defeat of the Armada initiated a great tradition, the second great tradition of English political history. Three times, at intervals of about a century, England fought to prevent a militarist Power—the France of Louis XIV and Napoleon and the Germany of Wilhelm II and Hitler—from mastering continental Europe and so dominating England; and each time it was England's destiny to do most to save the common cause of freedom.

The force of those two political traditions has been the stronger because from the outset they have been closely interlinked. The English wars of independence have all had an ideological background: the external and internal freedom of England were always inseparable: the survival of the English tradition of constitutional government was always at stake. From the sixteenth to the eighteenth century this issue was coloured with religion. Political liberty and Protestantism were kindred and allied causes: absolutism was backed by Rome. But in the eighteenth century the old religious antagonism, though it was never to be quite forgotten, died away. The issue became purely political. The question to be decided was whether parliamentary England could hold her own in fighting power and endurance against the massed and regimented forces of military despotism.

Owing mainly to this identification of external independence with domestic liberty, national sentiment was deeper and more widespread in England than in France before the French Revolution. It was not only the nationalism of a court and a governing class: it was a popular nationalism. Philip II could not possibly appeal to his subject peoples to fight for the Spanish Empire as Elizabeth could appeal to the English people to fight for England. Chatham was stronger than Choiseul because he had the people at his back. And, even when French nationalism rose to its height in Napoleon's France and German nationalism in Hitler's Germany, those other 'great commoners,' Pitt and Churchill, could inspire and direct the force of English nationalism at least as powerfully as their dictatorial opponents.

One further aspect of the English national tradition must be recorded. The freedom of England has never been an isolated cause. England fought her wars of independence in her own defence, but it was not the fate of England only that depended on the outcome. The repulse of the Spanish Armada saved the Dutch Republic from extinction. Marlborough's victories saved all Europe from French domination. When England stood alone against Napoleon, we were fighting, said Pitt, not only ' for our existence as a nation.' 'We are called to struggle for the destiny, not of this country alone, but of the civilised world,' and the pride we take in our efforts to ensure our own safety is heightened by the knowledge that we are holding out to nations ' bending under the iron yoke of tyranny ' a prospect ' of what the exertions of a free people can effect.'[2] When history so closely repeated itself on the eve of the Battle of Britain, Churchill, speaking as Pitt had spoken in the House of Commons, identified our cause as Pitt had done with the hope of freedom everywhere. ' Hitler knows that he will have to break us in this island or lose the war. If we can stand up to him, all Europe may be free. . . . But if we fail, then the whole world . . . will sink into the abyss of a new Dark Age.'[3]

Englishmen, it need hardly be said, have not always been true to this tradition. The record of every nation has its darker pages, and it will be evident in some forthcoming chapters of this book —to look no farther—that the English love of their own liberty has not always implied respect for other people's and that the spirit of English nationalism has been tainted often enough by selfishness and arrogance and lack of understanding. Englishmen should not forget, as they are apt to do, what they have done in

Ireland. Nevertheless, the main trend of English thought and conduct, the dominant note of the English tradition, has been humane and liberal; and an Englishman, weighing the good against the bad, may be pardoned for believing that the English nation in serving itself has not, on balance, done disservice to the world.

[1] G. M. Trevelyan, *History of England* (2nd ed. London, 1937), 233.

[2] *Pitt's War Speeches* (ed. R. Coupland; 3rd ed., Oxford, 1940), 328, 332.

[3] Winston S. Churchill. *Into Battle* (London, 1941), 234.

PART TWO

Wales and England
to the end of the Seventeenth Century

I. THE BIRTH OF WELSH NATIONHOOD

THE WELSH nation is rooted in its Celtic race, its Celtic tongue and its mountain homeland. That last geographical factor is by no means the least important. The Welsh mountains have not only coloured Welsh thought and helped to shape Welsh social life: they were the physical bulwark which protected Welsh nationality at a time when it would otherwise have been overwhelmed, and made possible its survival into the modern age.

The Romans penetrated the mountains and conquered Wales and built their forts and roads to hold it; but theirs was little more than a military occupation of strategic points. In that wild country Roman influence was as restricted as among the hills and moors of northern England. There were no such commercial or residential centres as fostered in the English south and midlands the growth of a Romanised upper class, no Romano-British towns, scarcely any villas; and Roman culture made little impression on the primitive tribal life of the countryside. But that does not mean that Wales gained nothing from the Roman occupation. It introduced the Latin alphabet. It taught, as the ' loan-words ' show, the use of better weapons and methods of war and of better housing and furniture and domestic utensils.[1] And above all else, there was one great Roman gift which the Britons of Wales shared with the Britons of England. Christianity was first established in the Romanised English towns, but it gradually filtered out into the country and penetrated not only into the rough English northland but also into Wales. There was nowhere any large-scale conversion. In Wales, as in England, Christianity, even when it became the ' official ' religion of the Empire, was the faith of a few; but, though Celtic paganism still dominated rural life, the little Christian Church maintained its footing. Like the Roman forts and roads, it survived the Romans' departure.

Not so the Roman system of government. With no legions at their back the Romanised British officials proved unable to prevent the revival of the old tribal feuds of pre-Roman days, and Britain soon split into a complex of chieftainships or little kingdoms in constant conflict with each other. But, if the Britons never formed a common front against their common enemies, they fought fiercely in defence of their own homelands. They drove the Picts and Scots back beyond the lowland belt between Forth and Clyde. They stubbornly contested the inward spread of the Anglo-Saxon settlements on the coast. They won victories such as those which the legend of a later day ascribed to Arthur. The battle of Mons Badonicus, fought about A.D. 500 at a place that cannot be identified, gave the Britons a long respite from aggression,[2] and it was not till the mid-seventh century that the invaders finally broke through into the West and, reaching the Bristol Channel and the Irish Sea, cut Wales off from the Britons of Cornwall in the South and from the Britons of Cumbria in the North. Those breaches were never repaired. Cornwall was ultimately merged in Wessex; the southern part of Cumbria in Northumbria, the northern in Scottish Strathclyde. But, if Wales was thus isolated, it was not subdued. The Welsh princes might render homage to Anglo-Saxon kings from time to time, but it was only a nominal submission. The invaders never pressed their conquest beyond the English midlands into the mountains and forests of Wales.

Those first two centuries after the Romans had gone were the heroic age of the Britons; and because the Welsh of Wales were the only Britons who were not destroyed or absorbed by the invaders, they became the sole inheritors and guardians of the great tradition of that age. The Arthurian legend is a good example. Modern scholarship agrees that Arthur was an historic person, probably a Romanised Briton who came to the front as a leader of horsemen against the heathen; but his field of action, it is now thought, was the North, rather than the South and West of the later romances; and there is no reason to suppose that he lived or died in Wales. Yet Wales appropriated him. He lay sleeping, it was said, in some Welsh mountain cave till the day when he would wake and come forth to reconquer and rule England. It was the same with the cultural tradition, with the language and the literature of the age. ' Welsh,' the analytic form of the old Brythonic language, was coming into general use among the Britons at that time; but after the subjection of the North it withered away till only the name of Cumberland preserved the memory of the Cymri[a] and, if it lingered longer in Cornwall, it was ultimately smothered by English. In Wales alone it has lived on, its usage uninterrupted from those far off days to our own. And with the language literature; for it is in this same heroic age that the stream of Welsh poetry which has continued flowing ever since first becomes visible to modern sight. Long before this time, in Britain as in Ireland, the Celtic custom had been established of maintaining poets or ' bards ' at

---

[a] The name *Cymri*, still preserved in *Cumberland*, is derived from *Cumbroges* (fellow-countrymen) and seems to have been adopted by the British in Wales and North-West England in the course of their struggle with the Anglo-Saxon invaders. *Wales* comes from Old English *Wealnas* (strangers) and *Welsh* from Old English *Waelise* (Lloyd i. 164, 191-2). Giraldus Cambresis (see pp. 27-29, below) was the first to explain (in his *Descriptio Kambriae*, i. Chap. VII) how the ' Saxons ' called ' extraneum omne Wallicum ' and ' gentes has sibi extraneas Walenses ' *Oxford English Dictionary* s. v. Welsh).

the courts of chiefs and princes whose task it was to sing the praises of their lords and glorify their ancestry. Hence this earliest surviving Welsh poetry is by no means primitive. In language, in convention, in technical skill, it is clearly the outcome of an old bardic tradition. It is 'typical heroic poetry.' It is mainly concerned with war—and with the pity as much as the glory of war—but, unlike most other heroic poetry, it does not take an epic mould. Like the best work of all the Welsh poets to come, it is lyric poetry. If narrative is needed, it is supplied by a sequence of lyrics as in Aneirin's famous *Gododdin*, a long poem, arranged in groups of rhyming stanzas, which ' immortalised the glorious three hundred who went forth at the behest of their lord, My-nyddawg Mwynfawr of Caer Eidyn (modern Edinburgh), and fell in an attempt to win back the old Roman fort of Catraeth (Catterick) from the Saxons of Deira.'[3] With Aneirin stands Taliesin, another sixth-century court bard, whose main theme was also the long struggle with the advancing heathen. These two poets were no more Welshmen of Wales by birth or domicile than Arthur. Aneirin lived in south-east, Taliesin in south-west Scotland. But, like Arthur, they were inherited, so to speak, by the only Britons who retained their freedom. They became the heroic patriarchs of Welsh literature.

The third thread of the Welsh tradition, unlike those others, was woven mainly in Wales itself. On the morrow of the Roman withdrawal Christianity won a hold on the Britons such as it had never had when it was safe beneath the Roman shield; and, until the link with Gaul was broken by the Saxon advance along the south coast, it was aided and fostered from oversea. Soon after the legions had gone, St. Germanus, once a soldier in Roman Gaul, crossed over to lead the Cumbrian Britons against the Picts. From Gaul, too, came the monastic movement which in the course of the next century spread rapidly over Britain. And nowhere was it stronger than in Wales. The heroic age was the age of the Welsh saints. In the generation after Germanus, St. Illtyd who had sat with St. Patrick at Germanus' feet in Brittany, settled in Glamorgan and created a famous centre of Christian learning in the monastery he founded at Llantwit Major. And Dewi or St. David, patron saint of Wales, who was born on the shore of St. Bride's Bay about 520 and died about 588, was Illtyd's disciple. By that time Wales was already dotted with monasteries and churches, and they grew steadily in number in the following century.[a] When St. Augustine landed in Kent in 597, bishops were already installed in what were to become the four cathedral sees of Wales; and together with a goodly company of abbots and divines, they took a leading place among the churchmen of southern Britain who met at a synod at Aust on the lower Severn to parley with Augustine in 602 (or 603). Augustine, according to Bede's account, made three demands. The British Churches must accept the Roman practice for fixing the date of Easter and for performing the rite of baptism, and they must co-operate with Augustine in preaching the gospel to the heathen conquerors of England.

It was probably the last of these proposals that was chiefly responsible for the breakdown of the conference.[1] The differences between Roman and Celtic rituals were the inevitable result of the seclusion of the British Isles from the Latin Christianity of Europe brought about by the heathen occupation of the Channel coast; and this, as time proved, was not an insuperable barrier to the unity of western Christendom. Nor had the British churchmen resented Pope Gregory's dispatch of a mission to convert the pagan kingdoms of England. The rupture of contact with Rome had not destroyed the Celts' respect for 'the head of the world's Churches,' as Columbanus put it; but it had made them less ready than the continental Churches to accept the Pope's ecclesiastical authority. And Gregory had made a diplomatic blunder. In his zest for the conversion of England he had failed to consider

[a] None of the churches survives because, unlike the stone Saxon churches in England, they were built of wood. (Lloyd, i. 220.)

the feelings of the British churchmen. For the best part of two centuries they had kept the faith alive, ' the one light in a great darkness,'⁵ while the hosts of Thor and Woden spread steadily over England. Latterly, moreover, they had founded a school of monastic piety and learning which was known and respected far beyond the bounds of Britain. Yet the status and welfare of these old Christians was, it seemed, a secondary matter. That Augustine's main task was the conversion of the English pagans was evident when he chose Canterbury for the seat of his new archbishopric; and from that far-off throne he was authorised, it appeared, to control and, at need, to discipline the British bishops most of whom were in Wales. Only on one hypothesis could the latter have been expected to submit to the authority of an Italian newcomer who yesterday had been no more than the prior of a Roman monastery—only if they had been prepared to subordinate all other considerations to a crusade for the conversion of England. And to this they were seemingly indifferent. Even among those Anglo-Saxons with whom they had made peace, they had made no attempt to proselytise. The great work done by the Celtic Church in the conversion of Scotland and northern England was of Irish origin, not Welsh. And the reason is plain enough. The Welsh Christians could never forgive the Anglo-Saxons for their brutal occupation and destruction of almost all their old British world. It was impossible for them to love those enemies. They hated them, and went on hating them after they had been converted. 'It is to this day the fashion among the Britons,' wrote Bede as late as 731, ' to reckon the faith and religion of Englishmen as naught and to hold no more converse with them than with the heathen.'⁶ At that time the Welsh Christians, alone of all the Christian Celts, still held aloof from Rome. In South Ireland, in Northumbria, in North Ireland, in Devon and Cornwall, at Iona, in Strathclyde, they successively gave way between 625 and 718. At last in 768, Wales succumbed. The Welsh Church accepted the ' Roman Easter ' and implicitly therewith the spiritual headship of Rome. It was the final step in the unification of western Christendom.

By the end of the eighth century the long war of independence came to an end. The object of the great earthwork known as Offa's Dyke (Clawdd Offa), which was built by the king of Mercia and overlord of all South England about 790 and still roughly marks the boundary between Wales and England, was to keep Welsh invaders out.[a] Like the Roman Walls in the North it was an admission that the limit of conquest had been reached. And thenceforward relations between the Welsh and their hereditary foes seem to have steadily improved. The enemy now were on their other flank, fierce Danes and Norsemen raiding from the sea. But the new dangers no more availed to unify Wales than the old. Between the principalities of Gwynedd, Powys and Deheubarth, into which at this time Wales was divided, and between lesser clans or tribes the old Celtic feuds and fighting persisted. For, while the Welsh were now masters of their national homeland and had inherited from their heroic age a national tradition, they were not yet a nation.

Towards the close of this period of conflict and confusion two Welshmen came to the forefront of Welsh history. Hywel the Good (*c.* 920–950) was the Alfred of Wales. He is thought to have taken Alfred as his model, and he certainly betrayed a singular respect for the English and their ways. ' By the Grace of God ruler of all Wales,' as his own famous code of law proclaimed him, he might well have deemed himself strong enough to assert the independence of his country in form as well as fact; but he readily rendered the allegiance required of him by Alfred's successors: he was, indeed, a frequent and friendly visitor at the English court. His great work for Wales was the codification of Welsh customary law. Local usages might long survive, but now

[a] It has been argued that the object of the Dyke was not military but administrative —to make an agreed frontier. Sir C. Fox, *The Boundary Line of Cymru: Proceedings of British Academy*, xxvi (1941).

only in subordination to a single body of law which was valid in all Wales. The code was, in fact, a national achievement, expressing a common way of thought about the conduct of Welsh life, manifesting a sense of national community. And there was more in it than that. A nation that obeys one law is on the way to becoming one state.[7]

But, as always, the unity which Hywel had given Wales was broken at his death; and for nearly a century, despite the occasional renewal of attacks from England and piratical raids from the sea, the Welsh reverted to their traditional Celtic civil strife. It was not till the eve of the Norman invasion of England that Gruffydd ap Llywelyn of Gwynedd emerged as master of Wales (1055)—'he was King' wrote the English annalist, 'over all the Welsh race'—but almost at once he was drawn into the whirlpool of English politics under Edward the Confessor and for the rest of his life was fighting battles, some of them victorious, with Aelfgar of Mercia as his ally and Harold of Wessex as his most formidable foe. Under this strain Welsh unity collapsed. Gruffydd at last was forced to seek refuge in the wilds of Snowdonia where he was hunted, betrayed and murdered by his Welsh enemies. They sent his head to Harold as the price of peace. Three years later Harold died at Hastings.[8]

2

William the Conqueror did not attempt to subjugate Wales or Scotland as he subjugated England. His march to the Forth in 1072 was not the opening stage of a conquest; it was a demonstration of force intended to overawe the Scots and so to make conquest unnecessary.[a] On the one occasion he invaded Wales his purpose was the same. In 1081 he marched as far as St. David's, relieving some isolated Norman garrisons on the way, and then withdrew, leaving the turbulent tribesmen of South Wales, for

[a] See page 66 below.

the moment at least, in a submissive mood. In any case, a full-scale conquest was probably beyond his power. The forest-clad mountains and the swampy wooded valleys of Wales were more obstructive to Norman horsemen than to Roman legions: in rainy seasons the rapid movement of the army was impossible. In three successive years (1094-96) Rufus invaded Gwynedd, and each time the only outcome was an ignominious retreat. It was not, indeed, till a new technique of fighting had been learned that the resistance of the Welsh mountaineers, old adepts at guerrilla warfare, could be crushed. Hence, though Wales suffered a kind of Norman conquest, it differed, as its Roman conquest had differed, from the kind inflicted on England. It was a gradual, piecemeal, creeping conquest, and two centuries passed before it was complete.

Full-scale conquest by royal armies having proved impracticable, the task of subjection was delegated to adventurous barons known as the 'Lords Marchers,' whose greed for land and lust for fighting could be slaked by the grant of feudal domains beyond the 'march' with licence to rule them and extend them as they pleased. Their advance was based on the three powerful earldoms of Chester, Shrewsbury and Hereford. Thence, with their troops of armed retainers, they pushed forward into Wales. At this point emerges the difference between the destinies of the North and the South which, in one form or another, has persisted to this day. Geography took charge of history. Along the rocky seaboard in the North, closely flanked by the great mountain *massif* of Snowdonia, the Normans, based on Chester, made little progress beyond Flint. It was otherwise in the South. There the broad maritime belt offered no serious physical obstacle to invasion, with the result that, at the death of Henry I, in virtually the whole of South Wales the old Welsh princes and chiefs had been ousted by the new Anglo-Norman Lords. In mid-Wales the invaders pushed steadily up the valleys, leaving the highlands between them in the occupation of the tribesmen.

To secure their advance they built at dominant points their massive Norman castles; but they made no attempt to settle the country with Normans. Except in Pembroke, where a twelfth-century settlement of Flemish farmers, weavers and traders, planted by sea and soon anglicised, gave it the name of ' little England beyond Wales,' there was no regular ' colonisation' of the Lordships; but to supply the needs of the Lords and their retainers an increasing number of English farmers and merchants followed on their heels and built up little townships in the shelter of their castles. Thus it came about that Welsh blood and ways of life were mingled with Norman and English. Not all the Welsh tribesmen withdrew into the hills before the invaders. Some of them remained within the Lordships, becoming vassals of the Lords and learning from the newcomers the arts of agriculture and trade. Miscegenation inevitably resulted. Some of the Lords themselves married daughters of Welsh chiefs, some of them spoke Welsh; and the government of their little realms was based on a varying mixture of Welsh custom and English law, of tribalism and feudalism. But the newcomers were never overwhelmed by their environment like their kinsmen isolated in the heart of Ireland. England lay close at their back. They were in constant touch with their relatives and friends in England; they participated from time to time in the turmoil of English politics; and they were constantly reinforced by new English immigrants. While, therefore, they might be affected to a greater or less extent by contact with the Welsh, they were not in danger of losing altogether their distinctive national character.

So the Norman Conquest did not give Wales what it gave England. The Normans consolidated the rival English principalities into a firm-knit state and so provided the internal peace and unity required for the growth of English nationhood. Wales, so far from being united, was partitioned. On one side of an irregular shifting line lay the Lordships of the valleys and the southern coast predominantly English and relatively civilised, on the other side the hill country, still wholly Welsh, still occupied by relatively backward tribesmen. Even the English part was not consolidated. The English state was not extended to cover it, nor was it organised as a separate principality. It remained a medley of petty sovereignties whose rulers were frequently fighting each other as well as the Welsh. Nor was any greater unity to be expected in the Welsh part. Tribal feuds persisted as of old. The princely houses, like the Lords Marchers, fought each other as well as the English, and even against the English they rarely fought together. Nevertheless, as before the Normans came, the possibility of national combination was always latent in the common love of freedom and the common hatred of the foreigners who were robbing them of it. Given the opportunity and another Gruffydd to lead them, the Welsh were capable of fighting as a nation; and there were two periods in the Middle Ages when both opportunity and leadership were forthcoming.

The first period began with a combined assault on the Lords Marchers when the death of Henry I in 1135 precipitated civil war in England, and it lasted till Edward I's invasion of 1277. Henry II himself twice led an army into the rough northern country, but he was baffled by forest and swamp and drenching rain and succeeded only in securing the nominal submission of Gwynedd. John went further than his father. He summoned all the princes of Wales to do homage at Woodstock (1209). But his royal authority was still only nominal and his invasion of Gwynedd (1211) had no more lasting result than Henry's. The Angevin kings, in fact, failed to achieve a real conquest of Wales, partly because the terrain and the climate made it a very difficult task, but mainly because they were preoccupied with their claims and wars in France and disputes with their barons at home. The Lords Marchers for their part were quarrelling with each other or with the King. Hence for over a century the process of gradual subjection was halted, and under a series of great leaders—Owain Gwynedd (died 1170), Rhys ap Gruffydd (died 1197), Llywelyn I (died 1240), Llywelyn II (died 1282)—the Welsh acquired a greater measure of political unity than they had ever had before. Neither Owain nor Rhys controlled all Wales, but the first and great Llywelyn assumed the leadership among the princes, composed their feuds, and summoned them on occasion to Councils at which he presided; and when his grandson, Llywelyn II, proclaimed himself Prince of Wales in 1258, his sovereignty in Wales was almost as complete and valid as the sovereignty of the English King in England. ' In those days,' wrote Matthew Paris, ' the Welsh . . . of the north joined together in indissoluble alliance with those of the south. Such a union had never before been, since north and south had always been opposed.'[9] The Welsh began, moreover, in this period to play their own part in the world beyond their borders. They joined in the domestic English conflict, now on the King's side, now against him. Llywelyn I's support was courted both by John and by the barons. He took the latter's side and obtained three clauses of Magna Carta to safeguard Welsh rights.[a] Llywelyn II, as the price of his alliance, gained from Henry III not only the overlordship of all the barons in Wales, but also the full cession of all the lands he had conquered from the Lords Marchers.[10] Owain sent an embassy to offer Louis VII of France his assistance against England. Llywelyn II made a military and commercial alliance with the nationalist leaders in Scotland. Though feudal homage might still be paid from time to time to the English crown, Wales was now virtually an independent national state.

[a] Clause 56. Welshmen illegally deprived of lands or liberties to recover them, Disputes on property in England, Wales and the Marches to be decided by their respective laws. Clause 57. Welsh property seized by Henry II or Richard and retained by John to be returned in due course ' in accordance with the laws of the Welsh.' Clause 58. Llywelyn's son and all other Welsh hostages to be surrendered immediately.

3

This political achievement brought all the latent forces of Welsh nationhood to life. An independent national state implied an independent national Church, and a persistent effort was made throughout this period to free the Welsh Church from Canterbury. The Normans had used the Church as an instrument of conquest.[11] They had tried to cut its old roots and to graft it firmly on to the southern province of the Church of England. A characteristic move, though inspired more by fashion than by policy, was ' the re-dedication of churches bearing the names of Welsh founders, unknown to the Christian world at large, to saints of wider reputation commemorated throughout the length and breadth of Christendom.' St. Teilo, St. Cynidr, St. Cynfal and many another ancient name succumbed to St. Peter, St. Thomas, St. Mary, St. Andrew and so forth. ' In the eyes of the Welshman it was the displacement of the ancient presiding genius of the place; the new patron might be dignified and worthy of respect, but he was not, like the old, rooted in the soil and endeared by a thousand happy memories.'[12] Of greater practical importance was the firm control of the Welsh sees. Many of the bishops chosen were Normans, not Welshmen, and all had been obliged to accept without question the rule of Canterbury. But now the Church asserted its claim to share in the national independence of the State. Not only was it strong enough to secure, with rare exceptions, the appointment of Welshmen to Welsh bishoprics: from the time of Owain Gwynedd onwards it repeatedly pressed the Pope to make St. David's an archbishopric of equal standing with those of Canterbury and York, and so free the Church of Wales from formal subjection to the Church of England.

If the first component of the national tradition was religion, the second was poetry; and the age of independence was the classic age of the bards. The springs of Welsh poetry had begun to run dry, but now they flowed again in full force and volume. It was a peculiar kind of poetry composed under conditions of peculiar formality. Only the professional court-bards could be poets, and most of the substantial body of medieval poetry that has survived was the work of a *pencerdd* or ' chief of song ' who stood at the head of his order and was allotted a ' chair ' at court. Like the members of a contemporary English guild, the bards were governed by an elaborate system of rules. Theme, form and even diction were prescribed. The themes were mainly, as in earlier days, eulogies of the prince, especially his prowess in war and especially in war against the English or ' Saxon ' invader; but, as time went on, religion, nature and love—the last in the conventional manner of the age—were also treated. The form was highly artificial. It was in this period that the system of *cynghanedd,* or the so-called ' strict ' metres as opposed to the ' free ' metres of a later time, developed its final form—a highly elaborate system of alliteration and consonantal repetition. And the diction was no less conventional. It was not the spoken language of the day but a purely literary language derived from the poets of the dawn. Composed for the ear, not the eye, and chanted to the accompaniment of the harp, it appealed to the emotions rather than the mind. Since most of it defies translation, only good Welsh scholars can appreciate its beauty. Of the many bards whose names and works have been preserved one stands high above the rest, Cynddelw Brydydd Mawr, ' Cynddelw the great poet.' [13]

Welsh prose shared in the national revival. Already before the Norman invasion Hywel the Good had done for Wales what his friend, Alfred, did for England: he had fathered the first-born work of prose written in his native language.[a] The great code of law which bears his name exhibits ' not only a wealth of legal and technical terms but also a highly developed syntax able to

---

[a] The earliest surviving piece of Welsh prose is dated a little before this; but it is only a fragment of twenty-four lines.

express with precision the finest distinctions and the most complicated niceties and ramifications of the legal mind. . . . Of its
kind it is prose of the highest order.'[14] From the morrow of the
invasion onwards into the period of the Princes a very different
sort of prose was being written. Together with the bards but on
a lower footing, a class of professional story-tellers had long
existed. A medley of myth and folklore, of war-heroics and
romance, their stories had hitherto been handed on from father
to son for oral telling only. Now they were written down, and
eleven of them were presently assembled in a collection known
as the *Mabinogion*, which is fortunately available for English
readers in excellent translations.[a] It is generally regarded as ' the
most artistic and delightful expression of the early Celtic genius
which we possess.'[15]

It was not, however, Welsh poets or prose-writers who gave
the strongest literary stimulus to the growth of a national spirit
in this age. Of the two writers who, more than anyone else, made
Wales known to herself and to the world, one was wholly, the
other three parts of Anglo-Norman blood. Geoffrey of Monmouth (died 1155) is far the more famous. His *History of the Kings
of Britain*, written in Latin but soon translated into many tongues,
was the first great collection of the Arthurian romances and its
effect on the literature of all western Europe was immeasurable;
and, while it made other countries aware of Wales and Welsh
traditions as they had never been before, it fostered the growth
of national self-consciousness among the Welsh themselves by
recalling, if in somewhat romantic guise, the glories of their
heroic past. Gerald of Barry (c. 1146-1223), better known by his
scholastic title as Giraldus Cambrensis, was born in South Dyfed
of Pembrokeshire. Nephew of an Anglo-Norman bishop of St.
David's, he adopted a clerical career, became archdeacon in his
uncle's diocese, and vainly aspired to obtain the bishopric itself

---

[a] The most recent and best is by Gwyn Jones and Thomas Jones, published in
Everyman's Library.

and to exalt it to the headship of an independent Welsh Church
freed from all control by Canterbury. But he was only three-parts
Anglo-Norman; his mother's mother was a well-known member
of the old Tewdwr family; and, though much of his life was
spent elsewhere, he spoke of Wales as his fatherland and regarded
himself as a great Welsh patriot. Nor was this merely a pose. He
took the keenest interest in all things Welsh—history, topo-
graphy, habits and customs and beliefs—in all that would now
be called the Welsh ' way of life.' He boasted of his knowledge
of the language, but his command of it was imperfect and he
wrote his *Itinerary of Wales* (1191) and *Description of Wales* (1194)
in the scholar's medieval Latin.[a] Based on his observations in the
course of a rapid official tour of Wales—he accompanied Archbishop Baldwin on a mission to raise Welsh recruits for the
Second Crusade—the books, more especially the first of them,
provide an incomparable picture of the life of twelfth-century
Wales, vivid, realistic, often amusing, always interesting. His
analysis of the Welsh character, both its good side and its bad,
suffers not unnaturally from overstatement; but for its time
it was a masterly essay in social science, and much of it still holds
good to-day. In particular he deplores the failure of the Welsh
to achieve political unity. The chief reason, he says, why the
Welsh do not enjoy the same happiness as other peoples is their
obstinate refusal to be subjected to the rule of one king.[16]

Giraldus, as it happens, was the first writer to put on record
what had, no doubt, been a notable feature of the Welsh tradition
from its earliest days—Welshmen's love of music and in particular
their inborn gift for choral singing. ' In their musical concerts
they do not sing in unison like the inhabitants of other countries,
but in many different parts; so that in a company of singers,
which one very frequently meets with in Wales, you will hear
as many parts and voices as there are performers.'[17]

[a] For a full analysis of the books, see articles by Thomas Jones in *The National Library
of Wales Journal*, vol. vi, Nos. 2 and 3 (Aberystwyth, 1949-50).

In this period, lastly, Welshmen began to think about their language and to realise that it was the most distinctive and vital element in their national life. It was not, of course, an academic appreciation of the linguistic aspect of nationality—such speculations lay far beyond their range of thought. It was simply a recognition of the fact that the English invasion was an invasion of English. The vast majority of medieval Welshmen spoke Welsh only, but more and more of them, at almost all levels of society, were learning to speak English too. Though several Lords, especially those who married Welsh wives, spoke Welsh at home, the official language of their little realms, the language of administration and the courts, was mainly English; and the Welshmen who took service under them or pleaded at their bars were obliged to acquire English. Even the countryfolk who brought their cattle to the little English market-towns picked up at least a smattering of English. To an intelligent Welsh patriot it must have become more and more evident that the foreign conquest was not only territorial; it was also linguistic. It was but one step in thought from that to link the independence of Wales with the survival of Welsh; and it is surely very significant that Giraldus should have shown himself to be aware of the conflict of tongues and what it implied. It is Giraldus who records the well-known answer of the old Welshman of Pencader in North Carmarthenshire to Henry II's question as to the effects of the English invasion. 'I doubt not, as oftentimes of yore, this race of mine may be brought low and much broken by the might of English arms. Yet the wrath of man, if God's anger be not added, will never utterly destroy it. For I am persuaded that no other race than this and no other tongue than this of Wales, happen what may, will answer in the great Day of Judgement for this little corner of the earth.'[a]

[a] In 1952, at the instance of *Plaid Cymru* (see page 374 below) a block of granite was erected at Penender with a Welsh version of this passage inscribed on it. It was unveiled by William George, 37-year-old brother of 'L.G.' (*Welsh Nation*, Oct. 1952, page 6.)

II. THE EDWARDIAN CONQUEST
AND ITS SEQUEL

WELSH INDEPENDENCE was the product of English weakness; it
was bound to collapse when England recovered her strength;
and Edward I, the greatest of the Plantagenets, was as ready to
take up Llywelyn's challenge to his overlordship in Wales as
Balliol's challenge in Scotland. The Edwardian conquest (1277–
78) was a real conquest. By the reduction of the Snowdon *massif*
in the heart of Gwynedd by a new strategy of encirclement and
blockade, the mountainous unruly North was now at last as
firmly subjugated as the more open and more settled South, and
massive castles were built, at Conway and Caernarvon for
example, to confirm the conquest. In 1282 a rising, in the course
of which Llywelyn was killed in a chance encounter, was easily
suppressed, and in 1284 Edward imposed a settlement intended
to secure for good the subordination of the Principality to the
Kingdom. 'Divine Providence,' ran the opening section of the
Statute of Wales, 'hath now of its favour wholly and entirely
transferred under our proper dominion the land of Wales with
its inhabitants . . . and hath annexed and united the same with
the Crown of the aforesaid realm as a member of the same body.'[18]
That part of Wales, accordingly, which had not been occupied
by the Lords Marcher—roughly the western half—was incorporated in the English structure of local government. Six shires
were carved out of it and committed to shire-administration, and
several of their towns chartered, roughly on the English model;[a]
and the English criminal law was introduced. But there the
process of assimilation stopped. In civil matters the Welsh were

[a] Pembroke and Glamorgan had been previously organised as 'shires,' but they
differed in important points from English shires.

allowed to retain most of their ancient customary law. No handicap was placed on their language, no restraint on their Church. Political subjection, in fact, was linked with cultural freedom. And, as if to show that union with England was not meant to obliterate the national tradition, Edward retained for the six shires the title of Principality, and in 1301 he named the child born him at Caernarvon in 1283 its prince.

This settlement, so liberal for its time, would soon have been undermined if Edward I's successors had not continued his pro-Welsh policy. As it was, within a decade of his death English officials, secular and ecclesiastical, were taking advantage of their position to acquire land by virtually compelling owners to sell. Disputes had arisen also over the retention of Welsh customs, and Welsh litigants were suffering from trials before English juries unacquainted with Welsh speech and law. In 1315, accordingly, Edward II issued two ordinances,[19] ' being minded,' as he said in their preambles, ' to do away with undue grievances and in the desire to confer more ample favour upon our aforesaid lieges for that we were born in the country of Wales.' Forced land-sales were forbidden. The customs in question were to be maintained ' just as in the time of the princes of Wales.' In litigation between Welshmen the jurymen and the law were to be Welsh; in mixed cases half the jury were to be English, half Welsh. Furthermore, whether or not Edward I had intended to summon representatives of Wales to the English Parliament, Edward II summoned 48 Welshmen in 1322 and 18 in 1326.[20]

It was not sentiment, of course, which prompted either the strong Edward or the weak to favour Wales. At a time of constant war, now with France, now with Scotland, Welshmen's loyalty to the English throne was of high practical value because they were, as they had always been, good fighters, rough maybe and disorderly but fierce in battle. The archers of South Wales were particularly formidable: the famous longbow was more a Welsh than an English weapon. Most of the troops which took part in the first Norman invasions of Ireland were Welsh; Welshmen fought for England at Falkirk (1298)[a] and at Bannock-burn (1314) and Welsh professional soldiers as well as Scottish were widely employed in continental Europe. Naturally, there-fore, Edward III continued his father's and grandfather's policy. It was with war in view that in 1343, in Parliament at Westminster, the Black Prince was ceremoniously crowned as Prince of Wales. In 1346 the attack on France was launched; and, if some Welsh professionals had taken service with the French King, a great many more Welshmen followed their Prince and made history across the Channel. One-third of the English army at Crécy consisted of Welsh archers and spearmen. And, despite the harsh treatment of Wales by Edward III's successors (to be recorded presently), Welshmen continued to fight for their English King. More than a century after the end of the Hundred Years' War, Englishmen had not forgotten that all Welshmen were not abed on Crispin's day, and it was the tradition of Welsh soldiership that enabled Shakespeare's audience to laugh at the national oddities of Fluellen and Glendower and yet applaud their manly bearing.

But all Welsh patriots were not minded to serve an English King. There were men like Owain of Wales, comrade of Bertrand du Guesclin, who fought for France at Poitiers and dreamed of recovering the independence of the Principality with the help of French and Spanish ships and troops. Twice he set sail from Harfleur in command of a French fleet, but he got no nearer the Welsh coast than Guernsey, where he landed with four thousand men in 1372 and ' discomfited the englisshmen in the yle.'[21]

[a] Five-sixths of the footmen at Falkirk were Welsh. J. E. Morris, *The Welsh Wars of Edward I* (Oxford, 1901), 287.

2

The subjection of Wales took the heart out of Welsh poetry. The national exaltation which had inspired the bards who sang the praises of the Princes could not survive their fall. The bitterness of defeat, the loss of independence, the arrogance of the ' Saxon ' conqueror, induced a mood of misery and hatred which in the famous elegy on Llywelyn composed by his favourite court-poet sinks to black despair.

> Woe is me for my lord. . . . Woe is me for the grief that he is fallen. . . . Mine it is to be wroth with the Saxon that he has overborne me, mine to complain bitterly in death's face, mine with good reason to reproach God who reft him from me. . . . Do ye not see the rush of the wind and the rain? Do ye not see the oaks beating together. . . . Do ye not see the sun rushing through heaven? Do ye not see that the stars are fallen? . . . Do ye not see that the world is done? A sigh to thee, O God, that the sea might come, overwhelming the land! Why are we left to wait?[22]

As time passed the Welsh spirit began to recover from the shock of conquest, and by the middle of the fourteenth century the springs of Welsh poetry were again flowing freely. But it was a new kind of poetry. With the loss of the Princes the bardic order seems to have lost something of its ancient prestige. The old stiff system could no longer be maintained. Poets broke away from the discipline which had so long prescribed the form and content of poetry. The *cywydd* (a kind of sonnet in rhyming couplets), hitherto regarded as an inferior kind of verse, took rank beside the classical *awd* (ode). The old rules as to theme, metre and diction were now widely disregarded. Patronage still demanded eulogy and elegy, but more scope was now given to love of nature and, though still in strictly conventional terms, to

33

love of women. In this new atmosphere of artistic freedom one of the greatest of all Welsh poets came of age.

Dafydd ap Gwilym (*c.* 1325-*c.* 1380) was a contemporary of Langland and Chaucer, and his place in Welsh literature is comparable with theirs in English. Hitherto the chief Welsh poets had belonged to the historic stronghold of Welsh nationalism in the North, but Dafydd was born in Dyfed, the south-west corner of Wales. In this area the old Marcher houses had recovered much of the property and authority they had lost to the Llywelyns, and had become again the centres of local culture. It was a Welsh culture: for the gentry who owed allegiance and rendered service to the Lords were Welshmen, and many of the Lords themselves, once pure Anglo-Normans, had by now become Welsh in speech and way of life and even, by intermarriage with the daughters of Welsh princely families, in blood. But it was Welsh with a difference. More English was spoken and read in Dyfed than in Gwynedd, and there was closer contact with Chaucer's England and the Continent beyond. Hence the South was quicker to feel the first breath of the Renaissance than the aloof conservative North, quicker to break away from the grip of the past and its age-old conventions. Dafydd personified this escape. The most startling novelty was his love-poetry—neither mystical nor romantic but personal and ardent and, though he could write pure love-lyrics, often laughingly lustful. But the theme that most inspired him was nature—the hills and woods and waters, the sequence of the seasons, the wild life of bird and beast—and it is this nature poetry that gives him his place in Welsh literature. ' At his best,' writes Sir Harold Idris Bell, ' he stands alone. Not a few critics, Welsh, English and continental, have regarded him as the greatest poetic genius the Celtic races have yet produced.'[23]

3

It seems strange that Chaucer and Dafydd were writing poetry so often gay and care-free in the second half of the fourteenth century. For England and Wales were both suffering at that time from the dreadful visitations of the Black Death and from the widespread unrest and disorder that ensued. In 1381 the social and political structure of England was shaken by the great revolt which is linked in the schoolbooks with the names of Wat Tyler and John Ball. Twenty years later came the rising in Wales which made Owen Glyn Dwr (Glendower) as outstanding a figure in Welsh national tradition as William Wallace in Scottish.[24]

Like many other lesser troubles of the time, it began with a quarrel between two local magnates. Descended from the ancient princes of Powys, a cultivated gentlemen and soldier, ' train'd up in the English court,' and owner of a large estate in North Wales, Owen became involved in a dispute with a neighbouring Marcher, Lord Grey of Ruthin. In the autumn of 1400 he took advantage of the general unsettlement after the fall of Richard II to try to enforce his claim in arms. Grey was a staunch Lancastrian, and whether for that reason or because Welsh tinder was only waiting for a spark, the local conflict precipitated a popular uprising which spread rapidly through all North Wales. The news of it reached Henry IV as he was moving south from the Scottish border and he decided to deal with it at once. Wheeling his army westward, he marched right through Wales, scattering the rebels and enforcing submission. But, as in earlier invasions, the Welsh leader could not be brought to bay, nor his forces rounded up; and, as soon as Henry had departed, they emerged from their mountain fastnesses and reoccupied the country. A second invasion in 1401 had the same result; and meantime the rising, which at the outset had been mainly due, like the English rising, to the economic consequences of the Black Death, had become a national revolt. The impulse was partly economic. The small peasant farmers and agricultural labourers were out against the landlords. But this conflict had a national colour; the former class were Welshmen, the latter Englishmen or Welshmen who had thrown in their lot with the English. And the rebellion revealed how deep and widespread was the hatred of the English conqueror. Edwardian statesmanship had soon been rendered useless by the arrogance and greed of the English officials and their Welsh friends and by the inevitable difficulty of doing real justice to Welsh claimants, Welsh usage and the Welsh language in English courts. For a century past the sparks of nationalism had been glowing beneath the surface, and now they burst into flame. All over Wales, in the more anglicised South as well as in the North, the countryfolk responded to the call of the blood and accepted Owen as their national deliverer. Welsh students hurried back from Oxford and Welsh labourers from the English border counties. And Owen sought to rouse the old Celtic spirit in other lands than Wales. At the end of 1401 he wrote to Robert III of Scotland and to the Lords of Ireland, calling on them to join in the fight against ' our and your mortal foes, the Saxons.'[25] The letters miscarried, but it seemed for a time as if Owen scarcely needed help from abroad. By 1404, so strong had his hold became on most of Wales outside the walls of the impregnable English castles, so fruitless it seemed to combat the tactics of guerrilla warfare, that Henry, distracted by conspiracies in England and hostilities with France and Scotland, decided to postpone the settlement with Owen.

Thus the phantom of Welsh freedom took shape once more, and Owen, now virtually as much the master of Wales as the great Llywelyn himself, assumed the status of a sovereign prince. *Owynus dei gratia princeps Wallie*—' Owen, by the grace of God, Prince of Wales '—so he styled himself when he sent his envoys to treat with Charles VI of France in the spring of 1404, and they for their part were greeted at the French Court as the envoys of the 'magnificent and mighty Owen, Prince of Wales.' Kings of France were always ready to take an interest in Wales—or in Scotland—in so far as it could be used to weaken England; and already, as it happened, the French had intervened on a small scale in Wales. A French squadron had attacked Caernarvon in 1403. Early in 1404 some two hundred French troops were in Anglesey. And now (July 1404) Charles concluded a firm alliance with Owen against 'Henry of Lancaster.' But the French assistance implicit in the treaty was slow to materialise. A fleet of sixty ships set out from the French ports in that year, ostensibly bound for Wales, but it spent the summer cruising in the Channel and returned to harbour in the autumn without having sighted the Welsh coast. Owen, meantime, was strengthening his position at home. Early in 1405 he entered into a trilateral compact with two English magnates, Northumberland, inveterate enemy of Henry, and Mortimer who aspired to his throne. The genuineness of this so-called Tripartite Indenture has been questioned, but the leading authority on Owen's career regards it as at the least a valid representation of the national ambitions cherished by Owen at that time.[26] They went far. Mortimer was to rule the south of England, Northumberland the north, and Owen's Wales was to push deep between them into the Midlands, the frontier running up the Severn to Worcester, thence across Staffordshire to the source of the Mersey and so to the sea. Certainly such a territorial programme was unlikely to be realised without substantial aid from France, and the force of 800 horsemen and 1800 infantry which landed at last at Milford Haven in the summer of 1405, proved inadequate. Carmarthen and Cardigan were captured, but, when Owen led the allied army through Herefordshire to confront Henry near Worcester, he found himself too far from his base of supplies and had to retire. It was the turn of the tide. Though Henry, despite the fresh levies he obtained from the neighbouring English counties, was unable to win a decisive battle, the allies were in no better case.

Towards the end of the year most of the French men-at-arms, disliking the climate, sailed for home. In the following spring Charles, realising that Owen could not now succeed in invading the heart of England, withdrew the rest of his force. And, while Owen still held his own in most of Wales, his power was beginning to decline. A few more years and he had lost it all.

An outline of the Wales he wanted can be gleaned from what he did and said in those few astonishing years of success. Politically, Wales, like England and Scotland, was to be a national state with its own king and parliament. Two parliaments were actually summoned, one at Machynlleth in 1404, the other at Harlech in 1405. Unlike Llywelyn's councils of chiefs, they consisted of representatives of the ' commotes ' or neighbourhoods, four from each. The ecclesiastical settlement was to match the political in national independence. It was the time of the papal schism, and Owen's ally, Charles VI, pressed him to break with Rome and treat with Avignon. Early in 1406, after consulting a council of Welsh magnates and clerics, Owen informed Charles that he would recognise Benedict XIII on certain conditions. [27] The most important of these was the Pope's concession of what Llywelyn in his day had asked—the restoration of St. David's to its ancient status as a national metropolitan archbishopric independent of Canterbury.[a] The other main conditions were no less nationalist in spirit. (i) Revenues of Welsh parishes were no longer to be made over to English monasteries and colleges. (ii) Only Welsh-speaking clergy should be appointed. (iii) Two universities should be created, one in North Wales, one in South, for clerical training.[b] Finally, Benedict was to bless the Welsh revolt as a holy war against the usurper Henry and his heretical subjects.

[a] Owen was apparently still thinking of the greater Wales of the Tripartite Indenture; for St. David's was to have for its suffragans not only the Welsh bishops, but also those of Exeter, Bath, Hereford, Worcester and Lichfield. Summaries in Lloyd, 119-121, and J. H. Wylie, *History of England under Henry IV* (London, 1884-98), ii. 312-313.

[b] The first Scottish university (St. Andrews) was founded in 1451.

An independent Welsh nation, embodied in a sovereign Welsh state, maintaining its own Welsh Church whose ministers would be taught to think as Welshmen, and preserving its own Welsh tongue—such was Owen's vision of a free Wales. But from 1406 onwards the chance of its fulfilment rapidly declined. Charles made it clear that no more French help would be forthcoming. Scotland's hostility was neutralised by the lucky capture by the English of the heir to the Scottish throne. In 1408 Northumberland was killed at Bramham Moor. And Owen, meantime, was losing his grip on outlying parts of Wales. A broad belt of the southern country and even northern Anglesey submitted to the English. The peasantry, it seems, having freed themselves from the worst of their economic bondage, were losing interest in the national cause, and the gentry, uncertain now of the issue, were beginning to trim their sails. As the spirit of national revolt grew weaker, the English troops, commanded in the North by young Prince Henry, steadily gained ground till Owen finally lost the two strongholds on which his power was mainly based—Aberystwyth in 1408, Harlech in 1409. That was the end. No longer a sovereign ruler but a hunted outlaw, Owen took refuge in the mountains and forests of his homeland where, impotent but uncaptured to the end, he faded out of history. When, soon after 1416, he died, Wales had already woken from the dream of a decade.

It was a harsh awakening.[28] The tide of warfare, ebbing and flowing, had injured and impoverished the countryside. Lands had been laid wate, monasteries wrecked, castles gutted, manor houses burnt, trees cut down, cattle slaughtered. The itinerary of John Leland, the antiquary, who traversed Wales about 1536-39, records ruin after ruin.[29] In Glamorgan one castle is ' al in ruins saving one high tower,' another is ' almost al donne.' The town of Radnor ' was defacyd in Henry the fowrthe days by Owen Glindowr.' In Montgomery only Welshpool castle stands. In Brecknock ' the people about Dinas did burne Dinas Castel that

39

Owne Glindour should not kepe it for his fortress.' But the scars of war were the least of the inflictions suffered by the Welsh on the morrow of the revolt. It had opened a new breach between Wales and England. Until the change that came with the coming of the Tudors, to be recorded shortly, Welshmen were disliked and feared in England. Welsh bards recounted, in somewhat emotional terms, the sharp hostility shown to them and their foreign speech in midland and northern England.[30] But the fear was more injurious than the dislike. The famous *Libell of English Policye*, written about 1436, makes a striking reference to the danger of another such rebellion as Glendower's.

> *Beware of Walys, Criste Jhesu mutt us kepe*
> *That it make not oure childes childe to wepe,*
> *Ne us also, if so it go his waye*
> *By unwarenesse; sethen that many a day*
> *Men have be ferde of here rebellione. . . .*
> *Loke wel aboute, for God wote we have nede*[31].

That was no idle scaremongering: it was what the English Government thought. From the outset of the rising onwards it maintained a system of stern repression. Between 1400 and 1402 no less than fourteen coercive Acts were passed, completely reversing the policy of the Edwardian régime. The inequality which had grown up more or less spontaneously between English and Welsh was definitely established by law. Civic privileges were now barred to all but Englishmen. No Welshman was to be ' accepted burgess, nor to have any other liberty within the Realm,' nor ' to purchase lands nor tenements within England nor within the boroughs nor English towns of Wales.' Welshmen and even Englishmen who had married Welshwomen were to be excluded from all office in Wales; and no Englishman could be convicted at the suit of any Welshman except by English judges and English jurymen. No Welshman was to possess or occupy a ' castle, fortress, or house defensive,' or to bear arms.

Congregations of Welshmen ' for to make or take any council '
were prohibited unless official licence were obtained for ' an
evident and necessary cause.' Nor was the political influence of
the bards forgotten. ' To eschew many diseases and mischiefs
which have happened before this time in the land of Wales by
many wasters, rhymers, minstrels, and other vagabonds,' no such
persons were to be in any wise sustained in Wales ' to make
gathering upon the common people there.' [32]

It was indeed a code for the suppression of rebels, not for the
good government of fellow-subjects, a foretaste of the Penal Laws
in Ireland; and since, when the revolt was over, English kings,
uncertain of their thrones, and English ministers harassed by
domestic and foreign enemies, were not minded to allow the
forces of Welsh nationalism to gather strength again, the code was
confirmed and renewed throughout the Lancastrian and Yorkist
period. Even under Henry V, who had tried repeatedly to come
to terms with Glendower in the latter stages of his revolt, and
who obtained such good service from Welshmen in his French
wars, special measures were enacted for the punishment of Welsh
crime.[33] And besides the garrisons of the royal castles and the
troops of the Lords Marcher a special force of a thousand men
was kept stationed in the heart of Wales to hold the country down.
Nor did the Wars of the Roses, though it divided their op-
pressors, bring relief to the Welsh.[34] For some years the struggle
centred round the March, and Welsh support was canvassed by
both sides: but if Welshmen fought for one side and were rewarded with the liberties of English citizens, they were liable to
proscription and execution by the other. Welsh society was rent
by family feuds between Yorkists led by the Herberts and Lan-
castrians led by the Tudors. Such Welsh patriots as held aloof
deplored the conversion of their country into a battlefield of
English factions, and called from time to time on the rival leaders
to join forces against the common enemy. ' Let not the Saxon
rule in Gwynedd and Flint,' wrote one of their bardic spokes-

men. ' Confer no office on the descendants of Horsa. Appoint as constables of castles throughout Wales men of thine own nation. Make Glamorgan and Gwynedd, from Conway to Neath, a united whole. And should England resent it, Wales will rally to thy side.'[35] True enough, the schism of Wales facilitated what was virtually an English monopoly of Welsh administration. Till some changes were made by Edward IV, almost all the county-sheriffs, constables of castles, chamberlains and justices were Englishmen. With the English garrison at their back, they did what they would with a subject race which had been put beyond the pale of law, and their oppressions and exactions were met by fierce reprisals. The records of Parliament and Privy Council throughout this period are incessantly occupied with the story of Welsh lawlessness and outrage. Bands of outlaws would gather in the mountains, descend upon some town on market day, and drive away the cattle. Pirates swarmed in the Severn estuary. The territories of the Lords Marcher became the scene of a grim irregular war. Travellers were ambushed and murdered on the road. One baron was assassinated in his own castle. No one's farm or crops were safe from arson or his flocks from pillage. ' In those days,' says a family chronicler, ' in that wide world every man stood upon his guard and went not abroad save in sort and so armed as if he went to the field to encounter with his enemies.'[36] In Wales, as in Ireland in days to come, subjection had resulted in demoralisation.

III. THE TUDOR ANNEXATION

DELIVERANCE CAME by a strange conjunction of accident and circumstance. Catherine, widow of Henry V, happened to fall in love with Owen Tudor, a member of an old Welsh family, who was beheaded by the Yorkists on the morrow of their victory at Mortimer's Cross (1461); and two of the sons of their secret marriage, Edmund and Jasper, created Earls of Richmond and Pembroke by their stepbrother Henry VI, loyally backed the Lancastrian cause in the Wars of the Roses. In the final stage of those wars Henry Tudor, son of Edmund by his marriage with the great grand-daughter of John of Gaunt, revived the Lancastrian claim to the English throne. Born in Pembroke Castle in 1457, he had spent the first fourteen years of his life in Wales, tended by a devoted Welsh nurse from Carmarthen, learning from her to speak Welsh as much as English. Thereafter he was compelled to seek refuge from Yorkist hostility in France and there he stayed for another fourteen years. In 1483 he decided to assert his claim to the English throne in person, and sailed for the Welsh coast to join in Buckingham's revolt in Brecon. But his expedition was dispersed by gales; the revolt collapsed, and Buckingham was executed. Two years later Henry tried again. Landing with some two thousand men at Milford Haven, he marched up the coast to the River Dovey and thence inland to Welshpool and on to Shrewsbury. His supporters had prepared for his coming. The bards, in particular, after some doubt and hesitation, had used their great influence with the people on his behalf and now welcomed the reappearance of a national hero whose task it was to ' tame the Saxons.' Readily accepting the rôle, Henry called on all Welshmen to help him wrest his crown from Richard, tyrant and usurper, and to restore ' this our said principality of Wales and the people of the same to their erst liberties, delivering them of such miserable servitude as they have piteously long stood in.'[37] But the response was not universal. In North Wales, where the heart of Welsh nationalism and the cradle of its historic champions lay, the coming of the ' Bull of Gwynedd ' was warmly welcomed; and two powerful chieftains, breaking through the trammels of English administration, led their wild tribesmen to join Henry at Welshpool. In the South the response was not so swift or sure; for the leading families had long wavered in their allegiance, backing York or Lancaster as their fortunes rose or fell. But, as Henry marched northwards, Rhys ap Thomas of Dynevor, the outstanding magnate of the South-West, made up his mind and, followed by the levies of the Herberts from Pembroke, joined Henry at Welshpool. As long, however, as the Stanleys, no less powerful in the North-East than Rhys in the South-West, hesitated, the issue was uncertain. But Henry, with the Red Dragon of Wales among his standards, marched boldly into England to confront the royal army, led by Richard III in person, at Bosworth Field. His courage was rewarded, Sir William Stanley took his side two days before the battle, and at the last moment, when battle was already joined, Lord Stanley followed suit and so decided the result.[38]

Crowned on the battlefield with dead Richard's crown, Henry VII based his title to the throne not on his descent from John of Gaunt and Edward III, but on the right of conquest; and, though his venture could not have succeeded without English support, the Welsh could claim that they had done more than anyone to set their countryman on the English throne. Naturally and happily they made the most of it; happily, because it gave them a providential chance of release at long last from the sense of national subjection. The Welsh had re-conquered England. Arthur had come down from his cave and seized the throne. And Henry, on his side, grasped the opportunity to bind the fighting spirit of Wales to himself and his house. He dispatched a commission to investigate and publish his Tudor ancestry. When, a year after Bosworth, his first son was born, he christened him Arthur ' in honour of the British race.'[39][a] And the Red Dragon was adopted in due course as the device of the House of Tudor and the sinister supporter of its coat-of-arms.[40] In Wales itself, meantime, the old system of subjection had dissolved. Already before Bosworth the most powerful man in South Wales had been a Welshman, and now Sir Rhys ap Thomas, who had been

[a] Prince Arthur died in 1502.

44

knighted on the battlefield, was further rewarded for his support in arms with a series of high offices. He became chamberlain of the royal domain in Carmarthen and Cardigan, constable and lieutenant of Brecon, and seneschal of Builth. He was virtually the ruler of South Wales. In Mid-Wales the President of the Council was an Englishman,^a but his lieutenant was a descendant of the princely house of Powys.^b Lesser offices, too, were now bestowed on Welshmen. ' For the first time in a century Welsh names appeared on the lists of sheriffs of the three North Wales shires, and the tribal chieftain William ap Griffith of Penrhyn [one of the two who had marched to Welshpool] became chamberlain of the principality of North Wales.'[41] Individual Welshmen, moreover, were now freely granted ' letters of denizenship ' which gave them the civil rights of Englishmen, and charters of the English model were granted, at a price, to the inhabitants of several lesser Lordships. The English practice, in fact, of treating Wales as a hostile and dangerous neighbour was completely discarded. The penal laws were forgotten. Parliament ceased to busy itself with Welsh legislation. Only one unimportant Act was passed with special reference to Wales.[42] The Welsh, in fact, were left more or less to themselves. ' They may now be said,' wrote an Italian diplomat in 1500, ' to have recovered their former independence for the most wise and fortunate Henry VII is a Welshman.'[43]

2

In fact, it was nothing like their former independence. A Welsh king in London was not the same thing as a Welsh prince in Wales. No one, except the distant king, rules Wales as the Llywelyns and Glendower had ruled it. The power of the Stanleys in the North was shaken by their mistaken hesitation at

^b Richard Pole, father of the Cardinal.
^a William Smyth, Bishop of Lincoln.

the time of the invasion. For ten years Henry bided his time, and then on a slender charge brought Sir William to the block. The power of Rhys ap Thomas in the South remained unchallenged till his death in 1525; but his young grandson and heir was not so fortunate. Arrested for a foolish armed intrusion into the Court of Sessions at Carmarthen, he was tried, imprisoned, released, imprisoned again and finally, in 1531, executed on a charge of treason—a significant prelude to Henry VIII's forth-coming policy in Wales.

In any case, the first need of Wales, and in particular of the western area occupied by the lesser Lordships of the March, was not freedom. It was government, the maintenance of peace and order, the rule of law. When Henry VII died, having charged his son—so the story runs—to have ' a special care for the benefit of his own nation and countrymen, the Welshmen,' he had done nothing to cure the anarchy bred in the years of repression. Nor for the first twenty years or so of his reign did Henry VIII do anything. Conditions in Wales went from bad to worse. Law-lessness increased, fostered by the continuing anomaly of the Lordships in which the King's writ did not run and fugitives from justice in one Lordship could find refuge in another. But it was not the domestic disorder of Wales that at last stirred Henry to action. It was external danger. In 1533 his quarrel with Pope and Emperor began the long sequence of conflicts with the absolutist powers of Europe which with intervals of peace or truce has continued ever since. And henceforward the relations between England and the other nations of the British Isles were mainly determined by the need for a common British front against the danger from abroad. There was no such front in 1533. It was only twenty years since Flodden and behind a flimsy truce Scotland was waiting for the first good chance of revenge. Ireland was in a state of chronic turbulence and rebellion. The execution of Kildare in 1534 was a sign that the attempt to govern Ireland through native Irish magnates had broken down. Scot-

land hostile, Ireland in revolt—only in Wales could Henry feel
secure in the event of a foreign war. And even in Wales it was
an imperfect security. Westwards of the narrows of the English
Channel South Wales was the nearest point for an invasion from
the Continent: Henry's father had landed there. The Welsh as
a whole were loyal to their Tudor king; there was no question
of rebellion or renewal of the old fight for independence. But in
the eastern half of Wales, the country of the Lordships, the royal
authority was not enforced; and the lack of an effective centralised
administration would be as helpful to a foreign invader as it had
been to Henry Tudor. England's security demanded that Wales
should be not only united in itself but also united as firmly as
possible with England. The manner in which Henry VIII met
that demand has been generally regarded as a fine example of
Tudor statesmanship.

First he enforced law and order. In 1534 Rowland Lee, a
militant bishop of the 'Wolsey school,' was appointed President
of the Council of the Marches with special powers for the punishment of crime. He used them to the full. With troops at his
back, he rode through West Wales hunting thieves. It was said
at the time that 5,000 felons were hanged within six years.[44] If
this had not been their Welsh king's doing such grim severity
might well have been regarded by the Welsh as a throw-back to
the days of national repression. As it was, its justice was not
questioned, and its results were remarkable. In a very short time
the March became as orderly and law-abiding as the neighbouring
English counties.

The second or constructive side of Henry's policy was not
postponed till Lee had done his work. In 1536 the whole political
and administrative system was re-modelled by two Acts of
Parliament.[45] In combination they extended to Wales the Tudor
programme of systematising and controlling government. To
that end Wales was to 'stand and continue for ever from henceforth incorporated, united and annexed' with England; and this

incorporation was to go much further than Edward I's, it was to go all the way. First, the whole of Wales, including the Lordships now at last abolished, was to be organised and administered in twelve shires as if it were a part of England. Secondly, all the King's welsh-born subjects were to ' enjoy and inherit all and singular freedoms, rights, privileges and laws within this his realm . . . as other the King's subjects naturally born within the same have, enjoy and inherit.' Thus, if incorporation with England was to be complete, to be practically fusion, it was to be fusion on terms of equality. A Welshman would stand on exactly the same civic footing as an Englishman. The law and the liberties it safeguarded would be the same; and it would be administered in the same way, save in so far as, by the later Act of 1542, a separate system of four judges' circuits was established, the ' Great Sessions of Wales.' The administration of all the twelve shires, new and old, would be on the English model. Magisterial powers, far wider then than now, would be exercised no longer by English officials but, as in England, by the local gentry. Last, but by no means least, Welsh representatives, who had never come to Parliament since the distant days of Edward II, were now to come there always. Knights for the Welsh shires and burgesses for the Welsh towns were to be summoned, as in England, to ' this present Parliament and all other Parliaments to be holden and kept up for this realm.' Thus, at a stroke, the Welsh became permanent partakers in a constitution which, even in Henry VIII's reign, was more liberal than that of any of the great states of Europe.

Political assimilation could go no further; as a separate body politic Wales had virtually ceased to exist. It retained its title of Principality. It retained in a modified form its old frontier, now permanently fixed by the demarcation of the new shires—an artificial frontier, it may be observed in passing, determined by the boundaries of the Border Lordships without regard for the race or language of their inhabitants, leaving in England the towns of Shrewsbury, where more Welsh than English was still spoken, and of Hereford, the trading centre of South Wales, and detaching from Wales without precisely annexing to England the whole shire of Monmouth which was almost as Welsh as Glamorgan. From a purely political standpoint the name and frontier of the Principality meant very little. They only meant, in fact, that Wales had a separate system of judicial administration.

But Henry wanted more than political assimilation. He wanted cultural assimilation too. Those were dangerous times, and to Henry's mind the less of local variety in speech and custom, the more uniformity in all ways of life, the stronger the State. There was little, if any, Welsh national sentiment in his Welsh blood, and he was determined that the new union should not be undermined by anything that made for separatism. This purpose was frankly stated in the preamble to the first Act of 1536. It referred to the past discord between the King's Welsh and English subjects, and attributed it to the discrepancy between their respective laws and customs and to the fact that the Welsh ' have and do daily use a speech nothing like nor consonant to the natural mother tongue used within this realm.' Provision was made accordingly to eliminate this troublesome variety. With certain exceptions, on which a commission was appointed to report, all ' sinister usages and customs ' were at once abolished; and in 1542, the commission having done its work, the imposition of English law was made final and complete. As to language, it seemed enough, and for a time it proved enough, to prescribe that all legal proceedings must be conducted in English and that the holder of any public office must be English-speaking. Henry, in fact, was trying not only to give the Welsh an English status but to turn them into Englishmen. But in so doing Henry, it need hardly be said, was not influenced by the theories about nationality and the importance of a national language and way of life which belong to a much later age. The idea that the Welsh were a nation in our sense of the word, and as such possessed national rights and values, could not have entered his mind. His policy was purely practical. He wanted security, and that implied as much unity and uniformity as possible in culture as in government.

Ultimately, as will be seen, this attempt to denationalise the Welsh broke down, and in any case, it should not be taken as a reason for condemning the settlement root and branch. For the material benefits of the peace and order it imposed are incontestable. Fields could be tilled in safety now and the grain carried safe to market. The towns became more busy and prosperous since the suppression of brigandage and piracy set roads and seaways free for the movement of merchandise. It is true that the subsequent praise of this Tudor peace was somewhat overdone. James I used it as an argument for the union of Scotland with England.[a] Sir John Davies echoed him in order to point the contrast with the failure of English policy in Ireland.[46] Burke's famous rhetoric about ' the day-star of the English constitution ' was inspired by his desire to extend its rays beyond the Atlantic. But there were Welshmen at the time who in praising the Tudor settlement were not concerned with any case but that of Wales. ' No country in England,' wrote George Owen, a Welsh landowner, in 1594, ' so flourished in one hundred years as Wales hath done, sithence the government of Henry VII to this time, insomuch that if our fathers were now living they would think it some strange country inhabited with a foreign nation, so altered is the countrymen, the people changed in heart within and the land altered in hue without, from evil to good, and from bad to better.'[47] And to that must be added the greatest service that the Tudors rendered to Wales. Taken as a whole and including as one essential factor in it the Welsh allegiance to the House of Tudor, it was the settlement of 1536 that saved Wales from the fate of Ireland—from taking, as the Celtic Irish took, the losing side in the two historic conflicts which rent and shook the

[a] See page 83 below.

British Isles in the course of the next hundred and fifty years, and from suffering the inevitable consequences.

IV. THE REFORMATION AND THE
REVOLUTION

THE REFORMATION was the immediate sequel of the settlement. Henry's breach with Rome coincided in time with his Welsh legislation, the dissolution of the Welsh monasteries with Lee's thief-hunting. If the Welsh had not been delivered from subjection just in time, if their rights had still been less than English rights, if the penal laws had still been in force, and if the King of England had still personified the hated ' Saxon,' the Welsh, it seems more than probable, would have fought for their old Roman Church if only because it was not the new Church of England. As it was, no serious attempt was made by Thomas Cromwell or his instruments to win their hearts and minds. In Wales, as in England, the materialistic side of the Reformation was manifest enough—the spoliation, cupidity, injustice. But there was little to be seen of its spiritual side. Churchmen of Bishop Barlow's character could not endow the Reformation in Wales with the moral loftiness it gained from a Cranmer or a Latimer in England. So it was with a more or less passive indifference that the Welsh submitted to the sequence of religious changes from Henry's reign to Mary's and from Mary's to Elizabeth's. Many Welshmen remained Catholics, but there was no such passion in their recusancy as inflamed the north and west of England, no ' Pilgrimage of Grace.' There was an active body of exiled Welsh Catholics in Rome, Milan and Douai, of whom the leading personality was Owen Lewis, once a young don at New College, Oxford, who was hoping to become Archbishop of York if the Spanish attack on England should succeed. But in Wales itself there was little treason. Only two Welshmen were executed for sharing in the plots to assassinate Elizabeth. Nor did the Jesuits try to do in Wales what, with such far-reaching results, they did in Ireland. It cannot be said, on the other hand, that Wales became widely or warmly Protestant. In England the Reformation had a strong ingredient of nationalism: it was a defiance of foreign interference in English affairs. But in Wales it made no such national appeal, and so failed to touch the springs of Welsh life and thought. The Welsh acquiesced in it, and that was all.

Their reaction to the Puritan Revolution and its aftermath was a similar story. Again it was comparatively negative. Deep as the influence of Puritanism on the Welsh was one day to become, it was slow in taking root. 'It is now full thirty years and upward,' wrote Penry, the Welsh Puritan, 'since Babylon hath been overthrowne in Wales. . . . But alasse, what shall we and our posterities be the better for this if Sion bee not built?'[48] This was partly because the ground had not been prepared for it to the same extent as in England and Scotland by the Reformation; partly because Puritanism was at first regarded as something alien imposed on Wales by England. Thus the Civil War affected Wales differently from Scotland and England. Since there were only a handful of Welsh Puritans, it could not be in Wales, as it was in Scotland, primarily a question of religion. Nor was the constitutional issue understood in Wales as it was in England. The claims of civil liberty made no deeper appeal to Welshmen in Pym's day than the claims of the Protestant conscience had made at the Reformation. Hence the Welsh reaction to the quarrel between King and Parliament was simpler and more personal than the Scottish or the English. It went back, so to speak, to Bosworth Field. It was mainly the tradition of loyalty to the Crown that, having kept Welshmen true to the Tudors, now kept them true to the Stuarts. There were moderates of the middle way like John Williams, Keeper of the Great Seal and Archbishop of York, who opposed Laud's policy and was tried and imprisoned, yet would not back revolt against the King. There was a small minority of Puritans, and amongst them a few wholehearted Parliamentarians. But only two of its twenty-four Welsh members took Parliament's side at the outbreak of the Civil War: the rest were all Royalists, and ten of them fought for the King. As for the rank and file of Welshmen, they followed the gentry's lead. Wales, especially Glamorgan, was the best recruiting-ground for the royal armies, and the sieges of the historic Welsh castles were among the most stubbornly contested of the war.[49]

But, except in so far as resistance to Cromwell's army in the second Civil War was regarded as resistance to English domination, the Welsh share in the conflict was not specifically Welsh: it was not inspired by nationalism. Nationalism was a far stronger factor both in Ireland and in Scotland because in each case the national religion was at stake. The Celtic Irish fought for James II as Irishmen because he was a Catholic. The Lowland Scots fought Charles I and Cromwell as Scotsmen because they were Presbyterians. But the Welsh did not fight as Welshmen, nor, like the English Cavaliers, as champions of the Anglican Church, but only as liegemen of the King. Wales, in fact, combined with the West Country and the Northern counties to make up the Royalist half of England.

After Worcester Wales was as firmly ruled by Cromwell as Scotland after Dunbar,[50] but neither country was denied a measure of self-government in his united Commonwealth. Wales recovered, Scotland obtained, its representation at Westminster. Owing to the exclusion of Royalists, there were only three Welshmen among the ninety surviving members of the Long Parliament in 1649. The Instrument of Government (1653) accorded 30 members out of 400 to Scotland and 28 to Wales. Among the members of the 'Rump' who re-occupied the House of Commons in 1658, there was no memorable Welshman.

Algernon Sidney, uncompromising and incorruptible republican of the classical aristocratic school, sat for Cardiff, but he was an Englishman, and out of tune with Welsh opinion. In politics, indeed, the Welsh Judge Jeffreys who tried him was a better representative of Wales. For throughout the period of strife and change the great majority of Welshmen stood rooted on the right —first Royalists, then Tories. Nowhere in Britain was there more enthusiasm for the Restoration, nowhere less enthusiasm for the ' Glorious Revolution.' Like most of the English Tories, the Welsh acquiesced in the Hanoverian succession, and, when the embers of the old fire flickered into flame in 1715 and 1745, their reaction was still much the same as Englishmen's. There were proportionately more Jacobites, perhaps, in Wales than in England, but they did not join the Scottish Jacobites in their desperate ventures to restore the Stuart dynasty. The Welsh help on which the Young Pretender counted in 1745 was not forthcoming. Only two or three Welshmen were with him at Derby. One of them was the leading Jacobite in South Wales, David Morgan, who opposed the retreat: he ' had rather be hanged than go to Scotland to starve.' He was hanged.

V. ANGLICISATION

BECAUSE THE reaction of Wales to the Reformation and the Revolution was not nationalist, Anglo-Welsh relations in that period of conflict were not exposed to the same strain as Anglo-Scottish and Anglo-Irish relations. The union of England and Wales stood firm; and the longer it lasted, the closer it became. Even the two distinctive Welsh institutions, the reconstituted Council of Wales and the Welsh Court of Sessions, only survived as long as they did because of the distance, far greater then than now in time, between Wales and London, and both of them ultimately disappeared. The Council was finally abolished in

1689; and, though the Court lasted on into the nineteenth century when it was replaced by two new circuits in the English system, there was nothing else political or governmental left to distinguish Wales from England when in 1746 the British Parliament, for legal convenience and to prevent misunderstanding, enacted that ' in all cases where the Kingdom of England, or that part of Great Britain called England, hath been or shall be mentioned in any Act of Parliament, the same has been and shall from henceforth be deemed and taken to comprehend and include the Dominion of Wales.'[51]

Nor was it only the separate political identity of Wales that the union had suppressed. The Welsh were beginning to lose their social and cultural identity as well. One of the chief factors in this process was the pull of the English metropolis. Many Welshmen had followed their Welsh king to London, seeking, naturally enough, to obtain rewards at court for their services at Bosworth. Henry was not unmindful of his obligation, and the number of posts he gave to Welshmen provoked some English jealousy, though nothing comparable with the coarse and violent anti-Scottish outburst in the days of Wilkes and the *North Briton*.[a] ' The poet, Skelton, ruefully recorded the device of St. Peter, who, being tired of the clamour of Welshmen in heaven, arranged that someone should shout the two Welsh words, *caws pôb* (toasted cheese), outside the gates, which were quickly shut when the Welshmen had all rushed out.'[52] Some of these new Londoners married English women and their descendants became less and less Welsh and more and more English. Two families thus founded became famous in the history of England. David Seisyllt had accompanied Henry Tudor to France. After Bosworth he served as a sergeant of the guard, and his son was a page at court who, in course of time, became the father of the great William Cecil of Elizabeth's day. The other historic personage was descended from Morgan Williams, a member of a

[a] See page 147 below.

Glamorgan family, who made his fortune as a brewer in Putney and married Thomas Cromwell's sister. Their eldest son, Richard, adopted his mother's family name, and one of his great-grandsons was Oliver Cromwell.

The place and prestige of the Welshmen in London reacted on the Welshmen of their class who stayed in Wales. Many of the gentry had profited greatly from the Reformation, acquiring large estates, together with their tithes, from the dissolution of the monasteries; and henceforward for many generations these big landed families were to dominate Welsh life. Naturally they took their tone in manners and dress and domestic life from their relations and friends in London; and, as elsewhere, the upper middle class, the clergy and the lawyers in particular, followed their lead. As elsewhere, too, successful business men in the towns strove to win a footing in this ' society.' Thus the gulf between rich and poor was widened, and it was now not only a difference in material things. As time went on, the landlords and their *entourage* became more and more anglicised; while the great majority of the population, mostly small peasant-farmers scattered along the hillsides fringing the great estates, remained Welsh in all their way of life. Language enhanced the difference. In ' society ' more English was spoken than Welsh, partly because it was ' fashionable ' or because Welsh landlords married English wives, but mainly as the result of Henry VIII's repressive policy. Welshmen who aspired to public office of any kind were obliged to learn English. So were lawyers and traders and anyone whose profession or business took him to the courts. For the language of the courts was English: if witnesses spoke Welsh only, their evidence had to be interpreted; it was very rarely that a judge knew Welsh. Welsh patriots soon saw what was happening, and castigated the snobs who wanted to be taken for Englishmen with all the bitterness of a losing cause. ' You will find some,' wrote an exiled Welsh grammarian as early as 1567, ' that no sooner see the River Severn or the clock-towers of Shrewsbury and hear the

Saxon say in his tongue " good-morrow," than they begin to forget their Welsh and speak it with a foreign accent; their Welsh is Englishfied, and their English, God knows, is too Welshy.'[53] Another student of Welsh, a generation later, fiercely attacked ' those who wish to destroy the language of the Cymry '; they were ' the dross and scum of the people.'[54] But vituperation could not save the language: creative work was needed to keep it alive, and during this period of decline literary Welshmen wrote little literature. Less than one-sixth of the two or three hundred books written by Welshmen or about Wales in the course of the century after the union were in Welsh.[55]

In the seventeenth century Welsh was still spoken, and Welsh only, by the great majority of Welshmen, the peasantry of the countryside; but its quality had steadily deteriorated. For the Reformation had done nothing for elementary education; and the grammar schools founded in several Welsh towns in the reigns of Henry VIII and Elizabeth for ' the better education and bringing up of poor men's children,' could not achieve that purpose for the simple reason that all the teaching was in English. Naturally, therefore, the schools became the preserve of anglicised society, while the poor grew up more or less illiterate. And, whereas the speech of the ignorant English villager was deeply affected by the noble language of the Bible and the Prayer Book he heard read in his parish church, the ignorant Welshman understood the English services of the new Church of Wales no better than the Latin masses of the old. The effect on the language was inevitable. Untaught to speak it well, unable to hear it spoken well, the mass of Welshmen spoke it worse and worse. It became steadily more vulgarised and more contaminated with English words. If nothing had happened to arrest its decline it must have shrunk in course of time into a rustic *patois* and ultimately ceased to be a living tongue.

Its salvation was not the result of deliberate policy: it was an incidental by-product of the religious changes. Already in Edward VI's reign and more so in Elizabeth's it was becoming evident that among other reasons for the failure of the Reformation to win a hold on the Welsh people was the fact that it could not use in Wales the two main instruments of its success in England, a Bible and a Prayer Book in the language of the people. It is significant that the first Welsh book, dated 1546, was a translation by John Price of an English manual called *The King's Primer*, which contained the creed, the ten commandments and the Lord's Prayer. About the same time a Welsh book of proverbs was published by William Salesbury, a lawyer of Llansannan who, like Price, had studied at Oxford. The third Welsh book, again by Salesbury, published in 1551, was a Welsh version of the portions of the gospels and epistles prescribed for reading on Sundays and Holy Days in the English Prayer Book. Those little efforts by individual Welshmen were the prelude to action by the Government. In 1563, the fourth year of Elizabeth's reign, an Act of Parliament[56] was passed requiring the four Welsh bishops and their colleague at Hereford to see to it that the Bible and the Prayer Book were translated into Welsh and copies of them placed in every church in Wales ' where that tongue is commonly spoken.' For financial and other reasons this Act remained inoperative, but its purpose was achieved by gifted and devoted Welshmen working on their own initiative and without any public funds to aid them. The Welsh New Testament and Prayer Book published in 1567 was mainly the work of Salesbury. The translation of the whole Bible published in 1588 was the wonderful single-handed achievement of William Morgan, a native of Caernarvonshire. He toiled alone for years as the needy vicar of a little rural parish in Denbighshire, but he was encouraged throughout by Archbishop Whitgift whose pupil he had been at

Cambridge, and the greatness of his work was recognised by his appointment to the bishopric first of Llandaff and then of St. Asaph.

The intent both of the English Act of 1563 and of the Welsh-men who achieved its object was purely religious: they were not concerned with nationality, with preserving or improving the Welsh language. Their aim was to make Welshmen better Protestants, not better Welshmen. The closing words of the Act, indeed, explained that, as a secondary advantage, the translations would help Welshmen to learn English by comparing them with the English version. Yet, in the event, the translations saved the language. The work of real Welsh scholars, they constituted a treasury of Welsh in its fullest and finest form. It is difficult to exaggerate what Cranmer's Bible did for English, but Morgan's Bible did even more for Welsh. It rescued it from vulgarisms and anglicisms, from dispersal into local dialects, from a general decay. It made it uniform, classical, permanent. And already in the earlier years of the seventeenth century more Welshmen were writing Welsh and it was better Welsh. But there was no sign yet of a real literary revival, and in any case the use of good Welsh was still confined to an educated *coterie*. As long as only a small minority of Welshmen had been taught to read, the deterioration of spoken Welsh was bound to continue. The Bible was in the church now, but it was not yet in the cottage.

Nor could the Welsh Bible have much linguistic value in an empty church; and, if at the end of the seventeenth century the Welsh were in danger of losing their language, the same could be said of their religion. The Anglican Church was still only the church of the anglicised upper class. Despite the individual efforts of such energetic bishops as Barrow, Lloyd and Beveridge, it had not won a hold on the Welsh countryfolk. It seemed, indeed, as if the Government and its clerical advisers, who con-trolled the policy and personnel of the Establishment, were not overmuch concerned to make the Church in Wales a Welsh Church. Only Elizabeth recognised that need. No less than thirteen of the sixteen Welsh bishops appointed in her reign were Welshmen.[57] After that, as before, the Welsh bishoprics were frankly treated as stepping-stones to more attractive English sees. At that time and for many years to come it was not expected that Welsh bishops, most of whom would soon be translated across the border, should be able to preach in Welsh. The episcopate, in fact, was mainly English. And there were scandalous cases of plurality and non-residence. 'Where so many of the churches,' writes an historian of the Church, 'were served by the poorly paid curates of non-resident incumbents, it is not surprising that services were cut down or omitted and that parochial visitation almost ceased.'[58]

In 1707 the union of Scotland with England was accomplished, and there were Scottish patriots who believed that doom had been pronounced on Scottish nationhood. The fate of Wales after 170 years of union with England might well have seemed to justify their pessimism. But the picture could be overdrawn. The Welsh national spirit was not yet by any means extinguished. The forces of assimilation had not yet destroyed the Welshman's love of his country or his pride in its historic past. In the journal kept by Defoe of a tour he made through Britain in the early years of the eighteenth century, there is an interesting entry, very English in tone, which shows that Welshmen, even of the anglicised class, for all their English speech and ways, were still indubitably Welsh. The English traveller commends the civility and hospitality of the Welsh gentry, and notes their delight at the stranger's interest in their country and their eagerness to tell him everything about it. 'They value themselves much on their antiquity, the ancient race of their houses, families and the like, and above all, on their ancient heroes, their King Caractacus, Owen ap Tudor, Prince Lewellin, and the like noblemen and princes of British extraction;

and, as they believe their country to be the pleasantest and most agreeable in the world, so you cannot oblige them more than to make them think you believe so too.'[59]

[1] J. E. Lloyd, *A History of Wales from the earliest times to the Edwardian Conquest* (London, 1911), 85-9.

[2] F. M. Stenton, *Anglo-Saxon England* (Oxford, 1943), 2-3.

[3] T. Jones, art on 'Welsh Literature' in *Chambers' Encyclopaedia* (ed. 1950), xiv. 520ff.

[4] See Lloyd, i. 172-8.

[5] G. M. Trevelyan, *An Autobiography* (London, 1944), 147.

[6] Lloyd, i. 371.

[7] Lloyd, 333-342.

[8] *Ibid.*, 364-371.

[9] Quoted by T. F. Tout, *History of England*, 1216-1377 (London, 1905), 76.

[10] Tout, *op. cit.*, 125.

[11] J. F. Rees, *Studies in Welsh History* (Cardiff, 1948), 21.

[12] Lloyd, 458-9.

[13] H. I. Bell, *The Development of Welsh Poetry* (Oxford, 1936), Chap. III.

[14] T. Jones, as cited page 27n. above.

[15] W. Lewis Jones in *Cambridge History of English Literature* (C.U.P., 1908), i. 253.

[16] *Giraldi Cambrensis Itinerarium et Descriptio Kambriae* (Rolls series, London, 1868), 225.

[17] *Ibid.*, 189.

[18] *Statutes of Wales*, ed. I. Bowen (London, 1908), 2. See Introduction, xxix-xxxvii.

[19] *Statutes of Wales*, 27-29.

[20] O. M. Edwards, *Wales* (London, 1920), 223-4.

[21] *Chronicles of Froissart* (trans. Lord Berners, London, 1901), ii. 392-3.

[22] Translation by H. I. Bell, *op. cit.*, 56-7.

[23] Bell, Chap. IV.

[24] The following paragraphs are mainly based on the late Professor Sir. J. E. Lloyd's *Owen Glendower* (Oxford, 1931).

[25] The text of the letters, the former in French, the latter in Latin, is printed in T. Matthews, *Welsh Records in Paris* (Carmarthen, 1910) 40ff., 112ff.

[26] Lloyd, 93. Cf. *Henry IV*, Act 3, Scene 1.

[27] The original of Owen's letter is in the Paris Archives and a copy in the P.R.O., Trans. For. Records, 135.

[28] W. Rees, 275-6.

[29] *Itinerary in Wales*, ed. L. T. Smith (London, 1906), *passim*.

[30] H. T. Evans, *Wales and the Wars of the Roses* (Cambridge, 1915), 3.

[31] ed. Warner (Oxford, 1926), p. 40, lines 784-793.

[32] 2 Henry IV, c. 12, 19, 20, 26, 27, 28, 29, 30, 31, 32, 34. *Statutes of Wales*, 31-36.

[33] 2 Henry V, Stat. 2. c. 5. *Ibid.*, 38.

[34] For a full account see H. T. Evans, *op. cit.*

[35] H. T. Evans, 171.

[36] Sir John Wynn, quoted by Bowen, *Statutes of Wales*, xlix.

[37] H. T. Evans, 221.

[38] W. G. Jones, *Welsh Nationalism and Henry Tudor*, in Transactions of the Cymmrodorion Society (1917-18), 1-59. David Williams, *op. cit*, 19-20.

[39] H. A. L. Fisher, *History of England*, 1485-1547 (London, 1906), 13.

[40] C. Oman, *History of England*, 1377-1485 (London, 1906), 492.

[41] D. Williams, 23.

[42] 1495: 11 Henry VIII, c. 33. *Statutes of Wales*, 47.

[43] *An Italian Relation of England* (Camden Society) quoted by D. Williams, *op. cit.*, 42.

[44] *Hist. MSS. Commission*, 1898, *Report on Welsh MSS*. i. p. x., cited by Fisher, *op. cit.*, 376.

[45] 27 Henry VIII c. 5 and c. 26, *Statutes of Wales*, 67, 75.

[46] J. F. Rees, 27.

[47] *Ibid.*

[48] Quoted by I. Jones, *Printing and Printers in Wales to* 1810 (Cardiff, 1925), 16 ff.

[49] For details of the Civil War in Wales, see J. F. Rees, chaps. v-vii.

[50] See pages 88-89 below.

[51] 20 G. II c. 42. *Statutes of Wales*, 206.

[52] D. Williams, 23.

[53] W. L. Williams, *op. cit.*, 298.

[54] *Ibid.*

[55] J. Rees and D. Brynmor-Jones, *The Welsh People* (London, 1900), 530.

[56] 5 Eliz. c. 28. *Statutes of Wales*, 149.

[57] D. Williams, 62.

[58] W. H. Hutton, *The English Church*, 1625-1714 (London, 1903), 359. See also M. G. Jones, *The Charity School Movement* (Cambridge, 1938), 270-277; and J. Rees and D. B.-Jones, 467-9.

[59] D. Defoe, *A Tour through the whole Island of Great Britain* (London, 1927 ed.), ii. 466.

PART THREE

Scotland and England
to the Union

I. THE MAKING OF SCOTLAND

THE EARLY divergence of Scottish history from Welsh was mainly due to geography. First, Scotland is four times the size of Wales and has provided a homeland for a proportionately larger population. Secondly, Scotland is twice as far as Wales from South-East England. Thirdly, Scotland is a mountainous country like Wales; but, whereas the Welsh mountains form a single mass covering most of Wales, the Scottish mountains, the true 'Highlands,' cover only about half of Scotland, north and west of a diagonal line running roughly from the neighbourhood of Aberdeen to Loch Lomond. South and east of that 'Highland Line' a lowland belt, with which only the much smaller seaboard of South Wales can be compared, stretches from the Firth of Clyde to the Firth of Forth and continues along the coast north-east to Moray Firth and south-east to the valley of the Tweed. Between this belt and England lie the so-called 'Southern Uplands,' a stretch of relatively bare, underpeopled, moorland country between the Cheviots and the Pentland Hills.

This geography made no broad difference to Scotland's history in the earlier age of race-migration—the Celts occupied the whole of Britain—but it had far-reaching effects on the course of the subsequent invasions. The Romans penetrated deep into Scotland. Three times they tried to subjugate the Highlands as they subjugated Wales; but the building of Hadrian's Wall between Solway and Tyne and Antoninus' Wall between Clyde and Forth was a confession of defeat, mainly due, it is supposed, to the difficulty of maintaining communications across the wild Southern Uplands with a distant base in England. Thus Roman civilisation made even less impression on Scottish life than on Welsh: it made none at all.

Scotland again, like Wales, was not submerged by the successive waves of invasion from continental Europe. The Anglo-Saxons' ' beachheads' were mostly in East Anglia and Kent. Thence they swept across England and made it their home. But the only part of Scotland they occupied was the south-east corner, the Lothian district, between Forth and Tweed. For several hundred years this area was included in the Kingdom of Northumbria. It was an Anglo-Saxon who re-named the rock-fortress ' Edwin's Burg.' It was not till about fifty years before the coming of the Normans that King Malcolm II recovered Lothian. Meantime another alien intrusion had been effected farther north. Danes and Norsemen raided and ravaged all up the east coast: the latter, rounding the northern tip, seized the Western Isles and ruled them right on into the Middle Ages. Limited though they were in scope, these invasions implied an infusion of new blood—Anglo-Saxon in the south, Scandinavian in the north; but the people of Scotland remained predominantly Celtic in race, though not so purely Celtic as the Welsh; and they retained, like the Welsh, their Celtic language (Gaelic), their Celtic tribal system, and, after the settlement of the missionaries from Ireland in Iona in 563, their Celtic monastic Christian Church.

The spread of Christianity over Scotland, it is thought, did most to help the Scots, in the centuries of fighting and confusion, to overcome the inveterate Celtic tradition of inter-tribal jealousy and conflict.[1] When Columba came to Iona, the tribes were grouped in four 'kingdoms'—one in the south-east covering Lothian, one stretching northwards from the Clyde to Pentland Firth, one on the mid-west coast, and one in the south-west (Strathclyde). All were Celtic, but Celtic with a difference. Picts predominated in the north, Scots in the south, Britons in the south-west. The last-named spoke Welsh, the rest Gaelic. Like the three smaller princedoms in Wales, these separate kingdoms were constantly at war; but in the period in which their rulers and peoples were being converted to Christianity—the period also of the Scandinavian invasions—a process of political consolidation was at work which began with the union of the northern kingdoms under Kenneth MacAlpin in 844 and came to its climax in 1018 when Malcolm II wrested the Lothians from Canute's England and his grandson, 'gentle Duncan,' inherited the throne of Strathclyde. When Duncan succeeded his grandfather in 1034, a generation before the Norman Conquest, the whole country north of the Tweed, save the islands off the northwest coast, became—if the language of a later day can be used of such primitive conditions—the national state of Scotland. The Welsh achievement never equalled this. Neither Hywel nor Gruffydd ruled Wales as effectively as their contemporaries, Malcolm and Duncan, ruled Scotland. More than a century passed before the Llywelyns could claim a comparable sovereignty, and, whereas the Welsh state they created collapsed within a few decades, the state of Scotland endured, with one brief interval, for nearly seven centuries.

The political unity of Scotland combined with geography to halt the Norman Conquest at the Tweed. In 1069 William marched north to stamp out rebellion in Northumbria, but he did not follow the stream of fugitives which his 'harrying' drove across the border. Scotland was not dangerously hostile; and the subjection of a warlike people, with the Highlands at their back, would at the best be costly in men and time. His immediate need was to complete the conquest of England, and it was not till that task had been accomplished that William came back to secure his northern flank. In 1072 he crossed the border and marched through Lothian to the Forth and the Tay with a fleet accompanying him offshore. It was a formidable exhibition of power, and the Scots, aware of the dreadful fate of their neighbours beyond the town, did not challenge it. They retreated as the Normans advanced: there was no fighting; and, having obtained a formal recognition of his overlordship from Malcolm III, the Conqueror withdrew.

The subsequent relations of Scotland with England were by no means always friendly. There was a second English invasion in 1080, a third in 1091, but not a fourth till 1296. The Scots for their part frequently raided and even aspired to annex the northern English counties. Scottish kings intervened on occasion in the domestic quarrels of England, as Llywelyn did, and more than once negotiated, like Glendower, with the court of France. But Scottish independence was not, like Welsh, a transient product of English weakness. Scotland stood on her own feet as firmly as France; and the controversy as to whether the King of Scotland did or did not pay homage to the King of England for permission to rule Scotland was mainly a matter of form. In fact, homage or not, he ruled it. And, as time went on, the two kingdoms settled down into more or less good-neighbourly relations.

This outcome was greatly aided by the gradual assimilation of Lowland Scottish nationality to English—a process which had begun with the Anglo-Saxon occupation of Lothian and was advanced a long step farther by the marriage of Malcolm III with the fugitive sister of Edgar the Atheling. Queen Margaret was proudly English and she did her best to anglicise her husband and his subjects. She made the court a centre of English culture;

she encouraged the use of the English language instead of Gaelic; she induced the Church, whose nominal submission to Rome about sixty years after the Synod of Whitby had not implied the discontinuance of Celtic prayers and practices, to conform more fully to the Latin usage now in force throughout most of Western Europe. Under her three sons, who succeeded in turn to the throne, this process of anglicisation was continued: under the last and ablest of them it was virtually completed. David I was almost an Englishman, he had spent his youth at the court of Henry I who had married his sister, he himself had married the daughter of an English earl. And in the course of his reign (1124–1153) he made half Scotland almost English. He invited English barons of his acquaintance—a Bruce, a Fitzalan, a Lindsay among them—to Edinburgh, and gave them feudal estates on which, like the Lords Marchers, they built their castles, assembled their retainers, and formed little foci of English life and influence. The outcome has been described as a ' bloodless Norman Conquest.' The old Celtic polity was gradually transformed into the feudal system which the Normans had forcibly imposed on England. The King was supported by a landed aristocracy. A *mormaer* was now an earl, a *toshach* a thane. The country was divided and organised in shires. Towns became chartered ' burghs ' on the English model. The Church of Scotland was more closely assimilated to the Church of England: Scottish bishops, like their English brethren, were appointed to high offices of State. English law was widely adopted or adapted. More and more Scotsmen spoke English. English trade and traders multiplied at the ports. It might be said, in fine, that the frontier between England and the south-east part of Scotland was losing most of its meaning. It marked a clear division between two separate states; but, save only in race—and blood was being mingled all the time—it was not so clear a demarcation of separate nations.

But only half Scotland had been anglicised. The new régime had been established in the Lowlands high-handedly indeed, but not by force; and sheer force would have been needed to impose it on the Highlands. There chiefs and clansmen steadfastly maintained their ancient Celtic customs and their ancient Celtic speech. The Highlands were to the Lowlands something like Wales was to England; and Highlanders hated as bitterly as Welshmen the foreign intruder and his foreign fashions. Several times they rose in arms to fight what they rightly felt to be a menace that threatened to destroy their traditional way of life. On Malcolm III's death his brother, Donald Bain, with the clans at his back, seized the throne, and in the four years before his expulsion he did what he could to undo Margaret's work and to drive out her Englishmen from Scotland. He was the last of the Celtic kings; subsequent risings were ineffective; but, when the last of them had failed (1235), the Celtic spirit was still alive. It was not to be finally repressed till another five hundred years had gone.

If the Celts had won, Scottish nationalism would have become predominantly Celtic, and Scotland's relations with England would presumably have been comparable with those of Celtic Wales or Celtic Ireland. As it was, the root of the modern harmony between Scotsmen and Englishmen lies in the fact that what Margaret and her sons did was never undone. It may well have seemed, indeed, by the end of the thirteenth century that in no long course of time social and cultural assimilation would lead to some kind of political combination. Why should two countries, whose domestic life had become so much alike, insist on remaining separate, independent, mutually foreign states? To the English Government this was a more vital question than to the Scottish: it was a question of strategic security. If England should go to war with France—and in fact the Hundred Years War was soon to begin—a disaffected Wales on her flank would be a tiresome handicap, but a hostile Scotland in her rear would be a serious danger. Clearly, therefore, the English Government was bound to make the most of any opportunity which offered for bringing about a closer union of Britain; and, as it chanced, a golden opportunity occurred in 1286 when, on the accidental death of Alexander III, his grand-daughter, Margaret, then living with her father, Eric of Norway, succeeded to the Scottish throne. In 1290 a council held at Brigham and attended by Scottish commoners as well as leading barons and ecclesiastics, approved the proposal of a marriage, backed by Edward I of England, between Margaret and the young ' Prince of Wales,' and concluded a treaty of alliance providing for the union of the English and Scottish Crowns. It was expressly a free compact between independent states, whose identity would remain distinct save only in the person of the monarch: Scotland, for example, was to have a Great Seal of her own. The validity of Scottish law and the preservation of her liberties and customs were guaranteed. The power to legislate for Scotland was specifically denied to any English parliament. The treaty was plainly an act of statesmanship, foreshadowing the ultimate achievement of the statesmen of 1707. But fate postponed the union of the Crowns for some 300 years and such closer union as it might have fostered for yet another century. The ' Maid of Norway ' died on her voyage to Scotland, and, as has happened more than once in British history, a lost chance of union was followed by a deepening of division. The treaty shows what good neighbours Scotland and England were before Margaret's death. Soon after it they became, and long remained, not merely strangers but bitter and bloody enemies.

The estrangement of Scotland was Edward I's doing. It was natural enough that he should take advantage of the disputed succession on Margaret's death to strengthen his influence in Scotland. He was, indeed, invited by the interim ' Governor ' and several party leaders to assist in deciding which of the rival claimants had the best title to the throne. It was natural, too, that he should open the proceedings by reviving the old claim to feudal overlordship. The assembled Scottish barons conceded it; and all the claimants at that time in the field bound themselves to accept his award 'as their Lord Paramount.[2] The hearing of the case, moreover, was elaborately judicial, and the ultimate choice of Balliol was just. But Balliol's character was not so strong as his case, and it may well have been his weakness that tempted Edward to assert through him, and so confirm, his own suzerainty over Scotland. Bullied and humiliated, the puppet was driven at last to cut the strings. After all, he was King of Scotland, and in 1295, relying on the backing of his people, he repudiated his homage and made a defensive alliance with the King of France, who for more than a year had been at war with the King of England. So began the liaison with France, the ' auld alliance,' which for more than 300 years was to distract and imbitter Anglo-Scottish relations.

Provocation had been answered by provocation; and Edward I was not the man to go back along a road he had once taken. He marched in force through Scotland, easily obtained the submission of the Scottish nobles, whose still purely feudal loyalties were unaffected by patriotic sentiment, and left the country strongly garrisoned, with three English delegates to govern it on his behalf over an empty throne.[a] But the subjection of Scotland was not so easy a matter as the subjection of Wales had been. Almost at once, the first war of independence broke out. The Scottish people had succumbed, save in the Highlands, to anglicisation, but they were not minded to submit to this kind of English conquest. Lacking the leader they needed among their feudal magnates, they found him in an unknown patriot who was a master of guerilla warfare. In the space of a few months (1297) William Wallace wiped out all English rule in Scotland. But the only lasting result of his triumph was the hold it had given him on Scotsmen's hearts. In 1298 Edward

---

[a] It was on this occasion that the stone on which Scottish Kings had been crowned at Scone was removed to Westminster.

again marched north, utterly defeated Wallace at Falkirk and so
broke the back of the rebellion. It was not, however, till 1304
that, having brought the unruly English barons to order and
made peace for a time with France, he was able to finish the work
of re-establishing his authority in Scotland. With the capture
and execution of Wallace, the last hope of independence flickered
out, and in 1305, at a council half composed of Scottish delegates,
a new constitution was drawn up. It confirmed Edward's direct
overlordship in Scotland, but it retained the separate Scottish
legal and administrative system to be manned, as before, mainly
by Scotsmen, and it extended its operation over the whole
of Scotland by annulling the Celtic laws and customs which
had survived in the Highlands as in Wales. It kept in being
the Scottish Parliament, still a purely aristocratic body; but
it is thought, though not known, that Edward intended
also to summon Scottish representatives to the English Parliament.[3]

It was a reasonable settlement. Edward had learned the lesson
that Britain could not be united without the recognition of a
separate Scottish nationhood, and he did not attempt any such
political amalgamation as Henry VIII, in very different circumstances, was to impose on Wales. But Edward had been wise too
late. By his previous attempt at a forcible subjection the 'Hammer
of the Scots' had awakened the spirit of Scottish nationalism. The
price which must be paid for the use of force is usually high, and
the behaviour of English officials and of English soldiers had left
an indelible mark. The flame of Scottish resentment which had
blazed out in Wallace's rising was rekindled by his execution.
Within six months of its enactment the new constitution collapsed
and the second war of independence began. This time it was a
Scottish noble who headed the rebellion. In 1306, Robert Bruce,
a patriot now like most of his kind, murdered his most dangerous
rival and seized the vacant throne. Old Edward, hastening to the
border, died on the point of crossing it; and Bruce used the

respite given him by the new king's weakness and his quarrel
with his barons to consolidate his position, to win the support of
the Scottish clergy, and finally to reduce the castles still held by
English garrisons. Stirling was the last of them, and it was on
his march to the relief of Stirling in 1314 that Edward II came to
Bannockburn.

Bannockburn was one of the most decisive battles ever fought
on British soil. The war continued in a desultory fashion for a
few more years, but it was certain now that England was not going
to conquer Scotland, and in 1327 the Treaty of Northampton
acknowledged the complete independence of Scotland under
King Robert I. If the Scots had lost Bannockburn, it may be that
their new nationhood would never have come to full fruition.
As it was, the wars of independence endowed the Scots with a
national pride they have never lost and a national tradition they
have never forgotten.

II. THE LONG FEUD

FROM BANNOCKBURN to the Reformation, a stretch of some 250
years, Scotland and England maintained an inexorable feud. The
border between them became a permanent battlefield, drenched
with blood and scorched with fire; and ferocious raids thrust deep
into the respective hinterlands. Pitched battles were fought from
time to time—Halidon Hill, Neville's Cross, Chevy Chase,
Homildon Hill—inspiring, as an Anglo-Scottish complement to
the bardic poetry of Wales, the immortal folk-song of the border
ballads. Year by year the unnatural gulf between the Lowland
Scots and the Northern English, two kindred peoples, speaking
the same language, was widened by savage deeds and savage
memories. But away from the border, at any rate, the enmity
was not so harsh or widespread in England as in Scotland. It is
usually the weaker party in a conflict that makes the bitterer foe;

and, if medieval Englishmen were often afraid of Scottish interference in their wars with France, they were never afraid of
Scottish domination, whereas the reason why all Scotsmen, save
a handful of selfish intriguers, hated England was that she had
tried, and might try again, to rob them of their national independence.

' So long as but a few hundred of us stand,' ran the famous
letter to the Pope drafted by Bruce's council a few years after
Bannockburn, ' we never will bow down to England. We fight
not for glory, pelf, honour, but for liberty, which lacking no
man of virtue may survive.'[4] For all these brave words, Scottish
liberty would still have been precarious if English power had not
been divided elsewhere. In 1337 Edward III claimed the crown
of France and began the war on which for a hundred years
England squandered the resources she might otherwise have used
for a settlement with Scotland. To the Scots, who could scarcely
hope that all their battles with England would be Bannockburns,
this new direction of English policy was naturally welcome, and
in plain self-interest they did what they could to aid the cause of
France. In 1372 the tie with France was renewed in more definite
and durable form. Welsh troops on the English side in the Hundred Years War[a] confronted Scottish troops on the French side.
Six years after Agincourt a Scottish army defeated an English
army at Baugé. Scotsmen fought to the last for Joan of Arc.
And more than once French forces were dispatched to Scotland
(as to Wales),[b] and took part in invasions of England. Thus, as
time went on, Scottish policy and sentiment became more and
more firmly attached to the ' auld alliance.' It was a twisting
away of Scotland's destiny from its insular to a continental setting,
and it was bound to affect the development of Scottish nationality.
The process of anglicisation had been abruptly halted by Edward
I and Wallace, and English influences were now replaced by

[a] See page 32 above.
[b] See page 37 above.

73

French. Scottish diplomats and soldiers frequented the French court. If Scottish students still went in intervals of peace to Oxford or Cambridge, they now went also in growing numbers to Paris or Orleans. When finally the Renaissance came to Scotland, it came, as Scottish 'baronial' architecture still bears witness, by way of France, not England. In every respect, indeed, the impact of the continent on the island, the merging of the Anglo-Scottish schism in a wider European conflict, was drawing England and Scotland farther apart. No one could have foreseen that in the end it was to bring them together.

Meantime free Scotland remained the poorer, weaker, less civilised of the two neighbour kingdoms. The life of medieval England, it is true, was not by any means well ordered. The French wars were an incessant drain on her manhood and money. Internally she was rent by the chronic feud between King and barons until at last it burnt itself out in the Wars of the Roses. Yet English life was becoming steadily more stable, more prosperous, more humane. Scotland, too, was advancing, but at a very much slower pace. The foundations, if no more than that, of popular government were laid when, in pursuance of an English precedent for once, Scottish burgesses as well as nobles were summoned to the Scottish Parliament (1326). Successive improvements in the administration of justice foreshadowed the great legal system of a later day. Cathedrals and abbeys were built matching their English counterparts in beauty. By the eve of the Reformation the national aptitude and zest for education were already so developed that three Universities were founded—St. Andrews (1451), Glasgow (1451) and Aberdeen (1494)—to serve an English-speaking population of only some two or three hundred thousand. But the background to such lights was dark. The Highlanders were left behind by the Lowlanders' advance. They still spoke Gaelic only, still clung to their rude clannish ways And in the Lowlands the feudal anarchy was worse than in England, the nobles more murderous, the churchmen more corrupt. Towns, trade, industry were slowly growing, but the mass of the people lived a bleak and stinted life, and Scotland as a whole was very much poorer than England.

It is idle to ask whether Scotland would have been better off if she had been united with England and shared her progress. For union at that time could only have been achieved by force and, if force had triumphed, the upshot would not have been a real and lasting fellowship of Englishmen and Scotsmen in one state. Force could only have thrust England's dealings with Scotland along the Irish road towards a greater tragedy. For, once the Scottish national spirit had been awakened, it became a psychological necessity that a union to be valid should be a voluntary union, without any sense of domination on the stronger side or subjection on the weaker, a union between nations which stood on an equal footing of national sovereignty. And for that the time was not ripe till another two centuries had passed. Thomas Carlyle understood. 'A heroic Wallace, quartered on the scaffold, cannot hinder that his Scotland become, one day, a part of England [Britain]; but he does hinder that it become on tyrannous and unfair terms a part of it. . . . If the Union with England be in fact one of Scotland's chief blessings, we thank Wallace that it was not the chief curse.'[5]

Scotland took her place among the new national monarchies of Europe in the reign of James IV (1488-1513), the most gifted of all the ill-fated Stewarts. What he did for Scotland was comparable with what Henry VII (1485-1509) did for England. He strengthened his authority over the whole country, bringing the Western Isles firmly and finally within the realm. He was not so careful a financier as Henry, but he vigorously promoted the growth of overseas trade, built for its protection a navy of thirty warships, and defended its interests at foreign courts. Never had the name of Scotland stood so high on the Continent.

At this time, also, the noble stream of Scottish poetry, which may be said to have begun with Barbour's romantic epic *The Brus* (Bruce), broke into full flow. It was the age of the makars, of Robert Henryson and Gavin Douglas and Dunbar, the greatest Scottish poet before Burns. Their poetry was written in the northern dialect of English which had long been spoken in civilised south-east Scotland. In that area, though not in the Highlands where the bards still chanted the praises of their chiefs, Gaelic poetry was dying out; but it is a mistake to suppose that Gaelic was the only national language of Scotland, as Welsh was the only national language of Wales. The Anglo-Saxon invaders never occupied Wales as they occupied south-east Scotland; and the language of the kingdom of Northumbria which stretched for several hundred years from the Humber to the Forth was roughly the same. When the Scottish frontier was advanced to the Tweed, and when, in course of time, midland English became the standard language of England, ' Scots,' as it came to be called, preserved its northern quality and drew farther apart, developing powers and beauties of its own. But it is important to remember that English was in origin as much a national language in South-East Scotland as in England.

Scotland's new strength in sea-power and trade, backed by the ' auld alliance,' was a challenge to England, and Henry VII's response was characteristic. He offered friendship. He over-looked James' support of Perkin Warbeck. He persuaded him, on the third asking, to accept the hand of his sister Margaret. In 1502 a treaty of peace was concluded—the first real peace and the first reaffirmation of Scotland's sovereign independence since 1328—and in 1503, to the music of Dunbar's famous poem, *The Thistle and the Rose,*[a] the Stewart and the Tudor were married. But, if this second attempt at a dynastic solution of the Anglo-Scottish problem was not wrecked at the outset like the first, it soon proved no less a failure. In 1509 pacific Henry VII was suc-

[a] This was the first use of the thistle as a symbol of Scottish nationality. (Terry, 149.)

ceeded by militant Henry VIII. In 1511 the latter joined a coalition against France. In 1513, James IV, loyal to the obligations of the ' auld alliance,' marched to his death at Flodden. The defeat was overwhelming. Yet, though the edifice of Scottish strength and prestige built up by James had crashed to the ground, the Scottish spirit was unbroken. Even Flodden could not undo what Bannockburn had done.

But Henry did not realise the strength of Scottish nationalism. True, he tried reconciliation first, proposing once more a dynastic settlement by a child-betrothal of his daughter Mary to James V. But on the rejection of his offer he unleashed the old savage border warfare. So, till a five-year truce was patched up in 1529, the tradition of hostility and hate persisted while within Scotland the schism deepened between those who wanted peace with England and those who, despite the grim lesson of Flodden, clung to France. It seemed, in fact, as if Anglo-Scottish relations were permanently to keep the pattern they had taken for the last 200 years when suddenly the international framework in which they were set began to shift.

Henry's breach with Rome in 1533 was the prelude to the conflict between the Protestant Reformation and the Catholic Counter-Reformation in which most of Europe was to be involved. Sooner or later, it was plain, England would have to fight, and, whether or not he realised the danger she was presently to run, Henry must have felt, more urgently than any of his predecessors, the strategic need of at least a peaceful, at best a united, Britain. In 1534 he began the pacification and annexation of Wales. In the same year he converted the truce with Scotland into a formal peace, strove to win over James to Protestantism, and offered again the hand of his daughter, Mary. But James preferred a different kind of dynastic settlement. In 1539 he married the daughter of Francis I of France and on her death within a year he married Mary of Guise. When he died in 1542, his first-born, Mary, was seven days old.

Maybe the double event gave Henry a chance of winning Scotland over, then and there, to England and the Reformation. Protestantism was growing fast in the Lowlands, stimulated by the burning of heretics and the notorious abuses of the Church, and soon to be further strengthened by the publication of an English version of the Bible (1544). The Queen of Scots was an infant: the Regent, Arran, a simpleton. But if there was an opportunity for statesmanship, Henry threw it away. To propose that the infant Mary should be pledged to his year-old son, Edward, was an obvious move. To try to enforce its acceptance should have seemed a no less obvious blunder. Yet that is what Henry did. In 1544-45 his army swept across Lothian. Multitudes were massacred, Edinburgh was burnt, Melrose and other abbeys and over 200 villages were destroyed. The invasion was repeated again in 1546, and again in 1547. The Scottish reaction to this ' English wooing ' was what might have been expected. Mary, now five years old, was promised not to the son and heir of Henry VIII of England but to the son and heir of Henry II of France. In 1548 a large French force was dispatched to Scotland, and, as a condition thereof, Mary was sent for safe keeping to France. ' Now,' said Henry II, ' Scotland and France are one State.'

The boast was premature, and it showed that Henry II understood the Scots no better than Henry VIII. Superficially it might perhaps have seemed that the French régime in Scotland during the next fifteen years was tantamount to its annexation. French troops were in the country, and the Regent's councillors, the Queen-mother, Mary of Guise at their head, were fastbound to Catholic France. But, underneath, Scottish nationalism was reacting against French hegemony as it had always reacted against English hegemony; and it was even more formidable now because religion had become its mainspring. Protestantism was still steadily spreading, and Protestantism was necessarily anti-French. The situation, in fact, was closely similar to that in

England; and in both countries the tension was resolved in a crisis lasting about five years and matched by a swift succession of dramatic events.

In England, Catholic Mary Tudor succeeded her Protestant brother on the throne in 1553, married Catholic Philip II of Spain in 1554, and set herself to undo the Reformation, restore the jurisdiction of the Pope and make England an instrument of Spanish policy. She died in 1558, and English nationalism, provoked by her subservience to foreign interests, welcomed the accession of Protestant Elizabeth, who rejected the widowed Philip's prompt offer of marriage, re-established the Protestant system, and began her long task of uniting and strengthening England against the forces of the Counter-Reformation.

In Scotland the assumption of the Regency by Mary of Guise in 1554 corresponded to Mary Tudor's marriage with Philip II: the Catholic cause was strengthened for the moment at the price of foreign ascendancy. In the spring of 1558, Queen Mary, now sixteen years old and still in France, married the Dauphin Francis, bestowed on him the ' crown matrimonial' of Scotland, and secretly signed a transfer of her royal rights to him and his heirs in the event of her dying childless. On Mary Tudor's death before the year was out, she claimed, by Catholic right of succession, the English throne, and adopted for herself and her husband the royal arms of England. In 1559 Henry II died, and Francis and Mary became King and Queen of France and Scotland together. Now indeed, they seemed to be, to all intents, ' one state.' But no sooner had the old Franco-Scottish *entente* thus reached its culmination than it collapsed. For the similar developments in Scotland and England had had similar results. In both countries nationalism had become identified with Protestantism, and in both the national spirit revolted against foreign Catholic domination. Thus, side by side with the sequence of events which seemed to be confirming the French hold on Scotland, a parallel sequence of events was leading to its destruction. In 1555 John Knox, with

Elizabeth's connivance, returned from exile and took the lead of the Reformation. In 1557 a powerful body of Protestant clerics and laymen—'Lords of the Congregation' they were presently called—leagued themselves by the first of the historic Covenants in open hostility to the Catholic establishment, demanded freedom to adopt the Protestant form of worship, and founded the first Scottish Reformed church at Dundee. In 1559, when the Regent denounced heresy and decreed the banishment of those who preached it, the challenge was answered by an outbreak of riotous attacks on Catholic buildings which began at Perth and swiftly spread the trail of irreparable destruction far and wide. In August the arrival of a fresh French garrison, a thousand strong and soon to be reinforced, brought the issue to a head. Already Knox and his colleagues of the Congregation had appealed for help in the only quarter whence it could be got; and Elizabeth was ready to send money, though not yet willing to send men. But early in 1560 Cecil overcame her hesitation. In February a treaty was concluded with the Scottish rebels at Berwick. In March an English army, with an English fleet to seaward, joined in the siege of the French at Leith. In June the Regent died. In July the Treaty of Edinburgh was signed, requiring the evacuation of all but a bodyguard of French troops. No claims were made for England, save only that the Queen of Scots must cease to bear the English arms: the ghost of English suzerainty was left in its feudal grave: it was not proposed that, for security, an English garrison should take the place of the French. This wise moderation was rewarded as it deserved. Scottish sentiment swung over from the old ally to the old enemy. ' An English army for the first time marched out of Scotland as a friend.'[6]

The crisis, however, was not yet over. When, on the death of Francis II at the end of 1560, his widow returned to Scotland, she found that her realm had already become Protestant in law. In the previous summer the Pope's jurisdiction had been abolished and the mass prohibited by Acts of Parliament, and at the same time the structure and doctrine of the Reformed Church, soon to be known as Presbyterian, had been established. But young Mary Stewart—still only nineteen—was as determined as Mary Tudor had been to undo what had been done; and it was not a desperate ambition. The wholehearted Protestants were as yet a minority in Scotland; in England, especially in the north, the Catholic cause was still strong enough to challenge the Elizabethan settlement; and in the background stood the gathering forces of the Counter-Reformation, headed by Spain and bent on overthrowing Protestant England whether by conspiracy within or by invasion from without. But, if Mary's designs were not by any means fantastic, her fate was only one factor in a wider complex and shaped by forces she could not control. The issue was not determined by her conduct during those seven wild years of her reign in Scotland—by the quarrel with Knox, the murder of Darnley, the elopement with Bothwell, the flight to England— nor by the pitiful part she played as Elizabeth's prisoner, nor by her ultimate execution in 1587. The issue was determined first by the detection of the conspiracies and the suppression of the Catholic revolt in England and next by the defeat of the Spanish Armada. In those decisive events Scotland was not called on to take part, but the leaders of her new Church, now also the leaders of the state, were well aware that Scotland's destiny was as much at stake as England's. The lesser kingdom could not hope to contest a Catholic triumph in the greater. Thus Scotland and England had been brought together across the gulf that had yawned so deep and long between them by their consciousness of a transcendent common cause—the protection of national freedom and the Protestant faith from the ascendancy of the Catholic monarchies of continental Europe.

III. BRITAIN IN THE SEVENTEENTH
CENTURY

THE SITUATION at Elizabeth's death in 1603 may well have encouraged the hope that the new friendship between the neighbour nations would endure. English sentiment accepted James VI of Scotland as James I of England because he was a Protestant. Scottish sentiment acquiesced in his migration from Edinburgh to London because he was a Scot. At the outset, therefore, the Scots did not feel, any more than the Welsh had felt in 1435, that the new régime implied the subjection of the weaker to the stronger nation. Like the Welsh, they were proud that a King of their blood should rule their old English enemies. But sentiment was not enough. To confirm it and make use of it so as to build a union of the peoples on a union of the Crowns, statesmanship was needed, and neither James I nor Charles I was a statesman. James was only half a Scot, Charles only a quarter. James revisited Scotland only once in the course of his reign, Charles only once before the Civil Wars. Both failed to appreciate— James not so crassly as Charles—the national pride of the Scottish people and the stubborn individualism of the Scottish character; and for that reason both adopted the fatal doctrine which has done more than anything else, perhaps, to injure the cause of international harmony in the world—that the logical, the desirable, the reinforcing complement of unity is uniformity. No fault can be found in the plea for union, the first statement of the case on record, which James addressed to his first Parliament. 'The union of these two princely houses,' he said, 'is nothing comparable to the union of two ancient and famous kingdoms. . . . If we were to look no higher than to natural and physical reasons, we may easily be persuaded of the great benefits that by

that union do redound to the whole island. If twenty thousand
men is a strong army, is not forty thousand a double the stronger
army? . . . Do we not remember that this kingdom was divided
into seven little kingdoms? And is it not now the stronger by
their union? And hath not the union of Wales to England added
a greater strength thereto? Which, though it was a great principality, was nothing comparable in strength and power to the
ancient and famous kingdom of Scotland? . . . Hath not God
first united these two kingdoms both in language and religion
and similitude of manners? Yea, hath he not made us all in one
island, compassed by one sea?'[7] So far, so good; but James
meant the union to be uniform. He wanted his single kingship
to be reflected in a single legal system and a single Church—' all
manners and statutes and customs welded into one as they are
all one body under one head.'[8] He proposed, in fact, to do with
Scotland what Henry VIII had done with Wales. His native
country would, he hoped, ' with time become but as Cumberland
and Northumberland and those other remote and northern
shires.'[9]

To press so hastily for an assimilation so complete could only
set back the cause of union. The English Parliament promptly
made it clear that they were not prepared to accept its commercial implications, a free share for Scotland in English trade
at home and overseas. How the Scots would have reacted to the
proposed abrogation of their laws and customs must remain
conjectural. There was no close discussion. The negotiations
James set on foot for the execution of his project soon petered
out; and the only advance he succeeded in making towards
assimilation was in the field of religion. He would have liked to
overthrow the whole Presbyterian system in Scotland, but it was
already too firmly rooted in the popular feeling of the countryside. With the aid, however, of a docile Parliament and even of
a submissive Kirk Assembly, he re-introduced episcopacy. This
in itself was a harmless victory. It accorded with a section of

Scottish opinion, restive under the claim of Knox's and Melville's Kirk to a parallel sovereignty with that of the State. But it was dangerous; it was meddling with Scottish nationalism at what had become its most sensitive point—its fierce resolve to have the kind of religion it liked. Dangerous, too, was James' dictatorial attitude. 'This I may say for Scotland,' he boasted at Westminster, 'and I may truly vaunt it. Here I sit and govern it with my pen. I write and it is done.'[10] But if it was true that James exercised more power in Scotland than any previous king, it was mainly because he was sitting at Westminster, because he had the strength, the prestige and the personal protection of the English State behind him; and to the Scotsmen who followed him south to an unwelcoming Court the reliance of their sovereign on his English ministers must have been obvious enough. Thus the favourable psychology of 1603 was steadily undermined. Scotsmen began to think that Scotland, after all, had been subjected to England, that the cardinal tradition of Scottish nationalism had been betrayed.

These suspicions were confirmed by Charles. Blind to the reaction it had already provoked, he pushed the policy of religious assimilation a long step forward. In 1637 he ordered the Kirk to use, in place of ' Knox's Liturgy ' which had been used for over seventy years, a modified version of Laud's English Prayer Book which the Scots regarded as ' much more Popish ' than the original. He could scarcely have made a more foolish mistake. For some time past the news from England—the uncompromising severity of Laud's High Anglican crusade, the notorious Romanism of Charles' French Queen—had awakened a smouldering fear that Protestantism was again in danger. The Prayer Book blew it into flame. The woman (if it was one) who threw a stool at the cleric officiating in St. Giles' was the forerunner of a national rebellion. Early in 1638, the leaders of the Kirk gathered at Edinburgh and ' renewed their covenant with God ' to save their country from ' the Popish religion and tyranny.' The document they drafted was called a National Covenant, and its reception was truly national. In the Lowlands, at any rate, the support it instantly obtained was practically unanimous. It was signed by multitudes in every shire and in almost every town, often amid scenes of passionate emotion. All but five of the Protestant nobles signed it. Since, moreover, its authors had shrewdly linked their denunciation of Roman doctrine with professions of loyalty to the Crown, it was signed by men who were presently to fight each other, by Montrose as well as Argyll. And it was national in another sense. It was a protest against an attempt to impose from England on the Scottish Kirk an English form of worship, drawn up by an English prelate. When the Central Assembly met in the following autumn, the universal temper was still fiercely nationalist. Ignoring, like the Long Parliament later on, the royal dissolution, it proceeded to sweep away all the ecclesiastical work that James and Charles had achieved. Episcopacy was abolished, the bishops excommunicated, the new Prayer Book banned, pure Presbyterianism re-established. Those professions of loyalty had sounded well enough, but in fact Scotland was now in full rebellion.

When the Covenant was drafted, Charles understood at once what the challenge meant, and with Laud and Strafford at his back he never thought of yielding. Nor did the Scottish leaders, aware of his difficulties with his English subjects. War was the inevitable result, the two Bishops' Wars (1639-1641) which were the first phase of the British Civil Wars and led to the British Revolution. It is only with the ' international ' aspect of that decisive chapter of British history that this study is concerned; and it is only, therefore, the effect of that period of convulsion on the relations between England and Scotland that calls for brief discussion.

From first to last, though their leaders often failed to recognise it, the basic issue was the same for both countries. Again they had a common cause—essentially the same as in Elizabeth's day—

the defence of civil and religious liberty against the system of absolute monarchy now spreading over continental Europe. But from the outset English and Scottish opinion differed on the relative importance of the two kinds of liberty. In England, closely as the religious quarrel was involved, it was primarily for civil liberty that the rebels fought. It was Parliament against the King. In Scotland, whose Parliament was still an unrepresentative and feeble body, possessing no political tradition, unable to act as the focus of a national revolt, it was religious liberty that came first. It was the Kirk against the King. Thus the Scottish rebels were not so much concerned as the English with the powers of the Crown. It might almost be said that they did not mind if the King were an autocrat provided only he were a Presbyterian. And with that attitude was mingled a strain of nationalism. Charles, after all, was a Stewart, and from the outset of the conflict Scottish pride was wounded by Englishmen's high-handed treatment of him. Hence the more universal revulsion in Scotland than in England against Charles' execution, the complete repudiation of Republicanism, the immediate recognition of King Charles II.

There was another and stronger reason why the two countries, or at least the dominant parties in them, were not kept together by the common cause. The Kirk's demand for religious uniformity made unity impossible both in Scotland and in Britain. The moral government established by the zealots of the Kirk, the powers exercised by its courts to punish ' sin,' the expulsion of ' back-sliders ' from public life, all this was a tyranny at least as intolerable as that of Charles' unparliamentary régime in England, and, like causes having like effects, it opened a steadily widening breach in the national unity of 1639. Unlike the Welsh, the Scots first took the field as a nation; but, before the fight was over, they were divided, like the Welsh and English, in two camps. The outstanding example is Montrose, the first Scot to cross the Tweed in the ' Bishops' Wars ' with Charles, the last to die for his son on the scaffold. Not content with splitting Scotland, the Kirk proceeded to split Britain by attempting to impose Presbyterianism on England. With that specific purpose the National Covenant of 1639 was transmuted into the Solemn League and Covenant of 1643. That was what the invading ' Army of the Lord ' demanded and what the Presbyterian majority in the English Parliament conceded. By a series of ordinances episcopacy was abolished and Presbyterianism established. How ironical it was! The Scottish leaders were trying to do to England *mutatis mutandis* exactly what Charles had tried to do to Scotland. They were betraying the same gross ignorance of their neighbours' character. And the Anglo-Scottish conflict they provoked was equally inevitable.

The decision lay with Cromwell and the army he had trained, and, while Cromwell, the idealist, did not believe in religious uniformity, Cromwell, the realist, knew that it was not practical politics. As for the soldiers at his back, the Independents, there were bigots among them as narrow as any ardent Presbyterian but they were ready to fight at need for freedom of conscience. That being so the attempt of the English Presbyterians in ominous imitation of the Kirk to enforce their doctrine and eradicate Independency in the army had led directly to the Revolution, to the domination of Parliament by the army, to Charles' death and Cromwell's ascendancy. So now it was the conduct of the Scottish zealots which brought about the forcible inclusion of Scotland in a British Union. When the leaders of the Kirk, in unnatural alliance with the Royalists, confronted Cromwell with their nineteen-year-old King, from whom they had extracted, without overmuch concern for his honesty, an acceptance of the Covenant and an admission of shame for his mother's idolatry, they were virtually declaring war, the last of the wars between Scotland and England. Its result was soon decided at Dunbar (1650), a Scottish disaster almost as overwhelming as Flodden and less undeserved. The defiant coronation of Charles in the

Royalist North at Scone a few months later and the diversionary invasion of England in the following year were desperate moves in a fight already lost. Worcester and Charles' flight to France ended the Civil War in Scotland and England alike (1651).

Scotland now lay at England's mercy as utterly as after Edward I's conquest; and the way in which Cromwell took advantage of it is one of his chief claims to greatness. His primary purpose was security. The execution of Charles had united almost all Europe against him; and, if he was presently to prove that his British Republic could play a more powerful part in the world than the English Kingdom had ever played, he had first to make sure of his base. And his base could never be secure—the strategic unity of the British Isles forbade it—unless Scotland and Ireland were linked with England in the common cause. So far from that, Ireland was always, and Scotland for the moment, on the Stewart side. To Cromwell, therefore, it seemed that the freedom of England could be preserved only by the drastic method of imposing a single unitary government on all three nations. Cromwell was very much an Englishman, and the external threat to English self-determination stung his English pride. ' I confess,' he blurted out to his troops in 1649, ' I have often had these thoughts with myself which perhaps may be carnal and foolish. I had rather be overrun by a Cavalierish interest than a Scotch interest, I had rather be overrun by a Scotch interest than an Irish interest. . . . The quarrel is brought to this state that . . . we must be subject to the kingdom of Scotland or the kingdom of Ireland for the bringing in of the King. It should awaken all Englishmen.'[11] A frank appeal to English nationalism; yet in his dealings with Scotland—whatever may be said of Ireland—Cromwell showed that his nationalism was temperate, conciliatory, at root defensive. After Dunbar he hoped for a friendly agreement between two self-respecting nations. He asked the Scottish leaders only to give England ' satisfaction and security for their peaceable and quiet living beside you.'[12] He had no desire for

conquest. Least of all did he want to dragoon the Scots into
religious uniformity; that was the charge he levelled at the Kirk.
But, since the Kirk zealots were still in control, conquest it had
to be, and Cromwell's conquest was the most thorough Scotland
had ever suffered; even the Highlands were combed and garrisoned. At the same time it was the mildest of all the English
conquests. No leaders were executed, no prisoners put to death;
only twenty-four prominent Royalists lost their estates, and the
conduct of the Puritan army of occupation was exemplary.

Cromwell's civil and religious settlement was similarly
moderate. The Kirk was left inviolate, still the established
national Kirk; but its civil powers were shorn away and the
General Assembly was dissolved. The Kirk courts were deprived
of the right to coerce anyone who did not belong to it. Nonconformity was not to be suppressed. Nor was the reform of the
civil administration a ruthless scrapping of Scottish institutions.
The old-established Court of Sessions, which had been twisted
into a Royalist instrument, was replaced by an English Commission of Justice. New magistrates' courts were created on the
English model. Survivals of feudal tenures and jurisdictions in
the Highlands were abolished. But no attempt was made to
'weld into one' the English and Scottish statute-books. The
result—Scotsmen themselves confessed it[13]—was a more honest,
impartial and efficient administration of justice than Scotland had
ever known.

Such was the Scottish background to the Union enacted by
the famous Instrument of 1653 for 'the government of the
Commonwealth of England, Scotland and Ireland and the
dominions thereunto belonging' and by the Ordinance of 1654.
At the outset of the Ordinance it was asserted that the people of
Scotland had been invited to join in a ' happy Union ' and through
their deputies had accepted the invitation. But in fact ' the Union
was an act of power, not of bargain.'[14] The English Commissioners' proposals were virtually demands and, as such, were not

contested. Nevertheless, it was not a one-sided settlement: it made, indeed, much the same concessions to Scottish sentiment and interest as the bilateral agreement which, fifty years later, brought about a more lasting union. Its two major breaches in the political structure of Scottish nationhood—the abolition of the Stuart monarchy and of the Scottish Parliament—were the inexorable conditions of any union at the time, and against them could be set, first, the inclusion of thirty Scottish members in the unicameral Parliament of the Commonwealth, second, the proportionate contribution of both countries to a common public revenue, and third, and far the most immediately important, the inclusion of Scottish trade in a single British commercial system. All goods, declared the Ordinance, were to pass between Scotland and England as freely by land or sea as between places in England, and between Scotland and the overseas dominions of the Commonwealth as freely as between England and those dominions. A last point, by no means negligible because it was a point of sentiment, was the prescription 'that the Arms of Scotland, viz. a cross commonly called St. Andrew's Cross, be received into and borne from henceforth in the Arms of this Commonwealth as a badge of this Union.'

Some such balance of national sentiments and interests was the indispensable condition of any valid union; but Cromwell's contemporaries in neither country had yet realised the necessity of compromise. At Westminster the settlement was not easily or quickly ratified. The merchants still boggled over free trade, and political nationalism went with economic. Scottish and Irish votes, it was pointed out, might be used to outnumber English. ' It is not for the honour of the English nation to have foreigners to come and have a power in the legislature,' said one member, a foreboding of the far-off day when the Irish members of the House of Commons would hold the fate of Governments in their hands. And, if such was the mood of English nationalists, the mood of Scottish nationalists, the weaker party to the settlement, was bound to be no less hostile. The Union, it was true, meant peace and security instead of war and invasion. The country was better governed than it had ever been. And, if the higher level of taxation customary in England pressed hardly on her poorer neighbour, the urban middle class, though not as yet the country-folk, were quickly discovering the material benefits of free trade —a lesson that was not forgotten in 1707. Yet the Scots, even those who confessed in their hearts the balance of gain that Cromwell's Union had bestowed on their country, could not be reconciled to it. It was not so much what it did as the way it had been done; it was a bargain in fact, but not in form; and, since national sentiment is often as much concerned with forms as with facts, Scotsmen welcomed even more joyfully than Englishmen the end of the ' usurpation ' and the return of their Stewart King.

Cromwell had spoken of his British Parliament as ' a strong treble cord twisted together which cannot be easily broken,'[15] but the Restoration untwisted it and Scotland was now again united with England only in the person of the King. All Cromwell's measures were swept away, his officials dismissed, his garrisons evacuated. A Secretary of State for Scotland, the unprincipled Lauderdale, advised his master in London. A Scottish Privy Council presently sat again in Edinburgh. The ' ancient ' Scottish Parliament met once more. But those were only the forms of national independence. In fact Scotland was ruled by an autocrat more French than Scottish, a thorough ' Londoner,' who never visited the country and the people for which in earlier days he had acquired a cordial dislike. There was no need for him to go: even more effectually than his grandfather he could govern Scotland with his pen. The Scottish Parliament was ultra-Royalist: its members far more obsequious than the Cavalier squires at Westminster. They left the executive unquestioned in the King's hands: they legislated as his agents bade them.

Charles II's Scottish policy was an echo of James I's. First, he recommended Union, but neither country was then in the mood for it, and the negotiations opened in 1670 soon broke down. Next, he determined to go at least as far as James in dealing with the Kirk. 'Covenanted' though he was, he promptly secured the restoration of episcopacy. Presentation to livings by laymen was also reintroduced. But otherwise, except for the continued suspension of the General Assembly, the Presbyterian system was left intact. Charles I's attempt to alter the liturgy was not renewed. As in James' day, this was not in itself an unreasonable settlement: a substantial section of moderate Presbyterians approved of it, and others were willing to acquiesce in it for the sake of peace; but the dour spirit of the founders of the Kirk was still alive, particularly in the south-western counties and mainly among humble folk, to whom it seemed plain that to submit to an episcopal régime was to violate the Covenant they had sworn to and break faith with God. The result was a non-conformist resistance more stubborn than the contemporary movement in England and far more brutally repressed. Easy-going Charles was not directly responsible for that black chapter of Scottish history. It was the work of more pure-blooded Scotsmen—Lauderdale, Rothes, and the new bishops—with the Scottish parliamentarians as their accomplices. What they tried to do was to make the Covenanters conform by force, and their methods were so harsh and after a time so cruel as to seem deliberately adopted in order to provoke rebellion: Lauderdale, indeed, in a moment of heat, declared he wanted a rebellion so that he could bring over Irish troops ' to cut all their throats.'[16] The persecution began when ministers who refused to conform were deprived of their livings; one-third of them, in the South-West it was almost all, thus lost their livelihood. Next, in betterment of the English Five Mile Act, recusants were forbidden to live within twenty miles of their parishes. When they persisted in preaching to their faithful flocks in open-air ' conventicles,' it was made a capital offence. Meantime conforming ministers were imposed on parishioners who hated and defied them, and talked or slept when forced under penalty to attend their services. Steadily the bitterness increased till in 1666 and again in 1679 it came to fighting. Both risings were easily suppressed. Some prisoners were hanged, others sent to convict-labour in the English transatlantic Colonies. Women were not spared. By the end of Charles' reign, thousands of sturdy Scots countryfolk had perished on field or scaffold, and many thousands more were brooding over their wrongs and the memories of their martyred dead.

And then history began to repeat itself. The intentions of James VII were soon as unmistakable to Scotsmen as those of James II to Englishmen. He made no secret of his Catholic faith and he scarcely made a secret of his hope to bring all Britain back to Rome with the help of Catholic France. Again, as in the days of Mary of Guise, the danger consolidated Scottish nationalism. Claverhouse could raise the Highland clans for James, but even before his death at Killiecrankie the dissident minority had no chance of thwarting the national will. The Scottish Parliament, however servile hitherto, could not combine devotion to the Stewarts with submission to the Pope. Nor could the Kirk remain divided on that issue: its moderates disliked fanatical Covenanters, but they detested Papists. So it was again a united nation that welcomed deliverance from over the border. In 1560 it had been Elizabeth. In 1688 it was William of Orange.

In almost all respects, indeed, the second crisis repeated the first. Again, while Romanism and absolutism were linked together, the English were more concerned about their constitutional freedom than their creed, and the Scots the other way about. And again the fortunes of Britain had become tied up with the fortunes of all western Europe. Now and for twenty years to come the issue was the same as it had been a century before. Like Philip II of Spain, Louis XIV of France was seeking to establish his ascendancy over all the countries within reach of his great military power; and for Louis as for Philip the chief bar to this ambition was the freedom of England. As before, therefore, the issue depended on the conduct of England, but, as before, not of England only. Even with the great William to lead her, it would have been difficult, it might have proved impossible, for England to preserve her freedom if Scotland as well as Ireland had remained loyal to the Stewarts and fought on Louis' side.

IV. PRELUDE TO UNION

IN 1688 the Union of the Crowns as a method of adjusting the relations between Scotland and England had been tried for a stretch of over eighty years, broken only by the brief Cromwellian interlude. After 1688 the experiment was continued for nearly twenty years and then finally abandoned. In 1707 the Union of Crowns was merged in a Union of Parliaments.

The cause of this conclusive change sounds paradoxical. The reason why, in the last resort, Scotland surrendered her national independence was because it had become a more real independence than it had ever been since 1603. For the Union of the Crowns under William III and Mary—and the Crown, of course, meant William, not James II's daughter—ceased to unite even to the extent it had before. In the first place the sentimental tie was broken. The Stuarts, after all, had been Stuarts, and William was a distrusted Dutchman. Secondly, if a Crown is to unite, it must have the power to do so and, though the Revolution had by no means introduced the parliamentary sovereignty of a later day, it had severely limited the royal prerogative. William had obtained his English throne on terms laid down by the Convention Parliament. Though he succeeded in retaining a measure of freedom in the control of foreign affairs, he was obliged to work with Parliament, not over its head. In particular his policy had to be defended by ministers who possessed the confidence of the House of Commons. It was the same in Scotland. The Scottish Convention Parliament dictated the terms of his accession. The Scottish Claim of Right echoed the demands of the English Declaration of Right. In Scotland, as in England, the executive dictatorship of a Privy Council, chosen and directed by an autocratic King, was abolished and with it the Committee of Articles which had virtually engrossed all the legislative power of the House it nominally served. Thus, at a stroke, the Scottish Parliament, which had always been far weaker than the English, acquired the same authority. Though still elected on an antiquated system and far from representative of the Scottish people, it became a powerful, independent, self-respecting national assembly.

Beside this independent Parliament now stood again an independent Kirk. The attempt to assimilate it in some degree to the English Church by superimposing episcopacy was once more abandoned. The ' prelates ' departed, never to return. Those Scotsmen who preferred an episcopal system now constituted a separate Episcopalian Church as much apart from the Established Church as the Presbyterian Church in England. The Kirk, moreover, recovered its General Assembly. In form, indeed, it was again the Kirk of the Reformation; but in spirit it had undergone a great and wholesome change. Only a small minority of Covenanters still claimed that the Kirk was the equal, if not the superior, of the State. The main body of its members had become convinced that, provided the Kirk were free to regulate its own affairs, it was best to let the old quarrel die and render to Caesar the things that were Caesar's. Thus it came about that, though the General Assembly still commanded a deeper allegiance from the Scottish people than Parliament, its proceedings became increasingly concerned with religion rather than politics. It was a happy ending to a tragic story. The factor in Scottish life which had done most to divide Scotland and had served also to divide

Scotland from England had been practically extinguished. The third element in Scottish nationalism, the traditional legal system, had suffered little disturbance except in Cromwell's time. With Parliament and Kirk stood the Scottish lawyers, a powerful profession, interpreting their own Scottish statute-book in accordance with their own Scottish procedure. It was a strong combination; and it stiffened the self-consciousness and self-confidence of Scottish nationalism.

In any event, no doubt, Anglo-Scottish relations would have been strained during the reign of William III. How distrustful was the Scottish mood was shown by the ease with which the ' massacre' of Glencoe (1692), an act advised by the Scottish administration as a salutary lesson to Highland Jacobites, was generally ascribed to ' English tyranny.' In an atmosphere so charged the effect of the Darien catastrophe was bound to be explosive. But it was also instructive; for in the glare of the explosion the inadequacy of the Union of the Crowns as a means of adjusting Anglo-Scottish relations was unmistakably revealed.

It has often been pointed out that the Scottish mind, which had been obsessed by religious controversy ever since the Reformation, was set free by the Revolution settlement to concentrate on more material things. And the economic condition of Scotland was a clear enough call to the energy and enterprise of Scottish patriots. The country was still miserably poor, its agriculture primitive, its trade restricted, its capital resources very small. England was immeasurably better off, and much of her wealth was notoriously due to her overseas commerce. So lucrative was the trade with the East that the East India Company was at constant war with ' interlopers' seeking to violate its monopoly. Westwards over the Atlantic lay a string of English colonies, from the Caribbean to Newfoundland, supplying England with sugar, tobacco and other raw materials and with markets for her manufactures. But the whole of this great field of business was reserved by the mercantile system exclusively to

Englishmen. Scotland and Ireland had no footing in it. The 'Trade Laws' or Navigation Acts of 1660 and 1663 barred them out as much as foreigners. Thus the only way open for Scotland to commercial expansion overseas was to do, on a scale proportionate to her capacity, what England had done; and two Scottish attempts had actually been made to found trans-Atlantic colonies. In 1621 James I granted Sir William Alexander the territory which has retained its name of Nova Scotia; but this was in an area claimed as a French preserve, and in 1632 it was formally restored to France. In 1684, a party of exiled Covenanters established a post at Stuart's Town in South Carolina; but this lay in Spain's preserve, and in 1686 the Spaniards wiped it out. Those were small adventures, and the project conceived by William Paterson, a Scottish founder and director of the Bank of England, was far more grandiose. With a daring and imagination worthy of the Elizabethans he planned to plant a colony on the isthmus of Darien or Panama. It lay, he pointed out, at the strategic centre of the American world. It would divert across the isthmus the course of trade between Europe and the Far East by halving the time and cost of the voyage. 'This door of the seas' he called the colony of his dream, and 'key of the universe.' Its colonisers would be able ' to give laws to both oceans and to become arbitrators of the commercial world.'[17]

For the execution of this tremendous project Paterson found, as it happened, an instrument ready to his hand. The first substantial result of the new Scottish spirit of commercial enterprise had been the formation of a joint-stock company, the Company of Scotland trading to Africa and the Indies. In 1695 the Scottish Parliament passed, and the King (on bad advice, he afterwards complained) assented to an Act [18] bestowing on the Company similar privileges to those bestowed by similar Acts on the great English Companies. It gave the Company a monopoly of trade with America for thirty-one years and with Asia and Africa in perpetuity. It empowered it to arm its ships and to plant colonies where no Europeans had previously settled and the natives were agreeable. It freed the Company's trade from all duties in Scotland for twenty-one years. A wholehearted concession; and at once, and inevitably, it raised a storm in England. It was fiercely, almost savagely, denounced in Parliament. It was an open challenge, it was argued, to the rights of the East India Company; it legalised ' interloping.' It meant that the centre of the Indian trade and of English investment therein would shift from London to Edinburgh. Nor did it threaten English business only. The English State would be involved if the Company ran into trouble; for the King's approval implied the King's protection, which only the English Navy could afford.[a] Fiery speakers even demanded an impeachment. And, if Ministers kept their heads, they were by no means out of sympathy with the rank and file. It happened that the Company was trying to raise subscriptions in the commercial cities on the other side of the North Sea: so the English Resident at Hamburg was instructed to use all his influence against the Company. He did so with effect.

If this display of English economic nationalism was natural enough at the time, no less natural was the passionate resentment it evoked in Scotland. Never since the days of the Covenant had Scottish national sentiment been so deeply and widely stirred. The cause of the Company became almost as sacred to Scotsmen as once the Covenant itself had been; and, when the lists were opened for raising £400,000—about half the total private capital available in the country[19]—most of the sum was quickly subscribed and the whole of it within six months.[b] Meantime the Company had changed its immediate objective. As its title showed, the promoters had first looked to West Africa and the Indies—and at various times those fields were explored by one or two of the

[a] Under the terms of the Act the King undertook to use his authority to obtain reparation for damage inflicted on the Company ' at the public charge.' That meant, of course, a charge on the Scottish revenue, but the only effective instrument for obtaining reparation would be the English Navy. See W. L. Mathieson, *Scotland and the Union* (London, 1905), 30-31.

[b] £220,000 was actually paid up.

Company's ships—but the Act had given them the same rights in America; and when Paterson, himself a director, observed that his colleagues had been shaken by the storm which the proposed invasion of the Indies had aroused in London, he seized the opportunity to persuade them to switch the *locale* of their first big enterprise right over to Darien.

That those Scottish business men should have allowed themselves to be so persuaded is another demonstration of the fervent nationalism which the conflict with English interests had awakened. Though the grim experiences of English colonisers in Virginia and elsewhere not so very long ago were on record and though the evidence as to the suitability of the site, the climatic conditions, the natural resources, was very slender and quite untrustworthy, the directors accepted Paterson's mad proposal—for mad indeed it was—without much hesitation. And that was not due only to Paterson's remarkable personality, his force in argument, his genuine enthusiasm. It was nationalism that overpowered the practical judgment of those Scottish men of business. The bigger, the more daring the enterprise, the better. They would show those arrogant Englishmen what Scotland could do on her own. If they succeeded, if they could hold the doorway to two oceans and impose on both their own ' Trade Laws,' then even the merchant princes of the India House might have to beg for terms.

In such high mood, in the summer of 1698, the first expedition sailed from the Road of Leith, bearing some 1200 settlers to found New Caledonia. It was one of the great days of Scottish history. The shore was packed with cheering crowds. Prayers were offered in the churches for the success of this ' national concern.' With the fortunes of the emigrants the whole future of Scotland seemed bound up. ' All our hopes,' wrote Fletcher of Saltoun, ' of ever being any other than a poor and inconsiderable people are embarked with them.'[20]

By the end of the year the settlers had reached their goal and begun to build and fortify New Edinburgh. But the only encouraging feature of their situation was the friendliness of the local Indians. Otherwise the outlook was bleak. There was no market among the Indians for most of the civilised commodities they had shipped. The promised forest of valuable logwood was not to be found. Eldorado was as elusive as it had been in Ralegh's day. Provisions, meantime, were soon running short, and disease had begun its fatal work. For the Company had chosen one of the most pestilential places in the world, a place where Europeans could not hope to live long till Colonel Gorgas' famous fight with the mosquito made possible the cutting of the Panama Canal. As the year drew on, the surviving colonists became more and more discouraged; and, when the news arrived that the Governors of the English colonies in the West Indies and North America had issued proclamations forbidding ' His Majesty's subjects . . . to hold any correspondence with the said Scots, nor to give them any assistance of arms, ammunition, provisions or any other necessaries whatever,'[21] they finally lost heart, abandoned their fort and their huts, and sailed for home.

The proclamations had taken them completely by surprise. They believed that they had a right to found a colony in any unoccupied area of the American coast. No doubt they remembered Stuart's Town, but they seemed to have believed that, if the settlement were strongly fortified, the Spaniards would let it alone. And, if they were attacked, they may, perhaps, have thought that they could count on English help, despite the ultimate possibility of commercial rivalry with the English colonies. In any case, the immediate and outspoken hostility of the Colonial Governors, representatives of a King who was also Scotland's King, astonished and dismayed them. Nor is this strange blindness to be wondered at: it had been shared by the promoters of the venture. It is difficult, indeed, to understand how a Scotsman of Paterson's ability, with his intimate experience of London, could have wholly failed to appreciate those cardinal factors in the

European situation which doomed the Darien expedition to disaster before ever it was launched. In the first place the Spanish Empire, though far gone in decay, was still an Empire whose very weakness made Spaniards all the more sensitive on the point of prestige. To plant a colony within the frontiers they had claimed for two centuries past was not only an insult; it was something like an act of war. And this colony was not planted, like Stuart's Town, on the outer fringe of the Empire, but at its very heart. It awakened memories of Drake's historic raids. In the second place this sharp affront to Spain ran directly counter to English policy. Elizabeth had abetted Drake, but William III could not possibly abet the Darien colonists. When the first expedition sailed, a war between a coalition which he headed and Louis XIV of France had only just ended in an inconclusive peace (1697). Spain had been a member of the coalition, and much of the fighting was in defence of the Spanish Netherlands. Nor had Spain's friendship lost its value when peace was signed. The death of her half-witted King without an heir was known to be imminent and the ' Spanish Succession,' the command of the vast Spanish realm in Europe and overseas, was bound to affect, one way or the other, the international balance of power. The peace, in fact, was only a truce. The check to Louis XIV's ambitions had merely hardened them. In 1701-02 war came again between another coalition and France, the decisive war which, thanks to the work which ' the greatest statesman in Europe ' had done before he died, to the genius of Marlborough and to English sea-power, finally thwarted Louis XIV's attempt to master Europe. No member of the Grand Alliance had more at stake than England; for, if Louis had prevailed, if his plans of invasion had succeeded, he would certainly have imposed the Stuart dynasty and the Catholic faith on all the British Isles. Clearly, then, the time of Darien was no time for quarrelling with Spain. If the King of Scotland could not openly obstruct a scheme which had enlisted the whole force of Scottish nationalism, the King of

England could see to it that nothing was done to help it. Hence the proclamations; and meantime the English ambassador at Madrid was charged with the awkward task of persuading the Spanish Court that ' the Kingdom of Scotland is entirely independent of the Crown of England '[22] and that the wearer of the latter could properly disown the foolish conduct of the former. The same distinction, for what it was worth, was explained by the Governor of Jamaica in a letter to the Governor of Cartagena.

In these circumstances New Caledonia had no chance of survival. Before the news of the evacuation reached Scotland, two more expeditions had been dispatched. The first was a small affair, a matter of reinforcement; and, finding the colony deserted, it withdrew. The second, which sailed in the autumn of 1699, carried some 1300 new settlers who, after hot debate, decided to hold their ground. With the aid of their Indian allies they boldly met and repulsed a Spanish advance overland; but, when a Spanish fleet of fifteen ships blockaded them, the end was inevitable. Had it been an English colony, the story would, of course, have been quite different. Not only were there enough English ships and English troops available in the Caribbean to repel any Spanish attack; the attack would have precipitated war in Europe. But for the lonely Scottish colony there could be no such defence or diversion. In the spring of 1700 the colonists capitulated and the incident of Darien was closed. It had cost the Company most of its ships, some two thousand lives, and about a quarter of a million sterling.

The story has been retold in these pages because it throws such a flood of light on the constitutional *impasse*. If England and Scotland had been governed by an autocrat, well and good. He could have favoured either kingdom as he chose or held the balance even. In any event, he would have made sure that his policy in one country did not conflict with his policy in the other. But William III was not an autocrat. Only by a use of his prerogative which would at once have been challenged as a violation of the

Revolution settlement could he prevent his two Parliaments from pursuing different courses. The Crown could not unite Britain then any more than the Crown unites the British Commonwealth to-day. In each of the non-Asiatic Dominions as in the United Kingdom the King is King in Parliament; and, though the personal influence which the Crown can exert in strengthening the sense of unity throughout the Commonwealth may be very great, that unity is maintained not by any institutions but by the fact that its separate Parliaments and peoples have common traditions, common interests and common ideals.

That, it need hardly be said, was not the state of affairs in Britain at the end of the seventeenth century. Before Darien Scottish dislike and jealousy of England were manifest enough. After Darien the antagonism was as bitter as in the far-off days of Wallace's execution. It is not too much to call it hatred.[a] For the intense emotion excited by the utter failure of their great ' national ' enterprise, the sense of humiliation and frustration, the wounded pride—it all vented itself on England. No Scotsman was held to blame for lack of knowledge or caution. The enterprise would have succeeded if England had not deliberately prevented Scotland from doing what she had so profitably done herself.

At this juncture the death of William III suddenly brought the constitutional relations between England and Scotland again to an issue. The succession of Anne to both thrones was not unwelcome to the Scots. She was not only a Protestant, she was a Stewart, daughter of James II (VII). But she had no surviving children, and by an Act of the English Parliament the English Crown would pass from her to the Electress of Hanover. There was no such Scottish Act. On Anne's death the Scottish Parliament would be free to dissolve the union of the Crowns and choose a sovereign, if it could find one, more congenial than a

[a] The popular mood was shockingly revealed as late as 1705 by the Edinburgh mob which terrorised the Council into acquiescence in the hanging of three innocent Englishmen. (Insh, 278-312.)

German princess. And since Jacobite sentiment was far stronger in Scotland than in England, it seemed not inconceivable that Anne's brother, one day to be known in England as the Old Pretender, might, Catholic though he was, maintain the Stewart succession to the Scottish throne. Of this dangerous possibility, directly affecting the strategic pattern of Europe, William III had been aware from the outset. In his first message to the Scottish Convention which put him on the Scottish throne he welcomed the suggestion for a closer union than the union of the Crowns. In his last death-bed message to the English House of Commons he declared that ' nothing can more contribute to the present and future security and happiness of England and Scotland than a firm and entire union between them' and that he would ' esteem it a peculiar felicity' if his reign should witness ' some happy expedient for making both kingdoms one.'[23] In her first speech from the throne Anne invited Parliament to ' consider of proper methods towards attaining a union between England and Scotland, which has been so lately recommended to you as a matter that very nearly concerns the peace and security of both kingdoms.'[24]

V. THE UNION

THE ENGLISH desire for Union, stronger now than it had ever been, was dictated by the international situation. With Anne's declaration of war on France in the spring of 1702 the decisive ten-year combat with Louis XIV had begun. As always, England's strategic strength lay in her insularity. As always, that advantage was seriously impaired by the fact that England was only half an island. And never before, not even in Elizabeth's day nor in Cromwell's, had the risk of a hostile Scotland threatening England's rear been so grave. Louis XIV had recognised James Stewart as King of both countries, and was in touch with the

Scottish Jacobites. Most of the Highlanders were Jacobite and Catholic, and there were many Lowlanders whose stubborn Presbyterianism was not wholly proof against the sentimental appeal of the Stewart cause, even if it were linked with memories of the ' auld alliance.' It was in the Lowlands, moreover, that the anti-English nationalism excited by the Darien catastrophe was fiercest, and it was still aflame. For those reasons, and also, perhaps, because Edinburgh was so much farther than London from the Straits of Dover and the Low Countries, few Scotsmen seemed to recognise, as clearly as John Knox and his followers in their day, the paramount common cause of Britain as a whole, to see that Scotland's freedom was as much at stake as England's in the European war. So the danger of Anglo-Scottish discord, even of conflict, in the middle of the war was real enough, and there was only one way of removing it. The Union of the Crowns must be submerged in a Union of the Parliaments. Only so could the Protestant succession to the throne be firmly secured. Only so could a divergence of foreign policy, as over Darien, be prevented. But unquestionably it would be a grievous sacrifice for Scotland. It meant that never again would Scotsmen be able to have the King of their choice. It meant that the home of their ancient Parliament, which had so recently acquired a new power and prestige in Scottish life, would become an empty shell and that their representatives would have to journey to faraway Westminster—fifteen days by road—there to be confronted by an overwhelming majority of Englishmen. It is not to be wondered at if Scotsmen regarded it as the end of Scotland's independence. True, that independence had been little more than nominal for a century past. ' Scotland from an international point of view was a geographical, not a political term; it had no fleet, and practically no army; it appeared in no treaty, and was represented at no foreign court; the Acts of its Parliament were liable to be nullified, though they could not be annulled, by English statutes; and the true seat of its government was not Edinburgh, but

London.'[25] Scottish patriots were aware of all that, but it was not the loss of an unreal political independence *in itself* that stirred them. Whatever its footing, Scotland was a national state, embodying the Scottish nation; and it was natural for Scotsmen in those days to believe that, if the state were lost, the nation would not long survive; that, when Scotland had been fused with England, Scotsmen would soon be transmuted into Englishmen. They could not know, as we know, that a nation can live and prosper without being incorporated in a uni-national State.

In the temper of Scottish nationalism at the time a voluntary union—and of course it could not be imposed—might well have seemed impossible; and it would indeed have been impossible if England had wanted not union only but also the uniformity which the Stewart Kings had aimed at. But, if English statesmanship merits the reputation it has acquired in the world of being rooted in practical common sense, then the conduct of English statesmen at this great crisis was an outstanding example of it. They confined the changes they proposed to the necessary minimum. They made no foolish attempt to tamper with two of the three institutional pillars of Scottish nationalism, the Kirk and the Law; and for the removal of the third they were willing to pay the necessary price.

What that price was had been made clear at every previous discussion of a union. It was Free Trade, the admission of Scotsmen on equal terms with Englishmen to a single British commercial system. For that boon the dominant section of the Scottish parliamentarians were prepared to sell their Parliament. It was the paradoxical result of Darien that it inflamed Scotsmen's hatred of England's ascendancy and at the same time convinced them that they must submit to it. For it had grimly demonstrated that only by union with their stronger and wealthier neighbours could they find an outlet for their new zest for commercial enterprise and a chance of escaping from their chronic poverty. The contrast with England's prosperity had long been painfully plain. It had recently been sharpened by the six ghastly years of failing harvests and starvation which had formed the domestic background to the tragedy of Darien oversea.[26] 'Was it entirely due to superiority of natural resources,' wrote a pamphleteer, ' that England was seven times as populous as Scotland and sixty times as rich; that Oxfordshire, not so large as Fife, produced almost as much in land-tax as the whole of Scotland; and that a town no bigger than Newcastle had more trade and paid more customs than all the Scottish burghs?'[27] Since, therefore, there was no alternative, hard-headed Scotsmen put sense before sentiment. They held it better for Scotland to share in the prosperity of a united Britain than to remain a nominally independent but ' poor and inconsiderable ' kingdom. The sequel was to prove them indubitably right.

Free Trade, then, was the price that England had to pay for union, and for English economic nationalism, for the champions —and who was not?—of mercantilism and the Navigation Acts, this was at least as hard to swallow as the loss of its Parliament to Scottish nationalism. Fortunately the English business men who shaped not only the opinion of the City but also to a large extent the policy of the Whig Party, were Hanoverians, anti-Jacobites. Gallophobes first and mercantilists second. They were ready to sacrifice all the fancied profits of monopoly to safeguard English liberty from a revival of Catholic despotism.

There was some hesitation, however, on the English side at the opening of negotiations between the Commissioners of the two countries in the autumn of 1702. Progress was slow. The Englishmen were lax in their attendance. Opposition to Union made itself heard. High Anglicans professed to dread the southward spread of an unmodified Presbyterianism in a united Britain. The Archbishop of York (it was reported) was stupid enough to suggest that the re-imposition of bishops on the Kirk should be made a condition of the settlement. Scotsmen, in fact, were keener now on Union than Englishmen, and, when the

Commission adjourned with nothing settled in 1703, the Scottish Parliament put three sharp turns on the screw. The Security Act provided that, on Anne's death without an heir, the Union of the Crowns would be dissolved by the choice of a Protestant Stewart sovereign for Scotland other than the English sovereign unless Scottish conditions, constitutional and economic, had first been satisfied. The Act anent Peace and War provided that, even if the Crowns remained united, Scotland should not be committed to war or to any treaty, political or commercial, with a foreign State without the assent of the Scottish Parliament. A third Act permitted the importation of foreign wines, including French, though England was at war with France. To such undisguised blackmail the English Parliament, emboldened by Marlborough's triumph at Blenheim (1704), retorted by the Aliens Act. It invited Scotland either to negotiate a treaty of closer union or to confirm the existing Union of the Crowns by acquiescing in the Hanoverian succession to both thrones. Failing both these alternatives it forbade non-resident Scotsmen to hold property in England and closed the border to Scottish coal, linen and cattle (about three-quarters of the total export trade) and to English wool. The tension created by his legislative duel was high and dangerous. For a sting in its tail the Security Act had provided for the arming and monthly training of local levies; and the English House of Lords had recommended that the militia should be called out in the northern counties and the fortifications of the chief towns repaired. If the rising hostility had not been checked, actual war might well have broken out—Godolphin indeed went so far as to say that it must be union or war[28]—and in that event the course of European history would have been changed. Happily the cooler heads on both sides prevailed. In 1705 the Scottish Parliament authorised the negotiation of a treaty and the English Parliament repealed the penal clauses of the Aliens Act. On April 22, 1706, newly and carefully chosen Commissioners, thirty-one for each country, met in London.

They were able to accomplish their task with remarkable speed because they began it in agreement on the basic principles —a legislative or ' incorporating ' union and free trade. At the outset, it is true, the Scottish Commissioners proposed a ' federal ' union,[a] and, if they had pressed the proposal, a long constitutional discussion must have ensued. But they did not press it. One of their own number put it on record that they, one and all, themselves ' considered it ridiculous and impracticable.'[29] It was, in fact, no more than a gesture for the benefit of the Scottish public, something to show that at least an attempt had been made to save their Parliament. It was not discussed in detail, and, when the English Commissioners promptly declared that they could ' treat on no kind of union but what was to be incorporating and perpetual,' it was withdrawn. There was no other conflict of principle, and the only closely contested point of detail was the number of Scottish representatives in the united Parliament. For the House of Commons the English Commissioners proposed 38, the Scottish asked for 50: it was settled at 45.[b] The number

[a] This proposal has nothing in common with proposals for federal devolution to-day. In 1707 Federalism had not yet acquired its technical modern meaning. The American Federation lay eighty years ahead, and it was ninety years before the Swiss Confederation became more than a league of independent Cantons. In 1707, in fact, Federation meant no more than Confederation—a league of States, not a Federal State. Thus the Scottish proposal did not contemplate a division of sovereignty between a ' central ' British Parliament and ' provincial ' English and Scottish Parliaments, but only an association of two equally sovereign Parliaments for dealing with certain common interests; and it is clear from an allusion to the ' States General ' in the record quoted above that the Scottish Commissioners had the Dutch Confederation in mind. It seems probable that the military and diplomatic power of the United Provinces, especially in William III's day, had given foreign observers a false idea of their constitutional unity. In fact they were no more than a league of seven sovereign Provinces which sent their delegates to the confederate assembly or States General to discuss such primary common interests as foreign policy and defence. The delegates varied in number, but voted as Provincial units. They acted on instructions which could not be varied without reference back to the Province. Agreement depended mainly on how far the dominant Province, Holland, could get its way. But the unity of action which impressed Europe was more in the executive than the deliberative field; and, while the executive authority in each sovereign Province was vested in its own Stadtholder, the wealthy and influential House of Orange was able to secure the election of one and the same member of the family as Stadtholder in most, and at last in all, the Provinces. Thus executive unity was brought about in practice without any explicit constitutional provision.

[b] There were—English and—Welsh members of the existing House of Commons. The population of England and Wales was about 6 million, of Scotland about 1 million. The English land-tax yielded £2,000,000, the Scottish only £3,600.

of Scottish peers to be admitted to the House of Lords was fixed at 16. On July 22, twenty-seven of the English Commissioners and twenty-six of the Scottish signed the Treaty of Union.

Its main provisions were as follows:

(1) The Kingdoms of England and Scotland were to be united in 'one Kingdom by the name of Great Britain,' with a flag combining the crosses of St. George and St. Andrew (i.e. the Union Jack).

(2) The Hanoverian succession to the throne of the United Kingdom in accordance with the English Act of Settlement (1701) was guaranteed.

(3) There would be one 'Parliament of Great Britain.'

(4) The Scottish legal system, with the Court of Session at its head, would be preserved 'in all time coming.' Only Scottish courts would deal with cases in Scotland, and their decisions would not be liable to review by English courts. (The possibility of ultimate appeal to the House of Lords, probably on purpose, was left uncertain.)[30]

(5) All subjects of the United Kingdom would enjoy 'full freedom and intercourse of trade and navigation' in all its territories and possessions, and be subject to the same regulations of trade by customs or other duties.

(6) Taxation henceforth would be uniform; but, since part of its proceeds would be applied to the service of the existing English public debt (about £18 millions), nearly £400,000 would be paid by way of 'equivalent' to Scotland to extinguish her public debt (£160,000), to refund the capital of the Darien Company, now to be dissolved, to finance the adjustment of the coinage and to promote industry and fisheries. Certain commodities, moreover, such as salt and malt, were to be exempted for some years in Scotland from the duties paid in England.

This Treaty, wisely generous to Scotland on its financial side, was tactfully submitted for approval first to the Scottish Parliament, where it was vehemently opposed by honest patriots like

Fletcher and by the Jacobites, but accepted by a large majority in both Houses. It remained to carry it into law, and the Queen's speech at the opening of the last session of the Scottish Parliament forcibly restated the case for ' an entire and perfect union.' ' It will secure your religion, liberty and property, remove the animosities amongst yourselves, and the jealousies and differences betwixt our two Kingdoms; it must increase your strength, riches and trade; and by this Union, the whole island being joined in affection, and free from all apprehension of different interests, will be enabled to resist all its enemies, support the Protestant interest everywhere, and maintain the liberties of Europe.'[31] But the opposition had been gathering strength all over Scotland; and, while the last and tumultuous debate proceeded within the Parliament House, the city outside was practically in the possession of a huge and disorderly mob, crying death to all betrayers of their country. Nor was the passage of the Act assured as long as the leaders of the Kirk hesitated to support it. It had been understood from the outset of the negotiations that the religious settlement would not be changed, but the question had been deliberately excluded from the Commissioners' consideration. Some fresh assurance, therefore, on this vital issue seemed required, and Parliament promptly provided it by passing an Act, presently incorporated in the Union Act, which guaranteed the Presbyterian worship, doctrine and government of the Scottish Church ' to continue without any alteration to the people of this land in all succeeding generations.' The conciliation of the Kirk proved decisive. On January 16, 1707, the Scottish Act of Union received the Queen's assent.

It was a free and an honest decision. Certain gifts and titles had been bestowed in the manner of the time; but the Scottish Union was certainly not, like the Irish Union, obtained by bribery. It was not, however, a majority decision. The mass of the people, in north and south alike, passionately nationalist, rating independence far above prosperity and unable to read the lesson of European politics, resisted to the last. In Scotland Union was achieved by a relatively small minority of Scottish patriots who were also statesmen.

The passage of the bill through the English Parliament was very much smoother. There was no substantial opposition. The Church of England required the same assurances which the Kirk had obtained and received, them in much the same form, a measure, incorporated like its Scottish equivalent in the Union Act, confirming for all time the Act of Uniformity and all other laws establishing and preserving the status, doctrine and organisation of the Church. No time was lost on other questions: nor were any amendments made, since that would have necessitated the risky reconsideration of the bill by the Scottish Parliament. All the clauses, with no word changed, were carried in both Houses almost within a month. On March 6 the Queen gave her assent. Nor in the English case was Parliament's decision at discord with the people's. Mercantilists grumbled at the loss of their monopoly. High churchmen shook their heads over the admission of Presbyterian nobles to the House of Lords. Jacobites sullenly bided their time. But there was no organised opposition. Englishmen, Whig or Tory, save only the minority who clung to the Stewarts and to Rome, had become convinced that the Union was a necessity for the strength and freedom of England.

The Union has proved so successful in creating unity that nowadays Englishmen and Scotsmen take it as almost a matter of course, a natural dispensation which seems to date from the dawn of time rather than the relatively recent age of Anne. Unless they are students of history, they do not realise what a great achievement it was. Two sovereign States merged their separate sovereignties into one. That had happened before in Europe, but only as the outcome of conquest or of intermarriage between autocratic dynasties. This merger was a deliberate act of policy, freely adopted by elected Parliaments. More than that, it was the voluntary merger of two countries which for four centuries past had been bitterly estranged and often at open war. Germans, at any rate before they became Nazis, were never more hated by Frenchmen than Englishmen were hated by Scotsmen in those not so very distant days. There is nothing, indeed, in the history of international relations to compare with such an ending to so long and fierce a feud. And no less remarkable than the decision itself was the statesmanship which put it into effect. Neither party, after the opening skirmish, tried to bully or over-reach the other. Both dealt with the business as a matter of give and take. And thereby they supplied the union with the psycho-logical conditions of success. The smaller, weaker country was bound to feel, at the outset at any rate, that it meant subordina-tion. But this sense of subordination was wholly different from the sense of subjection which was presently to poison the prospects of the Irish Union. It was a subordination freely accepted by the weaker party as the outcome of free negotiation in which, in status and in bargaining-power, it had stood on an equal footing with the stronger, and, if it had given much, had also taken much in return.

[1] C. S. Terry, *History of Scotland* (Cambridge, 1920), 12 ff.
[2] Terry, 61.
[3] T. F. Tout, *History of England, 1216-1377* (London, 1905), 228.
[4] Terry, 75.
[5] Quoted by Dicey and Rait, *Thoughts on the Union between England and Scotland* (London, 1920), 325, from *Past and Present* bk. i, chap. ii.
[6] Terry, 199.
[7] *Parliamentary History*, i. 979.
[8] Rait, 1020.
[9] *Ibid.*, 152.
[10] Notestein, *The Scot in History*, (London, 1946), 140.
[11] C. Firth, *Oliver Cromwell* (London, 1900), 257.
[12] *Ibid.*, 284.
[13] Nicol and Burnet, cited by Firth, 297.
[14] Terry, 407.
[15] *Ibid.*, 413.
[16] *Ibid.*, 445.
[17] G. P. Insh, *The Company of Scotland trading to Africa and the Indies* (London, 1932), 72-3.
[18] *Acts of the Parliaments of Scotland* ix., 377.
[19] Insh, 65.
[20] *Ibid.*, 117, 145.

[21] *Ibid.*, 149.
[22] *Ibid.*, 152.
[23] *Hansard*, v. 1341.
[24] *Ibid.*, vi. 5.
[25] W. L. Mathieson, *Scotland and the Union*, 122.
[26] G. M. Trevelyan, *English Social History* (London, 1944), 432.
[27] *A Sermon preached to the People at the Mercat Cross at Edinburgh*, paraphrased by W. L. Mathieson, 123.
[28] J. Mackinnon, *The Union of England and Scotland* (London, 1896), 222.
[29] Sir John Clerk's *Memoirs*, printed in *Select Documents for Queen Anne's Reign*, 1702-7 (ed. G. M. Trevelyan, Cambridge, 1929), 216-17.
[30] See Dicey and Rait, 191-200.
[31] Mathieson, 144-5. Dicey and Rait, 227-8.

PART FOUR

Britain
in the Eighteenth Century

WHEN ALL Britain was united in one tri-national State in 1707, it was an open question whether it would retain its 'plural' character or whether in course of time the weaker nationalities would be so absorbed into the stronger, the Welsh and the Scots so completely anglicised, that in the end the British State would have become uni-national and Great Britain no more than a greater England. In 1807 that question was no longer open. Both in Wales and in Scotland the eighteenth century witnessed a national revival, different in character according to the different circumstances, which made it almost certain that, when another century had passed, Britain would still be multi-national, that the Welsh and the Scots would still be nations.

I. THE WELSH REVIVAL

IN 1707 the national future of Wales, already so long united with England, was naturally far more precarious than that of Scotland, just entering on union. Of the two mainstays of the Scottish tradition of nationhood, the Welsh had neither. Henry VIII had abolished their law, and the Reformation had given them no

Welsh Kirk. The landed aristocracy and the urban middle class had adopted English speech and ways of life: only such pride as they took in the beauty of their country, and in their family history, distinguished them from Englishmen across a frontier which had lost its meaning. The process of anglicisation, it is true, had not yet extended to the poorer rural community, the peasant-farmers and their families who made up the great majority of the Welsh people. These country folk were still Welsh—in blood and temperament, in speech and domestic life, in the love of their mountain homeland and their memories of its ancient heroes. But they were almost wholly illiterate, and more than ' dumb loving ' of their land was needed to protect their national identity from the advance of modern civilisation or anglicisation—was it not the same thing?—which sooner or later must penetrate their valleys. The salvation of Welsh nationhood demanded intellectual and spiritual forces which in 1707 were dead or dormant: it demanded an educational and religious revival.

The fulfilment of that need is a famous chapter of Welsh history; but, while the eighteenth-century revival became ultimately a national revival, its promoters and leaders were not primarily nationalists. The group of churchmen and philanthropists who, prompted by Stephen Hughes and Thomas Gouge, founded the Welsh Trust towards the end of the seventeenth century, were only concerned to combat the notorious ignorance and the consequent irreligion of the Welsh poor.[1] They were a mixed Anglo-Welsh body, headed by Archbishop Tillotson; and one of the reasons why their operations were suspended after a few years was their inability to agree as to the language to be taught in their schools. Most of them took English almost for granted: the children must be taught, they held, ' to read our English Bible and be more serviceable to their country and to live more comfortably in the world.' But a resolute minority, following the lead of Stephen Hughes, insisted on Welsh. In the short time allowed it the Trust did useful work. It distributed Bibles and other religious literature, necessarily in Welsh, among the adult poor. For the children a number of schools were opened; about a thousand boys and girls were taught each year. In 1701 the Society for the Promotion of Christian Knowledge took over the Trust's work. It was a mainly English organisation, but it was warmly supported by well-to-do Welshmen, Sir John Philipps at their head, and in the course of the next thirty years nearly a hundred ' charity schools ' were provided for poor Welsh children.[2] It was on these founda-tions that Griffith Jones, ' the most distinguished figure in the history of education in Wales,'[3] began to build in 1737. Educated at a school in Carmarthen, he was a country vicar of the Anglican Church in South Wales, and, unlike some of his colleagues, an ardent Welshman. He was a devoted student and champion of the Welsh language, ' old, unaltered and unmixed, full, stately and masculine, and perhaps the chastest in Europe '; but, if he was more of a nationalist than his forerunners, his primary aim when he stared his ' circulating school ' was religious: to help his countrymen to understand the Christian faith and save their souls. Since his funds, raised to begin with from the pence of poor communicants, could not possibly cover the cost of all the new school buildings and teachers which the countryside required, he conceived the idea of shifting schools from village to village. It proved an astonishing success. Within ten years a hundred ' circulating schools ' had been set up; in thirty years, between three and four thousand. When Griffith Jones died in 1761, it was reckoned that nearly 160,000 children, who would otherwise have been quite illiterate, had received at least the rudiments of an education. And about thrice as many adults, it was reckoned, had attended the schools at night.[4]

The substance of this education was mainly religious: the Bible was the text-book; and, as the children who had learned to read it grew up, they brought a new leaven of literacy to the growing multitude of adult Welshmen who, as it happened, were being caught up, in these same years, in the sweep of a great religious revival. The old seed of Puritanism was bearing fruit at last. Small bodies of Nonconformists, Baptists and Independents and others, had survived the convulsions of the seventeenth century; and over a hundred Anglican clergy had been deprived of their livings after the Restoration. But in the earlier years of the eighteenth century the number of all the Nonconformists in Wales was probably not more than some 20,000, or about one-twentieth of the population; and in Wales as in England the new evangelical movement was started within the established Church. Howel Harris, its major prophet, was, like Griffith Jones, a life-long member of the Church of England. He, too, was the product of a Welsh school, and he too might have completed his education at Oxford if within a few days of his matriculation he had not yielded to an overmastering impulse to go and preach the gospel in his native land. From 1735 to 1751 he conducted an unbroken campaign of itinerant preaching over the whole of Wales. Scouring the country by day and night, repudiated by orthodox churchmen, persecuted by the social oligarchy, assaulted by hostile mobs and more than once in danger of his life, holding his meetings for safety sometimes high on a mountain side, some-times in the early hours of the morning, he brought vast multi-tudes of his countrymen under his spell and imprinted on their hearts his passionate personality and his Calvinistic faith. 'We preach primarily to the heart and the spirit of man,' he said. 'We agitate the soul to its very foundations.' His funeral at Trevecca, his birthplace, in 1773 was attended by some 20,000 people from all parts of Wales. 'Three platforms had been erected,' wrote Lady Huntingdon, ' and from them nine sermons were delivered. Fifteen clergymen administered the Holy Sacrament to the vast multitude, and the weeping was so great that it was with difficulty the final Burial Service was read.'[5] Whitefield and Wesley were both friends of Harris and frequently visited and preached in

Wales; but, since neither of them spoke Welsh, their influence was far less than that of Harris and his Welsh associates. Of the latter the foremost figure was Daniel Rowland, an Anglican curate who began preaching about the same time as Harris and of whom it is recorded that he sometimes administered the sacrament to a congregation of over two thousand and that once he preached without pause or interruption for six hours.[6] And in the footsteps of these pioneers trod a growing company of preachers in whom the ancestral Welsh gift of eloquence found new vent in a spate of fervent oratory, clothed in the language of the Welsh Bible. Forerunners of the great nineteenth-century Welsh school of preaching, these were the men who reanimated Welsh religion. Their appeal was mainly, as Harris said, emotional: they provoked, as similar salvationists elsewhere and at other times, some strange manifestations of religious hysteria; but it was a real religion that they taught. It has never been seriously questioned that they wrought a deep and lasting change in the spiritual and moral life of the great mass of Welsh countryfolk. And its organisation was Welsh. When the Methodist community became the chief vehicle of the revival, its members worked for many years in partnership with the English Methodists—the first site of Lady Huntingdon's training college was in Wales (1768)— and they remained, like their English brethren, more or less uncomfortably, within the fold of the Anglican Church; but, when the final schism came in 1811, their Calvinistic Methodist Church was separated not only from the Anglicans but also from the Wesleyans. It was a distinct Welsh Church. And it was a Church of the common people, as democratic in personnel and government as the Presbyterian Kirk in Scotland, but not, like the Kirk, established and safeguarded by the State. When, moreover, as the nineteenth century drew on, the dissenters became a great and growing majority, it was the Church to which the bulk of Welshmen adhered. The Anglican Church of Wales retained its hold on most of the upper class; but it was in Nonconformity, in

Methodism and other sects, Baptist and Independent, which shared in the rival, in the plain grey stone chapels that were soon to be built all over Wales, that the spiritual life of most Welshmen was henceforward to be centred. The revival, in fact, gave Wales, what the Reformation had given Scotland but what Wales had lacked since the far-off days of Celtic Christianity, a national Church.

The revival was not only spiritual or moral; it was also intellectual. While it was greatly aided by the new elementary education of the Circulating Schools, it inspired itself a new kind of adult education. The thirst for adult education had already shown itself in the number of adults who attended the Circulating Schools on week-day nights; and, while the Sunday Schools which spread over England towards the end of the eighteenth century were only for children, the Sunday Schools established in Wales, mainly by the efforts of Thomas Charles, a Methodist preacher and organiser, became primarily schools, or what would nowadays be called 'study circles,' for men and women. Once the opposition of strict Sabbatarians had been overcome, they spread fast and far till they had become a universal Welsh institution. ' On Sunday the whole country was turned into a school.'[7] Hour after hour these Welsh folk of all ages sat listening to the reading of the Bible and debating its meaning till their minds were stocked, sometimes overstocked perhaps, with texts, and the geography of Palestine became more familiar to them than that of Wales itself.

So great was the demand for Bibles that, though the supply of them was rapidly increased—several editions of 10,000 and 15,000 had been provided by the Bible Society by 1768—there never seemed enough. An English tourist recorded the excitement aroused in a little country town by the arrival of a cartload of New Testaments. The people, peasants for the most part, rushed out to meet the cart, dragged it home, quickly distributed the precious books, sat up far in the night reading them, and took them to the fields next morning to read in the noonday break.[8]

The educational effect of the Sunday Schools was profound. It was impossible for Welsh countryfolk, hitherto illiterate, to study so closely such an incomparable treasury of history and thought and literature as the Bible, however narrow or naïve their understanding of it, without an immense enrichment of the mind. It was, of course, a crude, unsystematic, amateurish kind of education, but it was very much better than no education at all, and it steadily improved in scope and method. And its hold on Welshmen was all the stronger because it was not organised or financed by the State or by an established Church. It was home-made. Like the religious revival with which it was so closely linked, it was the work of the Welsh people—another manifestation of the reawakening of the Welsh national spirit. Nor is that the only debt Wales owes to the Sunday Schools. They were the nursery of modern Welsh democracy. Peasants and artisans and middle-class folk sat together in complete equality. All the teachers were unpaid and many of them were recruited from the field and workshop. Leadership was solely a matter of merit. It is hard to overvalue, indeed, what Wales has owed in political training as well as in cultural growth and vigour to the Sunday Schools.

Lastly, the rival directly brought about a regeneration of the Welsh language. The great Welsh preachers preached in Welsh; and the language of the Sunday Schools was Welsh. Hence multitudes of Welshmen were now hearing, as never before, the classical Welsh of their Bible read aloud and listening to sermons steeped in it and discussing themselves its chapters verse by verse. The result was almost automatic. They began at last to speak their tongue again as it should be spoken.

2

There was now again good Welsh for them to read. Morgan's Bible had raised the writing of Welsh prose to the highest level; but one result of the Reformation and the conflicts it provoked was to divert the great bulk of Welsh prose into a single channel. From the sixteenth century right on into the nineteenth it was mainly concerned with religious controversy and exposition; and, though this did not always inhibit good writing, the effect on style and scope and originality was inevitably cramping. Welsh poetry, meanwhile, was recovering from a long decline. Though linked so firmly with England by the Tudors, Wales had had no share in the glory of Shakespeare's day or Milton's. True, Henry Vaughan (1622-95) was a Welshman. Born near Brecon, he went to Jesus College, Oxford, and after studying law in London for a time he returned to Wales and presently settled down at Newton-by-Usk, where he stayed for the rest of his life. But, if Vaughan was a great Welsh poet, he did not write Welsh poetry. He has, indeed, been described by his most recent English biographer as the ' most Welsh of all who have written English poetry.'[9] In fact, Vaughan was the first great practitioner of what has become celebrated in our own day as the Anglo-Welsh school, the school of Welshmen writing in English. Good Welsh poetry was also written at this time, notably by Morgan Llwyd, the mystic. One other Welsh literary figure emerges from this barren age, who was far better known in Wales than Vaughan. Rhys Prichard (1579-1644), vicar of Llandovery, was no poet, but he wrote a number of homely religious rhymes which were ultimately published, at the instance of Stephen Hughes, with the title of *Canwyll y Cymry* (The Welshmen's Candle). They were so immensely popular that Prichard may almost be counted as a forerunner of the religious revival. For generations after he was dead the rhymes were still remembered and recited in the cottage-homes of Wales.

At last, in the second half of the eighteenth century, in the days of Griffith Jones and Howel Harris, the springs of Welsh poetry began to flow again. The first impetus came from a gifted family in Anglesey, the Morris brothers, Lewis, Richard and William. Lewis was no mean poet, but the main interest of all three was antiquarian. They were ardent students of the Welsh language and literature; they collected and copied medieval manuscripts; they brought to life again the moribund study of the classics in intellectual circles. Linked with them was the Reverend Evan Evans (1731-89), or Ienan Brydydd Hir, who, like Lewis Morris, was both poet and scholar. And from the same *milieu* came Geronwy Owen (1723-69) who is widely regarded as one of the greatest of modern Welsh poets. He typifies the transition to the modern democratic conception of poetry as belonging to and, often as not, composed by the common people. The son of a drunken Anglesey tinker, Owen was educated at Bangor and at Jesus College, Oxford; taught for a time at Donnington School near Wellington; moved to London where he served as secretary to the Cymmrodorion Society; and finally migrated to Virginia where he held for two or three years the mastership of William and Mary College in Williamsburg. The great vogue of his poetry in Wales was the more remarkable because of its sternly academic character. 'His themes are often remote from popular interest, and his treatment of them is austere and even arid.' But his technique was masterly, especially in his handling of *cynghanedd*, and it was mainly on that account that his poetry was so widely read and admired—an early manifestation of what is now a commonplace, the high level of Welsh folk culture. The cottager still loved to sing the rhymes of the Welshmen's Candle, but now, as education spread, he was becoming better acquainted with classical Welsh poetry and even wrestling with the mysteries of the old traditional metres. Nor was all Owen's poetry academic. He could descend from Miltonic heights to more personal themes—his faith, his love of his craft, and his longing for his homeland. 'Where I played of old,' he wrote of Anglesey (Môn), 'are men who know me not; a friend or two may remember me, scarce two where once were a hundred. I am a man cut off, obscure, an exile from Môn, a stranger to our ancient tongue. . . .'[10]

Roughly contemporary with Owen were two other poets who differed as much from him as they did from each other. Thomas Edwards or Twm o'r Nant (1739-1810) was famous in his day for his verse 'interludes' or 'moralities,' playlets in which two or three characters personify virtues and vices and suffer the appropriate results. His writing rarely rose to poetry, but 'he had a fund of humour and a capacity for effective satire, much shrewd practical wisdom, a gift for epigrammatic phrase, and occasionally a certain dramatic impressiveness.'[11] His attitude was scarcely puritanical. He abominated Calvinism. He was quite out of tune with the religious revival. And yet it was no accident that his popularity coincided with it. It was another symptom of the intense interest in morals it inspired.

The second poet, on the other hand, was closely associated with the rivival. Hitherto the traditional Welsh love of community singing had been obliged to confine itself in church and chapel to chanting the metrical version of the Psalms. Thus a real need was met when the Reverend William Williams (1717-91) of Pantecelyn near Llandovery, commonly known by the name of his birthplace, began to write the hymns which set him high—at the very top, it has been claimed—among Christian hymn-writers of all time. He wrote many other poems, including two long religious epics in the Miltonic manner, but it was the hymns that won him his immense popularity. Many of them were not the more or less formal statements of faith and doctrine which most modern hymns provide. They were the inflection, rather, of personal religious experience, of the communion of the single soul with God; and this was in the closest harmony with the spirit of the revival.

An important part in the cultural renaissance was played by the Welsh Societies. The best-known of them, the Cymmrodorion and the Gwyneddigion, were founded by Welshmen in London in 1751 and 1771. Branches of them and of several other similar societies were presently established in Wales till in course of time there was not a town, scarcely even a village, which did not have its little society or literary club. With this was linked the revival of what has now become a famous national institution. The first eisteddfod (session) of which an authentic record has survived was held at Carmarthen about 1450. It was a gathering of bards, and already, it appears, competition in poetry was a feature of it since the poet Dafydd ab Edmwnd was awarded the ' chair.' There was another such meeting in 1523, and in 1568 ' an eisteddfod was held at Caerwys in Flintshire, when a commission was granted by Elizabeth's government to certain North Wales gentlemen to grant licences to the bards, in order to distinguish them from the sturdy vagabonds who infested the countryside.'[12] Eisteddfodau were occasionally held in the seventeenth century, but nothing is known about them. In 1789 the festival first appears in its modern form. In that year two eisteddfodau were held, with the aid of the Gwyneddigion Society, at Corwen and at Bala. Thenceforward regional eisteddfodau were held from time to time, but it was not till the coming of another cultural campaign in the later years of the nineteenth century that the great national festival of our own days came into being.

The revival of the eisteddfod brought to the front the extraordinary figure of Edward Williams or Iolo Morganwg (1746-1826). The son of a Glamorgan stonemason, he made a living first from his father's craft and later as a bookseller and a land agent; but his life was given to Welsh literature and lore. He sought for, studied and copied early MSS., and took part in publishing the first edition of the poems of Daffyd ap Gwilym and the great collection of medieval prose and poetry known as the *Myvyrian Archaiology of Wales*. So far, so good; but that was not all he did. A sturdy radical, as honest in most things as he was poor, careless of money, not to be bribed, he yet thought fit to tamper with those ancient texts he seemingly loved so well. He not only altered and expanded freely. He inserted whole poems in the *corpus*; for he was no mean poet himself and the best of his poems, as it happens, were those he fathered on poets of the past. Contemporary men of letters were completely deceived; it was not indeed till the twentieth century that his fabrications were fully and finally exposed. It was this strange abnormal genius who provided the fictitious material, much of it supposedly Druidic in origin, for the institution of the *Gorsedd Beirdd Ynys Prydain* or ' Court of the Poets of the Island of Britain ' with the Arch-Druid at its head and its three ranks of Druids, Bards and Ovates. In the summer of 1792 the first gorsedd was held, not at some legendary site in Wales, nor even at Stonehenge or Avebury, but —doubtless because most of the interested Welshmen lived in London—on the unromantic slopes of Primrose Hill.[13]

3

Religion, education, language, literature—in all this cultural realm Welsh life achieved its great renaissance in the course of the eighteenth century; and the process, though not directly nationalist in origin, became steadily more and more suffused with national sentiment. This did not mean that Wales was drawing away from England. There was no renewal of the antagonism or separatism of an earlier day, no weakening of the ties that had so long bound the neighbour countries together. If Welsh nationhood was stronger in 1800 than in 1700, so was the union of Wales with England. In public life Welshmen became more and more identified with Englishmen. The Welsh M.P.s, mainly representing, like their English colleagues, the landed gentry, were mostly members of the Tory Party. There was no difference between Welshmen and Englishmen in the House of Lords. There was no Welsh Party, pursuing distinctive Welsh policies or promoting distinctive Welsh interests. It was the same in other things than politics. Welshmen, like Scotsmen, were steadily crossing the border to seek a livelihood in England—Geronwy Owen spent most of his days there—and sharing with Englishmen in public, professional, cultural, commercial life. Several of them rose to the front rank. Sir Thomas Trevor (1658-1730) became Attorney-General in 1695, Chief Justice of Common Pleas in 1701 and Lord Privy Seal in 1726. Lord Kenyon was Attorney-General in 1782, Master of the Rolls from 1784 to 1788, and Lord Chief Justice from 1788 to 1802. Richard Price (1723-91), the philosopher and publicist, was a native of Glamorgan. Sir William Jones (1746-94), the famous Orientalist, was the son of an Anglesey yeoman. Owen Pughe (1759-1835), who compiled the standard English-Welsh dictionary, came from Merioneth. The great Robert Owen (1771-1858) was born and died at Newtown.[a] Nor was Welsh participation in English life confined to life in England. Already in the Elizabethan age Welshmen had begun to share in the exploration of the New World. Welsh names are recorded amongst those who sailed with Drake and took part in Ralegh's ill-fated Virginian settlement. Beside the great Elizabethan soldier, Roger Williams (1540?-95), stand seamen like Mansel (1573-1656) who became Vice-Admiral of England, Button (? -1634) who, a few years after Hudson's death, penetrated into Hudson Bay and discovered the Nelson River, and the famous Henry Morgan (1635?-88) who began his career as a pirate and ended it as Governor of Jamaica. Welshmen also rank high as colonial pioneers. A purely Welsh colony,

[a] Mrs. Siddons (1755-1831) has been called Welsh; but she only happened to be born at Brecon when her father was acting 'on tour' there.

called Cambriol, was founded in 1616 at the easternmost point of Newfoundland; but, though it escaped the tragic end of Scottish Darien, it wilted under the hardships of the North Atlantic winter, and, after some twenty years, mainly for financial reasons, it petered out. Pennsylvania was not founded by a Welshman, but most of its early settlers were Welsh Quakers: the district in which they settled is still known as the 'Welsh Tract.' In the eighteenth century Welshmen served as Governors of Nova Scotia, Bermuda, Barbados and Trinidad, and Welsh ambassadors and ministers served with distinction at foreign courts: Sir Arthur Paget (1771-1840) at Vienna and Constantinople, Sir H. W. W. Wynn (1783-1856) at Berne and Copenhagen, Sir Charles Vaughan (1774-1849) at Berne and Washington. Among the founders of the East India Company was Thomas Middleton of Chirk Castle, and Welshmen served, though not in such disproportionate numbers as Scotsmen, with the Company: one of them was Sir Harford Jones (1764-1847) who was the Company's chief agent in the Middle East and its envoy in Persia at a critical stage of the Napoleonic War.

In the economic field, also, the association of Welshmen with Englishmen steadily increased as the eighteenth century drew on. Before the advent of the Industrial Revolution and long after it, the Welsh economy was mainly pastoral. The Welsh mountains were classed by Adam Smith in 1776 with the Scottish Highlands as seemingly 'destined by nature to be the breeding countries of Great Britain.'14 Agricultural technique was still quite primitive: corn was grown only for local consumption. Most of the land was under pasture for the breeding of cattle and sheep; and the chief markets for them and for wool and butter were over the border, not only in the towns of the western English Midlands but as far afield as London. This old-established economic link still held, but it was completely overshadowed by the interlocking of England and Wales in the Industrial Revolution. Whatever may be said of the less happy social aspects of that far-reaching change in the way of British life, it remains a fact that, without the inventiveness and enterprise and energy of the industrial pioneers, Wales—and England and Scotland too—would have been unable to cope with the growth of population without widespread destitution and large-scale emigration. Wales with its mineral wealth could share in the new industrial livelihood. Ireland, lacking minerals, could not.

South Wales, endowed with coal and iron and access to the sea, was one of the districts of Britain in which the Industrial Revolution may be said to have begun; and, as it happened, it was English initiative that introduced the new technique of iron-working which was in course of time to transform the whole life of the country. Smelting iron with charcoal had long been practised here and there in richly wooded Wales, but in 1759 John Wilkinson, the first great ironmaster of the new régime, extended his business of smelting with coke or coal from Shropshire to South Wales. The chosen site was Merthyr Tydvil. It lay on the edge of the outcrop of a vast unexploited coal-field, and alongside the coal thus easily obtainable was plenty of limestone and other minerals needed for the operation of blast furnaces. John Guest, whom Wilkinson and his partners sent as manager of their new enterprise, was the founder of one of the two great ' dynasties ' which were to control the South Wales iron industry for a century to come. The founder of the other was Richard Crawshay, a Yorkshireman, who in 1786 obtained the lease of the Cyfarthfa estate, also at Merthyr, from the son of Anthony Bacon, a London merchant, who had first acquired the lease in 1765. Other ironmasters began to operate in the same ' mineral kingdom ' as the Guests and Crawshays till by 1815 a line of furnaces and factories stretched east and west from Merthyr for twenty miles. Meantime the growth of the industry had been accelerated by a great improvement in the means of transport from the inaccessible hill-country to the port of Cardiff, some twenty-five miles away. After 1790 the old, slow business of conveying the iron products on mule-back was done away with by the building of the Glamorganshire Canal. At the outset of the nineteenth century the shadow of the ' iron age ' was fast advancing. Already Merthyr was the largest town in Wales; its population was nearing 8,000 while Cardiff's was less than 2,000. And already the output of iron from South Wales was about one third of the total output of Britain.[15] By the end of the century, moreover, coal mining had begun to yield more coal than the ironworks needed and to develop an export trade on its own, while copper-smelting and the tin-plate industry were growing fast round Swansea. Till the growth of an overseas trade in the nineteenth century the main market for this swelling industrial production—for iron and coal, for copper and tin, as for cattle and sheep—was England; and from England in return began to flow a stream of English business men, technicians and artisans to take a hand in the transformation of South Wales.

The change wrought by the Industrial Revolution was less drastic and less lasting in North Wales for the simple reason that, the coal located there being poor and hard to work, the advent of steam inevitably drew the new industry to the better and easier seams in the south. Other minerals, it is true, were available. Lead had been regularly mined from the close of the seventeenth century onwards in Flintshire and neighbouring counties, but in the latter years of the eighteenth century this industry was over-mastered by the competition of richer ores from oversea. Copper-mining on a substantial scale began in Anglesey and at one or two points of the opposite mainland in the 1760s; but, as time went on, most of the metal was shipped to Swansea to be smelted. The most prosperous and enduring industry was the slate industry, mainly based on the quarries of Caernarvonshire and Merioneth. Besides minerals and various minor industries there was an important textile industry; and for textiles as well as iron the Industrial Revolution meant the coming of a new age. From about 1780 the new methods of spinning and weaving cotton were spreading out from Lancashire not only into Yorkshire and the English midlands but also into the valleys of North Wales, soon dotted with cloth-mills driven by their streams. The woollen industry, long fed from the backs of the mountain sheep, was less quickly affected by changes of technique and, since it was therefore less subject to invasion by English technicians, it remained, more than cotton and far more than iron in the South, Welsh in management and labour force. But textiles could not do for North Wales what coal and iron did for the South: the stimulus of the Industrial Revolution was transient; before it reached its climax in the nineteenth century North Welsh textiles, like those of Ireland and South-West England, were being driven from the market by the great businesses of Yorkshire and Lancashire.[16]

Thus the opening stage of the Industrial Revolution had different results in North and in South Wales. And it was more than an economic difference: it directly affected the growth of Welsh nationhood. For, already at the outset of the nineteenth century, the Industrial Revolution was deepening and confirming the trends which had divided Wales since Norman times. The South was becoming steadily more industrial, more urban, more anglicised, while the North remained pastoral, rustic, more purely Welsh.

4

There was one unifying force which operated at this period to override local differences and rouse in all the British islanders a sense of common patriotism. The onset of the Industrial Revolution roughly coincided in time with the revival of the fight with France. The Seven Years' War broke out in 1756. France joined in the War of American Independence in 1778. The war with the French Republic and Napoleon began in 1793. And throughout this constant conflict, since France was so near a neighbour and possessed a military strength far greater than

Britain's and a sea-power able on at least one occasion to challenge Britain's mastery of her own home waters, there was often danger of a French invasion. Against that danger, Englishmen, Welshmen and Scotsmen stood together as one man. Long gone was the day when Owen Glendower welcomed to Wales the troops dispatched by his ally, the King of France, to help him against England. Welsh regiments fought beside the English regiments of the British Army on the Continent and overseas: the most famous was the Royal Welch Fusiliers raised first as 'Lord Herbert's Regiment of Foot' in 1688, raised again in 1756 and in 1760. Welshmen, too, served readily in the militia. It is a remarkable fact that Howel Harris himself enlisted in it in 1759, stood on guard on the east coast of England, and, rising to the rank of Captain-Lieutenant, remained under arms till the peace of 1763. Five members of his family joined the regular army and served in the North American campaign, besieging Louisbourg, fighting under Wolfe at Quebec: only one of them came safe home.[17]

The outbreak of the French Revolution had much the same effect on Welsh opinion as on Scottish or English. In none of the three countries was the reaction distinctively national. In all of them the Revolution had its friends and its enemies, its sceptical Tories, its enthusiastic Radicals. Its foremost Welsh champion was Richard Price, whose notorious sermon at the meeting-house in the Old Jewry in 1789 provided Burke with a text for the introductory pages of his *Reflections*. Price was a Londoner, but there were other Welshmen who preached the revolutionary cause in Wales, founded branches of the Corresponding Society and the 'Friends of the People,' and denounced in prose and verse the wickedness of kings and priests. But in Wales, as in Britain as a whole, most of the early champions of the Revolution were shocked and sobered by the excesses of the Jacobin régime, and thenceforward the French had no more chance of popular support in Wales than in England or Scotland.

Striking evidence of this may be found in the story of the French invasion of Pembrokeshire in 1797—a story so fantastic that it would be unbelievable were it not fully attested not only by English official records but also by the archives of the revolutionary government in Paris.[a] The operation, it appears, was planned by General Hoche towards the end of 1796 as a subordinate or diversionary annex to his main design, the invasion of Ireland. While a French fleet with a substantial force of regular troops sailed for the Irish coast, a small body of irregulars was to descend on Bristol, set it on fire, and then, crossing the Channel, march through Wales to Chester and Liverpool. Ransom levied on those cities would be distributed among the poor who would be incited to rise against the Government and plunder the property of the well-to-do. The composition of the force was as curious as the design. It was to consist of 600 gaolbirds released from the prisons of North-West France and 600 convicts taken from the galleys. The command was entrusted to Colonel Tate, a native of South Carolina, now seventy years old, who had fought in the War of Independence and whose only qualifications for this post would seem to have been that he spoke English and still hated Britain. A last absurdity was the mistiming of the enterprise. The invasion of Ireland had been repulsed at Bantry Bay, and Hoche himself had gone to fight on the Rhine, before the expedition was ready to sail. Yet the original plan was persisted in. In mid-February two frigates and two smaller ships sailed from Brest with the 1,200 felons on board and made for the Bristol Channel. But finding the easterly wind too strong, they abandoned that part of the scheme, and, rounding St. David's Head, disembarked the troops on the rocky coast near Fishguard in the late afternoon of February 22, 1797, and then sailed off to a rendezvous in the Irish Sea. Save for a handful of men in the fort at Fishguard there were no troops to oppose the landing, and

[a] A detailed and fully documented account is available in *The Last Invasion of Britain*, by Commander E. H. Stuart Jones, R.N. (Cardiff, 1950).

the invaders scrambled ashore in the gathering darkness and camped near the edge of the cliff. Next day some high ground, about two miles inland, was occupied, and about half the force was dispersed in patrols over the countryside to search for food, fuel and transport for the march through Wales. The tricolour had been hoisted on a commanding height, but any hopes Tate might have had that the peasantry would greet the invaders as friends and deliverers were soon dissipated. The patrols found that almost all the little farmhouses and cottages had been hurriedly deserted. Breaking in, the half-starved felons found a good stock not only of food but of drink: for, as it happened, a ship with a cargo of French wine had recently been wrecked on that part of the coast. Most of the patrols were soon gorged and drunk. Observing that the invasion had come to a halt, the country-folk began to creep back towards their homes. They armed themselves with shotguns, scythes, pitchforks, spades. They stripped the lead from the roof of St. David's Cathedral and cast it into bullets. . . . Meantime the volunteer forces in the neighbourhood, yeomanry and 'fencibles,' had been quickly mobilised and by nightfall they were concentrated, about 500 strong, at Fishguard. An attack on the enemy's position was planned for next morning, but in the course of the night, aware that most of his troops were in a state of drunken mutiny and believing that British regulars were approaching from the east, Tate surrendered.[a]

This queer story has been told in some detail because of the light it throws on Welsh sentiment in the early stages of the long war with France. In Ireland French invaders were welcomed, but not in Wales. And the scene of the little play was not set in anglicised south Pembrokeshire or 'little England beyond Wales.' It was in the northern part of the county where the people were wholly Welsh in blood and speech and life. Yet the

[a] A number of Welshwomen, in their red cloaks and high hats, had gathered on the high ground to watch events. Stuart-Jones has shown from French documents that there is probably some truth in the local legend that Tate mistook those women for the expected regulars.

reaction was as immediate and violent as it would have been in Kent or Kircudbright. And, as the war with the Republic merged into the war with Napoleon and the danger of invasion grew, Welsh patriotism was indistinguishable from English or Scottish. It was a British war and its heroes British heroes. Some of Wellington's foremost generals were Welshmen—Sir Stapleton Cotton who closed his long career as a Field Marshal and Lord Combermere; Sir Edward Paget who commanded the reserve at Corunna and directed the first Burman war; and Sir Thomas Picton, the hero of Vittoria, who fell at Waterloo.[a] There were distinguished Welsh sailors too—Admiral Hughes who fought Suffren in the Indian Ocean during the War of American Independence, and Admiral Foley who led the English line into action at the Nile and stood at Nelson's side at Copenhagen and heard him say that he could not see the signal for withdrawal with his blind eye.

The association is significant. Of all the heroes of the war the Welsh, like the English, put Nelson first. Far more than their own Picton or Hughes or Foley they idolised the English sailor; and mainly, no doubt, for that reason Welsh sentiment was much more deeply stirred by Trafalgar than by Waterloo. 'With mingled emotions of joy and sorrow' the *Cambrian*, the first and at that time the only daily newspaper published in Wales, reported the 'victory achieved by *Britain's* darling son.'[18] The *Cambrian* was produced in Swansea, and Swansea was then the chief town and port in the anglicised industrial area on the coast. But in rural Wales, in districts in west and central Wales which were at that time as Welsh in blood and speech as north Pembrokeshire, the reaction to Trafalgar was the same. Carmarthen was illuminated and the mayor and corporation 'paraded the town, preceded by the Carmarthen Volunteer Band playing 'God Save the King' and 'Rule Britannia' and occasionally a solemn dirge (104th Psalm) with drums muffled. When the procession reached a large

---

[a] There is a statue of Picton at Carmarthen, his birthplace.

bonfire which had been made in Market Street, they found several large bowls of punch awaiting their arrival, and a number of loyal and patriotic toasts were drunk in copious libations.' At Llanelly, guns were fired, bells set ringing, and the streets illuminated. Aberystwyth was ' stunned ' at the news, but ' in an instant the town was a blaze of light.' And so at Brecon and ' various other places in Wales.'[19]

The eighteenth century had witnessed the revival of Welsh nationhood. The life of Wales had become more Welsh than at any period since the Tudor annexation. But it was a purely cultural revival: there were no politics in it. The Welsh had not forgotten their ancestral hatred of the ' Saxon '; but the antagonism was latent now: it only showed itself in the social rift between the anglicised landowners and the countryfolk. Memories of conquest and subjection had faded away. Nobody dreamed now of recovering Welsh independence. And this acquiescence in the political unity of England and Wales—it was the same, as will be seen, in Scotland—was confirmed by the common experience of the Napoleonic War. The primary factor in England's great political tradition—the defence of England and thereby of Europe against military despotism—had never been purely English. From the time of the Spanish Armada and on through the series of wars with France, Wales—and Scotland, too, in a different fashion—had been linked with England in resistance to continental absolutism. It might be said, indeed, that the tradition had been a British tradition from the outset. But it was Napoleon who first impressed on all thoughtful Britons the significance of the world setting in which their tri-national island stood and the strategic necessity of its unity. If Britain had been divided in itself as the British Isles were divided, Napoleon would have won the war.

II. THE SCOTTISH REVIVAL

AT THE outset of the eighteenth century Scottish nationhood was far more robust than Welsh. Wales had been conquered by England at the end of the thirteenth century, and, with brief intervals of precarious independence, had remained subjected to England till the union of 1535. The English conquests of Scotland, on the other hand, had all been transient; the Scottish nation had never been subjected to the English, save only for a time under Cromwell; and it was an independent national State which by a voluntary bilateral compact was united with England in 1707. Clearly, therefore, *a priori*, the chance of resisting national submergence was much stronger in Scotland than in Wales, and it was reinforced in Scotland by the preservation of a national Church and a national system of law. Yet the Scotsmen who opposed the Union of 1707 believed that it would inevitably result in the absorption of Scottish into English nationality; and forty years later, when all that remained of the old tradition of national antagonism to England might seem to have flickered out with the collapse of Jacobitism, the Union was still unpopular and the pessimistic patriots still unconverted. But in the course of the next fifty years the life of Scotland underwent a transformation as astonishing as that of Wales. In 1815, while a Scottish patriot might still be anxious lest in this or that particuar the old Scottish ways were being overgrown by English, he could not seriously believe that Scottish nationhood was in danger of extinction.

Indeed for more than a generation after the Union the danger lay the other way. Scarcely had that great act of statesmanship been achieved when Scottish nationalism began to react against it; and, before the eighteenth century was half-way through three attempts were made to break up the Union settlement by force of arms and either to subject all Britain to the rule of a Scottish king or to make Scotland again a separate sovereign state.

The cause of this reaction was partly economic, partly political. The commercial benefits which had mainly determined the acceptance of the Union were slow to mature, and meantime the pressure of the higher rate of English taxation and such other grievances as the malt tax and the suppression of smuggling[a] made the Union increasingly unpopular. On the political side the discontent was deepened by the enactment of a series of measures by the Tory Parliament towards the end of Queen Anne's reign —the Treason Act, the Toleration Act, the Patronage Act—which were regarded in Scotland as violating in spirit, if not in letter, the solemn compact of the Union.

These discontents gave Jacobitism its chance, and the Union was not a year old before the first armed attack was launched on it. There were only some 1,500 ill-equipped troops in all Scotland at that time; and Louis XIV was ready to back the Jacobites more vigorously then than at any later period. In March 1708, five men-of-war sailed from Dunkirk with transports carrying a French force about 5,000 strong. It seems more than probable that its landing would have precipitated a widespread rising and that Scotland would have become again, if only for the moment, a separate Stuart kingdom. But the invaders did not land. A British fleet under Admiral Byng[b] was on the watch; and, when, on the day after they had reached the Firth of Forth, the French observed it in the offing, they fled away northwards up the coast. So hot was the pursuit that James' request to be set ashore was rejected, and he was carried back with his French supporters to Dunkirk.

In 1715 again the chances of invasion were by no means desperate. German George I could not make the same appeal to

[a] Hence the Porteous Riots familiar to readers of *The Heart of Midlothian*.
[b] Father of the admiral who was executed in 1757.

Scottish loyalty as Stewart Anne, and, if only the 'Old Pretender' had been willing to change his faith, all Scotland would have backed him. As it was, if the Kirk's heart was moved, it kept its head. It would not have a Catholic King. So, though the High-landers, north and east, rose in force, their advance on Edinburgh was checked by Argyll, and it was an army of less than 2,000 that ventured across the border and surrendered to the English troops which barred their path at Preston.

The situation in England was similar. Only long-sighted Englishmen realised that Union was a permanent necessity. On the short view the overthrow of French ascendancy in Europe in Marlborough's wars had invalidated what had been in 1707 the supreme argument for Union, the strategic security of England; whereas its greatest drawback, the concession of Free Trade, still rankled in mercantilist minds. To back out of the Union, how-ever, was one thing: it was quite another to accept a James III in England. The Catholics, who except in the far North had little influence, might be wholehearted Jacobites; but the Anglican Tory squires, sons of the Cavaliers, however much they disliked the Hanoverian and his Whig supporters, were not prepared to fight for another Stewart. So only a handful of Northern Catholics rallied to the 'Old Pretender.'

The odds were still heavier against the 'Young Pretender.' By 1745 Scotland had begun to settle down to the Union. A new generation had grown up. Memories of past conflict in the Lowlands were becoming overlaid by the present enjoyment of peace and security and the fruits, now just beginning to be realised, of the economic side of Union. And the Highlands were now less restless and less dangerous. A prudent clemency had been shown to the Jacobites after 1715,[a] and Wade's great system of roads had made it far easier for troops to deal with a rising in any part of Scotland. Since in England, too, the Hanoverian monarchy had had time to take root, the chance of a widespread rising to put the Stewart on the throne was much fainter in 1745 than in 1715. The only hope of success, indeed, lay in foreign aid; and in the spring of 1744 it seemed it would be given. Louis XV suddenly made up his mind to invade England. An army of invasion, 10,000 strong, was gathered at Dunkirk. A naval squadron was provided to convey the transports to the Thames. *Efflavit Deus.* In two successive gales several of the French ships were wrecked. The invasion was called off, and Louis, for the time being, lost interest in the Jacobite cause. But the impetuous young Charles Edward was not deterred. In the summer of 1745 he landed, almost alone, on the Highland coast; and, though his prospects were so much weaker, he achieved a far greater initial success than his father. He occupied Edinburgh, proclaiming King James VIII and appealing to Scottish nationalism by proposing to recall the extinct Parliament, and then marched into the very heart of England. But at Derby the tide turned. The Pretender's forces, mostly raw Highlanders and Irishmen, were less than 6,000 strong; he obtained a bare 200 recruits in Lancashire; and, though Louis XV's interest in the Jacobite adventure had so far revived that he signed a treaty binding him to render aid, the ' auld alliance ' proved as ineffective as it had always been. Money was sent and arms and six small cannon; but the project of 1744 was not revived: there was no French invasion of England. The march to Derby, indeed, would not have been accomplished if England had not been denuded of troops or if Cope had been a better soldier or if the Protestant population of northern England had been less apathetic in face of the strange invasion. As it was, by the time the Pretender reached Derby, troops had arrived from the Low Countries with Cumberland in command; and, since only the young adventurer wanted to go on, the retreat from Derby began, a retreat which led right back to the Highland Line and ended in the slaughter of the clansmen at Culloden.

The Pretender's escape added one more romantic chapter to the tradition of Scottish nationalism; but the Jacobite cause was now no more than a romance: for all practical purposes it was dead. And, as will presently be recorded, the old Celtic life of the Highlanders did not long survive it.

2

There were many more Scotsmen in England in 1807 than in 1707. The Union of the Parliaments had renewed the current of migration started by the union of the Crowns. With the rump of the Scottish Parliamentarians, the forty-five commoners and sixteen peers who left Edinburgh for London, went a number of Scotsmen who, like those who had followed their Stewart King in 1603 to curry favour at his court, were hoping to share in the distribution of the posts and pensions notoriously associated with the operation of eighteenth-century politics. Some of them went far. To name only the most successful, John Stuart (Earl of Bute) became *de facto* Prime Minister in 1760; Thomas Hay (Earl of Kinnoul) Chancellor of the Duchy in 1753; Alexander Wedderburn (later Lord Loughborough) Solicitor-General in 1771, Attorney-General in 1778, and Lord Chancellor in 1793; Henry Dundas (later Lord Melville) Home Secretary in 1791, Secretary of State for War in 1794 and First Lord of the Admiralty in 1804. Nor was it only in the political field that Scotsmen could better their fortunes over the border. Scotland was still vastly poorer than England. In every walk of life the standard of living was much lower. A Scottish judge was paid £700 a year, an English £2,000. A Scottish university professor's salary was £100 to £150, a clergyman's averaged £50 to £60, a parish schoolmaster's about £12.[20] And money was not the only magnet. Ambitious Scotsmen felt that London offered more scope for their talents than Edinburgh; well-to-do Scotsmen—and all Scots were not poor—were attracted by the greater amenities of English life; they bought estates in England, sent their sons to English public schools, married their daughters into English 'society.' It was a multifarious invasion and its result was remarkable. In a very short time Scotsmen had won their way to the front rank not only in the public services, military, naval, imperial, but in the whole field of professional and cultural life. William Murray, better known as the great Lord Mansfield, became Lord Chief Justice in 1756, Drummond Archbishop of York in 1761, Douglas Canon of Windsor in 1762 and afterwards Bishop of Carlisle and of Salisbury. In the same period the professional world of London contained John Hunter surgeon, William Fordyce physician, Robert Adam and his brothers architects, Robert Strange engraver, Allan Ramsay portrait-painter, and among men of letters Thomson, Smollett, Boswell, Campbell.[21]

For this great company of Scotsmen Scotland had ceased to be home. Nearly all of them were Londoners. And there was little, if anything, distinctively Scottish in their life and work. The politicians, it is true, formed a compact Scottish group in Parliament, but that was mainly because the Scottish system of representation was even more anachronistic than the English—there were only some 4,000 parliamentary voters, about half of them 'fictitious'[22]—so that the Scottish M.P.s were more easily subject to management and, as an English M.P. complained, 'always voted as they were directed.'[23] The selection and behaviour of the Scottish peers was subject to the same control. Hence, while there was a Scottish parliamentary 'bloc,' there was no Scottish Party, just as there was no Welsh Party. On the accession of George III the 'bloc' became an adjunct of the English 'Court Party' and it remained an adjunct of the English Tory Party till the reform of the representative system in 1832. Only on three occasions could the conduct of the Scottish parliamentarians be described as national. The first was the Porteous Riots. A bill, harshly penalising Edinburgh, was carried in the Lords, but vigorously opposed by Scottish members in the Commons and substantially modified as a result. The second occasion was the Militia Bill of 1757. The Seven Years War laid all Britain open to attack, but Scotland was excluded from the operation of the bill for fear lest Jacobitism might still have life enough to make the arming of the people dangerous. Regarded as a slight on the honour of the nation, this precaution was angrily denounced in Scotland and opposed, without effect, by Scottish members of both Houses. The third occasion was the Roman Catholic Relief Bill of 1778. A measure relieving Catholics in England from certain disabilities which in fact had long ceased to be enforced passed through Parliament without serious opposition; but, when another bill was introduced to extend similar relief to Catholics in Scotland, it was hotly attacked by the Scottish members. And in that they again were truly representative. Scottish Protestants as a whole had retained to a greater degree than English the fierce anti-Roman spirit of the Reformation; and in 1779 something akin to the temper of 1559 flamed out again. While the Kirk soberly disapproved the bill in General Assembly and resolutions were carried and petitions organised elsewhere, the mob once more took charge in Edinburgh and Glasgow, looting and firing Catholic buildings. The Government bowed to the storm it had unwittingly aroused. The bill was withdrawn.[a]

Those three were the only occasions during the first century of the Union on which the Scottish members of the united legislature acted as Scotsmen; and the Scottish share in the executive was similarly unaffected by distinctive national aims or policies. The separate Scottish Privy Council was retained at the passing of the Union Act as a sop to Scottish sentiment, but in the very next session an Act ' for rendering the Union of the two

---

[a] The shocking ' Gordon Riots' in 1780 showed that anti-Popery, if not so strong as in Scotland, was by no means defunct in England. It is an interesting fact that the same unbalanced Scotsman, Lord George Gordon, who held a seat for an English constituency, took the lead in both fields. He went to Scotland to organise the agitation in 1779 and returned to England to head the movement which brought about the catastrophe of 1780 (J. P. de Castro, *The Gordon Riots*, Oxford, 1926). The Scottish Bill was withdrawn, but the English Act was not repealed.

Kingdoms more entire and complete' decreed that there should be only one Council and provided for the exercise of the Scottish body's incidental functions by the Justices of the Peace.[a] In 1746 the Secretaryship of State for Scotland was likewise abolished. But those changes were not meant, of course, to exclude Scotsmen from the government of Britain. At least one Scotsman was always needed in the Cabinet as an adviser on Scottish affairs and as leader of the Scottish parliamentary 'bloc.' After 1745 it was usually the Lord Advocate, whose ancient office, first mentioned in the reign of James III,[24] had been retained at the Union as the necessary complement to the retention of Scottish Law. Argyll[b] from 1725 to 1761, Dundas from 1791 to 1805 was not only, so to speak, the Scottish Minister, but the sole Scottish Minister. The whole administration of Scotland was concentrated in their hands—Dundas was dubbed by his countrymen 'King Harry the Ninth'—and they not only secured the appointment of many Scotsmen to posts in England and in British services oversea, they saw to it that the tradition, never substantially broken save by Cromwell, that all posts in Scotland should be held by Scotsmen was rigidly maintained. Despite the growing number of Scotsmen in well-paid office in England, English statesmen did not question this Scottish monopoly of Scottish office: wisely, since the administration of Scottish affairs by Scotsmen was one of the main factors in maintaining Scottish acquiescence in the Union.

In that sense the Scottish share in British government was national, but not in any broader sense. There was no distinctive Scottish interest or objective in British policy. The Scotsmen in the Cabinet were virtually indistinguishable from its English members in their attitude towards the American Colonies or the French Revolution and its sequel or towards India or Ireland. When George III, on an impulse of his own, closed his first speech from the throne with the declaration that he ' gloried in the name of Britain '[25] his use of the word was correct in more than a

[a] 6 Anne, c. 6.
[b] His title was Earl of Islay from 1715 to 1743 when he succeeded to the dukedom.

formal sense. Throughout his reign he was King of a country whose Parliament and Government had become completely unitary in respect of all British as distinct from party local affairs. It was not a combination, an adjustment, between two national politics: it was a fusion. But, if so, were not those predictions of the doom of Scottish nationhood coming true? Were not those many able Scotsmen who were making their careers away from Scotland in danger, as time went on, of forgetting they were Scotsmen? It is difficult to imagine Scotsmen in any circumstances losing their pride in their past; but, as it happened, any such risk as there may have been was nullified by two developments.

The first arose from the fact that national fusion is a two-sided business. If Scotsmen in England had wanted, like those ' Englishfied ' Welshmen in the sixteenth century,[a] to forget their origin, they could not have done it: it was made impossible by the attitude of their English neighbours. The Scotsmen's invasion of England, their trespass on Englishmen's monopoly of place and power, had not, of course, been welcome. It was likened, indeed, to a ' plague of locusts.' But at first there was little, if any, malice in this resentment. Englishmen grumbled at Scotsmen's advancement, ridiculed their national peculiarities of speech and behaviour, scoffed at their pride in their native land; but they did not hate them. In this, as in so much else, Dr. Johnson was a typical Englishman. His notorious antipathy to Scotland and all things Scottish did not go very deep. He certainly saw nothing to admire in the bare unwooded scenery. 'Seeing Scotland, is only seeing a worse England. It is seeing the flower gradually fade away to the naked stalk.'[26] ' The noblest prospect which a Scotchman ever sees is the high road that leads him to England.'[27] And he really hated oatmeal porridge. Quite genuine, too, was his dislike of Scottish ' clannishness ' in England. Why are all the Adam brothers' workmen Scots?[28] Why does Boswell employ the only

[a] See page 57 above.

Scottish shoeblack in the town?[29] [a] But observe the note of humour. For Johnson, in fact—and he made no secret of it—the Scots were a theme on which he enjoyed ' letting himself go'; and, under pressure from the patient Boswell,[b] he admitted that he could not explain the cause of his ' antipathy.'[30] But his long, and in those days arduous, journey through the Highlands to the Western Isles in the autumn of 1773 was proof of his deep interest in old Gaelic Scotland, and there was much he found there that appealed to his conservative instincts. He was impressed by the Highlander's hospitality and good manners. ' Civility seems part of the national character of Highlanders.' He noted and did not disapprove their family pride. ' Every Highlander can talk of his ancestors.'[c] He confessed there was no Gaelic literature, but he deplored the decline of the spoken language and listened with delight to Gaelic songs whether in the drawing-room or in the harvest-field. He could not question the value of the recent transformation of Highland life—the end of the old blood-feuds, the coming of law and order and safety on the roads—but he was deeply distressed by other aspects of the change—the degeneration of the chiefs ' from patriarchal rulers to rapacious landlords,' the desperate poverty of the clansmen, and the great stream of emigration over the Atlantic that was depopulating the mountain country.[31] It was this understanding, this display of an English nationalist's better side, that made the *Journey to the Western Islands of Scotland* so notable a book. Scotsmen have often confessed that Johnson showed in it a truer insight into Scottish or at any rate Highland character and a deeper respect for its virtues than any other writer of either nation in that age.

[a] Johnson only once—in one of his strange talks with Wilkes—descended to making a joke of Scottish poverty, and it was Wilkes who gave him the lead. Boswell's *Life*, (Oxford, 1904), ii. 408.

[b] Boswell's reaction to the insults so freely lavished on his country is one of the most amusing features of the immortal biography; and so are Johnson's laboured attempts to salve the wounds, ' I will do you, Boswell, the justice to say that you are the most *unscottified* of your countrymen.' ' You are a Scotchman without the faults of a Scotchman.' *Ibid.*, i. 504, ii. 263.

[c] Like the Welsh, see page 60 above.

Johnson was the stoutest of Tories. He accepted a pension from Bute. He was quite unaffected, therefore, by the nasty storm of anti-Scottish prejudice which was whipped up by Whig partisans at the outset of George III's reign. The Whigs were infuriated at the young King's success in breaking down the ' oligarchy ' they had so long maintained, and some of them and their hangers-on vented their spleen on the Scots. The dumb subservience of the Scottish parliamentary ' bloc ' was bad enough: it was worse, it was intolerable, that George should choose his ' dearest friend,' Bute, to be the chief tool of his attempt to restore the authority of the Crown. Bute, as it chanced, was not at all a typical Scot. He was highly anglicised. His most valuable family connections were English. Yet, as long as he held office, it was roundly asserted that Scotland was ruling England. Strafford's Irish army had never been forgotten; it was soon to be recalled in the debates on the Quebec Act; and, though the earlier years of George III were not seriously comparable with the later years of Charles I, it was put about that the King was using the barbarians from beyond the border to destroy the liberties of Englishmen. It was not Bute only, nor the Scottish members of Parliament, that were pilloried. Scotsmen of every sort or station—Chief Justice Mansfield for example—were reprobated or ridiculed for being Scotsmen. And to what lengths these partisans allowed themselves to go! The scurrility of Wilkes' *North Briton*, significantly named, is not surprising; nor are ' Junius' ' venemous libels on the Scottish character—' they cordially love themselves and as cordially hate their neighbours '; ' when treachery is in question ' (Wedderburn is the butt) ' we should make allowances for a Scotchman.'[32] Nor is the treatment accorded to needy Scottish wayfarers as described by Smollett in the opening chapters of *Roderick Random*[a] to be wondered at when pamphleteers and journalists, aided by Churchill on the stage,

---

[a] For horseplay and scurrility, see Bohn's edition, page 90. ' Lousy Scotch ' as an abusive epithet, pages 141, 192.

147

were deliberately inflaming the narrow nationalism of the man in the street. But it is strange to find almost as crude a prejudice in high political circles among men who should have known better. Horace Walpole was intensely Whiggish and always a querulous critic, but it was going rather far to complain that the Scots were lending 'all their mischievous abilities' to ruin the constitution out of mere envy of the English.[33] And other than pure-blooded Englishmen joined in the hue and cry. Anglo-Irish Shelburne, writing to Welsh Richard Price in 1783, described the Scottish nation as a 'set of innate cold-hearted impudent rogues . . . I can scarce conceive a Scotchman capable of liberality.'[34] It is startling, surely, to find a statesman of Shelburne's calibre, even in a black mood and in a black year for England, indulging in such rant.

This exhibition of an ugly English nationalism was enough in itself to prevent Scotsmen in England from forgetting their origin. But something meantime was happening to Scotsmen in Scotland. Those emigrants, after all, were only a tiny fraction of the Scottish people; and, whatever their fate might be in London, their fellow-countrymen who stayed at home were in no danger at that time of overmuch anglicisation. Forces were at work which were soon to make the Union a reality, but for at least a generation after 1745 the effect of the Union was by no means unifying. It was only on those few particular occasions or when confronted in wartime with a common danger that Scotsmen took any interest in English affairs. One reason for this was distance. In 1758 the mail-coach, running once a month, took from ten and a half to twelve and a half days to cover the 300-odd miles between Edinburgh and London. As late as 1790 letters spent four days in the post.[35] Stale news is not exciting, and the Scottish newspapers were few and their circulation small. On the constitutional issues, moreover, which made the stuff of politics at Westminster between 1760 and 1783 Scotsmen could not share the zest and understanding which Englishmen had acquired from their parliamentary past. Hence a general indifference to London politics, a sort of isolationism, which was naturally stiffened by the behaviour of Wilkes' Londoners. But the chief reason why Scotland in this formative period lay aloof from England, keeping to herself, was not a lack of interest in what was happening beyond the border: it was an absorbing preoccupation with what was happening within it.

The first event was an economic transformation which set Scotland free at last from the poverty that had always cramped her life. It began with agriculture. Soon after the Union Scottish landowners, not too proud to seek advice from England where agricultural technique was immeasurably more advanced, began to revolutionise their methods—abolishing the antediluvian ' run-rig ' system, carving out manageable farms, levelling, walling, hedging, draining, planting trees for shelter, and so forth—with such remarkable results that in Lothian first and then in other Lowland districts the countryside became the home of a well-manned, happy and increasingly prosperous agrarian community. By the end of the century it was English farmers who were seeking advice across the border.[36] There was a similar advance in commerce and industry. The price for which Scotland had sold her independence was beginning to be paid. If the Union by extending English mercantilism to Scotland cut down the old Baltic and German trade of the east-coast ports, it more than compensated by opening the colonial trade in North America and the West Indies to the merchants of the Clyde. They made the most of their opportunity. Their chief imports were sugar, rice and tobacco, especially the last. In 1775, when the American Revolution abruptly destroyed the trade, half the import of tobacco into Britain came to Glasgow, and half its re-export to continental Europe went from Glasgow. Most of the goods shipped in return were manufactured in England,[a] but the share

[a] Readers of *Redgauntlet* will remember the Tory Laird's contempt for Edinburgh tradesmen and their English wares. " Can they not buy our own Scottish manufactures, and pick their customers' pockets in a more patriotic manner ? " " Then the ladies must

of Scottish industry was growing—linen, thread, stockings, leather-goods, hardware. The shipping of the Clyde increased sixfold. Glasgow in 1707 was a little country town, beside an undredged river ' fordable on foot,' with a population of about 12,000: in 1807 it was a city and a port with an open channel to the sea, its population over 70,000. Paisley, likewise, was fattened by what it made out of thread, linen gauze and such like from a village of 3,000 into a town of 25,000. Linen held the lead, more than compensating for the temporary swamping of Scottish by English woollen goods and presently enabling Glasgow to recover from the loss of American tobacco; but heavy industry now also took the field. Scotland, like Wales, was one of the areas in Britain in which the Industrial Revolution started; and the exploitation of its underground wealth of coal and iron may be said to have begun when on an Englishman's initiative and with English plant and artisans, the famous Carron works were opened in 1759.[a] In 1806 there were 29 blast furnaces in Scotland with an output of over 23,000 tons. Three further developments quickened the pace of economic progress—first, James Watt's invention of the condensing steam engine, first used at Carron; second, a vast improvement in transport, the building of good roads by the ' turnpike trusts ' and the cutting of the great canal from Forth to Clyde (1768-90); third, the expansion of the banking system in a form that favoured the enterprise of small-scale capital. The results of it all were impressive. The Industrial Revolution had not attained its full scope by the end of the eighteenth century; Scotland was not yet wealthy, but it had ceased to be desperately poor. And the business of making a better living was enough to occupy the minds of Scottish farmers, merchants, shipowners, cotton-spinners, iron-founders, bankers,

---

have fashions." " Can they not busk the plaids over their heads, as their mothers did ? "

[a] John Roebuck's work in Scotland was contemporary with John Wilkinson's in Wales; see page 129 above.

and in their degree, of Scottish peasants and artisans. No room was left for politics. The empty Parliament House at Edinburgh no longer seemed to matter. London was as far away as derelict forgotten Darien.[37]

The second great event in Scotland after 1745 was the social and cultural transformation of the Highlands. The immediate sequel to Culloden was 'Butcher' Cumberland's brutal punishment of the Jacobite clans; but the Government's policy thereafter was notably lenient. There was no repressive legislation comparable with the penal laws in Lancastrian Wales or in contemporary Ireland. The clansmen were disarmed. By a foolish provision which applied to loyal as well as rebel Highlanders and was strangely not repealed till 1782, the wearing of the kilt was forbidden. Jacobite estates were confiscated, and their revenues applied to the building of roads and schools and other public purposes; but only some eighty individuals were exempted from a general Act of Indemnity. Most of them had escaped oversea and, as time went on, many of them made their way home unmolested. In 1784 the forfeited property was restored to its old owners. These conciliatory measures took the sting out of Jacobitism. It ceased to be a conspiracy keeping Highlands and Lowlands apart. It remained a romance in which all Scotsmen could share.

This happy result might not have been achieved if the risings of 1715 and 1745 had not made it clear that a primitive and a progressive society could not go on living side by side. But Englishmen and Lowland Scotsmen alike were now convinced that the Highlands must be ' civilised.' With one bold stroke the ancient clan-system was destroyed: Highland land-law became the same as Lowland: ' hereditary jurisdictions ' were abolished: quasi-tribal warrior chiefs were converted into peaceable landlords (1747). The immediate economic results were bad. The Highlands were overpopulated for pursuits other than fighting

151

and raiding; and the chiefs were less considerate of their tenants than they had been of their vassals. The growth of sheep-farming increased the destitution of the peasantry, and thousands would have starved if they had stayed at home. But the new industrial development offered them employment in the Lowland towns, and for the more adventurous the Union had opened a door to a new life overseas. It is estimated that 30,000 Highlanders emigrated between 1745 and 1775, mostly, it seems, to Canada.

The abolition of the clan-system had left the Highlanders still very different from their neighbours in other things than their greater poverty. With few exceptions they spoke Gaelic only. Many of them were Catholics, some virtually pagans. Almost all of them were grossly ignorant. Without some change in this cultural field the process of assimilation would have been quite incomplete, and nothing is more remarkable in the whole story than the way in which that change was brought about. It was partly the Kirk's doing, partly the work of the S.P.C.K. which, as has been seen, was engaged on the same task at the same time in Wales.[38] Two spurs had prompted them to action at the outset of the eighteenth century: first, the notorious lack of schooling in the vast neglected parishes in the Highlands and the Western Isles; second, the vigorous attempt of the Catholic missionaries, now headed by a bishop for the first time since the Reformation, not only to maintain but to extend their hold on Jacobite areas. By the joint efforts of the Kirk and the Society as many schools were built as their meagre funds allowed. Some of these were the Kirk's parish schools, but most of them were ' charity schools ' as in Wales, and in many cases they were mobile, anticipating the Welsh ' circulating schools.' ' In districts where the children were few and the homesteads scattered the itinerant schoolmaster gave what instruction he could for a few months and went his way.' Starting with five in 1711, the ' charity schools ' numbered 150 in 1750 and 189 in 1809. Thus a fast-increasing number of 'little savages' were becoming literate, and, since the teaching was based on religion, were growing up to be good Presbyterians. The expansion of 'Popery' was checked. Since, indeed, there were very few Catholic schools, many Catholic parents allowed their children to get their education where alone it could be got.

Lastly, language. One of the aims of the educational campaign at its outset was the elimination of Gaelic, 'the rude speech of a barbarous people.' The English Bible was the text book, and unhappy schoolmasters had to try to expound it to children who knew no English. Its translation into Gaelic was stubbornly opposed[a] until it was discovered that the children were being taught to read aloud the English version quite correctly but without knowing what it meant. In 1766 schoolmasters were instructed to teach both languages. In 1767 a Gaelic New Testament was produced, and a Gaelic Bible some forty years later. But it could not do for Gaelic what the Welsh Bible did for Wales. The Gaelic of the Highlands was a spoken language only; unlike Welsh, it had no great literature; and while it continued to be spoken—it is still spoken—in some districts, more and more Highlanders learned English. It was not only an instrument of education, it was also, as in Wales, a means of economic advancement. For a man seeking a job in the Lowlands its practical value was obvious.

When Dr. Johnson travelled north in 1773 he was disappointed to find that the wild Highlanders he had expected to see no longer existed, 'so quick, so great and so general' had been the 'change of national manners.'[39] In that respect, indeed, the results of the great educational movements launched about the same time in two old Celtic areas of Britain were quite different. In Wales the process of assimilation with England was checked: Welsh life

[a] 'Their language is attacked on every side,' protested Dr. Johnson. 'Schools are erected in which *English* only is taught, and there were lately some who thought it reasonable to refuse them a version of the holy scriptures, that they might have no monument of their mother-tongue.' (*Journey*, 91.)

became more Welsh. But the life of the Highlands, which in all the elements of nationality had differed from Lowland life even more than Welsh from English, was so changed, it was so much assimilated, save only in the distant Western Isles, to the life of the Lowlands, that the two nationalities—and they had in fact become separate nationalities—were at last combined in one.

3

With economic transformation and national consolidation went a third outstanding feature of eighteenth-century Scotland, the most remarkable of them all—the coming of the 'golden age' of modern Scottish culture. It was as if the escape from poverty, like some sudden change of climate, had enabled the Scottish genius to break through the stiff soil and come all at once to its full flower. Two of the blooms alone would have sufficed to make Scotland famous—David Hume (1711-76) and Adam Smith (1723-1790). But Hume had great companions in philosophy—Thomas Reid (1710-91), George Campbell (1719-96), William Robertson (1721-93), James Beattie (1735-1803)—and a great successor in Dugald Stewart (1753-1828). Nor was Adam Smith the sole inventor of political economy: in some respects he was anticipated by James Stuart Denham (1712-80). There were great names, too, in physical science—William Cullen in medicine[a] (1710-90), James Hutton in geology (1726-97), John Leslie in chemistry as well as mathematics (1766-1832). Since nearly all these men were teaching at the Universities, it must have been for serious-minded Scottish students a time when it was 'bliss to be alive.' And that wonderful summer of philosophy and science passed into a no less wonderful autumn of poetry and prose. The age that linked the eighteenth with the

[a] Hunter is not mentioned here, as his career was mainly in London; see page 142 above.

nineteenth century was the age of Burns (1759-96) and Scott 1771-1832).

This swift storming of the heights was a purely Scottish achievement. Save in so far as its prose was modelled on the English style, it owed little to England. It was the work of Scotsmen living most of their lives in Scotland. And it restored to Edinburgh the prestige of a national capital, whose life, if less exciting and romantic than in the old historic days, was incomparably more brilliant. From Hume's time to Scott's and on to the days of Jeffrey and the *Edinburgh Review* it was one of the three or four leading intellectual centres of Europe. What a change since 1745! Linked with the growth of prosperity and the civilisation of the Highlands, the flowering of Scottish culture completed the process of national transformation which, as Scott observed in 1815, in little more than fifty years had rendered ' the present people of Scotland a class of beings as different from their grandfathers as the existing English are from those of Queen Elizabeth.'[40] But, if it was a Scottish achievement, it had done little to stimulate national consciousness till the advent of Burns and Scott. Though the famous men at Edinburgh had turned their backs on London, though they were critical of English ways and doings and sharply resented the slanders of Wilkes and his allies, they were yielding unconsciously—or so it seemed—to the subtle influences of anglicisation. They talked ' broad Scots ' in private, for instance, but in public they studiously affected an English accent. Their interests, moreover, were not in the past, but in modern theology, modern philosophy, modern science. Macpherson's forged epic of a Scottish heroic age (Ossian) might enjoy a passing vogue. An eccentric antiquarian like David Erskine might erect a colossal statue of Wallace on his estate and present President George Washington with a snuff-box made from the wood of the tree in which Wallace took shelter. But by and large the cultivated world seemed to be losing its pride in Scottish history and the traditional life of the Scottish folk.

Whatever the strength of that tendency may have been, it was destroyed by Burns and Scott. Both were passionate patriots.[a] Both set themselves to preserve the heritage of Scottish life. With Burns it was the language. His purpose, he said of the poems he published in 1786, was to express the feelings of himself and his rustic fellow-countrymen ' in his and their native language.'[41] With Scott it was history. ' By such efforts, feeble as they are,' ran the preface to *Minstrelsy of the Scottish Border*, his first important book, ' I may contribute something to the history of my native country, the peculiar features of whose manners and character are daily melting and dissolving into those of her sister and ally.'[42] As everybody knows, they both achieved their object to the full. Immeasurable indeed was the effect of Burns' poetry and of Scott's historical ballads and novels in reviving Scotsmen's love of Scotland's life and their pride in her past.

Because of the rustic language of his greatest poems, Burns appealed mainly to Scotsmen, but Scott's influence was world-wide. It was first felt in England. Englishmen, who with very rare exceptions had known and cared nothing about Scottish history and life, may be said to have discovered Scotland by reading Scott. A new stream of English tourists followed in Johnson's footsteps and took more delight than he in Highland scenery. More serious-minded travellers sought the ' Wizard's ' acquaintance and sat at the feet of the famous Scottish professors.[b] Next to England, it was in France that the Scottish achievement was acclaimed. Voltaire made a quip about the versatility of Scottish genius. Hume was lionised in Paris. And, while the fame of the philosophers spread to centres of learning beyond France,

[a] ' The spirit of Wallace,' wrote Burns, ' poured a Scottish prejudice into my veins, which will boil along there till the floodgates of life shut in eternal rest.' Quoted by W.P. Ker, *The Politics of Burns* in *Two Essays* (Glasgow 1918), 39.

[b] Besides such Scotsmen as Scott, Sydney Smith, Mackintosh, and Brougham, many English visitors attended Dugald Stewart's famous lectures, including in his later years Palmerston and Lord John Russell. Palmerston used to say that he profited little from his English education at Harrow and Cambridge and that he acquired ' whatever useful knowledge and habits of mind ' he possessed at Edinburgh. Terry, 595. H. C. F. Bell *Lord Palmerston* (London. 1936) i, 6.

the Waverley novels, translated into many languages, conquered the whole of literate Europe and America. Scotland—it was emphatically not North Britain—had recovered her place on the map of the world.

4

In Scotland as in Wales the national revival had no disruptive or separatist effect. Side by side with it, in both countries, a process of British consolidation was at work. It was more striking in Scotland than in Wales because Scottish nationalism was stronger than Welsh and because the union with England was so much more recent. It was not centuries ago, it was only yesterday, that the Scots had been an independent nation. But the reasons for the closer connection with England were the same—a steady increase in the current of migration, in social intercourse in inter-marriage, in the business associations prompted by the onset of the Industrial Revolution,[a] and, above all else, in the recognition of a common British interest in face of continental Europe. At the time of the Union, as has been seen, Scotsmen were much less aware than Englishmen of the danger of French aggression; but in the subsequent period of constant war with France they saw, as clearly as in Knox's day, that Scotland's freedom was no less at stake than England's. Though the ' auld alliance ' had been so important and persistent a factor in Scottish history—far more so than in Welsh—and though as late as 1745 a minority of Scotsmen were still prepared to welcome a French invasion to help them against England, the Scottish people joined in the new sequence of wars with France as spontaneously and unanimously as the English.

Scottish regiments had fought beside English long before the Union. The Scots Guards were raised in Scotland in 1660, the

---

[a] About 1787 John Gladstone, a Scot of Highland blood, exchanged a business partnership at Leith for one at Liverpool, where his son William Ewart was born in 1809.

Royal Scots (1st Foot) and the Scots Fusiliers (21st Foot) in 1678, the Second Dragoons, the oldest regiment of Dragoons in the British Army and famous in later days as the 'Scots Greys,' in 1681, and the Seventh Hussars in 1690. The 25th Foot, with their characteristic motto, *In veritate religionis confido*, were raised at Edinburgh in 1689, and in the same year the 26th Foot, known later as the 'Cameronians,' were raised from that recently persecuted sect in the Glasgow area. Most of these regiments fought in Marlborough's great battles on the Continent. The continuing tension in Europe and the wars which broke out in 1739 and 1756 led to the raising of more Scottish regiments. In 1739 the six companies which Wade had enlisted for road-making from the loyal Highland clans were raised to eight and became the 'Black Watch.'[a] In 1741 the 47th Foot were raised in Scotland. At the Siege of Quebec they were known as 'Wolfe's Own,' and thereafter a black 'worm' was worn in the lace of their uniforms in memory of Wolfe. The 55th Foot were raised in 1751, the 87th and 89th in 1759, the 93rd and 101st in 1760 and the 105th in 1761. The Scotsmen who manned these regiments came either from the Lowlands or from the anti-Jacobite Highland clans. But in 1757, by an often-cited stroke of statesmanship, Pitt enlisted in the common cause the fighting spirit of the clans who had risen for the Pretender in 1745, and two regiments were raised from the Frasers, Macdonalds, Macleans, Macphersons and the like.[b] For the American War and the wars with the French Revolution and Napoleon, thirteen more regiments of foot were raised in Scotland; and, if Horace Walpole may be trusted, the Royal Marines, when first raised in 1755, were 'almost all Scots.'[43]

The conduct of the rank and file of these Scottish troops on the battlefield—in Europe, in North America, in India—quickly gained them the reputation of great fighters; and there were

[a] From their black, blue and green tartan. They were listed as the 42nd Foot (Highland Regiment).

[b] Pitt gave the command of one of these regiments to the son of the rebel Lord Lovat, executed in 1746. It was listed as the 78th Foot (Fraser's Highlanders).

Scottish officers who attained high place and fame. Lord Loudoun was Commander-in-Chief in America in 1756 and second in command in Portugal in 1762. James Murray took over the command when Wolfe fell on the Heights of Abraham in 1759. Hector Munro won the battle of Buxar in 1764. And there was one great Scottish seaman—Adam Duncan, victor of Camperdown (1797). In the civil services, too, in this critical half-century, Scotsmen played a distinguished part. Andrew Mitchell was British ambassador in Frederick the Great's Berlin in 1756. The East India Company's administration, thanks to Dundas, was heavily manned by Scotsmen, and John Macpherson became Governor-General of India in 1785. James Murray, just mentioned as a soldier, was appointed first civil Governor of Canada in 1763, and there were three other Scottish colonial Governors at that time.[44] A little later the first names appear on the great roll of Scottish explorers and missionaries in Africa. Mungo Park set out for the Niger in 1795. John Campbell landed at the Cape in 1813, Robert Moffat in 1816, John Philip in 1819.

This fine record of service was certainly one of the chief factors which made for the consolidation of the Union in this period. It fulfilled a psychological need. It not only gave Scotsmen a sense of comradeship with Englishmen, in battle, in camp, in office, in council; it made them feel they were not subordinate or ineffective partners in the common cause; they were ' pulling their weight.' The record was also the right answer to English jealousy and prejudice. The ' locusts,' it appeared, were not so useless and destructive after all. If the antagonism of Bute's day had faded out from Englishmen's minds by 1815, it was largely due to the recognition of what Scotland had done for Britain since 1745.

The elder Pitt, personifying in this matter as in others the English spirit at its best, did not need to be taught Scotland's value to England and the Empire by what Scotsmen did. He took it for granted from the outset. In 1749 he boldly supported the unpopular proposal to recoup Glasgow for the fine exacted by the 'Young Pretender.' 'There are not many cities in the United Kingdom that have so often and so remarkably distinguished themselves in the cause of liberty.'[45] Though associated with Wilkes for a time in politics, he abominated the *North Briton*— 'odious and dangerous writing' he called it[46]—and he did his best to combat the animosity it roused. And in 1766 he put in words what he had done in act when he raised those ex-Jacobite regiments in 1757. It was in the course of the famous speech in which he pleaded that the American colonists were entitled to an equal share with Englishmen at home in the heritage of English liberty. He attacked Bute, but not as a Scotsman. 'I have no local attachments,' he went on; 'it is indifferent to me whether a man was rocked in his cradle on this side or that side of the Tweed. I sought for merit wherever it was to be found . . . I found it in the mountains of the north. I called it forth and drew it into your service, a hardy and intrepid race of men. . . . They served with fidelity as they fought with valour, and conquered for you in every part of the world. Detested be the national reflections against them! They are unjust, groundless, illiberal, unmanly.'[47]

The sense of a common cause was by no means confined to the Scottish members of the services, military and civil: it was shared by the Scottish people. Throughout that series of historic crises—the Seven Years War, the American War, the French Revolution, the Napoleonic War—the reaction of the Scottish and the English peoples was the same. How Scottish public opinion resented the exclusion of Scotland from the Militia Act of 1757 has been recorded, and the resentment was deepened when the danger of French invasion was brought home to Scotsmen in 1760 by the descent on the coast of Belfast Lough of a French squadron whose objective was thought to be the Clyde. But that did not prevent Scotsmen from sharing to the full in the excitement and enthusiasm roused by the triumphs of the war. Wolfe, in particular, was quite as much a hero in Scotland as in his own country.

The Scottish attitude to the American Revolution differed from the English only in so far as less interest was taken in it—save in Glasgow, smitten so hard by the loss of American tobacco—and there was less inclination to question the Government's case. There was no Scottish Chatham or Burke to lead a Whig revolt: the Scottish members in both Houses solidly supported North: and when the quarrel issued in a war which spread to Europe, Scottish patriotism was at least as much aroused as English. In 1778 that daring sailor, smuggler and slave-trader, Paul Jones—a native, as it happened, of Kirkcudbrightshire—after a destructive raid on Whitehaven, landed on the Scottish side of Solway Firth and looted Lord Selkirk's mansion. In 1779 he captured some prizes off the east coast and threatened an attack on Leith. This second incident sent a wave of patriotic fervour through all Scotland. Town after town voted funds for fitting out armed ships or providing bounties for seamen willing to serve in them. The rejection of another appeal for a Scottish militia did not check the rising ardour. Volunteers were enrolled and drilled and marched through the streets with the magistrates and civic officials at their head.[48]

It was the same with the French Revolution. That great convulsion sharply divided British opinion, but not on national lines. Scottish Tories were at one with English Tories, and Scottish Radicals with English Radicals. The fall of the Bastille in 1789 was welcomed by such liberal-minded Scotsmen as Dugald Stewart and William Robertson with the same satisfaction, if more soberly expressed, as by Fox. Mackintosh answered Burke. The Dundee Whig Club and Stanhope's Revolutionary Society presented similar addresses of congratulation to the States General and the National Assembly. In 1792 associations of Friends of the People were established in Scotland as in England;[a]

[a] Contact was made with Irish agitators. At a meeting in December, 1792, a strongly

and in 1793 they invited the London Corresponding Society, whose founder, Hardy, was a Scot, to an 'international' Convention at Edinburgh. It was under the influence of the few Englishmen who attended it that the threatening language was used that brought about its forcible dispersion. For in Scotland the same kind of agitation was met by the same kind of repression as in England. It only differed in the degree of its harshness. No Braxfield disgraced the English trials.

Nor was there any national divergence when the war with the French Revolution was merged in the long struggle with Napoleon. In both countries the gravity of the position was not fully understood at first. When the Militia Act of 1797 at last gave Scotland the equal treatment so long demanded, the immediate paradoxical result was an outbreak of serious rioting in some districts; but the cause of it was not so much lack of patriotism as a dislike of compulsory long-term military service for which there seemed to be no urgent need. Some class-feeling, too, had been whipped up by agitators in industrial centres on the ground that the Volunteers, who had been raised in 1794[a] as in 1779 in place of militia and were drawn mainly from the upper and middle classes, were exempt from the militia ballot. But the disorder was local and soon suppressed, and, when the menace of Napoleon could no longer be ignored, when (as a contemporary put it) 'instead of Jacobitism, Invasion became the word,' it was as if the days of John Knox and the Spanish Armada had come back again. Lord Cockburn, the great Scottish judge, was then a

---

worded address was presented from the United Irishmen. In 1794 the refusal of a group of Irish students to acknowledge the national anthem at an Edinburgh theatre led to a riotous battle with a party of young Tories. Scott used to boast that he had been one of its leaders. Craik, 421.

[b] Burns, who had favoured the Revolution at the outset but, like many others, had been repelled by its excesses, was one of those Volunteers. In his masterly essay on *The Politics of Burns* (Glasgow, 1918), the late W. P. Ker pointed out that Burns was a champion of the Union and the British Navy, and identified himself with British politics. It was for the Dumfries Volunteers that he wrote (1795) 'Be Britain still to Britain true among oursels united.' Young Scott was also one of the earliest Volunteers; and Cockburn recalled the zest he took in Cavalry exercise, charging the French invaders represented by a turnip on a pole. 'Cut them down, the villains,' he would mutter, 'cut them down!' Henry Cockburn, *Memorials of His Time* (Edinburgh, 1856), 195-6.

young member of the Bar, and he left on record a graphic description of that militant time. ' After the war broke out again in 1803,' he wrote, ' Edinburgh, like every other place, became a camp and continued so till the peace in 1814. We were all soldiers. Professors wheeled in the College area; the side arms and the uniform peeped from behind the gown at the bar and even on the bench; and the parade and the review formed the staple of men's talk and thoughts. . . . Brougham served the same gun in a company of artillery with Playfair[a] . . . Francis Horner[b] walked about the streets with a musket, being a private in the Gentlemen Regiment. . . . I, a gallant captain, commanded ninety-two of my fellow creatures from 1804 to 1814. . . . The parades, the reviews, the four or six yearly inspections at Dalmahoy, the billetings for a fortnight or three weeks when on ' permanent duty' at Leith or Haddington, the mock battles, the marches, the messes—what scenes they were! And similar scenes were familiar in every town and in every shire in the kingdom. . . . Any able-bodied man, who was *not* a volunteer or a local militiaman, had to explain or apologise for his singularity.'[49] Nor, of course, were the Scotsmen who had migrated to England any less patriotic. It was a Scotsman, Thomson, who had written ' Rule Britannia' in the course of an earlier war (1740). It was another Scot, Campbell, who wrote ' Ye Mariners of England' (1801), ' Hohenlinden (1803), and ' The Battle of the Baltic' (1805). Campbell, indeed, who was born in Glasgow in 1777, had come to identify himself with the English tradition of resistance to tyranny in the past as well as the present. In ' Men of England' he acclaimed the glory of Hampden, Russell, Sydney.

> *They defied the field and scaffold*
> *For their birthright—so will we.*

[a] Henry Brougham, Lord Chancellor, 1830-34. John Playfair, Professor of Natural Philosophy at Edinburgh, 1805.

[b] M.P. from 1806 till, with two short intervals, his death in 1817.

Thus the struggle with Napoleon—the common danger, the common endurance, the common victory—completed the process of welding the Scottish people with the English and Welsh. Doing ' great things together,' they had acquired something like a new British nationhood, a composite nationhood in which each of the component nations retained its distinct national identity, its national spirit and tradition. What Chatham, English of the English, felt about united Britain in 1775 has been recorded above. Let Wordsworth speak for the England of 1809. An ardent champion of small nations, he writes with high approval of the memories of Scottish and Welsh patriotism still alive in Britain—' the flashing eye, and the agitated voice, and all the tender recollections, with which the names of Prince Llewellin and William Wallace are to this day pronounced by the fireside and on the public road.' Yet he takes the value of political unification for granted. ' Who does not rejoice that former partitions have disappeared, and that England, Scotland and Wales are under one legislative and executive authority? '[50]

For Scotland let Scott be spokesman. There was never a more passionate Scottish patriot. It is betrayed in almost everything he wrote, in the manner of his home-life, in his talk. One day, in 1808, he was walking away, with Jeffrey and other progressives, from a meeting at which he had fiercely opposed some alteration of procedure in that citadel of Scottish nationalism, the judicial system. When his companions began to make a joke of it, ' No no,' he broke out, ' 'tis no laughing matter; little by little, whatever your wishes may be, you will destroy and undermine until nothing of what makes Scotland Scotland shall remain.' ' And so saying,' Lockhart records, ' he turned round to conceal his agitation—but not until Mr. Jeffrey saw tears gushing down his cheek.'[51] To the end of his life this sensitiveness, this anxiety lest Scotland should be gradually absorbed into England, persisted. No Scotsman, on the other hand, was a more wholehearted champion of the Union. He had no doubts about the case for it at the time it was achieved. ' Since St. Mungo catched herrings in the Clyde,' says Bailie Nicol Jarvie of Glasgow, ' what was ever like to gar us flourish like the sugar and tobacco trade? Will anybody tell me that and grumble at a treaty that opened us a road west-awa' yonder?' And he had no real doubts either, despite those occasional qualms, about the Union in his own day. He was the most loyal of British subjects. Pitt was *his* venerated leader, Nelson and Wellington *his* heroes. And in the famous introduction to *Marmion* (1808), the tale of ' Flodden's fatal field,' he appropriates, as a Briton and like Campbell, great English names of an earlier day. After the tributes he pays to Nelson and Pitt and, with a fine candour for so high a Tory, to Fox too, he owns his own literary debt to ' the mightiest chiefs of *British* song '— Spenser, Milton, Dryden.

[1] M. G. Jones, *The Charity School Movement* (Cambridge, 1938), 282 ff.
[2] *Ibid.*, 289-293.
[3] *Ibid.*, 297.
[4] D. Williams, 147.
[5] I. Jones, 143, 151.
[6] Lecky, 107-8.
[7] O. M. Edwards, 391.
[8] M. G. Jones, 321.
[9] F. E. Hutchinson, *Henry Vaughan* (Oxford, 1947), 164.
[10] Bell, 120-123.
[11] *Ibid.*, 128.
[12] D. Williams, 272.
[13] Bell, 124-6. D. Williams, 272.
[14] *Wealth of Nations* (ed. E. Cannan, London, 1904), i. 425.
[15] J. F. Rees, 132-6.
[16] A. H. Dodd, *The Industrial Revolution in North Wales* (Cardiff, 1933); I. Jones, Chap. X.
[17] Davies, 210-11.
[18] *Cambrian*, Nov. 9, 1805.
[19] *Ibid.*, Nov. 11, 1805.
[20] Sir Henry Craik, *A Century of Scottish History* (Edinburgh and London, 1911), 235.
[21] Terry, 564.
[22] Mathieson, 17-21.
[23] *Ibid.*, 22.
[24] J. Mackinnon, *Constitutional History of Scotland* (London, 1924), 144, 247.
[25] *Parliamentary History*, xv. 982.
[26] Boswell's *Life* (Oxford, 104 ed.), ii. 189.
[27] *Ibid.*, i. 285.
[28] *Ibid.*, i. 568.
[29] *Ibid.*

[30] *Ibid.*, ii, 459.

[31] *Journey to the Western Islands of Scotland* (Paisley, 1907), 51, 77, 174, 91, 93, 97, 136.

[32] *Letters of Junius* (ed. C. W. Everett, London, 1927), 14, 196.

[33] *Memoirs of George III* (London, 1894), iv. 84. For his sneers at the traditional treachery of Scotsmen and so forth, see *Letters* (1913-15 ed.), x. 204, xi. 222, xii. 252.

[34] Lord Fitzmaurice, *Life of Shelburne* (London, 1912), ii. 308.

[35] Terry, 565. Craik, 228 n.

[36] G. M. Trevelyan, *English Social History*, 450-1.

[37] For an outline of economic developments in the eighteenth century see J. Mackinnon, *Social and Industrial History of Scotland since Union* (London, 1921), Part I; H. Hamilton, *Industrial Revolution in Scotland* (Oxford, 1932), Banks, Chap. XII.

[38] The following paragraphs are based on Dr. M. G. Jones' invaluable work, already cited.

[39] *Journey*, 90.

[40] Quoted by Terry, 563.

[41] Terry, 583.

[42] Quoted by John Buchan, *Sir Walter Scott* (London, 7th ed., 1946), 61.

[43] Details and dates in R. Triman, *The Regiments of the British Army*, London, 1878 Walpole, *Memoirs of George III*, iv. 353.

[44] Mathieson, 47 n.

[45] B. Williams, *Life of Pitt* (London, 1913), i. 174.

[46] *Ibid.*, ii. 157.

[47] *Ibid.*, ii. 189-190.

[48] Craik, 363.

[49] H. Cockburn, *Memorials* (London, 1856), 187-195.

[50] *Convention of Cintra* (Oxford, 1915), 163-4, 170, quoted by Dicey and Rait, 325

[51] J. G. Lockhart, *Life of Scott* (Edinburgh, 1837), ii. 110, quoted by Buchan, 83

PART FIVE

Wales
in the Nineteenth Century

ALL THE other factors which, visibly and invisibly, had been making for the unification of tri-national Britain were immensely reinforced by the common experience of the English, Welsh and Scots in the world crisis in which the eighteenth century closed and the nineteenth opened. The war with Napoleon far more than the previous conflicts with continental militarism made the island peoples conscious that they were making history together; and, since historical tradition is the mainspring of nationhood, it was at this period that a new composite nation, a British nation, may be said to have come into being. Its growth was strengthened by the dominant rôle of Britain in the political and economic history of the nineteenth-century world. Though the senior partner's name might still be used, especially by foreigners, to cover the whole firm, 'Britain' and 'British' came into their own. It was the age of the *Pax Britannica*. Britannia ruled the waves. Britain was the workshop of the world. British trade followed the British flag. The British Empire grew to its zenith.

Naturally this growth of a common British patriotism blunted, to some extent and for a time, the sense of national differences. The fact that England was so much larger and stronger and richer than Wales and Scotland was forgotten. The threat of anglicisation lurking in those superiorities seemed to have lost its sting. No one apparently save Scott and no one certainly of Scott's prestige had any misgivings as to the possibilities of Welsh or Scottish nationhood losing its distinctive character and being merged completely in the British amalgam. That, no doubt, is one reason why for the first thirty or forty years of the peace the rise of nationalism in continental Europe and the new conception of its meaning and its claims made no deeper impression on Welsh and Scottish than on English thought. Sympathy with the efforts of small continental nations to obtain their freedom was a British heritage from the Napoleonic age: it had become part of the British tradition; and Welshmen's and Scotsmen's share in it had no distinctive tone or warmth. The cause of Italians, Poles, Hungarians appealed to them as it did to Englishmen, no more and no less. It was the same with their interest or lack of interest in the new philosophy of nationalism. It was the same, too—and this was still more significant—with their reaction to the Irish national revolt. Even Celtic Wales was not more stirred than England by the fate of Celtic Ireland in O'Connell's day; and this was not wholly due to the anti-Catholic sentiment of Welsh Dissent or to dislike of uncongenial Irish immigrants. The Welsh had no sense of a common cause with the Irish. Too long a time had passed since they, too, had been a subject people seeking to wrest their freedom from their foreign conquerors.

Thus for more than a generation after 1815 there was nothing in Wales or Scotland to compare with the nationalist movements in continental Europe or in Ireland. No ' Young Wales ' or ' Young Scotland ' took their stand beside ' Young Italy ' and ' Young Ireland.' It was not till the century was well advanced that a pale reflection of Irish nationalism flickered up in Wales and Scotland, not till its last quarter that Welshmen and Scotsmen followed the Irish lead and began to talk about Home Rule.

I. THE TRANSFORMATION OF WALES

BY MID-VICTORIAN times the Industrial Revolution, rising to its climax, had transformed the life of Wales. But it was a lopsided transformation. South Wales was changed far more than North. The share of the South in the immense material progress of the Iron Age was much the greater share: how much greater the statistics of population are enough in themselves to show. At the first official census in 1801, the population of Wales was 587,245: at the census of 1851 it was 1,163,139 or roughly double; and of that increase the two counties in which industry was mainly located, Glamorgan and Monmouth, accounted for over one-quarter.

Northern and Central Counties

			1801	1851
Anglesey	..	..	33,806	57,237
Caernarvon	..	..	41,521	87,870
Denbigh ..	..	..	60,299	92,583
Flint ..	..	..	39,469	68,156
Merioneth	..	..	29,506	38,843
Montgomery	..	..	48,184	67,335
Cardigan	..	..	42,956	70,796
Radnor ..	..	..	19,135	24,716
Brecknock	..	..	32,325	61,474

Southern Counties

			1801	1851
Monmouth	..	..	45,586	157,418
Glamorgan	..	..	70,879	231,849
Carmarthen	..	..	67,317	110,632
Pembroke	..	..	56,280	94,140

This southward distortion was inevitable. Even if the stimulus given to local industries in the earlier stages of the Industrial Revolution had proved lasting, the economic balance in North Wales could not have been radically altered. By natural law it continued to depend for its livelihood mainly on its flocks and herds and crops: and in the generation after 1815, while the trade in cattle and sheep and their products remained steady, the profits of agriculture fell. It had gained, though far less than in Scotland, from improvement in technique:[a] it had shared in the boom created by all Britain's need of corn in the war years: but it also shared in the post-war slump. Less and less wheat was grown. Labour began to drift away either eastwards to Cheshire and Lancashire or southwards to the industrial area. And the tide of emigration was presently swollen not only by the collapse of the woollen industry but by the growing attraction of urban life. The building of the mid-Wales railway from Welshpool to Aberystwyth made no difference. It had been hoped that the railway would help to revive the old local industries by providing easier access to English markets. In the event the local markets were swamped with English goods.[1]

The contrast deepened as time went on. Caernarvon maintained its strength through its slate quarries: Flint, with a coalfield of its own, shared presently in the great industrial development of Merseyside; but in the mainly agricultural counties emigration grew till in the end it exceeded natural increase. The census of 1941 revealed that in the ninety years since 1851 the population of Montgomery had fallen to 49,610, of Brecknock to 59,020, of Radnor to 22,730, and of Cardigan to 55,960.[b]

Meanwhile a very different picture was taking shape in the South. The miners were burrowing ever deeper into the ' hills of

[a] The result of enclosures was less marked in Wales than elsewhere. Enclosure was old-established; there was no open-field system, and it was mostly waste land and mountain pasture that were affected. A. H. Dodd, 56.

[b] Pembroke, detached from the industrial growth of the neighbouring seaboard, has suffered with the North. Its population in 1801 was 56,280, in 1851 94,140, in 1941 92,480.

coal.' The grim array of ironworks was steadily spreading east
and west of Merthyr. The annual output of iron rose from 78,000
tons in 1815 to 450,000 in 1840. Newport, Cardiff, Swansea, now
girt with metal works and factories, were soon to threaten
Merthyr's lead in urban population and later on, when the
industrial centre shifted to steel and tinplate works nearer the ports,
to leave it far behind.

	1801	1851	1941
Cardiff	1,870	18,351	211,300
Swansea	6,831	31,461	139,000
Newport	1,423	19,323	95,000
Merthyr	7,704	63,080	61,800

Meantime the growth of the coal industry, no longer tied up with
iron, was stimulated by the coming of coal-burning railway
engines and steamships. In 1841 the Taff Vale Railway was
opened from Merthyr to Cardiff. From 1847 onwards a network
of lines struck out from Swansea into the anthracite area. Between
1845 and 1852 the South Wales Railway, subsequently absorbed
into the Great Western, advanced from Gloucester all the way to
Milford Haven. At Cardiff and Swansea, moreover, the docks
were growing with the growth of exports.

This vast industrial expansion called for a much large labour
force than the native population of the southern counties could
provide, and the current of immigration set going in the earlier
stages of the Industrial Revolution swelled into a flood.[a] Some
of the newcomers came from rural North Wales. Many came
from Ireland, selling their unskilled labour for miserable pay in
the docks and ironworks of the coastal belt and up the mining
valleys, undercutting wages and degrading the standard of life as
in Lancashire and South-West Scotland. But the great majority

[a] Welshmen were emigrating from South Wales as well as North in search of better
working conditions in Northern England or of a new life overseas, but the number of
immigrants was far greater.

of immigrants naturally came from neighbouring England. Englishmen were invading North Wales also. Since the time of the Tudor conquest of Ireland, they had been constantly coming and going, and sometimes staying, along the main Irish road from London to Holyhead. The Union of 1800 swelled this traffic, and it was swollen again when the Irish mail line of railway was carried over the Menai Bridge to Holyhead (1848-50) and when seaside resorts developed at Llandudno and its neighbours. Presently the scenic beauty of the west coast also attracted English residents. But the total English immigration into all the rest of Wales was far surpassed by that which streamed into the industrial South. Nor was it only an inflow of English labourers. English works managers, technicians, railwaymen, bankers, shopkeepers were gaining a foothold in this fast-growing industrial society.

The transformation of South Wales was not, of course, a peculiarly Welsh phenomenon. The Industrial Revolution, like the Napoleonic War, was for all Britain (but not for all Ireland) a common experience. Its main features in the English ' black country ' or Tyneside or the industrial belt in the Scottish Lowlands were the same as in South Wales—the decline of agrarian life, the drift of labour from field to factory, the monstrous growth of the industrial towns. There were, however, certain aspects of the Welsh experience that were not shared by England. Though Welshmen, Scotsmen and Irishmen were steadily drifting into England, the impact of immigration from without was much weightier on little Wales than on England seven times its size and with a population sixteen times larger in 1801; and, whereas in England incoming Welsh and Scottish labourers, though not to the same extent the Irish, were absorbed into English culture and ways of life, the reverse occurred in Wales. South Wales had always been more subject and susceptible to English influence than the North, and the process of anglicisation was inevitably quickened by the increase of English immigration. The Industrial

Revolution was no respecter of nations. It made for uniformity in speech and social habit. Welsh labourers in mine and factory still spoke Welsh, though more and more of them began to pick up English too, and the life of the valleys running up into the coalfield was still indubitably Welsh. But English speech and English ways were steadily gaining ground at higher social levels and in the towns. Incoming English managers and business men did not learn Welsh. Their dependents or customers learned English if they did not know it already. And many of them did know it; for it had long been taken for granted that a Welshman must speak English if he wanted to get on in life. The children of poor families were sent to school mainly, if not solely, to learn English, and in many South Wales schools at this time English was the only language of instruction in all subjects.[a] Before long, in Monmouth and Glamorgan—and the same was true of northern Flint—an increasing proportion of Welsh-born folk not only spoke English at home as well as out of doors but were beginning to lose their hold on their native tongue. The same sort of process was at work in social life. Long ago, as has been seen, the landlord class all over Wales had become more or less anglicised, speaking English only for the most part and Anglicans to a man, while their tenantry spoke Welsh and, since the revival, were mostly Nonconformists. Class and culture were now similarly associated in the South. In the rural areas and in the bleak mine valleys peasants and workmen were slow to change their way of life; but in the towns the fast-expanding middle class adopted English manners as well as English speech. The industrial magnates imitated their English colleagues, and the clerks and tradesmen imitated them. Anglicisation became in course of time the hall-mark of worldly success. The well-to-do business man thought it vulgar to speak Welsh. He attended church, not chapel. He sent his children to expensive English schools. His house, his horses and carriage, his domestic arrangements, his wife's dresses

[a] See page 210 below.

173

proclaimed his attainment of a footing in English ' society.' His business visits to London, pleasantly diversified by a meal at a smart restaurant and a stall at the theatre, detached him still further from the stern, old-fashioned, Puritan tradition of Welsh Wales.

The pull of London, indeed, was irresistible—much more so for South Wales than for Scotland. As the nineteenth century drew on, Cardiff might grow to half the size of Edinburgh, but Edinburgh had been for centuries the capital of Scotland when Cardiff was an unknown fishing village; and with none of Edinburgh's historic memories Cardiff—and Swansea and Newport—were far less able to resist the magnet of London. It was much more than a social pull. Big business makes for centralisation and London was the only possible centre. Welsh mine-owners and iron-masters might make fortunes, but the Industrial Revolution in Wales was largely financed in London. And the course of the railways pointed the moral. The whole of the British network radiated from London. The main lines in North and South Wales ran direct to London. The minor lines through Central Wales linked up with the London line at Ruabon and Shrewsbury.[a] And when the British Parliament began to grapple none too soon with the more shocking social results of the Industrial Revolution, when the State began to extend its functions far beyond the limits of an earlier day, the new administrative system was based on London. Necessarily so; for since the State was a unitary State, the scope of its activities could be determined only at Westminster and their control vested only in Whitehall.

History, it seemed, was repeating itself. As in the sixteenth and seventeenth centuries, Welsh life was yielding to English pressure. The spirit of the eighteenth-century revival had spent

[a] The east-west direction was in any case imposed by the lie of the land. The valleys run that way. A north-south line through the heart of Wales was scarcely possible. Even to-day there is no main north-south road.

its force. Of its two great instruments, Nonconformist religion was still the strongest power in the lives of most Welshmen, but it was not yet consciously associated with national sentiment. Popular education had not maintained its early momentum, and preoccupied as it now was with teaching English, it was ceasing to be the means of preserving and improving Welsh. Was the national tradition fading out? Did the closer partnership with England brought about by war and economic change imply the decay and eventually the extinction of Welsh nationhood? It would not have been unreasonable to ask such questions in the generation after Waterloo.

II. INDUSTRIAL AND AGRARIAN UNREST

THE UNREST and agitation which spread among the workers, industrial and agrarian, from 1815 onwards was again a common experience in which all Britain shared. The grievances of Welshmen in the mines and metalworks—low wages, long hours, bad housing, the exploitation of female and child labour, the truck system—all this was felt in English and Scottish industry as much as in South Wales. It was the same in the rural areas. Welsh and English peasantry suffered together from the effects of agricultural depression and the rigours of the new Poor Law. And poverty and discontent had the same political background. The anomalies of the old system of parliamentary representation were not, of course, peculiar to Wales. If Merthyr was unrepresented, so was Birmingham. Reform was a common cause—the smoke over Bristol in 1831 must have been welcomed by many Radicals across the Channel—and common, too, was the disillusionment which followed the passing of the Reform Bill, the efforts of the working class to obtain redress by its own combined exertions, the increase of strikes, the growth of Trade Unionism, the rise of Chartism. The Welsh part in all this agitation was not a symptom of Welsh nationalism in revolt. On the contrary, just as the Industrial Revolution in Wales was mainly the work of Englishmen, so in its origins was the attempt at counter-revolution, if so it may be called, in the thirties and forties. The first Unions in the coalfield were branches of a Lancashire organisation. The first Chartist groups were founded on the Birmingham model. The National Convention met, of course, in London.[2]

Yet, like the Industrial Revolution as a whole, the agitation it provoked in Wales assumed in some respects a Welsh complexion, and it betrayed at times the fact that underneath the cause that the Welsh workers shared with Englishmen lurked a latent sense of national antagonism. As has been seen, the owners, the employers, the administrative staff were almost wholly English. ' In the works,' reported the Education Commissioner for South Wales in 1847, ' the Welsh workman never finds his way into the office. He never becomes either clerk or agent. . . . His language keeps him under the hatches, being one in which he can neither acquire or communicate the necessary information.'[3] To some extent, therefore, there was a nationalist flavour in Welsh strikes.[a] Nationalist, too, was the antagonism roused by the infiltration of 'foreign' labour—Cornish tin miners and skilled iron-workers from the Midlands and Yorkshire. The arrival of Northumbrian miners provoked a riot at Wrexham in 1826.[4] But the English immigrants were not so fiercely hated as the ignorant, ill-conditioned Irish who would take wages on which the poorest Welshman could scarcely keep alive.[5] There was often savage fighting on Saturday nights; and Irish blacklegs were among the victims of the ' Scotch Cattle ' bands[b] which from 1832 to 1834 committed a series of outrages, mainly in Monmouthshire, beating up blacklegs, wrecking their homes and blowing out furnaces.[6] Nor was the Welsh workers' hatred of the Irish

[a] In R. Llewellyn's popular novel, *How Green Was My Valley*, a Welsh miner speaks of founding a union ' to fight against the bloody English.'
[b] Their badge was a red bull's head with hearts impaled on its horns.

tempered when they found them siding timidly with the employers. When Chartism came to a head at Newport, it was observed that only one Irishman was involved in the rioting, while one hundred of the special constables enrolled at Cardiff were or were said to be Irish.[a] The cup was full when O'Connell, who at that time was in alliance with the Whig Ministry and believed that Chartism was drifting into revolutionary violence, publicly declared all Chartists to be traitors.[7]

It was in Wales, as it happened, that some of the most spectacular events of the Chartist movement occurred. The outbreak at Llanidloes in the spring of 1840, when the town was held for a week by a Chartist mob,[8] was comparable with the riots at Birmingham and other places; but nothing happened in England to match the march of some five thousand Welshmen down from the coal valleys through the darkness and drenching rain of a winter night into Newport, headed by its sometimes mayor, John Frost. They seem to have expected that the English Chartists would follow their example in the Midlands and that these combined demonstrations would so frighten Parliament that it would at least be willing to receive and discuss the Chartist petition. They carried arms of a sort, but they apparently supposed that they would not have to use them, and, when they were confronted by a company of the 45th regiment posted in a hotel and firing began, they broke up and made off. It was, in fact, a pitiful fiasco, but the news of it shocked and alarmed a British public that had not yet forgotten the red days of the French Revolution. The march, it was widely believed, had been planned as the first step in a concerted revolutionary rising to overthrow the Government and establish a Chartist régime. The trial of Frost for high treason was a *cause célèbre*. The long forensic duel, the summing up and the verdict, the sentence to the barbarous death still meted out for treason—these furnish a

[a] The Cork police offered to serve in South Wales. N. Edwards, *The Industrial Revolution in South Wales* (London, 1924).

dramatic chapter for the otherwise somewhat prosaic story of the Chartist movement.[a]

If nationalism had been an active, self-conscious force in Welsh life at this time, the agitation which culminated at Newport might well have assumed a nationalist complexion. For, though Welsh and English Chartists were at one in assailing the British Government and Parliament as then constituted, it would presumably have made a difference to the Welshmen that the Government contained no Welsh Minister and the Parliament only thirty-four Welsh members out of 615. But the notion of Welsh subjection to a predominantly English State seems to have died at Bosworth Field and more than a generation was yet to pass before it was reborn. Those occasional betrayals of a latent national antipathy were not the outcome of any nationalist movement. They had nothing to do with the politics of nineteenth-century nationalism in Ireland or on the Continent.[b] Frost's political philosophy was much the same as Cobbett's: it had no nationalist ingredient;[c] and when he or his fellow-leaders declared that the 'people of Wales' were determined to have their rights, they were not voicing any separatist sentiment; they only meant that the British parliamentary system in which the Welsh had their share must be radically reformed. It was a delegate from Liverpool who bade the men of Merthyr to remember Owen Glendower.[9] It was at an anti-Chartist meeting at Coalbrookdale that Chartist agitation was denounced as the work of Englishmen who had been paid to come and stir up trouble in Welsh Monmouthshire.[10] But nobody remarked after Newport that the trouble was suppressed by English soldiers who were paid to do it and shot down twenty Welshmen and wounded several others in the doing. It

[a] A detailed narrative is given in D. Williams' exhaustive and scholarly biography, *John Frost* (Cardiff, 1939).

[b] Subscriptions levied for the cost of the Convention were called 'national rent' (D. Williams, 106), but this was merely an imitation of O'Connell's technique, and the epithet which meant much in Ireland was meaningless in Wales.

[c] The language used at public meetings and in the political newspapers was English as much as Welsh.

was, in fact, a domestic quarrel, a conflict between Welsh classes, and such faint national colour as it possessed was due to the fact that most of the upper and middle class were anglicised in speech and custom and most of the working class were not. It was Welshmen who held a banquet in honour of the 45th and lionised Lieutenant Gray—an Irishman as it happened—who was in command at the hotel. It was Welshmen who on the platform, in the Press, and sometimes in the pulpit demanded vengeance on the ' rebels.' It was a court of Welsh magistrates who prolonged the preliminary inquiry into the guilt of Frost and his colleagues for more than a month in trying to make sure of a conviction for high treason. The two counsel, on the other hand, who brilliantly defended Frost at his trial were Englishmen,[a] and so was the Lord Chief Justice[b] who presided and summed up strongly for acquittal. When the jury, after less than half an hour's deliberation, returned a verdict of guilty, he duly pronounced the death sentence, but he ultimately succeeded in persuading the Home Secretary to commute it to transportation for life.

Chartism was mainly an industrial movement: its Welsh arena was the coalfield and the ironworks in the south and the wool mills in Montgomery and Merioneth.[c] The agrarian unrest which developed alongside it in the rural areas was necessarily associated with it to some extent: for the peasants, too, were in revolt against the existing social system, and ' revolutionary demagogues,' as a witness before the Commission of 1844 termed the Chartist agitators, toured the country trying to set tenants and landlords at variance.[11] It was probably no mere coincidence that the first agrarian outbreak occurred a few months before the

[a] Fitzroy Kelly, afterwards solicitor-general, attorney-general and lord chief baron and Sir Frederick Pollock.

[b] Sir Nicholas Tindal.

[c] The first Chartist outbreak was at Carmarthen, but it was an affair of the town rather than the country. Llanidloes was a centre of substantial immigration, and the outbreak there was due more to xenophobia than to Chartist propaganda. The signatures of the Chartist petition recorded in Glamorganshire in 1839 numbered 18,884, in Montgomeryshire 3,461, in Cardinganshire 1,026. D. Williams, 156.

march on Newport; but the two movements were not closely co-ordinated, and, while Chartism began to fade out after 1839, the agrarian unrest increased till in 1843-44 it reached its climax in the extraordinary affair of the Rebecca Riots.

Rural Wales at this time was a patchwork of big estates and little farms. The status and condition of those who occupied the farms as tenants of the landlord were much lower than those of the average English farmer: they might be called peasant farmers, and they usually ran their farms with the labour of their own families. Never well off, they suffered severely from the general depression and at the time of the outbreak their lot had been worsened by a series of wet seasons and bad harvests. Their chief grievance in these years of depression and poverty was not high rents or insecurity of tenure or the new Poor Law: it was the heavy fixed payments for tithes and Church rates; and the spark which exploded their discontent into violence was the extra cash burden of the turnpike tolls. The General Highway Act of 1835[12] had resulted in the creation of bodies of trustees charged with the duty of maintaining roads and empowered to set up toll gates to meet the cost. Many new gates were erected and the rate of toll was increased. The collection of it, which had hitherto been lax, was now stiffened by the employment of professional toll collectors.[13]

The outbreak of 1839, when a number of gates were broken down on the border of Pembroke and Carmarthen, was transient and did not spread. But the organised campaign of gate-breaking which began in those same counties at the outset of 1843 was extended into Cardigan, Radnor and Glamorgan, and lasted till the spring of 1844. A great number of gates and toll houses were destroyed—in Carmarthen alone at least seventy out of about one hundred.[14] The magistrates, who were often in tacit sympathy with the law-breakers and had no rural police at their disposal, were quite unable to suppress the disorders. They occurred without warning and always during the night in country which in daytime was wrapt in peace. The leader of the campaign was never identified. He was known as ' Rebecca '—why is not quite certain[a]—and signed manifestos and letters to the newspapers with the name. His lieutenants were called his ' daughters.' Stranger still was the mummery with which the operations were conducted. The band of farmers, sometimes two hundred strong or more, all on horseback and carrying all sorts of arms from guns and pistols to spades and sledge hammers, were dressed in women's gowns and bonnets. They rode up to the chosen toll-gate in the middle of the night, firing guns and blowing horns, and dismounting advanced upon the gate. Rebecca led, pretending to be old and blind and feeling her way with her staff. When, to her surprise, she came up against a gate, she complained to her daughters that her way was barred, and, after some further colloquy, she bade them remove the obstacle.[b] Thereupon the gate was broken up and the posts sawn off. Next the toll-house was demolished. As a rule no personal violence was done. The toll-keeper had usually had warning of the attack in an ill-spelt letter from Rebecca and had made off. If not, he was given time to remove his furniture and household goods. Rarely, if ever, was there any looting. Their task accomplished, Rebecca and her

[a] At an early stage of the movement it was put about that the name was derived from *Genesis* xxiv, 60: ' And they blessed Rebekah and said unto her, Thou art our sister, be thou the mother of thousands of millions, and let thy seed possess the gates of those which hate them.' Historians have accepted this derivation, but Mr. H. T. Evans has argued that at the outset the name was taken either from that of the woman who provided the dress for the first ringleader or from that of the wife of the first toll-keeper whose gate was attacked. H. T. Evans, *Rebecca and her Daughters* (Cardiff, 1910), 9.

[b] A contemporary description of a gate-breaking on April 7, 1843, contains the following colloquy.
Rebecca (*hobbling up to the gate and feeling her way with her staff*): Children, there is something put up here. I cannot go on.
Daughters: What is it, mother? Nothing should stop your way.
Rebecca: I do not know, children, I am old and cannot see well.
Daughters: Shall we come on, mother, and move it out of the way?
Rebecca: Stop; let me see (*feeling the gate with her staff*): it seems like a great gate put across the road to stop your old mother.
Daughters: We will break it, mother. Nothing shall hinder you on your journey.
Rebecca: No; let me see, perhaps it will open. (*Feeling the lock*) No, children. It is bolted and locked, and I cannot go on. What is to be done?
Daughters: It must be taken down, mother, because you and your children must pass.
Rebecca: Off with it then, my children. It has no business here.

daughters mounted their horses, and, with another burst of gun-fire and horn-blowing, trotted off home to restore their petticoats to their wives and become the sober farmers of the morning.[15]

While the gate-breaking continued unabated, the scope and objectives of the outbreak widened. Chartists enlisted in Rebecca's family and gave the movement a more political flavour. In the summer of 1843 some two or three thousand people gathered at Rebecca's bidding in the mountains, carrying placards inscribed in Welsh not only with ' Free Tolls and Freedom ' but also with ' Liberty and better Food,' and, descending on Carmarthen, they set fire to the Poor House and would have gutted it if troops from Cardiff had not arrived in time. A little later a Rebeccaite Conference near Llandilo listed nine demands: the first was still the abolition of the toll-gates, but the next four dealt with tithes, church rates, the Poor Law and rent. At another mass meeting in the hills north of Swansea, a petition to the Queen was drafted in which the toll-gates similarly figured as only one of several grievances. And, as the scope of the movement expanded, its methods became more violent. The more active magistrates received threatening messages. Ricks and farm buildings were fired. Houses were forcibly entered and tithe owners were sometimes compelled to restore to the farmers the money they had paid. The capture of a leader from time to time and his sentence to transportation failed to stop the disorders; but, when it was observed that the gates were not rebuilt, when police were drafted in from London and more troops stationed in the disaffected counties, and when finally the Government appointed a Royal Commission of inquiry, the movement rapidly declined. It survived into the new year and then soon petered out.

The sequel was happy. Public opinion in England, informed by some frank reports from the special correspondent of *The Times*, recognised the strength of the case against the toll-trusts. The burden of the evidence before the Royal Commission was the same. In 1844, accordingly, an act was passed reorganising the whole system of turnpikes in South Wales on a uniform and equitable basis.[16a]

The significance of the Rebecca Riots for the present study lies in the fact that they were a purely Welsh affair. Rebeccaism was not, like Chartism, an extension of an English movement into Wales. The grievance which precipitated the outbreak was a local grievance; and the men who took part in it, both the leaders and the rank and file, were all Welshmen. Yet the undercurrent of national sentiment, of resistance to English domination, seems to have been even feebler in Rebeccaism than in Chartism. The Education Commissioner for Central Wales in 1845 commented, it is true, on the Welsh countryman's ' intense national distrust of foreigners,' and believed that the Rebecca agitation would have been more serious and widespread if it had had better leadership. But there is very little evidence to suggest that rural Wales was on the brink of a national revolt. One of Rebecca's earlier letters, threatening an English gate-contractor, shows that the far-off origins of Welsh nationhood were not forgotten. ' It is a shameful thing for us Welshmen,' it began, ' to have the sons of Hengest have a dominion over us.'[17] A manifesto of 1839 bade the insurgents in one district not to ' blame or injure the native magistrates of your native country ': the only guilty men were ' two Sassenachs ' who possessed no qualifications for their office.[18] That no Englishman should be appointed to a stewardship or governorship in South Wales was one of the demands put forward at the Llandilo conference; but it figured only sixth on the list. Welsh nationalism, as was soon to be apparent, was not dead, but it was certainly asleep, and Rebecca did no more than Frost to waken it.

Why was this so? Why was not unrest in rural Wales tinged,

[a] 7 and 8 Vic. cap 91.

like unrest in rural Ireland, with the colour of a national revolt? The situation in both countries was broadly alike. On both Nature had imposed a predominantly agrarian economy. In both the peasantry were of the ancient Celtic stock and in both the land which had once belonged to them had been acquired for the most part by English invaders. In each country the issues between tenant and landlord were the same—high rent, insecurity of tenure, compensation for improvements and so forth. The grievance most deeply felt in Wales, till the question of the tollgates cropped up, was the payment of Church tithes. So it was in Ireland, and both for Welsh and for Irish the grievance was accentuated by the fact that the Church to which the tithes were paid was not the Church to which with few exceptions the countryfolk belonged. But these points of similarity were completely overshadowed by the points of difference. It was not only that the Irish countryfolk were far worse off than the Welsh, far poorer, more ignorant, less skilled in agricultural technique and that, unlike the Welsh, they had no contiguous industrial belt to relieve the pressure of growing population on the land. The conflict between landlord and tenant was immeasurably more bitter and violent in Ireland than in Wales. The curse of Ireland was 'absentee landlordism.' But with few exceptions the Welsh landlords lived on their estates, often running 'home-farms' themselves, usually interested in the improvement of their tenants' holdings, and the best of them, if at any rate they could speak Welsh, maintaining the same sort of friendly relations with the tenantry as the good kind of English squire. Equally wide was the difference on the point of nationality. Most of the Anglo-Irish landlords living in England had become, it might be said, more English than Irish. But in Wales, while, as has been seen, the industrial magnates were mostly recent English immigrants, the landowning families had been so long established in the country and so closely linked by inter-marriage with its native people that, while they had retained their English speech and manners and their

English Church, they had become authentic Welshmen. A Welsh farmer, therefore, however deep his grudge against his landlord, could not curse him for an Englishman. There was a difference, too, between Irish and Welsh tithes. The Church which the Non-conformists were obliged to support was at any rate a Protestant Church. So agrarian unrest in Wales never acquired the dreadful character of agrarian unrest in Ireland. There was no ' land-war.' Even less than the Scotch Cattle could Rebecca and her daughters be likened to the murderous gangs which terrorised the Irish countryside. And for the same reasons the agrarian disturbances, like the industrial, were a matter of social, not of national, dispute. If a Welsh patriot had addressed a gathering of Welsh peasants in the language with which O'Connell intoxicated his Irish audiences, if he had told them what a wonderful country Wales would be if only it were freed from the rule of the British Parliament, they would hardly have understood what he meant.

Perhaps the most clinching evidence of the absence of any strong national sentiment in Rebeccaism, of its complete detachment from the Irish mood, is to be found in a letter which Rebecca addressed to *The Times*[19] in the autumn of 1843, applauding the Government's decision to send a Commission of Inquiry to Wales. ' We know,' she wrote, ' that England will do more for oppressed Welshmen than Wales itself with its jobbers and degenerate gentry would ever have done.' Little did she know what actually England was about to do for Wales. That first inquiry prompted a second, and the second did something that Rebecca had not thought of.

III. THE INQUIRY OF 1846

IT WAS widely held that the outbreaks of lawlessness in Wales were mainly due to the ignorance of the working class. The remedy for unrest, it was thought, was not repression, but more and better education. 'It should be borne in mind,' said Welsh-born William Williams, M.P. for Coventry, quoting a visitor to Wales, in 1846, 'that an ill-educated and undisciplined population, like that existing amongst the mines in South Wales, is one that may be found most dangerous to the neighbourhood in which it dwells, and that a band of efficient schoolmasters is kept up at a much less expense than a body of police or soldiery'; and he moved for an inquiry into the state of education in the Principality, 'especially into the means afforded to the labouring classes of acquiring a knowledge of the English language.'[20] The Government favoured the proposal, and appointed three Commissioners to carry it out—R. R. W. Lingen, J. C. S. Symons and H. V. Johnson. They divided the country into three sections,[a] and after six months' exhaustive investigation submitted what was virtually a unanimous report: the statement of the facts and the conclusions drawn from them in their separate reports were very much the same.

The Commissioners were English gentlemen, lawyers by profession, intelligent, capable, conscientious. They visited every educational institution, however small and humble, in their respective sections, and their reports thereon were well and clearly written. But the state of education and the means of improving it could not be studied only in the schools; and, though they had Welsh-speaking assistants, they were debarred from direct contact with the life of the Welsh poor, and from a real understanding of their customs and traditions, by the fact that they knew no Welsh. For information in that field they had to rely on those English-speaking members of their own class with whom they naturally associated and those English-speaking witnesses who gave evidence before them. Thus their opinions were bound to be influenced by those of anglicised Welsh society—the landed gentry, the leading townsmen and the Anglican clergy—who were separated

---

[a] Lingen: Carmarthen, Glamorgan and Pembroke. Symons: Brecknock, Cardigan and Radnor. Johnson: North Wales.

as has been seen, from the mass of the poorer folk in town and country by a wider gulf than that which divided the corresponding classes in England.

The Commissioners' description of working-class education was bound to be depressing. If it was bad enough in England at that time, it was much worse, in quantity and quality alike, in Wales. The old-established Grammar Schools had been reinforced by some new foundations in the eighteenth century; but they were still too few and too small, and they catered, as they had always done, for the anglicised middle class, not for the mainly Welsh-speaking poor. The pioneer work of the Circulating Schools, vital as it had been in its day, had not gone much beyond teaching poor children to read their Welsh Bible, and not many of them now survived. The Sunday School movement, on the other hand, was relatively young and fast expanding, and the Commissioners, as will be seen, fully recognised its value; but, as they pointed out, its teaching was confined to religion. For almost the only secular education worth the name the Welsh poor were indebted to their share in the fruits of the campaign launched in England by Lancaster and the undenominational British and Foreign School Society in 1808 and by Bell and the Anglican National Society in 1811. But the progress of that campaign in Wales had been much slower than in England, partly because the Welsh countryside was poorer and more backward, partly because of the obstacles created not only by the deeper schism between Church and chapel, but also by division in the latter's ranks. In 1843 there were only two British schools in North Wales, and not many more in the South. Most of the poor children were thus obliged to seek such scraps of secular education as could be got for a few pence a week at the so-called ' private adventure ' schools; and, while a few of those were redeemed by their masters' exceptional personality, the majority of them were wretchedly inadequate—a small bare room, no proper equipment, few books, and, worst of all, a teacher who, often as not, was only half-educated himself. Almost any man who lost his job could turn to teaching for a livelihood. The teacher's profession, said one of the Commissioners, who never minced their words, ' is one of the last esteemed and worst remunerated: one of those vocations which serve as the sinks of all others.'[21]

Those were the facts, and the Commissioners' clear and candid presentation of them could not be contested. Nor, perhaps, could they be blamed if they tended to apply a linguistic test to education and to identify Welsh children's ignorance in general with their ignorance of the English language in particular. For it had been taken for granted in the parliamentary resolution which constituted their terms of reference that the education needed for the Welsh poor was education in English. That was the standpoint from which the first and ablest of the three reports set out. ' My district,' it began, ' exhibits the phenomenon of a peculiar language isolating the mass from the upper portion of society '; and it went on to show how ignorance of English prevented the working man from rising in the social scale both in industry (as quoted above) and in agriculture. ' His social sphere becomes one of complete isolation from all influences save such as arise within his own order. . . . He is left to live in an underworld of his own, and the march of society goes so completely over his head that he is never heard of except when the strange phenomenon of a Revival or a Rebecca or Chartist outbreak calls attention ' to the peculiar character of his life.[22] On the isolating, depressing and demoralising effects of speaking only Welsh, all the Commissioners were agreed. ' The Welsh language,' says Symons, ' is a vast drawback to Wales and a manifold barrier to the moral progress and commercial prosperity of the people.' It ' bars the access of improving knowledge to their minds.'[23] Because of their language, says Johnson, the mass of the Welsh people were inferior to the English ' in every branch of practical knowledge and skill.'[24] In one field, in particular, in the administration of justice, ' the evil of the Welsh language is obviously and fearfully great. . . . It distorts the truth, favours fraud and abets perjury.'[25]

This fierce attack on Welsh was not inspired only by the belief that the folk who spoke it could not join in the ' march of progress' without learning English. The Commissioners were also convinced that there was nothing to help them in Wales. ' There is no Welsh literature worthy of the name.'[26] Something had been done, it was admitted, in intellectual circles to encourage an interest in Welsh poetry and music. The Eisteddfod, for instance, had been revived. But they had failed to give ' that character of solidity and usefulness which might have been given to Welsh, literature.' There is ' no book on geography, history, chemistry, natural history or any of the useful arts and sciences which owes its origin to an Eisteddfod except two or three treatises on agriculture.'[27] Of some four hundred Welsh books in circulation, three-fourths were concerned with religion and poetry and only one-eighth with scientific subjects.[28] The periodicals which, apart from the Bible, provided almost the only reading for the poor were ' almost exclusively ' religious and bitterly sectarian at that.[29]

The conclusion was implicit in these criticisms. Somehow or other the Welsh must get rid of their language. ' This disastrous barrier to all moral improvement and popular progress in Wales ' must be broken down. It would not be an easy task: for the Welsh poor not only had a fuller command of their language than the English poor:[30] they loved it. ' If interest pleads for English, affection leans to Welsh. The one is regarded as a new friend, the other as an old one to be cherished for himself and especially not to be deserted in his decline.'[31] Only in Welsh, moreover, could a Welshman give full rein to his natural gifts of speech. How, then, can this ' old and cherished ' language be done to death ? It cannot be ' taught down ' in the schools; ' for, so long as children are familiar with no other, they must be educated to a considerable extent through the medium of it. . . . Still less, out of school, can the language of lessons make head against the language of life.'[32] These were intelligent observations, and, if the Commisioners had been able to grasp all that they implied, they might have thought twice before pronouncing their drastic sentence. But they had made up their minds. For the sake of Wales Welsh must go; and fortunately there were two forces at work which might be counted on sooner or later to bring it about. The first was the widespread desire among the working classes themselves that their children should learn English because it would enable them to ' rise in life.' The other was the extent to which English, borne on the flood of immigration and economic expansion, was already penetrating Wales. It was seeping up the main roads. It would flow still faster along the coming railways. The end, it seemed, could not be long delayed. Already, ran one sanguine sentence, English was ' in process of becoming the mother-tongue of the country.'[33]

It is not surprising that the Commissioners should have swept aside the ancient language of Wales as ruthlessly as Macaulay, a decade earlier, had swept aside the ancient languages of India. For in one respect both they and Macaulay were right. It was incontestable that an adequate knowledge of modern civilisation was almost as unattainable in Welsh as in Arabic or Sanskrit. And had it not been taken for granted in their instructions that the ignorance of the Welsh working classes meant that they were ignorant of English ? It might at first sight seem more surprising that the Commissioners were not content to stress the manifest value of English: that they denied any value at all to Welsh: that they seemed, indeed, to regard it as an ' evil ' not only because it was an obstructive rival to English, but in itself. They were unaware, no doubt, that the pioneers of education for the poor in Wales had been ardent champions of Welsh,[a] and that the revival of the language had been one of the main factors in saving Welsh

[a] See page 117 above.

nationhood from decay and dissolution. But in any case such a modern interpretation of what had happened in the eighteenth century would have had little meaning for them. Nationality was not understood in early Victorian England as it is understood to-day.[a] Few, if any, Englishmen can have thought much as yet about the value of a nation's language to its mind and soul, or realised that, if it lost its language, the best elements in its life might be cut from their roots and wither. Such ideas would have seemed fanciful to the Commissioners. Knowing no Welsh, unable to read Welsh poetry, they did not trouble to consider whether English might be acquired without discarding Welsh. It is safe to say that the notion of a bi-lingual Wales never entered their heads. Nor, finally, is it to be wondered at that they so unmistakably identified the ' march of progress ' with material advance and so complacently assumed that the best service that could be rendered to Welshmen was to make them more like Englishmen. For they were living in the intellectual climate of Macaulay's England. The reign of the ' Philistines ' was at hand.

This frontal attack on the Welsh language was linked with a less direct attack on Welsh Dissent. The Commissioners, who were presumably Anglicans or at any rate not Nonconformists, did not go so far as to suggest that Dissent was an ' evil.' On the contrary, they were plainly impressed by the vigour of the religious life which centred in the chapel. To the Sunday Schools in particular they paid a warm and evidently genuine tribute.[b] They were ' the main instrument of civilisation ' in most of the countryside. The morals of the people were most degraded where their influence was least felt.'[34] A striking description of their

[a] See page 168 above.

[b] They had been given a lead in this matter in their instructions from the head of the department (Kay Shuttleworth) which appointed them. ' The Sunday Schools must be regarded as the most remarkable, because the most general, spontaneous effect of the zeal of Christian congregations for education. Report of the Commissioner of Inquiry into the state of Education in Wales, *Accounts and Papers*, 1847, vol. 27, pt. i, iv.

friendly democratic atmosphere has been quoted on an earlier page.[a] Nor was their value moral or social only: they were ' real fields of mental activity.'[35] It was not the zeal of Welsh Dissent that the Commissioners found fault with. Except, perhaps, in the curious lack of reference to Welsh preaching, they seem to have outgrown the distaste of eighteenth-century English society for ' enthusiasm.' Nor did they press their criticism of the polemical tone of some of the religious teaching or its pre-occupation with the niceties of theological controversy. What troubled them most about it was its monopoly of the educational field. They con-trasted ' the energetic working of the missionary spirit in religion ' with ' the neglect of secular education.'[36] The books, the periodicals, they were almost all religious. The people knew their Bible from end to end, but what else? They were ' better versed in the geography of Palestine than of Wales.'[37] The Commis-sioners did not say outright that there was too much religion in the educational activities of Welsh Dissent, but they did say that there was too little interest in the secular stuff of modern life and thought. They seem to have realised that to remedy that weakness might be no easier than to suppress the Welsh tongue: for the chief merit of the religious system—its spontaneous, popular character—seemed in that respect a disadvantage. It had been created by the poor, it belonged to the poor, and its leaders and teachers were drawn from the same class and were therefore not fully alive to the social and intellectual deficiencies of a life to which they and their fathers before them had been accustomed.[38] This limitation of outlook, this aloofness from the surrounding world, was at root the reason why the Commissioners linked their criticism of Welsh Dissent with their attack on the Welsh language. Each in its degree, they held, though one much more than the other, was responsible for the isolation which kept the Welsh working classes from sharing in the ' march of progress.' And here again there was substance in their criticism. Only a

[a] See page 120-1 above.

bigoted sectarian could deny that the education of the chapel at this time was too narrow in its scope and too disputatious in its method.

The Commissioners had been instructed to keep in mind ' the amount, character and condition of the population and the means available in the district for the maintenance of schools.' That was a sensible injunction, but unfortunately the Commissioners made too much of it or at least of one item in it. They were shocked, it appeared, by what they were told about the character of the Welsh workers, and in a number of outspoken sentences scattered throughout their reports they delivered judgment on their morals. It was at least as stern and sweeping as their condemnation of their language. ' The Welsh,' they admitted, ' are peculiarly exempt from the guilt of great crimes. There are few districts in Europe where murders, burglaries, personal violence . . . are so rare '[a]—and this meritorious record, they suggested, was mainly due to Welshmen's ' natural benevolence and warmth of heart.' ' On the other hand,' they went on, ' there are, perhaps, few countries where the standard of minor morals is lower.' Not only were ' cleanliness and decency ' neglected: ' side by side with warmth of religious feeling there was widespread disregard of temperance, of chastity, of veracity and of fair-dealing.' Of these immoralities the worst and most common was sexual incontinence. It was ' the besetting sin . . . the peculiar vice of the Principality.'

These painful accusations were backed by the circumstantial evidence of numerous Welsh witnesses, mostly clergymen, Nonconformist as well as Anglican, and magistrates, and there was no reason why the Commissioners should disbelieve them. But their bearing on the problem of teaching Welsh children English was somewhat indirect, and it seems strange that they should have

[a] Major crimes were twice as numerous in Hereford as in neighbouring Radnor or Brecknock.

thought it necessary to set them forth in their reports and in such indiscriminating terms. They probably knew little about rustic morals in England and still less about the vices of the slums; for the social conscience of the English governing class had only just begun to be awakened to an interest in such matters. Yet they seem to have taken for granted that the charges they made against the Welsh were not to be matched elsewhere. Did they imagine that the English poor were incomparably cleaner, more decent, more chaste? Were liars and cheats and drunkards so much less often to be found in other countries? They must have known better than that, and surely they should have made it plain that the moral failings they thought it their duty to denounce in Wales were not unknown among their fellow-countrymen or, for that matter, anywhere else.

Still stranger was the official publication of the full text of the reports. For surely the authorities should have foreseen—they can scarcely have wished to provoke—the inevitable reaction. All Wales, it need hardly be said, was up in arms. Rural North and urban South were at one. The anglicised upper class may have agreed with much of what they read in the reports, with the statement of the case for teaching English and with the criticism of Nonconformist education; but they were Welshmen after all, and proud of it, and they were wounded to the quick when they found Wales pilloried before all the world for its unusual immorality. Even the feud between Church and chapel was for the time forgotten. Naturally the most vehement protests came from Welsh-speaking Nonconformists, but English-speaking Anglicans quickly made it plain that they shared the majority's resentment at the insult to all Wales, and English Bishop Thirlwall and English Dean Cotton joined in the indignant chorus. Welsh sentiment, it may be said, had never been so unanimous. And the strength and heat of it were unmistakable. Even to-day ' the *brâd* of the Blue Books '—a word meaning ' treachery ' and coloured with dark memories of old domestic strife[a]—has not been forgotten.

In cool retrospect it may seem, perhaps, as if too much was made of what after all might be regarded as no more than a failure in tact, however gross, on the part of Englishmen who were honestly trying to help Wales. And it is true that the agitation on the platform and in the Press was often excessive. The value of the information to be found in the reports was ignored. So were the tributes, and there were several, to Welshmen's natural gifts. But to students of the psychology of nationalism, especially in small and sometime subject nations, the uproar excited by the *brâd* will seem natural enough. The worst of it, no doubt, was the public indictment of Welsh ignorance and depravity; but that was by no means all. The Welsh language had been calmly consigned to the rubbish heap. If the kind of religion which most Welshmen had adopted had been more respectfully treated, it was enough for the angry critics that it had been criticised, that it had even been suggested that there was too much of it. Their language and their religion—they would not have described those things as two vital elements of their nationhood. That was not the language of the day. But they would have claimed that those were their own distinctive Welsh possessions, and, while hitherto they had taken them more or less for granted, now that they were publicly disparaged they realised how proud they were of them. That is why the educational inquiry of 1846 was such an important event in the history of Wales. It made the Welsh more conscious of their nationhood: it stung Welsh nationalism awake.[b]

[a] The use of the word suggests that it was not so much the English Commissioners as the Welsh witnesses who were held responsible for the ' stab in the back.'

[b] Speaking in the House of Commons as Minister of Education in 1946, Mr. R. A. Butler said: " We have also had some courses initiated in the Welsh language. I regard as obscurantist the attitude of the Commission of Inquiry exactly a hundred years ago which went to Wales and took the view that to keep alive a knowledge of this beautiful tongue was tantamount to crippling Welsh initiative and penalising Welsh endeavour. I wish now, a hundred years later, to make amends for that attitude." *Hansard*, H. of C., 1946, v. 380, c. 1411.

IV. EDUCATION

It has been said that the history of Wales in the Victorian age is a history of education; and there is truth in that overstatement. For, while most chapters of Welsh history in these years are part of a common British history, the building from base to summit of a complete educational system in Wales was a distinctively Welsh achievement. It was aided, of course, by the Welsh share in the financial resources of the British State, but it was mainly due to the zeal and energy of Welshmen. It embodied in schools and colleges and libraries and in a regiment of teachers and students the reawakened spirit of Welsh nationhood. That is the aspect of it with which this book is concerned, and ony the barest summary of the actual process can be provided here.[a]

It began, as it was bound to do, at the level of primary education; and, before the Commissioners of 1846 exposed Welsh ignorance so brusquely to the world, Welshmen, with Hugh Owen in the lead, had begun to grapple with the desperate need for more and better education for the children of the working classes. From 1843 onwards many more schools, both Anglican and Nonconformist, were provided; in 1845 a Non-conformist South Wales Education Committee was formed and in 1846 an Anglican Welsh Education Committee; and the first Welsh teacher-training college was opened at Brecon in 1846. Thus the campaign was already under way when it was so vigorously reinforced by the publication of the ' Blue Books.' Wales had been pilloried for its ignorance, and the only effective response Welsh patriots could make was to set themselves to raise the standard of their children's education to a level no English critic could condemn. It took time, but in the course of two

---

[a] Useful introductions to the subject will be found in *Education in Wales, 1847-1947*, a pamphlet published by the Welsh Department of the Ministry of Education (H.M.S.O., 1948), and in T.I. Ellis' *The Development of Higher Education in Wales* (Wrexham, 1935).

generations it was done. Already by 1870 hundreds of new schools were scattered over Wales, and after 1870 hundreds more 'Board Schools' were built under Forster's Act. At the end of the century every Welsh child was receiving a free primary education of much the same quality and under much the same conditions as English children.

By 1900 a Welsh system of secondary and higher education had also been built up. On the recommendation of the Aberdare Committee of 1880 the provision of secondary or intermediate schools—'County Schools' they came to be called—began in 1894 and steadily continued till most of the market towns of Wales possessed them. To finance them the Welsh Intermediate and Technical Education Act of 1889[a] authorised the newly-created County and County Borough Councils to levy a half-penny rate to be supplemented by a Government grant of pound for pound.[b] This novel legislation—hitherto only primary education had been assisted by the State—was applied to Wales alone at that time, and a vital part of its operation, the examination and inspection of the County Schools, was entrusted in 1896 to a purely Welsh body, the Central Welsh Board.[c] It remained to crown the educational structure with a University, and that also had been done by 1900. Besides the Training Colleges, which had grown to four by 1880, a University College had been opened at Aberystwyth in 1872. A second was opened at Cardiff in 1883 and a third at Bangor in 1884. In 1893 these colleges (to which Swansea was added in 1920) were united by royal charter to constitute the University of Wales. The University, said Rosebery, embodied ' the spirit of nationality in its best form.'[39]

This Welsh educational system was partly financed by the

[a] 52 and 53 Vic. cap. 40.
[b] Voluntary subscriptions were supplemented on the same scale.
[c] The Board consisted of 80 members (3 ex-officio, 71 elected by certain educational bodies, 6 co-opted) all of whom had had experience of educational work in teaching, administration or planning. None of the 80 were women. There was an executive Committee of 15. T. I. Ellis, 88.

British Treasury and partly administered by the British Government. After 1896 the Intermediate Schools were controlled by the Central Welsh Board, but the control of the primary schools was still vested directly or indirectly in the Board of Education, and when the Education Act of 1902 provided for the establishment of State secondary schools, the supervision of them was also entrusted (in 1904) to the Board of Education. There was thus a conflict of authority in the secondary field, and on the introduction of another Education Bill in 1906 a strong section of Welsh opinion pressed for a unified Welsh administration of all Welsh schools. As the outcome of a national conference at Cardiff, a clause, mainly the work of D. Brynmor Jones, was inserted in the Bill, establishing a Council of Wales to take over the existing functions of the Board of Education and the Central Welsh Board, and, while empowered to raise money on its own authority, to administer the funds supplied by Parliament for all Welsh education except at the University level. This was a thorough-going plan of functional devolution, but it failed to secure unanimous support in Wales, and it was so sharply attacked in Parliament that the Government, despite its great majority in the Commons, withdrew it. The autonomists' agitation, however, was not wholly unproductive. To assuage their disappointment—so it is supposed—the Board of Education created in 1907 a Welsh Department, staffed by Welshmen, to deal with its duties in Wales. This was a notable concession to Welsh sentiment. It might be described as devolution at the centre. But it was not the devolution to the circumference which the autonomists desired, and in 1908, after a conference at Shrewsbury, a Bill was drafted, again by Brynmor Jones, to establish a Council of Education for Wales. It followed the lines of the abandoned clause of the 1906 Bill, but it took one long step beyond them. The educationalists were not the only champions of autonomy. In political circles, too, for some years past, schemes of devolution covering a wider field than education had been canvassed,[a] and the Education Bill now drafted was linked with these schemes in proposing that the Council should be appointed by and responsible to a Secretary of State for Wales. But the scheme never got as far as the House of Commons. Like its predecessor of 1906 it failed to obtain sufficient agreement in Wales. The main crux on both occasions was the distribution of seats on the Council as between the local authorities and the educational experts on the one hand and as between North and South Wales on the other. Discussion of this issue continued for some years, but it was still unsettled when all such domestic questions were thrust into the background by the outbreak of war in 1914.

To many Welshmen this failure to secure complete autonomy for the Welsh educational system seemed a minor question. It did not lessen the value of the work that had been done. It did not seriously affect its national character. It was mainly, it seemed, a matter of form. Whoever controlled it, the system was bound to depend largely on State aid, and, since in the normal course the Minister would act on the advice of his Welsh Department, the control was Welsh control of a sort. And in all other respects—in the patriotic impulse that had created it, in the character it had assumed, in most of the manpower that worked it—the system was as purely Welsh as the children and the students that it served. It was, in fact, a national system, the first and most striking expression in institutional terms of the reawakened consciousness of nationhood.

There are two primary documents for the study of this chapter of Welsh history—the report of the Commissioners of 1846 and the report of the Aberdare Committee of 1880—and nothing more plainly reveals the nationalist complexion of the educational campaign than the contrast between them. The first never mentioned the Welsh nation: it ignored the claims of

[a] See pages 222ff., below.

nationality: it made no secret of its authors' hope that in the interest of Wales most of the distinctive features of Welsh life would disappear: it was essentially a plea for assimilation, for anglicisation. The Aberdare report, on the other hand, was essentially a plea for the recognition and preservation of Welsh nationhood; and the contrast was not entirely or even mainly due to the fact that the Commissioners of 1846 were Englishmen and Aberdare and most of his colleagues Welshmen.[a] The chief reason was the lapse of time. In 1880 far more was known and understood in Britain about the meaning and function of nationhood than in 1846. Between those years the problem of Irish nationalism was forcing its way to the front of British politics. It was the time of Gladstone's early moves in Irish affairs, of the disestablishment of the Anglican Church of Ireland, of the foundation of the Home Rule Association, of the rise of Parnell. And concurrently a fresh wind of continental thought about nationality was blowing across the Channel. It was the time of Garibaldi and Kossuth, of Mazzini and Cavour, of the controversy between Mill and Acton on the relations between a nation and a state. Hence the contrast between those documents. Unlike the Commissioners of 1846, the Committee of 1880 could understand that the question of Welsh education was inseparable from the question of Welsh nationhood, and they prefaced their recommendations with a declaration of nationalist doctrine which is historically so significant and bears so closely on the subject of the present study that it deserves to be quoted in full.[40]

The first thing to be noted is that Wales has a distinct nationality of its own. The fact that Welshmen are thoroughly loyal to the Government under which they live, that they are satisfied to possess the same institutions and to be governed

[a] Henry Austin Bruce (1815-1895), created first Baron Aberdare in 1873, was born at Duffryn in Glamorgan and was M.P. for Merthyr Tydvil from 1852 to 1868. The other Welsh members of the Committee were Earl Cawdor, Henry Richard, John Rhys and Lewis Morris.

by the same laws as Englishmen, that there is no agitation among them for a separate existence, though it tends to make their nationality less obtrusive and exacting, in no way destroys its reality. The spirit which elsewhere[a] manifests itself in struggles against the supremacy of a dominant race is in Wales content with maintaining the continuity of the national life, preserving the traditional sentiment of the race, and following those ideas and usages which are distinctive and characteristic of the nation.

The sentiment of nationality cannot be ignored and ought not in our opinion to be discouraged. Some of the witnesses who gave evidence before us expressed themselves strongly as to what they designated Welsh narrowness and provincialism, and seemed to us to be of opinion that whatever is specially characteristic of the people should be got rid of. To this end they contended that Welshmen should as much as possible be educated out of their own country and that no encouragement should be given to institutions specially adapted to the national characteristics of Wales or likely to perpetuate distinctively Welsh sentiments or ideas.

That narrowness or provincialism, whether Welsh or English, should be corrected, and, as far as may be, replaced by breadth of view and comprehensiveness of thought will probably be admitted without controversy, but this may be done without destroying the Welsh type of character or converting the people of Wales into Englishmen. That system of education is most desirable for Wales which, while preserving the national type, improves and elevates it, and at the same time gives opportunity for the development of any literary tastes or intellectual aptitudes which may be characteristic of the nation.

The existence, therefore, of a distinct Welsh nationality is in our opinion a reason for securing within the limits

[a] Ireland is evidently in the Committee's mind.

of Wales itself a system of intermediate and higher education in harmony with the distinctive peculiarities of the
country.

To this new self-conscious cultural nationalism a Welsh
University seemed the most important part of the educational
system. It was not only that a native University, however small
and new to start with, would bring the meaning and value of
higher education ' more closely home to the daily life and thought
of the people ' than the ancient English Universities ' with all
their prestige.'[41] A Welsh University, such as Owen Glendower
had dreamed of long ago,[a] was the natural and needful expression
of Welsh nationhood. There were old-established Universities in
Scotland. In Ireland Trinity College, despite the status it had
enjoyed since Elizabeth's day, might not be regarded as a national
institution; but the creation of the four Queen's Colleges created
in 1845 and, still more, the new-born Royal University of
Ireland (1879), were manifest concessions to Irish nationalism.
And both the Scottish and the Irish institutions had been generously
financed from British funds.[b] Was Wales, it was asked, to be the
only nation in the multi-national United Kingdom to be denied
its legitimate status in the academic world?

It was this jealous pride in Welsh nationhood that impelled
so many gifted Welshmen at that time to devote their lives to the
advancement of Welsh education and in particular to the making
of a University. To them it was ' national service ' in the full
sense of both words. T. C. Edwards, the first principal of the
first University College at Aberystwyth, hailed his appointment
as bringing true the dream he had cherished since boyhood of
doing something ' to serve Wales.'[42] When J. Viriamu Jones
abandoned a promising career at Sheffield to start the second

[a] See page 38 above.
[b] The ' Royal University ' was granted £1,000,000 from the endowment of the
disestablished Church. In the year 1880–81, the Scottish Universities received a Treasury
grant of £18,992, the Queen's Colleges £22,826. *Report of the Committee on Intermediate
and Higher Education in Wales*, A and P. 1881, xxxiii, 66.

College at Cardiff, ' no nobler task,' he said, ' could fall to the lot of any Welshman.'[43]

This was genuine nationalism, but it was only cultural nationalism. All the leading educationalists of that day were as contented as the Aberdare Committee with the existing political status of Wales. ' The revival of the Welsh national spirit,' said J. V. Jones, would lead to ' a closer union with England.'[44]

V. LITERATURE AND LANGUAGE

THE GROWTH of cultural nationalism in Wales was accompanied, naturally enough, by one of those outbreaks of literary and particularly poetic energy which had occurred from time to time in the past. The circumstances were not encouraging. There were now few well-to-do Welshmen who wanted to read Welsh books or patronise their authors; and the creative spirit was cramped by the inhibitions of the rigid puritanism which dominated most Welsh minds. But these handicaps were overcome. There was an outflow of poetry which in volume alone was ' extraordinary for so small a nation,' and the best of it has been highly praised by those who are best qualified to judge.[45] Two poets stand out above the rest for the hold they won on Welshmen's hearts—John Ceiriog Hughes (1832-1887), known as Ceiriog, and William Thomas (1832-78), known as Islwyn. Ceiriog's songs were ' sung from end to end of Wales and by all classes.' An English critic has acclaimed him as ' unequalled throughout our islands, save by Burns alone, for his gift of writing songs whose appeal united all classes of his countrymen.'[46] Islwyn, ' the most philosophic of Welsh poets,' was ' the very antithesis of Ceiriog,' but his intensely religious, mystical, melancholy poetry made a strong appeal to the Welsh temperament.[47]

Prose, as the Commissioners of 1846 complained, was mainly

confined to religious books and periodicals. Except in anglicised society whose needs were met by English books, there had been little demand for secular literature in Welsh, but a new kind of Welsh newspaper had already come into being which discussed political and economic questions. Two men above all others may be called the fathers of the modern Welsh press. The first was William Rees, known as Hiraethog, who founded *Yr Amserau* (*The Times*) in 1843. The second and greater man was Thomas Gee whose journal, the *Baner Cymru*, was started in 1857 and amalgamated with *Yr Amserau* in 1859. Through its columns Gee did more than anyone else to influence Welsh political thinking in the second half of the nineteenth century. He became one of the oustanding personalities of the national revival, and his services to it were not confined to journalism. In 1847 he began and in 1858 completed the publication of D. S. Evans' Welsh-English Dictionary, and in 1854 he began to publish in monthly parts a Welsh encyclopaedia for the composition of which he enlisted all the best writers of his day. Its last and tenth volume appeared in 1878.[48]

Welsh literature and an interest in all things Welsh would not have developed in this period as they did without the aid of the Welsh Societies. The most famous of them, the Cymmrodorion, was founded (as has been recorded earlier) in London in 1751 and was revived in 1873. Its main purpose, like that of the Cymreigyddion, the Cymdeithas Cymraeg and others, was chiefly to bring together Welshmen living outside Wales to discuss and promote Welsh cultural interests. For a time, therefore, they consisted mainly of groups of exiles in the larger English towns. But in the course of the nineteenth century branches of them were established in almost all the towns of Wales.[a] The lectures

[a] A Union of Welsh Societies was formed in 1913. By 1927, 85 Societies had joined it with a total membership of about 10,000. *Welsh in Education and Life* (H.M. Stationery Office, 1927), a masterly report on Welsh cultural development by a departmental committee of the Board of Education.

delivered and the papers read at the meetings of these Societies did much to enlighten the Welsh public about the past of Wales. Much of the popular tradition was shown to be legendary. Long-cherished beliefs about the primitive heroic age were pruned away. Iolo Morganwg's fraudulent reconstruction of druidic ceremonial was exposed. The work done by the more learned Societies, such as the Cymmrodorion and the Cambrian Archaeological Association, laid the foundations of the modern scientific study of Welsh history.

It was the Gwynnedigion Society which had been responsible for the revival of the Eisteddfod at Corwen in 1789,[a] and thenceforward the number of small local Eisteddfodau steadily increased. In 1858 it was decided that over and above these local gatherings a single National Eisteddfod should be held every year at some chosen place. For a time this project was obstructed by financial difficulties, but after 1880, when the National Eisteddfod Association was founded, the great festival soon acquired the elaborate and impressive character it wears to-day; and there can be no dispute as to the influence which it increasingly exerted on Welsh life. It stimulated literary activity: it was a feather in a poet's cap to win the Crown for free or the Chair for canonical poetry and in a prose writer's to win the essay prize.[b] The drama was similarly encouraged by the rival production of plays, but it was music, perhaps, that gained most. The old Welsh gifts of choral singing and harp-playing and the peculiar art of singing to the harp were raised to the highest level of technique by the competition of local choirs, especially children's choirs, and harpists from all over Wales. But the Eisteddfod did more than stimulate Welsh culture: it made the common people of Wales aware of it. Gathering in thousands to the festival, listening in eager silence to the sequence of literary and musical performances, they realised that the art displayed before them was the national art of

[a] See page 125 above.
[b] See Professor T. Jenkins' authoritative essay on 'The Development of Nationalism in Wales' in *Sociological Review*, xxvii (1935), 163-182.

Wales, and felt, more deeply than lectures and books and newspapers could make them feel, a pride in being Welsh.

It seems to have been the Eisteddfod more than anything else that awakened an interest among English intellectuals in the new flowering of Welsh culture. It was so, at any rate, with Matthew Arnold. At the Eisteddfod at Chester in 1866, one at the last held beyond the border, he was an honoured guest. 'When I see,' he wrote in answer to the invitation, ' the enthusiasm these Eisteddfods can awaken in your whole people, and then think of the tastes, the literature, the amusements of our own lower and middle class, I am filled with admiration '; and he dwelt on the benefit Wales could confer on England by infusing English ' Philistianism ' with Celtic sensitiveness and spirituality. ' No service that England can render the Celts by giving you a share in her many good qualities can surpass that which the Celts can at this moment render England by communicating to us some of theirs.' There followed his famous Oxford lectures on the study of Celtic literature in which, while deprecating overstatements of the difference between Celt and Saxon and claiming a ' Celtic fibre ' in the English spirit, he contrasted the temperament and worldly fortunes of the steady-going, practical, utilitarian, successful Saxon with those of the imaginative, impulsive, sentimental Celt, impatient of realities, always ready, as Henri Martin, the French historian, had said, ' to react against the despotism of fact,' and therefore always losing ground in the material work-a-day world. It was characteristic of English culture, he declared, that Celtic studies had never been seriously pursued in England, and he closed his course of lectures with an appeal for the establishment of a Celtic chair at Oxford

The lectures were published and in his introduction Arnold cited a shocking example of what might be described as English nationalism in Philistine costume. The Chester Eisteddfod and

Arnold's reaction to it were the subject of two angry leaders in *The Times* which reproduced with painful exactness the sentiments of the notorious 'Blue Books' of 1846. 'The Welsh language is the curse of Wales. Its prevalence and the ignorance of English have excluded and even now exclude the Welsh people from the civilisation of their English neighbours. An Eisteddfod is one of the most mischievous and selfish pieces of sentimentalism which could possibly be perpetrated. It is simply a foolish interference with the natural progress of civilisation and prosperity.' And so forth. . . . Arnold's comment is interesting. 'What I said to myself as I put the newspaper down was this: " Behold England's difficulty in governing Ireland! " ' On one point, however, Arnold's opinions were more in line with *The Times*, and have been cited against him by Welsh nationalists. He held that 'the natural course of things irresistibly tends' towards 'the fusion of all the inhabitants of these islands into one homogeneous English-speaking whole' and that the practical contribution of Welsh culture to that of England and the world at large must be made in English. ' For all modern purposes, let us all as soon as possible be one people; let the Welshman speak English, and if he is an author, let him write English.'[49]

Arnold's appeal for an Oxford chair bore fruit. In 1877 a chair of Celtic, associated with Jesus College, was founded at Oxford and another at Edinburgh in 1882. The first occupant of the former was Sir John Rhys (1840-1915). The influence of this great Celtic scholar was immense, and it was mainly his pupils who filled the chairs of Welsh language and literature created in rapid succession at the new University Colleges. The most eminent of these was Sir John Morris-Jones (1864-1929) who, himself a gifted poet, built up at Bangor a school of students and writers of Welsh poetry, an example to be followed later on by two other professor-poets, W. J. Gruffydd at Cardiff and Gwyn Jones at Aberystwyth. Nor was history behindhand in the general advance of scholarship promoted by the growth of the University.

The early and medieval history of Wales was now written at last at the highest academic level by J. E. Lloyd of Bangor.

At the heart of this cultural revival lay a paradox. While interest and pride in the national tradition were growing, its most vital and distinctive element was losing ground. Already in the forties English was spoken as much as Welsh by the townsfolk of the South. Chartist meetings usually opened with prayers in Welsh, but, often as not, the speeches that followed were in English.[50] Some thirty years later[a] it was calculated that while the great majority of Welsh Nonconformists spoke and worshipped in Welsh and while newspapers and periodicals with a combined circulation of over 150,000 were printed in Welsh, already about one-third of the total population of nearly 1,500,000 habitually spoke English. Nor was the advance of English and the retreat of Welsh likely to slow down. Every day the material and social forces making for anglicisation were gaining strength. To anxious champions of Welsh culture in the eighties it might have seemed as if their language was already withering under the curse which the ' Blue Books ' had laid on it.

Such fears were slow to take shape. Strange as it seems to-day, the leaders of the cultural revival in its earlier stages took little interest in the language save as a subject of purely academic study and were not concerned about its preservation. Most of the local patrons of the chief Societies in those days were drawn from the anglicised upper class, and their proceedings were largely conducted in English. The Cymreigyddion, for instance, invited a sarcastic comment from Commissioner Symons. It ' holds meetings at Abergavenny,' he wrote, ' where a band of literati promote Welsh literature by making English speeches once a year in its defence.' Even the Eisteddfod was drifting with the tide. The most prominent man of letters associated with it, Gwallter Mechain (1761-1849), complained in his old age that the intentions

[a] After the census of 1871. Linguistic statistics first appeared in the census of 1891.

208

of those who had promoted its revival in 1818 were being, ' in one Eisteddfod after another, diverted by the saxonism of traitors from cherishing our own native gifts.'[51] But the Saxonists prevailed. Most present-day visitors to the Eisteddfod are probably unaware and would be surprised to learn that right on into the later years of the nineteenth century its proceedings were conducted, its presidential addresses spoken, its judges' awards composed, in English.[52]

There were several reasons for this drift. It must be remembered once more that the philosophy of nationalism was only slowly coming into vogue and that the nearest exponents of it, the Irish, were not at that time claiming that their native language was an essential element in their nationhood. It must be remembered, too, that most of the educated Welshmen of that day were members of an anglicised society who, in so far as they were interested in Welsh traditions, regarded them as belonging to the past rather than the present or the future. Welsh, which few of them could speak or read, might be worthy of study, but as a language so far gone in its decline as to be almost as ' dead ' as Greek or Latin. Others were defeatists who, much as they might love the language, had come to acquiesce in what seemed to be its inevitable fading-out from living speech. Others again were optimists to whom it seemed that, since the great majority of Welshmen still spoke Welsh, the language was in no serious danger of extinction.

This last opinion could scarcely have been held by anyone who realised what was happening in the schools. The language, in fact, was being steadily done to death on the lips of the younger generation. Whatever else in their reports might be contested, the Commissioners of 1846 told the truth when they said that knowledge of English was essential if the children were to ' get on ' in later life and that their parents were aware of it; and not only on the morrow of the Commission but on through that period when schools were multiplying fast, the school-managers for the most part sympathised with the popular demand for English and did their best to meet it. Not only was all instruction given in English despite the fact that many teachers' command of it was bad and their teaching consequently worse: the use of Welsh by the children among themselves was penalised. In many schools a board, labelled 'Welsh stick,' was hung round the neck of a child caught speaking Welsh and passed on to subsequent culprits till the last day of the week when the child who happened to be wearing it was flogged.[53] [a] The parents seem to have acquiesced in these draconic measures; but it would be quite wrong to suppose that their keen desire that their children should learn another language implied that they did not care about their own. They were incapable of understanding that, if this educational policy were consistently maintained, their children's children would one day speak no Welsh. And, if the thought could have crossed their minds, they would have been reassured by better-educated folk. The Aberdare Committee, for example, were ardent nationalists, but, as practical men, they did not question the need for Welshmen to speak English, and they reported with satisfaction the progress which the knowledge of it was making. But that did not mean, they pointed out, that Welsh was in any immediate danger. ' Such is the attachment of the Welsh to their own language and literature, so deeply interwoven are they with their daily life, their religious worship and even their amusements, that ... the Welsh language will long be cherished by the large majority of the Welsh people.'[54] But how long? Two, three generations? The issue would be decided in the schools. If Welsh were banned in them, its doom, soon or late, was certain. And what would happen to Welsh culture when it lost its language?

Twenty or thirty years earlier it would have seemed eccentric or perverse to ask such questions, but it was impossible for the

[a] The authors of *Welsh in Education and Life* pointed out (page 2) that boys in English schools were similarly punished in the sixteenth century for speaking English instead of Latin.

group of educationalists who were now campaigning for a Welsh University to acquiesce in the prospect, however distant, of Welsh ceasing to be a living language; and, led by Thomas Powell, Professor of Welsh at Cardiff, Dan Isaac Davies, an inspector of Welsh schools, and O. M. Edwards who from his fellow's rooms at Jesus College, Oxford, was appealing to Welsh pride in Welsh tradition in a series of eloquent and widely-read Welsh books, they joined with the Cymmrodorion in founding in 1885 the Society for the Utilisation of the Welsh Language in Education. They won their first victory in 1888 when the ban in the schools was broken. On the recommendation of the Cross Commission it was decided that teaching might now be given in Welsh as well as in English, that Welsh might be taught as a class-subject as English was now taught in English schools, that the teaching of Welsh history and geography should be encouraged, and that Welsh grammar might be taken as a specific subject in the higher standards. This last concession meant that Welsh would now rank with Latin, French and German as one of the languages required for admission to teachers' training colleges. These regulations, like the similar concessions that were made to Gaelic in Scotland and to Erse in Ireland, were proof of the sympathy felt at the Board of Education with the aspirations of linguistic patriots; but they were only permissive regulations, and many schools in Wales did not adopt them. In some cases the headmaster and members of his staff could not speak Welsh themselves. In others the controlling managers of boards had no liking for the change. Thus for more than a decade the campaign for Welsh in the schools was halted, but with the passing of the Education Act of 1902, which transferred the control of the schools to a ' Local Education Authority' for each county, the campaigners' difficulties were very greatly lightened. ' Now instead of being faced with the hopeless task of convincing hundreds of different authorities they would confine their attention to about a score.'[55] The results were soon apparent.

When the Welsh Department of the Board of Education was established in 1907, one of its first official documents stated that the Welsh language had already been introduced, with the Board's 'entire approval,' as a subject and as a medium of instruction, in 'almost every county in Wales.'[56]

Before 1914, then, the battle for Welsh in the schools had been won or nearly won. It was none too soon. To sceptical minds it might have seemed too late. For during the period in which the battle was being fought, the language was still losing ground among the people as a whole. In the census of 1891 the number of Welsh folk who spoke Welsh was counted for the first time. It was counted again in the censuses of 1901 and 1911. The results were as follows:

	Total Population over 3 years[a]	Speaking Welsh	Speaking English only
1891	1,685,614	898,914	
1901	1,864,696	929,824	928,222
1911	2,247,927	977,366	1,208,282

Thus, while in those twenty years, the total population increased by 33 per cent, the number of those who spoke Welsh only or both Welsh and English, rose by only 7 per cent, while the number of those who knew no Welsh rose by 56 per cent. In other words, an increase in the knowledge of English, which everyone held to be on all acounts desirable, was accompanied by a decrease in the use of Welsh. And that, of course, was what the Commissioners of 1846 and those Welshmen who in their hearts agreed with them had hoped would happen.

A brief digression is needed here to record what might be called the Welsh 'diaspora.'[57] From its earliest stages Welshmen had shared with the other peoples of the British Isles in the current

[a] The figures for 1891 are for the total population over *two* years of age.

of migration across the Atlantic, and in course of time they built up Welsh communities which proudly maintained their Welsh speech and customs. One of these was founded in the seventeenth century at New Haven in Connecticut by David Yale whose son Elihu made a fortune in the Company's service in India, and when a college was established at New Haven in 1700 he presented it with books and other gifts. Hence the name of the famous University.[a]

As individuals, also, Welshmen played their part in the public life of the old thirteen colonies and in the revolution which severed them from Britain. One of the writers who did most to promote it from the other side of the Atlantic was Welsh Thomas Price; and it is said that no less than eighteen of the fifty-six signatories of the Declaration of Independence were of Welsh descent. Certainly the man who drafted it was Welsh in blood and sentiment. 'The tradition of my father's family,' wrote Jefferson, ' was that their ancestor came to this country from Wales, from near the mountain of Snowdon.'[58] It is claimed, too, that several of the revolutionary generals were of Welsh origin.

Welshmen have not been so prominent in the public life of the United States as Irishmen; but there are Welsh communities in many American cities to-day where Welsh is still spoken and newspapers printed in Welsh. One of these Welsh groups is in South, not North America. Mainly inspired by Michael Jones, a somewhat eccentric Independent minister and a stout hater of England, a party of some 150 Welsh men and women sailed from Liverpool in 1865 to the River Chabut which flows into the Atlantic about 700 miles south of Buenos Aires, and settled along its banks on land given them by the Argentine Government. Like other infant colonies—Scottish Darien, for instance—it had a hard time at the outset; it suffered grievously from drought and famine and flood; but, with the help of the Argentine and also

---

[a] As a tribute to Yale's memory one of the towers of the University is a replica of the tower of the church at Wrexham near the original home of the Yales.

of the British Government, 'Y Wladfa' survived. It is there to-day, some 80,000 strong, spreading eastwards, through Patagonia to the foothills of the Andes. But it has not fulfilled its founder's dream. Welsh Nonconformity survives, a little oasis in a Catholic world; but Welsh blood has mingled with Spanish, and the Welsh language has been forced by official decree for some time past to compete with Spanish in the schools. It has, indeed, less chance of survival in Patagonia than in present-day Wales.[59]

VI. RELIGION AND POLITICS

MORE THAN a generation passed before the national revival which started in the cultural field in the eighteen-forties acquired a political complexion. There were no real politics at all in Wales till the sixties, no national politics till the eighties.

Before the Reform Act of 1832 the working of the parliamentary system in Wales was still quasi-feudal. To a greater extent than in England the seats in the Commons were regarded as the property of the great landed families. Contested elections were rare, and, when they did occur, they were not conflicts between Whig and Tory principles but only a trial of strength between rival families. Henry Richard, M.P. for Merthyr Tydvil from 1868 to 1888, described the conduct of the electors in the days of his youth as 'less that of citizens contending for their rights than that of clansmen vehemently battling for their respective chieftains.'[60] Nor did the Reform Act make much difference. It was not till the extension of the franchise in 1867 and the emergence of Gladstonian Liberalism that the social unrest which had found vent in the Rebecca and Chartist Riots could express itself in electoral terms. In 1868 the Liberals won 21 seats, the Conservatives only 9; there were two more Conservative wins in 1874, but thenceforward until the rise of the

Labour Party the Welsh seats presented an almost unbroken Liberal front. In 1880, the Conservatives won only 2 seats, in 1885 only 3, in 1899 only 4, in 1892 only 2. The contrast with the balance of parties over the border was marked. In England the urban vote was mainly Liberal, the rural vote mainly Conservative. In Wales the Liberals were as strong in the country as in the towns.[a]

One reason for this, but not the chief reason, was the character of agrarian unrest in rural Wales. In the industrial areas the Welsh workers were on much the same footing *vis-à-vis* their employers as the English workers. The grievances of the South Welsh miners, for example, were much the same as those of the miners in Yorkshire or Durham. Trade Unionism came like Chartism from England, and the Welsh Unions were fused from the outset with the English. But in the country the status of the tenantry, as has been noticed, was lower. They were smaller and poorer men, their tenures were less secure, their rents rose as steadily and more steeply, and their conflict with their landlords—except in those few cases where the landlord was less anglicised than most of his class, took pride in his Welsh descent, spoke Welsh and took an interest in Welsh customs and traditions—was sharpened by a stronger sense of social schism. Thus, when agrarian discontent flamed up in violence, as in the 'tithe war' of the eighties, the antagonism, though incomparably less fierce than in Ireland, was fiercer than in England. And it was not only on the tenants' side. As soon as the landlords realised that their old ascendancy was in danger, they used the powers they still possessed without stint or scruple. After the Liberal victory in the elections of 1868 many tenants who had not voted, as they had always voted in the past, for their landlords' candidates, were evicted; others had their rents raised while those of loyal voters were reduced; Liberal shopkeepers were boycotted. Naturally this headstrong victimisation was not forgotten when the Ballot Act

[a] For Scotland, see pages 266, 268-9 below.

215

of 1872 enabled the tenants to vote against their landlords with impunity. And the breach thus opened was never closed. In England there were many Liberal landlords and many Conservative farmers and peasants. In Wales, the landlords put aside their old family feuds and drew together in a solid Tory *bloc* confronting an equally solid Liberal *bloc* of peasant-farmers.[a]

But the distinctive, the dominant feature of Welsh politics was not the class-conflict, agrarian or industrial; it was their association with religion. They were more than associated: they were well-nigh identified. By the end of the nineteenth century politics in Wales had become religious and religion had become political almost to the same extent as in sixteenth-century Scotland.

Ever since the eighteenth-century revival religion had been far the strongest force in most Welshmen's lives, moulding their opinions, controlling their social conduct, monopolising most of their books and newspapers, inspiring most of their poetry. Till the closing years of the Victorian age, the mainspring of Welsh thought and conduct was still to be found in chapel and Sunday School, in domestic Bible reading, in hymn singing indoors and out, in an occasional revivalist outbreak. It was a tremendous moral force which was generated in the power-house of Dissent; and, as nineteenth-century life and thought became more and more democratic, it became also a political force. For democracy was a challenge to privilege, and the most glaring example of privilege in Wales was not the squire's broad acres nor the industrialist's wealth, it was the status of the Church of England. English Nonconformists, scattered over a country which was still predominantly Anglican, might acquiesce in the historic claim of

[a] A wealth of information on agrarian conditions in Wales is to be found in the exhaustive report of the Royal Commission on Land in Wales and Monmouthshire (*Accounts and Papers*, 1896, 34). Details of the victimisation in 1868 are given in the report of the parliamentary committee appointed to investigate it.

a Church which, after all, was an English Church; but in Wales the dissenting congregations, for all their sectarian disputes, confronted the Church as a solid body supported by the great majority of the population and differing from their English brethren in their national character. An earlier chapter has shown how the Church from the time of the Reformation onwards failed to win a hold on Wales and how the growth of Nonconformity fulfilled a need which it had not met. At the opening of the nineteenth century its only chance of extending or even holding its ground was to recognise the distinctive character of Wales and to modify its policy accordingly. But this did not happen. With one or two exceptions—Thirlwall was the most notable—the rulers of the Church in Convocation and in Parliament continued to treat Wales as if it were a westward extension of England. 'Wales,' said the Bishop of St. David's in 1886, ' is at present nothing more than the Highlands of England without a Highland Line: it is a geographical expression.' [61] The most striking example of this attitude was the personnel of the episcopate. From 1715 to 1870 not a single bishop in Wales was a Welsh-speaking Welshman.[a] In a frame of mind in which such an astonishing dispensation seemed natural and proper the Church was bound to resist to the bitter end the Dissenters' plea that in Wales the Church, since it was not, as in England, the Church of the majority, ought not to enjoy the privileged position of a State-established Church. And that being so, Dissent for its part was bound to take to politics. The State had established the Church in Wales: only the State could disestablish it. From about 1870 onwards it became the supreme objective of Welsh Dissent, sustained with all the power at its command, to obtain an Act of Parliament disestablishing and disendowing the Anglican Church in Wales.

This issue transcended all others. It pervaded all Welsh life.

[a] English Thirlwall learnt Welsh well enough to preach in it. The first Welsh-speaking Welsh bishop since 1715 was Joshua Hughes who was appointed bishop of St. Asaph by Gladstone in 1870.

It deepened and embittered the class-conflict: for nearly all one side in it were Nonconformists and nearly all the other side were Anglicans. And more than anything else, more than the cultural revival, more than the educational crusade, it vivified the new consciousness of nationhood. More than anything else, too, it awakened a sense of national antagonism. The fight for Disestablishment was directly and openly a fight with Canterbury. The analogy with Knox's Scotland again holds good. Welsh religion had become not only political but also nationalist.

The conflict with the Church did more than make Dissent political; it also determined what its politics should be. Before 1843 the political opinions of the various congregations had not been by any means unanimous. The Calvinistic Methodists for the most part had stood firmly on the Right: there was much more sympathy for radical ideas and movements among the Independents and Baptists. But these differences were dwarfed by the common antagonism of all the chapels to the Church; and, when in 1843 a clause in Graham's Factory Bill offered the Church an authority it had not hitherto possessed in non-sectarian education, they instantly closed their ranks. This unity was stiffened by the ' Blue Books,' and it grew stiffer still with the growth of the demand for Disestablishment from 1870 onwards. On that issue sectarian schism was impossible, and it was, broadly speaking, as a single body that the Dissenters in due course voted the Conservative Party out of Wales.

The chief reason for their electoral choice was plain. They may not have realised how little sympathy the cause of Disestablishment would obtain in either parliamentary camp, but they believed, and rightly, that a Liberal Government was more likely to support it than a Conservative; and this belief was fortified when Gladstone, in the teeth of fierce opposition, disestablished the Church of Ireland in 1869. But there were other reasons for the leftward choice. In Wales as in England there were

ertain political causes which, because they were essentially moral
auses, made a strong appeal to the ' nonconformist conscience.'
n the domestic field it was, first and foremost, the control of the
iquor trade. In foreign affairs it was pacifism and hostility to
vhat came to be called ' jingoism ' or ' imperialism.' It is signifi-
ant that the first Welsh M.P. to acquire a reputation outside
Wales was the above-mentioned Henry Richard who was an
rdent pacifist. He was also a Welsh patriot: he was one of the
irst to challenge the indictment of the ' Blue Books,' he was in
he forefront of the educational campaign, and his championship
f Welsh interests in the House of Commons earned him the title
f 'M.P. for Wales.' But he was better known, and not in Britain
nly, as ' The Apostle of Peace.' Secretary of the Peace Society
rom 1848 to 1884, he pleaded the cause of arbitration and dis-
rmament in and out of Parliament and took a leading part in
rganising the series of Peace Congresses held at Brussels, Paris,
rankfurt and London. He was the only Welshman of his
lay whose name was known and honoured in the world at
arge.[62]

Disestablishment, agrarian and industrial reform, temperance,
pacifism, those were the causes—the first standing out above the
others—that, because they were all more likely to be favoured by
the Liberal than by the Conservative Party, drew the Welsh
Nonconformists, townsfolk and countryfolk alike, into the
Liberal fold. And before long their party allegiance was tightened
by the overpowering impact on Welsh sentiment of the Liberal
leader's personality. The admiration, the veneration, felt in
Wales as in Scotland for Gladstone in his prime was more than a
matter of politics. On the primary issue, indeed, he was out of
sympathy with the Welsh mind. Ardent champion of the Church
of England, he might ultimately be brought to acquiesce in Welsh
Disestablishment, but he was not one of those who foresaw that
the Church would be stronger when at last it ceased to be the
established Church *in* Wales and became the disestablished Church

of Wales. But Gladstone's personality transcended his politics and there was something in his appeal to the Welsh temperament that might almost be described as the ' call of the blood.' Gladstone was pure Scot, Lowland on his father's side, Highland on his mother's. So, though not a Welshman, he was at least half a Celt. And when he spoke to huge Welsh audiences, the flashing eye, the evangelistic fervour, the copious and sometimes cloudy eloquence, the wonderful voice, the relentless appeal to a moral idealism which, as his critics might have put it, defied ' the despotism of fact '—all this proclaimed the Celt and made so much the easier his conquest of Celtic hearts. That Gladstone, great as was his power in England, was still more powerful in Wales and Scotland is an interesting comment on the racial composition of the British people.

For a time, however, Gladstone's hold on Wales was not secure. As long as he hesitated to commit himself to Disestablishment, the Welsh Liberals were not fully absorbed into the Liberal Party.[a] It was an alliance rather than a merger. The Welsh Liberals were Nonconformists first and Liberals second. When the Education Act of 1870, based as it was on a compromise, failed to give them all they wanted for their schools and when, worse still, in 1871 a Welsh member's motion in favour of Disestablishment was met by Gladstone's firm refusal to treat the Church in Wales as he had so recently treated the Church in Ireland, their allegiance to the party wavered. At the elections of 1874, while the Liberals gained Merionethshire, they lost Caernarvon, Cardigan, and Carmarthen. But Gladstone's campaign against the Turks and Disraeli's new ' imperialism ' combined to restore the Liberal ascendancy, and when the ' Newcastle Programme ' of 1892 made Disestablishment the second plank of its platform, the party's hold on Wales was unshakable

[a] As late as 1890 T. E. Ellis, the leading Welsh M.P., wrote to a friend: ' I am still quite dissatisfied with the G.O.M. . . . Not one word has he said to indicate that he realises that the Church in Wales is a sore, crying grievance. No, not one word.' T. I. Ellis, *Thomas Edward Ellis* (Liverpool, etc., 1948), ii., 172.

until, as time went on, it was challenged by another party of the Left.

By 1880 the cultural revival and the religious conflict had brought Welsh nationalism back to life. But it was not yet political nationalism. The champions of Welsh education and the Welsh language were not thinking in political or constitutional terms. The Nonconformists were seeking freedom from a pre-dominantly English Church, not from a predominantly English Parliament. They were separatists only in religion. Nor is it surprising that Welsh nationalists were slow to follow the example of nationalism in other countries, to seek to give their national spirit a political body, to want some measure of national self-government. In the first place they did not feel that the participa-tion of Wales with England and Scotland in one democratic multi-national State implied the subjection of Wales. Unlike Irish or Italian or Hungarian nationalists they were not rebelling against the misrule of a foreign Government. Secondly, while, as will be seen in the next section, they shared in the keen interest aroused in England by continental nationalism, the only nationalist movement which was closely and continuously forced on their attention was the Irish, and for the cause of Irish Home Rule they felt as yet no sympathy at all. Their sense of kinship with another Celtic country had been dimmed, as has been seen, by the kind of Irish Celt which had swarmed into the Welsh labour market. It was altogether extinguished by the Irish demand for Home Rule. The spirit of John Knox was at work again. The fact that Home Rule meant Rome Rule was distasteful enough to English Anglicans: to Welsh Calvinists and their kindred it was utterly detestable. And this prejudice was hardened in Wales as in England by Irish political methods, by the black record of violence and crime. A change of attitude began when Welsh intellectuals took to reading about the Irish rebellion of 1848 and the young patriots who kindled it. But it was not till Gladstone took the stage that the Welsh people as a whole were converted to Home Rule. And the effect of his crusade was not confined to the Irish issue. When he expounded, as nobody in Britain had yet done, the meaning and the claims of Irish nationhood, he made Welshmen think about their own. Was not Wales a nation too? Though the geographical setting and the historical background were so different, had it not similar claims? Scotland had its own legal system, its own established Church, and in the administrative field a Scottish Secretary in London and a number of Scottish offices in Edinburgh. Ireland had an Irish Secretary of State and an Irish Executive at Dublin which, however unpopular, was now mainly manned by Irishmen. Wales alone had no Welsh institutions, no Welsh minister, no Welsh department. Was that the reason—the chain of thought ran on—why Welsh needs were apparently less understood and more neglected than Scottish and Irish needs, why agrarian reform in Ireland had moved so much faster than in Wales, why the generous aid to Irish and Scottish higher education had been withheld from Welsh? Could Welshmen expect better treatment as long as the only political expression of their nationhood, the only political instrument for the protection and promotion of their national interests, was an unorganised group of representatives in a Parliament in which they were outnumbered by the representatives of England, Scotland and Ireland by twenty to one? Such were the thoughts that prompted Welsh politicians to take their first steps along the Irish road.

In Scotland also (as will be recorded in the next chapter), Gladstone's Irish crusade had made Scotsmen begin to think that what seemed good for Ireland might be good for Scotland too, and the sudden emergence of national sentiment in both countries was a phenomenon that could not be ignored in England. Englishmen who had long taken the indissoluble unity of Britain for granted were reminded that Scotland was and Wales claimed to be a nation and were forced to admit that, if nationhood implied the right to some form of national self-government, the implication could not, at least in theory, be confined to Ireland. Thus the idea of 'federal devolution'[a] of dividing the United Kingdom into national provinces, each with its own legislature and executive for the conduct of its domestic affairs, and each represented in a sovereign Central Parliament and Government dealing with their common affairs—began to win the place in British political thought which, though often overshadowed and at times wellnigh forgotten, it has never lost. It was not a wholly novel idea. It had been broached in 1844 as a means of dissolving the union with Ireland; but at that time there was little understanding of what it meant and the discussion of it quickly flickered out. Much more substantial was the project of Home Rule-all-round propounded by Isaac Butt, the moderate-minded leader of the Irish Nationalists from 1870 to 1878. His primary aim was to secure or restore a separate Parliament for Ireland, but, unlike his successors he did not insist on this concession being made to Ireland first and separately. He proposed that England, Scotland and Ireland, 'united as they are under one sovereign,' should combine in a common Parliament for the conduct of their common affairs, 'while each of them should have its own . . . domestic Parliament for its internal affairs.'[63] But the time was not ripe for such revolutionary doctrine. Public opinion in the seventies in England, Scotland and Wales alike was by no means ready to concede Home Rule for Ireland and still less to contemplate a 'federal' scheme for the whole of the United Kingdom. Gladstone is a good example. His conversion to Irish Home

---

[a] None of the proposals made now or later for devolution was strictly federal. Federalism is a division of power between the Central and Provincial Parliaments and Governments. The Centre and the Province is equally self-governing in the fields allotted to them by the constitution. This is not the case in any of the devolution schemes. In all of them the Central (or Imperial) Parliament retains its sovereignty complete and unshared. The Provincial Parliaments are subordinate, not co-ordinate authorities. Their decisions can be overridden and their powers altered or annulled by the Central Parliament. The term 'federal,' however, has been so commonly applied to the devolution schemes that it seems pedantic to abstain from its use in these pages.

Rule was several years ahead. In Butt's time he opposed it, and, among other arguments, he pointed out that what was given Ireland could not logically be withheld from Scotland and Wales —a consummation which he evidently regarded at that time as almost ridiculous. ' If the doctrines of Home Rule as established in Ireland,' he said in a speech at Aberdeen in 1871 which was often uncomfortably quoted afterwards, ' I protest on your behalf that you will be just as well entitled to it in Scotland.' And it was the same, he went on, with Wales where the strength of national sentiment was manifested by the fact that far more Welshmen spoke their old Celtic language than Scotsmen or Irishmen.[64a] In that same speech, however, he showed himself aware of a problem in which the whole of the United Kingdom, and not Ireland primarily or particularly, was involved—the problem of parliamentary congestion. The British Parliament, he said, ' does a great deal more work than any other legislative assembly in the world.' And, eight years later, in the course of his Midlothian Campaign, he threw out the suggestion, as the next chapter will record, that all-round devolution might, after all, be considered not with special reference to Ireland but only as a means of easing the intolerable burden laid on Parliament.[b] It was not Gladstone, however, who brought devolution for a passing moment to the front of British politics. When, converted at last, he produced his scheme of Irish Home Rule in 1885, it was Chamberlain and his fellow Radicals who came out for all-round devolution as a more acceptable alternative. But Gladstone regarded it as falling far too short of what was needed to meet the Irish claim; and, when the crisis came and Gladstone was defeated and Irish Home Rule seemed dead, the victorious Unionists were no longer interested in alternatives.

But Irish Home Rule was not dead. Nor was devolution. The two causes had become interlinked. And now Gladstone, the Irish

---

[a] He seemed to suggest that the great majority of Welshmen spoke nothing but Welsh; but the passage may have been badly reported.

[b] See pages 296-7 below.

Home Ruler, became, honestly and naturally enough, a friend, though a somewhat tepid friend, of all-round devolution. It was an ironical reversal of his earlier attitude. In 1871 he had attacked Irish Home Rule because it might lead on to Home Rule in Britain. In 1879 he had aired the notion of Home Rule-all-round but solely as a means of relieving parliamentary congestion. But the elections of 1885 had revealed that, while the majority of Englishmen were against Home Rule for Ireland, the majority of Welshmen and Scotsmen supported it; and, though there was as yet little public demand for Welsh Home Rule and even less for Scottish, it seemed to Gladstone that, if such a demand developed, both on principle and in policy, it should not be discouraged. Home Rule for Ireland must still have priority; but Welsh and Scottish backing of it might be reinforced if it were regarded as something Wales and Scotland too, could have later on if they wanted it. Hence the theme of Gladstone's famous speech at Swansea in the summer of 1887.[65] It was a great occasion. For over four hours a host of Welshmen bearing Liberal banners marched past the old statesman. ' 12-4½,' he noted in his diary, ' the astounding procession. Sixty thousand! Then spoke for near an hour.'[66] Among the shouts of ' Home Rule for Ireland ' which greeted his rising were also some shouts of ' Home Rule for Wales '; and, after congratulating ' the most Protestant country in the whole world ' on its determination to do ' full justice to Roman Catholic Ireland,' he went on to declare that he did not agree with those Englishmen who refused to recognise Welsh nationality.[a] Wales was a nation, and if her national interests had been neglected it was because she had been too patient and too silent. ' Wales has not told her own tale. . . . It is time your representatives [in Parliament] . . . subject to the claims of imperial patriotism, laid their Welsh heads together and

[a] Early in the speech Gladstone, turning towards his wife who sat near him, claimed, though wholly Scottish, ' to speak in a certain sense as a man of Wales.' In 1840 he married Catherine Glynne, whose ancestry went far back into North Welsh history, and since eighteen he had lived at her family home at Hawarden in Flintshire.

considered what are the fair claims of Wales.' He did not know
he said, if there was any demand for Welsh Home Rule—one
voice cried ' yes '—and he left it at that. But the purport of all
he had said was unmistakable. It was a direct encouragement of
Welsh nationalism. It was an invitation to Welsh politicians to
form, if not a Welsh parliamentary party, at least a Welsh cabal.
It was an intimation that, if Wales wanted Home Rule and could
make a good case for it, she ought to have it.[a]

VII. YOUNG WALES

In Wales as in England the nineteenth-century concept of
nationalism had become familiar long before Gladstone's speech
at Swansea. It came from continental Europe by way of Ireland.
The writings of Thomas Davis, leader of Young Ireland from
1842 till his early death in 1845, were widely read, and taught
Welsh readers not only about the idealistic side of Irish nationalism,
but also much they had not known before about nationalism on
the Continent. This knowledge was deepened by William Rees,
better known as Gwilym Hiraethog, who in the column of his
newspaper, *Yr Amserau*, and in the popular lectures delivered all
over Wales so impressed Welsh sentiment that Mazzini, Garibaldi
and especially Kossuth were heroes in Wales at least as much as in
England.[67] But the Welsh were slow to apply the moral to themselves. They sympathised with Italians and Hungarians struggling
against oppression: they learned in time to admit the claims of
Irishmen; but they did not feel—why should they?—that Wales
likewise was a subject nation needing freedom. As early as 1846,
it is true, Hiraethog, who corresponded with Mazzini, proposed
in *Yr Amserau* that the Welsh M.P.s should ' resolve themselves

[a] John Bright, who had parted from Gladstone over Home Rule, sharply criticised
this speech. Why, he asked, had Gladstone ignored the claims of Ulster, which had a
population 300,000 greater than Wales, while he treated Wales to ' a flattery which, if
not insincere, seems to me childish.' *Annual Register*, 1887, 105-7.

into a united Welsh party,'[68] but his was a lonely voice and nobody seems to have listened to it. In 1868 a wider and more lasting movement began in the South, and, aided by the growing heat of the religious conflict and the outbreak of the ' tithe-war,' spread gradually northwards into rural Wales. But it lacked effective leadership till in the eighties two remarkable young Welshmen, Thomas Edward Ellis and David Lloyd George, made their appearance on the political stage.

Ellis was born in 1859 on a Merionethshire farm of purely North Welsh stock. From schooling at Bala he went on to the recently founded Aberystwyth College and thence to New College, Oxford, where in the course of obtaining a degree, he was captivated by the writings of Mazzini[a] and Thomas Davis, and became an ardent nationalist. A short apprenticeship as a political private-secretary and journalist prepared his path to politics. In 1886 he stood as Liberal candidate for Merionethshire and won. Like all Welsh Liberals he put Disestablishment at the head of his programme; but he already differed from most of his colleagues in believing that the way to get Welsh wishes met was the Irish way, and he began his election address—' I solicit your suffrages as a WELSH NATIONALIST.'[69] A few months later he became the first president of the Cymru Fydd (Wales of the Future), a society which was formed in London in 1887 and soon spread its branches over Wales. The ' Young Wales ' movement it embodied, like its forerunner, Davis' ' Young Ireland,' was nationalist in all respects. It wholeheartedly supported the cultural revival. A national literature, inspired by Welsh history and tradition, was one of the instruments which, as Ellis put it, would prove that Wales ' had not finished her course ' and make her again, ' as she was in days gone by, a power among the nations of the world.'[70] But ' the chief aim and purpose ' of Cymru

[a] His devotion to Mazzini outlasted his youth. On a holiday in the Austrian Alps in 1899 he climbed the Stelvio and wrote: ' We reached the top of the Pass and stood opposite the marble which marks the boundary between Austria and free Italy, and we blessed and blessed again the work and memory of Joseph Mazzini.' T. I. Ellis, ii, 91.

Fydd, ran a manifesto of 1888, was 'to facilitate the attainment of a National Legislature for Wales, with full control over all purely Welsh business, and a Welsh Executive responsible to it and the Imperial Parliament where Wales would still be represented.'[71] This was a somewhat amateurish conception of devolution—for how could an executive be responsible to two legislatures?—but its intent was no more than devolutionary: it was not in the least separatist. Cymru Fydd, said one of its adherents in an exposition of its aims in 1894, was not mad enough to dream of reviving Welsh independence. ' It is recognised not only that union with England is inevitable, but that it provides the best opportunity that Wales could have to deliver her mission—if mission she has—to the world. The one condition that is insisted upon is that the connection shall not be made closer at the expense of Welsh nationality.'[72]

No one responded more eagerly than Ellis to Gladstone's Swansea speech, and he succeeded in persuading some, but by no means all, of the twenty-eight Welsh Liberals in the Commons to regard themselves, like most of the Irish members, as an independent party, ready to vote against Liberals as well as Tories. And certainly his little group were neither silent nor patient. They constantly intervened in debate, and in the discussion of the Tithes Bill of 1891, they even outdid the Irishmen in the technique of obstruction. But as long as the Tories were in office, it was useless to pursue Cymru Fydd's ' chief aim and purpose.' Quadrilateral Home Rule was no more practical politics than bilateral. But, if nothing could be done at the high ' federal ' level, the debates on the Local Government Bill in 1888 provided an opportunity of trying to do something at the level of local government. The system established by the Bill was a uniform system for all Britain, but it could be given, so to speak, a national twist, and to that end Ellis moved an amendment proposing that an advisory Welsh Council should be set up to supervise the operation of the new machinery in Wales. Such a Council, the amendment ran on—driving in the thin end of the wedge—could lighten the increasing pressure of business on the House of Commons by discussing such questions as education, fisheries, crown lands and public works in Wales and so become—the wedge was driven home—' a real, solid and effective measure of decentralisation.'[73] But the House, it need hardly be said, did not favour this insidious approach to national devolution, and the amendment was withdrawn. The Act as passed, however, contained a section[a] which, though not nationalist in its intention, could be put to nationalist use. Joint Committees of County Councils might be formed ' for any purpose in respect of which they are jointly interested.' The Welsh Home Rulers decided to take advantage of this opening and at a conference at Shrewsbury at the end of 1891 a Joint Committee was actually formed ' to confer upon matters of interest to the Counties and County Councils of Wales .'[74] Earlier in that year, the attempt to build some sort of national structure on the new County system had been put into legislative shape. A National Institutions (Wales) Bill was introduced in the Commons by Alfred Thomas (M.P. for Glamorgan E., and afterwards Lord Pontypridd), with the backing of Ellis, Lloyd George and seven other Welsh members. Adopting and elaborating the proposals of Ellis' amendment, the Bill authorised the setting up of a National Council for Wales representing the sixteen Welsh counties and county borough councils to ' discuss and inquire into such matters as they shall deem of common interest to Wales.' More than that, the Council was empowered to pass legislative measures ' in the nature of private bills ' concerned with Welsh public works. More still, a Welsh Education Department was to be established which would do the work at that time done in Wales by the Board of Education and would be authorised, in particular, to make regulations for the teaching of Welsh in schools. To crown this devolutionary system, a Secretary for Wales was to be appointed to take over

[a] 51-52 Vic. cap. 41, section 81.

the functions of most of the existing departments of Government 'so far as they relate to Wales.' Two conferences were held at Llandrindod Wells to discuss this Bill, and early in 1892 it was reintroduced in an amended form, again by Alfred Thomas but this time with seventeen backers. The National Council was now to consist of elected representatives of each parliamentary constituency in Wales as well as the representatives of the County and county borough councils. Most of the administrative functions transferred under the first Bill to the Secretary for Wales were now to be vested in the Council or in a Local Government Board for Wales responsible to the Council. The cost of the Council, which in the first version of the Bill was to be borne by the local councils, was now to be defrayed by Parliament.

These proposals offered Wales more national autonomy than Scotland possessed but far less than Gladstone wanted to give Ireland. They were nothing like Home Rule. Nor were they an essay in federalism. The Council was to be a deliberative but, save only for private legislation, not a legislative body. The Bills, in fact, were mainly measures, and somewhat clumsy measures, of administrative devolution. But, however well they had been drafted, nothing could have come of them. They were dropped as soon as introduced. They were, in fact, no more than a gesture, a demonstration that a body of Welsh opinion wanted a measure of national self-government and had begun to think out its practical implications.

Though nothing concrete was achieved and though, despite his great prestige in Wales, Ellis had failed to rally more than a fraction of Welsh opinion to the cause of Welsh Home Rule, he believed—and the young enthusiasts of Cymru Fydd believed with him—that its ultimate triumph was assured. In acknowledging a national testimonial in the autumn of 1890, 'The great current of the time,' he said, 'is sweeping to nationalism. Wales in throwing in her lot with Ireland in the Home Rule struggle has struck a blow not only for the national rights of another Celtic country but also for her own.' The awakening of a new national spirit, he went on, is manifested in the fight for the land, in the tithe-war, in the educational campaign, in the new interest in the Welsh language and literature. ' But over and above all that, we shall work for a legislature elected by the manhood and womanhood of Wales and to them responsible. It will be the symbol and cement of our unity as a nation, our instrument in working out our social ideals . . . the deliverer of our message and example to humanity.'[75] A fine oration in the Mazzini style, but over-sanguine. Thirty years later Ireland was still without Home Rule, and fifty years later the cause of political nationalism in Wales, as in Scotland, was still regarded by most Englishmen as an idle dream.

It was soon apparent that for Welsh nationalism, at any rate, the current was running the wrong way. When, in the autumn of 1891, the Liberal Party committed itself at last to Welsh Disestablishment, and in the ' Newcastle programme ' ranked it second only to Irish Home Rule, they robbed the nationalists of their argument that Disestablishment could only be achieved by an independent Welsh party on the Irish model. Such disloyalty to the Liberal Party was now, it seemed, as needless as it was unpleasant. The next setback to the nationalists was the loss of their leader. When the Liberals came back to power in 1892, Gladstone offered Ellis the ministerial post of Junior Whip; and, convinced after searching thought that he could better serve the interests of Wales inside the Government than outside, he accepted it. Gladstone was not ungrateful: he appointed the Land Commission in 1892 and gave the University its charter in 1893; but he spent most of what strength he still had on the second Home Rule Bill, and it was not, as will be seen, till after his retirement in the spring of 1894 that a Welsh Disestablishment Bill was introduced.

Ellis was promoted to be Chief Whip in the Rosebery Government, and after its fall he continued to take a leading part in the counsels of the Liberal Party till his premature death in 1899. He was a Welsh nationalist to the end, but he was an honest man, and after 1892 he was a Liberal first and a nationalist second.[a] For that reason alone—and there were many others— the title of ' The Parnell of Wales ' given by some of his followers in the brief heyday of his fame proved to be an almost ludicrous misnomer.[b]

It has been suggested that, if Ellis had chosen otherwise, if he had persuaded all the Welsh Liberal members to follow him in demanding ' Home Rule-all-round,' Gladstone, with a majority of only forty, would have been forced to yield. But that is a more than usually idle speculation. For the Irish Nationalists, who numbered eighty-one, would certainly have voted Gladstone out of office if he had broken faith with them and held up Home Rule for Ireland in order to fit it into a quadrilateral system for the United Kingdom.

VIII. LLOYD GEORGE

THE LEADERSHIP of Welsh nationalism, vacated by Ellis's election to the Ministry, was assumed, in fact, if not yet in form, by the youngest and most brilliant of his former comrades. Like Ellis, Lloyd George was of humble country stock, originating on his father's side in Pembroke, on his mother's in Caernarvon. He was born in 1863 at Manchester, and, on his father's death in the following year, he was taken by his mother to the little village of Llanistumdwy near Criccieth. He went, when he was old enough, to the local National School whose master was, as it happened, an unusually gifted teacher; but, as the boy grew up,

[a] Campbell-Bannerman said at his death: ' He was the most perfectly honest and loyal of men.' Ellis, ii. 298.

[b] Of the complete contrast in personality as well as in political methods and manners it is enough to say that Ellis was known in the House and not only among Welsh M.P.s as ' Our Tom.' Not even his Irish followers would have wanted or dared to call Parnell ' Our Charlie '!

he obtained a wider and deeper education from his uncle, Richard Lloyd, the intellectual village cobbler and a man of remarkable strength of character and singleness of mind. He had been thoroughly grounded in the Welsh Nonconformist tradition when he began his career as a solicitor at Portmadoc; and he soon acquired a more than local reputation as an outspoken champion of tenants and tithepayers in the courts. His interest in politics developed early. Readers of the *North Wales Express* would have been surprised to learn that the lofty denunciations of Toryism, which appeared in its columns under the name of ' Brutus,' had been written by a youth of seventeen.[76] He was soon taking part in political debates. The first of his speeches to be reported—he was then nineteen—was an attack on Irish landlordism and the second an attack on the British occupation of Egypt. A chance meeting with Michael Davitt in 1886 won him to the cause of Irish nationalism and a little later he first met Ellis and at once became his friend and follower. In the course of the next few years the younger man became known throughout the country as a more eloquent, more high-spirited, more combatant spokesman of young Wales than his gentler leader. At a great Liberal meeting at Liverpool in 1889 he claimed that Welsh nationalism was not anti-Liberal; it was ' Liberal enthusiasm worked up to a glowing red by the blasts of patriotism.'[77] At Cardiff in the following year he claimed as full a measure of Home Rule for Wales as that which was offered to Ireland, and pointed out that all the arguments for Irish Home Rule applied to Wales and none of the objections. Wales had no Ulster problem. Welsh politics were not stained with crime. Nor in the Welsh claim to self-government was there the faintest tinge of separatism. He closed his speech with the demand that in the world-wide conflict between right and wrong Wales should no longer serve as ' the standard-bearer of another nation,' but do battle for the right under her own Red Dragon as of old. A self-governing Wales would hold up before other nations the example of ' a people who had driven oppression from their hillsides and initiated the glorious reign of freedom, justice and truth.'[78] Heady stuff, perhaps, but potent at election time. Two months later the young patriot—he was still only twenty-seven—snatched from its age-long masters, by the margin of eighteen votes, the Tory strong-hold of Caernarvon Boroughs.[a]

He quickly made his mark in the House of Commons, and, when he took Ellis' place, it was soon clear that the Government now had to deal with a more militant, more unruly spokesman of Welsh claims. When there were signs of wavering and delay over Disestablishment, Lloyd George and three of his Welsh colleagues resolved that, if the Government continued to evade the fulfilment of its promise, they would snap the ties of party discipline and vote against them. They did not force the issue so long as Gladstone, whom Lloyd George regarded as ' the biggest political figure in our history '[79] mainly because of his unselfish championship of subject nations, was in office, but immediately after his retirement in the spring of 1894 they openly rebelled. They still stood alone however; the other Welsh Liberals refused to break with their party, and it was probably due to Ellis' influence with ministers that a Disestablishment Bill was at last introduced. It passed its second reading in April 1895, but, while it was in committee, the Rosebery Government was suddenly defeated on a relatively trivial issue and resigned. At the subsequent elections the Liberals lost only six of their twenty-eight Welsh seats, but in the United Kingdom as a whole the Tories obtained a majority of 152. For the next twenty years Disestablishment remained with other Liberal causes on the shelf.

At the outset of his long years in opposition Lloyd George attempted to rally the surviving Liberals, weary of the Irish fight which had broken the party and brought it to defeat, to the less

---

[a] Lloyd George retained his seat till, a few months before his death in 1945, he went to the House of Lords.

desperate policy of quadrilateral Home Rule. For five years the Scottish nationalist M.P.s had kept the idea alive, insisting in a series of resolutions that whatever was done for Ireland must be done for Scotland also;[a] and in 1894 the recurrent motion for Scottish Home Rule had been supported for the first time by a Welshman, Herbert Lewis (Flint). Welsh legislation, he had argued, was as much obstructed as Scottish, and, if Scotland had Home Rule, Wales must have it too.[80] The motion was carried by 180 votes to 170. In the following year, when, owing perhaps to Lewis' intervention, the Scottish resolution was expanded to cover Home Rule-all-round, it was seconded by Lloyd George. Welsh nationalism, he contended, was moderate and reasonable. Wales had no desire whatever to be an independent republic; but it suffered like Scotland from parliamentary congestion and delay. This was familiar ground, but he made one new point. Home Rule-all-round, he said, would ' foster the spirit of local patriotism,' the spirit to which the British Army had so successfully appealed in raising its Welsh and Scottish regiments. . . .[81] This time the motion was defeated by 128 to 102. But Lloyd George persisted. Early in 1896 he convoked a meeting at the House of Commons to discuss it. There was little hostility but no enthusiasm; nor had any been awakened when, in 1898, Herbert Roberts (Denbigh) introduced another resolution for ' Home Rule-all-round.' He made a forcible reply to Balfour's charge that devolution would be fatal to the unity of the United Kingdom and the British Empire. 'That view,' he said, ' is entirely wrong. I speak, as I have a right to speak, on behalf of Wales, and I say that there is no portion of the United Kingdom which is prouder of the British Empire than Wales.' In his plea for domestic self-government there was not ' the shadow of a desire to impair the supreme authority of this Parliament or to advance one single step along the road to separation.'[82] It was wasted breath. Not enough Welsh or Scottish members had

[a] See page 300 below.

attended the debate to prevent the House from being counted out

There was only one way to overcome such indifference Gladstone's question at Swansea must be answered. Parliament must be shown that, whatever Scotland thought, Wales at any rate *did* want Home Rule. So, for the next two or three years Lloyd George continued to preach devolution in Wales. And, like the Scottish nationalists before him, he argued the case for it on wider ground than national needs alone. Social reform for the United Kingdom as a whole, he declared, even if the Liberals were in office, would be gravely obstructed and delayed by the congestion of parliamentary business. ' Parliament,' he said, ' is at least thirty years in arrears.' The recognition and redress of social evils, moreover, in every part of the country needed closer contact with the facts than Westminster could provide. He wanted ' local Parliaments ' to serve as ' so many searchlights to flash into all the dark places in the land.'[83] Cymru Fydd responded, but that was not enough, and for many months Lloyd George strove to bring the whole body of Welsh Liberalism into line with Cymru Fydd. But to persuade the old-established party organisations to merge their independence in a cause which, whatever its merits, was not an official ' party plank ' was a formidable task. In North Wales Lloyd George finally succeeded, but in South Wales he failed, mainly owing to the opposition of one strong man. D. A. Thomas, the coal magnate, one day to become Lord Rhondda, was an ardent Welsh Liberal. He had been one of the rebel four. But, while he was hot for Disestablishment, he did not want Home Rule. It was not only a matter of personal rivalry, not only that he disliked the idea of the South Wales Liberal Federation of which he had long been president being merged in a wider organisation which was seemingly to be headed by Lloyd George. His attitude reflected the old split between North and South. Year after year, the process of anglicisation had been steadily continuing in the great industrial belt. More and more Englishmen were settling there. More and more Welshmen, even in the mining valleys, were speaking English. Commercial and financial ties were being strengthened. Cardiff and Swansea were drawing still nearer to London. The desire for Welsh self-government was bound, therefore, to be weaker there than in the less industrial, less anglicised North; and Thomas was only one of many South Welshmen who turned their backs on Cymru Fydd. The breach was fatal to the nationalist cause. After 1898 Young Wales collapsed as quickly as Young Ireland after 1848.

Lloyd George could fight for a losing cause—and retrieve it —but not for a lost one. And he had already begun to think that the things he wanted for Wales—Disestablishment and social reform—might after all be more easily obtained by a united British Liberal party than by an independent Welsh one. Disestablishment could not be brought about by devolution: it would rest with the United Kingdom Parliament, and the only way to get it was to break the veto of the House of Lords. As to social reform, Lloyd George's horizon had been widening during the last few years. Hitherto he had known little of life beyond the bounds of Wales, but the repute he had won as a Liberal speaker had carried him to public platforms far afield, and he had discovered that the English poor were suffering from the same grievances as the Welsh and that the measures required to remedy them were likewise the same. Why, then, should English and Welsh reformers fight separate battles? Why not fight together and share the gains? Such were the reflections which were gradually converting the greatest Welshman of the age from a Welsh politician into a British statesman.

This process was confirmed by his opposition to the South African War (1899-1902). There was a Welsh colour in it; for Wales was a small nation, with an historic tradition of fighting for freedom, and Wales, like the little Boer Republics, was a land of farmers. But most of Lloyd George's campaign was fought in England, and he emerged from the ordeal—an ordeal on which his whole career and once, maybe, his life itself had been at stake —as the most eloquent and forceful leader not of Welsh pro-Boers only but of all the British Radicals. It was the same when, on the morrow of the war, he took the lead against the Education Act of 1902 both in Parliament and in the country. Again his opposition was salted with nationalism: for Nonconformists resented the payment of rates for the upkeep of Anglican schools more fiercely in Wales than in England because they regarded the Church in Wales as a 'foreign' Church. But again it was a question of principle which knew no frontiers; and the English Nonconformist conscience was at one with the Welsh. Thus, when in 1906 the Liberals returned at last to power in unprecedented strength, it was not as a favour to Wales that Lloyd George was given office in Campbell-Bannerman's Government. He no more went to the Board of Trade because he was a Welshman than his chief went to 10 Downing Street because he was a Scotsman.

Five years later he could claim that his choice of the best way to serve Wales had been justified. He had launched his great programme of social reform from which Welshmen were to benefit equally with Englishmen and Scotsmen. He had brought Disestablishment again to the front, and no independent nationalist could have championed it with greater force and fervour. 'To insist,' he said, ' on treating a faith which the Welsh people do not accept as if it were their national creed . . . is the most intolerable of all oppressions.' Promoted to the Exchequer in the Asquith Government, he had led the attack on the Lords with a Celtic fire that shocked Mayfair and delighted Limehouse, and had framed the famous budget which precipitated the constitutional crisis and led through two elections to the Parliament Act of 1911. In 1909 Asquith had again introduced a Welsh Disestablishment Bill, and after 1911 the Lords could not kill it, they could only delay its enactment. It received the royal assent in September 1914, but, war having broken out, it was accompanied by an Act suspending its operation for a year or till the war ended. . . . Could more, could as much, have been achieved for Wales if Lloyd George had persisted in a fight for Welsh Home Rule which he could not possibly have won?

Home Rule-all-round, it is true, had by no means faded out of politics. On the contrary, public interest in it had been steadily growing since the early years of the century. The theme of parliamentary congestion and of 'federal' devolution as the most effective means of relief was often ventilated at public meetings and in the Press. But the problem of congestion by itself would not have brought 'federalism' to the front of the political stage. It was Ireland that put it there. When Irish affairs came again to a crisis, when the Parliament Act was passed, and when in 1912 the third Home Rule Bill was introduced with the knowledge that this time the House of Lords could only hold back its enactment for three years, then 'federal' devolution was vigorously canvassed, but not so much now because it would relieve congestion as because it offered the only hope of agreement on Ireland between the conflicting parties whose antagonism had now become even fiercer than it had been in 1885. It was, in fact, a revival, in similar, if graver, circumstances, of Joseph Chamberlain's 'alternative' policy. But it could no more be made a basis of agreement from 1911 onwards than in 1885. The Liberal Party, it is true, were now committed to the 'federal' principle. When Asquith introduced the Home Rule Bill, it was intended, he declared, to be the first instalment of Home Rule-all-round— 'the first step and only the first step in a more comprehensive policy . . . the emancipation of the Imperial Parliament from local cares and local burdens.'[84] But that, of course, was not acceptable to the Conservatives. Still Unionists-all-round, some of their more moderate leaders might be willing to contemplate the possibility of a 'federal' scheme but only if Ireland were not given priority or special treatment but classed with England,

Scotland and Wales in a single and more or less symmetrical act of 'federation.' The discussion, however, continued on the platform and in the Press. Among the protagonists were T. A. B. Brassey (afterwards second Earl Brassey), Liberal M.P. for Hastings, who continued the personal campaign begun in 1906 in favour of a 'federal' United Kingdom as an essential prelude to Imperial Federation, and J. Murray Macdonald, Liberal M.P. for Stirling, who expounded, more clearly than anyone else, the case for devolution as a means of relieving congestion. As the Irish situation worsened, many other publicists joined in the discussion, till there was scarcely a number of any of the chief reviews which did not contain an article on the ' federal solution.'[a] The most influential of these writers was F. S. Oliver. A Conservative whose celebrated life of Alexander Hamilton had made him an authority on federalism and who was closely acquainted with some of those moderate leaders of his party, he published a series of letters in *The Times* in 1910 under the *nom de plume* of ' Pacificus.' They were an eloquent and reasonable plea for a non-party ' federal ' settlement, and the book in which they were reprinted in 1911, *Federalism and Home Rule*, was widely read. But discussion, however sober, and argument, however non-partisan, were of no avail.

Meantime the Scottish and Welsh nationalists, who were more interested in obtaining Home Rule for themselves than in obtaining agreement on Home Rule for Ireland, continued their campaign in Parliament. The Scottish Liberals had put devolution on their programme in 1908 and subsequently introduced a number of Home Rule Bills and resolutions.[b] The Welsh Liberals for their part were content to speak and vote for Scottish motions till in 1914 they followed the lead given by the Government of Scotland Bill in the previous year and introduced a

[a] See, for example, articles by J. A. R. Marriott in the *Nineteenth Century*, Nov., 1911, and May, 1912; Lord Charnwood, *ibid.*, April, 1913; Lord Dunraven, *ibid.*, June, 1907; Nov., 1913, and June, 1914; and unsigned articles in the *Round Table*.

[b] See pages 304-6 below.

Government of Wales Bill. It was fathered by E. T. John, the member for Denbigh, a Middlesbrough industrialist and a zealous, if somewhat uninspiring, Welsh patriot. His Bill embodied a full-scale 'federal' scheme. Wales was to have a single-chamber Parliament of ninety-five members and a Government consisting of a Lord President, representing the King, and an Executive Committee composed of the ministerial heads of Welsh Departments. Parliament would have power to legislate for Wales except in those matters which had been reserved to the control of the United Kingdom Parliament in the Irish Home Rule Bill, and to levy any taxes in Wales other than customs duties. But this wide measure of devolution was not to affect the sovereign legal authority of the United Kingdom Parliament 'over all persons, matters and things in Wales,' and the existing thirty-four Welsh seats therein were to be retained 'until English affairs are dealt with by an English legislature.'[85] John introduced the Bill on March 11, 1914, with a short speech in which he pointed out that the principle of separating the management of Welsh affairs from that of English had already been conceded in such institutions as the Central Welsh Board and the Welsh Department of the Board of Education.[86] The Bill was read a first time, but not a second. The war had already begun, and nothing more was to be heard of devolution for a time.

When, just a century after Waterloo, the cause of freedom in the world was challenged again, all minor loyalties in Britain were merged once more in the sense of common citizenship in a Commonwealth which, true to the British tradition, took the lead in resistance to aggressive Continental militarism. Once more the English, Welsh and Scots did 'great things together.' But the Welsh who fought Wilhelm II were different from the Welsh who fought Napoleon. For the intervening century had seen the growth of a nationalist movement which had failed in the political field but succeeded in the cultural. Wales was now

Welsh and Scottish Nationalism

conscious of its nationhood. And this consciousness was strengthened by the character of the war. The Austrian attack on Serbia and the German invasion of Belgium had made the freedom of small nations the first of the issues for which the Allies fought; and Lloyd George could bid his fellow Welshmen remember how much the world has owed to ' the little five-foot-five nations.'[87] And this feeling among Welshmen that the world-war was in a special sense their war was immensely enhanced when a Welshman assumed the main direction of it. The coming of yet another world war and another great war leader has dimmed the memory of the paramount place which Lloyd George held for a few decisive years in the conduct of the British war effort and the councils of free Europe. But in fact his power and prestige from 1917 to 1920 were comparable with Churchill's from 1940 to 1945. He exercised, like his great successor, the kind of democratic dictatorship which the British parliamentary system permits in an emergency. And this kindled in his fellow-countrymen, irrespective of class or party, the same sort of pride, though now far more consciously national, as their ancestors had felt when Henry Tudor won the English crown on Bosworth Field.

[1] Dodd, 269, 277. E. J. Jones, *Some Contributions to the Economic History of Wales* (London, 1928). C. P. Gasquoine, *The Story of the Cambrian* (Oswestry, 1922).
[2] D. Williams, 105, 115.
[3] *Report of the Commissioners of Inquiry into the State of Education in Wales* (A. & P., 1847, vol. 27), Pt. i, 4-5.
[4] A. H. Dodd, 399-400.
[5] D. Williams, *Modern Wales*, 230.
[6] N. Edwards, *The Industrial Revolution in South Wales* (London, 1924), 95-100.
[7] *Ibid.*, 240.
[8] D. Williams, *Modern Wales*, 237.
[9] D. Williams, 340.
[10] *Ibid.*, 154.
[11] *Report of the Commissioners of Inquiry for S. Wales* (A. & P., 1844, xvi), Q. 1754.
[12] 5 and 6 W. IV, cap. 50.
[13] *Report of the Commissioners of Inquiry for Wales*, p. 2.
[14] *Annual Register*, 1843, 257-263.
[15] Full description in H. T. Evans, *op. cit.* Outline in *Annual Register* as cited above.
[16] *Report* (as cited above), Pt. ii, 65.
[17] *The Times*, Sept. 6, 1843.
[18] H. T. Evans, 30.

[19] Sept. 6, 1843.

[20] *Hansard*, H. of C., 1846, v. 84. c. 848.

[21] *Report of the Commissioners of Inquiry into the State of Education in Wales: Accounts and Papers*,1847, vol. 27, pt. i, 33.

[22] *Report*, pt. i, 3.

[23] *Ibid.*, pt. ii, 66.

[24] *Ibid.*, pt. iii, 61.

[25] *Ibid.*, pt. ii, 66.

[26] *Ibid.*, pt. ii, 66.

[27] *Ibid.*, pt. iii, 330-31. An interesting note on the Eistedfoddau.

[28] *Ibid.*, pt. iii, 59-60.

[29] *Ibid.*, pt. ii, 66-7; pt. iii, 61.

[30] *Ibid.*, pt. iii, 61.

[31] *Ibid.*, pt. i, 6.

[32] *Ibid.*, pt. i, 7.

[33] *Ibid.*, pt. i, 7.

[34] *Ibid.*, pt. iii, 59, 64.

[35] *Ibid.*, pt. i, 4.

[36] *Ibid.*, pt. iii, 59.

[38] *Ibid.*, pt. i, 5.

[38] *Ibid.*, pt. iii, 63.

[39] Crewe, *Life of Rosebery* (London, 1931), 469-70.

[40] *Report of the Committee on Intermediate and Higher Education in Wales*, A. and P. 1881, xxxiii, 46-7.

[41] *Ibid.*, 67.

[42] T. I. Ellis, 22.

[43] K. V. Jones, *Life of John Viriamu Jones* (London, 1915), 111.

[44] *Ibid.*, 293.

[45] H. I. Bell, *The Development of Welsh Poetry* (Oxford, 1936), 148-159.

[46] R. C. K. Ensor, *England*, 1870-1914 (Oxford, 1936), 335-6.

[47] H. I. Bell, 154-5.

[48] I. Jones, 261-2

[49] *The Study of Celtic Literature* (popular ed. 1891, reprinted 1929), x-xiii, 10-11, 15, 85-93, 148, 152.

[50] D. Williams, *John Frost*, 165 and *passim*.

[51] *Welsh in Education and Life* (cited p. 204n. above),75-6.

[52] *Ibid.*, 76.

[53] *Report*, iii, 19. *Education in Wales*, 1843-1947, 17.

[54] *Aberdare Report*, 47.

[55] *Welsh in Education and Life*, 71.

[56] *Ibid.*, 87.

[57] These paragraphs are based on D. Williams' authoritative study *Cymru ac America* (*Wales and America*), Cardiff, 1946.

[58] D. Williams, *op. cit.*, 49.

[59] *Ibid.*, 274-5.

[60] *Letters on the Social and Political Condition of the Principality* (London, 1876), 80. Quoted by D. Williams, *John Frost*, 6.

[61] W. Watkin Davies, *Lloyd George*, 1863-1914 (London, 1939), 116.

[62] C. S. Miall, *Henry Richard* (London, 1889).

[63] *Home Government for Ireland. Irish Federalism, its Meaning, its Objects and its Hopes* (London, 1874), 16.

[64] *The Times*, Sept. 27, 1871.

[65] *The Times*, June 6, 1887.

[66] J. Morley, *Life of Gladstone* (London, 1903), iii. 386.

[67] D. Williams, *A History of Modern Wales*, 274.

[68] March 26, 1846, cited by T. Evans, *The Background of Modern Welsh Politics* (London, 1936), 230.

[69] T. I. Ellis, ii. 42.

[70] W. Watkin Davies, *Lloyd George*, 73-4.

[71] E. L. Chappell, *Wake up, Wales!* (London, 1943), 22.

[72] W. L. Williams, *Cymru Fydd: its aims and objects* (Cardiff, 1894).

[73] *Hansard* (April 13, 1888), cccxxiv, 1249.

[74] Chappell, 25.

[75] J. V. Morgan, *Welsh Political and Educational Leaders in the Victorian Era* (London, 1908), 395.

[76] M. Thomson, *David Lloyd George* (London, 1949), 61-2.

[77] *Ibid.*, 83-4.

[78] H. Du Parcq, *Life of David Lloyd George* (London, 1912-14), i. 87-9.

[79] T. Jones, *Lloyd George* (Oxford, 1951), 276.

[80] *Hansard*, 1894, vol. 22, col. 1300.

[81] *Hansard*, 1895, vol. 32, col. 531-4.

[82] *Hansard*, 1898, vol. 54, col. 1690.

[83] T. Jones, 34.

[84] *Hansard*, H. of C., 1912, vol. 36, col. 1403.

[85] Text of the Bill and explanatory memorandum in A. and P., 1914, iii, 69.

[86] *Hansard*, 1914, v. 59, col. 1235-8.

[87] Speech to a Welsh gathering in London, Sept. 19, 1914. *The Times*, Sept. 20.

PART SIX

Scotland
in the Nineteenth Century

Nationalism in Scotland is rooted in the same broad facts and ideas as in Wales; but geography and history have given it a different character. Scotland is more than four times the size of Wales, its present population more than twice as great. And the most densely populated area in Scotland is much farther away from the centres of English wealth and power than the corresponding area in Wales. Glasgow is about fifty miles farther than Cardiff from Manchester, ninety miles farther from Birmingham, 180 miles farther from London. Modern transport, it is true, has transformed the meaning of distance, but it has not, as the saying goes, 'annihilated' it; and before the railways were built it was easier for an Englishman to find work and a new home in Wales where the industrial belt lay just across the border than in Scotland where some fifty miles of agrarian uplands intervened. Thus the life of Lowland Scotland was less exposed than that of South Wales to English immigration and anglicisation. But geographic or demographic factors in the shaping of Scottish nationalism were far outweighed by the force of history. At the outset of the nineteenth century it was less than the span of two men's lives since Scotland had been a national State with a great and unbroken tradition as old as England's, whereas such imperfect and transient

245

Statehood as the Welsh had once possessed had disappeared long before the eighteenth century. It was that historical fact, far more than the relative smallness of Wales, that made it possible for Englishmen ill-acquainted with Welsh life to question whether Wales was really a nation. No one has ever had any doubts about the reality of Scottish nationhood.

I. SCOTT'S LAST YEARS

IN WALES, as has been seen, the anglicised and anglicising element in society was the Tory upper class, and the revival of Welsh nationalism, when it came, was mainly the work of middle-class Liberals. In Scotland it was the other way about. For the Tory noble houses and the landed gentry, with their memories of the rôle their ancestors had played on the stage of history when Scotland was a Stewart kingdom, it was a matter of family pride to exalt the past, to cling to tradition, to seek to save what remained of Scottish ways of life and speech from the insidious pressure of English influence. It was the Whigs, the Hanoverians, the party led by the professional middle class who were the anglicisers, the assimilationists, in Scotland. To the intellectuals of the *Edinburgh Review* the traditional idiosyncrasies of Scottish life seemed out-moded, rustic, provincial. Jeffery, it was said in Tory circles, had 'lost his broad Scotch and acquired narrow English.'[1] But on one point the nationalism which had survived in Scotland and the nationalism which presently revived in Wales were wholly unaffected by differences of class or party. Neither betrayed the faintest tinge of separatism. Not for a very long time, not indeed till our own day, did anyone in either country question the necessity of a united Britain.

Scott in his prime has already been cited as the outstanding example of what Scottish nationalism meant both in its depth of feeling and in its practical good sense. It was the same to the end of his life. It was Scott, for instance, who brought about the visit of George IV to Edinburgh in 1822 and arranged and presided over the pageantry at Holyrood which, with its elaborate ceremonial and its rich display of kilt and tartan, bore witness to the ' Wizard's ' minute and loving knowledge of the old romantic Scotland of the Stewarts. But Scott—and all Edinburgh ' society' with him—rendered the Hanoverian a genuine homage such as he could scarcely have obtained in London so soon after the scandal of his Queen's trial. In 1826, on the other hand, when a bill was introduced at Westminster which *inter alia* forbade the Scottish banks to continue their old-established custom of issuing £1 notes, he was roused to a passionate protest against ' the disposition to change everything in Scotland to an English model;'[2] and the vehement letters he published under the pseudonym of Malachi Malagrowther raised such a storm in Scotland that the bill was withdrawn. ' If you *unscotch* us,' he wrote to Croker on that occasion, ' you will find us damned mischievous Englishmen.'[3]

It seems improbable that Scott seriously believed that Scottish nationhood was too weak to resist a spiritual English conquest; but he was anxious about it, and his anxiety would have been deepened if he could have foreseen how greatly the forces of assimilation were to be strengthened after his death in 1838. ' *Moriturus bos saluto*,' he said when the Radical mob had howled him down at Jedburgh in the course of his electoral anti-Reform campaign.[4] Did he realise that the Scotland he had known was dying too? Three months before his death the enactment of the Reform Bill had set Scotland side by side with England on the path to democratic politics. A few years later the advent of the Iron Age brought the Industrial Revolution to its climax in Scotland and England alike. And the effect of those developments in integrating British life was to prove no less potent than the effect of the Napoleonic war.

II. HIGHLANDS AND LOWLANDS

DOWN TO the Southern uplands the physical structure of Scotland and Wales is broadly similar, and the difference between the mountainous North and the low-lying southern belt—more strictly, in the Scottish case, the midland belt—has been one of the main factors in shaping the history of both countries throughout its course. In both countries the contrast between North and South was accentuated by the Industrial Revolution. In Scotland as in Wales the coal and iron fields are located in the South, and the outstanding feature of Scottish as of Welsh life from the later eighteenth century to our own day has been the growth of industry and population in the South and the decline of agriculture and population in the North. The Scottish statistics tell the same tale as the Welsh.

	1801	*1901*	*1931*
Scotland	1,608,240	4,472,000	4,842,000
Highland Counties[a] ..	381,576	418,950	370,426
Lanarkshire	147,692	1,339,289	1,585,968

This demographic contrast was sharper in Scotland than in Wales[b] because economic conditions in the Highlands—the long harsh winter, the vast stretches of inhospitable moor and forest—were more adverse than in the Welsh North, and the southward drift of population to the industrial belt was accompanied by a much larger flow of migration oversea. The lot of the Highland smallholder or 'crofter' was far harder than that of the Welsh peasant-farmer: it was nearer the Irish level. Already when the clan-system was abolished, the population of the Highlands was

[a] Argyll, Inverness, Perth, Ross and Cromarty, Sutherland, Caithness.

[b] See Welsh figures, page 169 above.

248

greater than the land alone could feed; yet it continued to increase in defiance of economics right up to the middle of the nineteenth century, just as it increased in Ireland up to the Great Famine. In both cases the main factor in making this increase possible was the cultivation of potatoes, and the Highlands consequently suffered, though never so terribly as Ireland, from the blight. Serious famines occurred in 1837, 1846 and 1850. As early as the seventeen-eighties attempts were made to ease the pressure on the land by moving crofters from the glens to the coast, but it was not easy to convert lethargic and feckless peasants who hated the sea into efficient fishermen. Another form of relief was provided for a time by the expansion of the kelp industry— the manufacture of potash by burning seaweed—but it needed fiscal protection to keep it alive and it was killed outright by the competition of German potash and Peruvian iodine, leaving its employees without a livelihood. And, meantime, the means of subsistence on the land were being straitened by large-scale en- closures. The growth of sheep-farming was bad enough for the peasantry; it needed much less labour than agriculture and most of the shepherds were brought from the Lowlands. Worse, since it had practically no economic value, was the increasing reserva- tion of huge areas for ' deer-forests.' In 1882 they covered nearly two million acres, in 1912 over three and a half. Much of this wasted ground—it was estimated at one-third by the Crofters Commission of 1883—could, at a cost, have been brought under cultivation; and its locking-up solely for the purpose of shooting deer was fiercely denounced by Lowland champions of the Highlanders. The clearances and enclosures, moreover, whether for deer or for sheep or for the consolidation of large farms, were often carried out with a hasty ruthlessness which bears comparison again with what happened in Ireland. The process of eviction, wrote J. S. Blackie (1809-95), who founded the Chair of Celtic at Edinburgh University in 1882, was ' harsh, cruel and tyran- nical'; and he argued that, while the Highlands were certainly overpopulated, it should not have been the people that were made to suffer for it.[5] Blackie was a passionate and outspoken Tory nationalist; but, though, unlike Scott, he betrayed a marked strain of anti-English feeling, he could not say that the plight of the Highlands was England's fault. It was partly due, no doubt, to the *laissez-faire* indifference of a predominantly English Parliament; but the major blame lay nearer home. In the Highlands as in Celtic Ireland the chief culprits were the landlords; and, while in Ireland nearly all the landlords were of Anglo-Irish stock, in the Highlands nearly all of them were Scotsmen.[a] It must not be supposed, however, that more enlightened landlords could have made it possible for the Highland population to make a living in their ancestral homes. There were no country towns and not enough ' cottage industry ' to make up for the decline of agriculture in the face of world-production and world trade. Nothing, in fact, could have prevented the dispersion of the surplus population, and the landlords were only accelerating and exacerbating an inevitable process.

Lloyd George once observed that the Celtic peasantry of the British Isles secured a hearing for their grievances only when they took to violence; and, though the ' Crofters' War ' in the early eighties was immeasurably less murderous and protracted than the ' Land War ' in Ireland, it was a more serious affair than the ' Tithe War ' in Wales.[b]

Meanwhile the outflow into the industrial South and overseas, which had begun in Dr. Johnson's day, was continuing in growing volume throughout the nineteenth century and on into the twentieth. Clearance and eviction were not the only purgatives. Improved communications made it easier for Highlanders to discover and pursue the chances of a better living in the industrial belt; and the parish schools were teaching the raw Highland youth not only the English language but something also about the

[a] A reasonable statement of the landlords' case will be found in the Duke of Argyll's *Scotland as it was and as it is* (Edinburgh, 1887).
[b] See page 215 above.

opportunities awaiting them in the outer English-speaking world. It has been said, indeed, that the Highlands were depopulated as much by the schoolmasters as by the landlords. It was a painful business. In Scotland as in Ireland the sorrows of exile and the breaking-up of homes were real enough. But for the Scottish as for the Irish emigrants it is incontestable that, once the rupture was over, the great majority of them had a happier, freer, more prosperous life than they could have had in any circumstances if they had stayed at home.

Those Highlanders who did stay at home were fast losing what was left of their distinctive character. The process of assimilation, of absorption into a common Scottish nationality, had begun concurrently with the opening stages of the Industrial Revolution: it was speeded up by the improvement of communications, by the schools and, above all, by the Kirk. By 1815 the rural population of the Highlands had become predominantly Presbyterian. The subsequent increase in the number of Roman Catholics in Scotland was mainly due to Irish immigration into the industrial area. In the Highlands they were now scarcely to be found outside the narrow ' Catholic Belt ' stretching eastwards from the Southern Hebrides. And, having lost their old religion, the Highlanders were losing their language too. In the Highlands as in Wales the native Celtic tongue was being steadily overborne by English; and Gaelic had much less chance of survival than Welsh. It was spoken by a far smaller proportion of the population. Statistics are not available till 1891, but the census of that year recorded that 50.2 per cent of Welshmen could speak Welsh and only six per cent of Scotsmen Gaelic. Nor had the Gaels the legacy of native prose and poetry which gave the Welsh the springboard of a linguistic and literary renaissance. No old Gaelic prose had been preserved and the surviving old Gaelic poetry does not match the Welsh in amount or in quality. J. S. Blackie, for all his love of the Highlands, regarded much of it as ' scarce

worthy to be called poetry at all.'[6] Most of it is the work of the
medieval court-bards, who, like their *confrères* in Wales, were concerned to extol the ancient descent and warlike exploits of the
chiefs they served, and, like them, had little mercy for Scandinavian or Saxon foes. 'The Macgregor,' for instance, is exalted
as the man 'who plunders the Saxons and fattens the Gael with
their gold.' The most ferocious imprecation is one of the latest,
an 'incitement to battle' which appears to have been written
on the eve of the campaign which closed at Flodden.[7]

> *Burn their women, lean and ugly!*
> *Burn their children, great and small!*
> *In the hut and in the palace,*
> *Prince and peasant, burn them all!*
> *Plunge them in the swelling rivers,*
> *With their gear and with their goods;*
> *Spare, while breath remains, no Saxon,*
> *Drown him in the roaring floods!*

In the seventeenth and eighteenth centuries there was a number
of gifted Gaelic lyric poets, mainly inspired by the romance of
Jacobitism, and there was one outstanding writer of sacred poetry,
Dugald Buchanan (1716-68). But the most famous name in this
period is that of James Macpherson (1736-96) who fabricated the
Ossianic epics. Only two major Gaelic poets emerged in the
nineteenth entury—John Morrison (1790-1852), the 'poet black-
smith,' and William Livingston (1808-70), who was, incidentally,
a fierce hater of England; but neither of them could be set beside
Ceiriog or Islwyn. Nor did the Gaels keep up to the same extent
as the Welsh the tradition of folk-poetry. 'At the dawn of the
nineteenth century every district in the Highlands had its native
poet while, a century later, not a single Gaelic bard of known
reputation existed anywhere within its borders.'[a] Traditional

---

[a] This statement was made by an eminent Celtic scholar, the late E. C. Quiggin,

singing and dancing lasted longer; but in the course of time they were frowned away by the Kirk. 'Have you no music, no singing, no dancing, now at your marriages?' asked a lover of Gaelic speech and custom on a visit to the Hebrides in 1899. 'May the Possessor keep you!' replied the good wife, 'you are a stranger in Lewis or you would not ask. It is long since we abandoned these foolish ways. In my young days there was hardly a house in Ness where there was not two or three who could play the pipes or the fiddle. . . . A blessed change came over the place. . . . The good men and the ministers who arose did away with the songs and the stories, the music and the dancing. . . . They made the people break and burn their pipes and fiddles.'[8] Both in Wales and in Scotland Calvinistic austerity was the most formidable enemy of Celtic culture. In Wales it delayed and obstructed its revival. In Scotland it did more than anything else to kill it.

Backed by so meagre a literature and faced by the Kirk's disapproval of Celtic tradition, the spoken language seemed doomed to extinction. In the schools which spread across the Highlands from the late eighteenth century onwards there was for a time the same attempt as in Wales to stamp out the 'barbarous' speech. The teaching was in English; children were punished for speaking their mother-tongue, even in the playground, and the latest culprit in the week was made to wear, just as in Wales, a badge of his or her disgrace. The practical argument in favour of English, now slowly creeping up into the Highlands from the Lowlands as it crept up into the Welsh mountains from the English border, was also the same. To escape from agrarian destitution, to obtain a job in the industrial belt, to seek a new life overseas, it was essential to speak English. 'The population,' wrote a Census Commissioner, probably a Lowland Scot, in

in an article on *Celtic Literature* in the twenty-first edition of the *Encyclopædia Britannica*. But it is contested by a present-day champion of Gaelic who declares that the popular tradition is 'still fully alive.' T. L. Campbell, *Gaelic in Scottish Education and Life* (Edinburgh, 1943), 38.

1871, ' are cut off from emigrating to the towns from a want of knowledge of the English tongue.' ' The Gaelic language,' he went on in a tone that echoes the Welsh Commissioners of 1846, ' may be what it likes, both as to antiquity and beauty, but it decidedly stands in the way of the civilisation of the natives making use of it. . . . It ought, therefore, to cease to be taught in all our national schools; and, as we are one people, we should have but ONE language.'

This attack on Gaelic was not, it should be noted, an English attack like that in Wales on Welsh. Like the controversy in the Kirk, it was a domestic Scottish affair. Educational policy was decided in London, but it was guided by the Scottish Educational Department in Edinburgh. And that in its turn reflected the dominant Lowland opinion which, led by the Kirk, desired to suppress a language which belonged to the past and still smacked of Popery. But the onslaught was checked by the somewhat tardy recognition of the fact that Highland children who spoke Gaelic in their homes, like Welsh children who spoke Welsh, were incapable of fully understanding lessons given in a ' foreign ' tongue. It was also realised that, for children who were mostly utterly illiterate, teaching *in* Gaelic involved teaching *of* Gaelic; and it was for the latter that the Gaelic Society of Inverness (founded in 1871) petitioned the House of Commons in 1875 and sent deputations to the Scottish Secretary in 1877 and 1879.[9] Meantime many of the schoolmasters and the local authorities they served had been won over by experience to the Gaelic cause. In 1877 the Highland School Boards were asked in an official circular whether they were in favour of teaching in Gaelic, and the result was striking. Twelve made no return. One thought it ' might be an advantage.' Twenty-five were against it. Sixty-five approved.[10] The official response was to insert an article in the Scottish Code of 1878 making the teaching of Gaelic permissive; but nothing more was done till the Crofters' Commission of 1883-34 not only recommended that Gaelic teaching should be ' not merely permitted but enjoined,' but also declared that ' the Gaelic language, in virtue alike of its being the vernacular tongue of so considerable a population and of its now recognised place among ancient languages,' was entitled to be treated, as it already was in Ireland, as a specific grant-aided subject like Latin or French.[11] To those arguments the Education Department bowed in part. Gaelic teaching was still to be permissive only, but Gaelic was added to the list of specific subjects. And here the matter rested. When an appeal for further concessions was made in 1897, the Scottish Secretary made it clear that Gaelic was not to be imposed on all the Highland schools— that, while it was not to be repressed wherever it was needed for the better learning of English, neither was it to be artificially fostered where that need did not arise.[12] So, at the outset of the twentieth century, the materialist motive still held the field. When Professor J. Watson delivered his inaugural lecture in Blackie's old chair at Edinburgh in 1914, he complained that Gaelic was far worse treated in Scottish schools than Erse in Irish schools or Welsh in Wales. ' The only recognition of it is in temporary oral use as a means to the acquisition of English. . . . Such an attitude to Gaelic is unjustifiable on educational grounds and unfortunate for our interests as a nation.'[13]

The professor did not mean, of course, that Scottish national culture could ever again be Gaelic, but only that Scottish life would be the poorer if Gaelic were no longer spoken in the Highlands. And that, it seemed, was going to happen. Between 1901 and 1931, while the population of the Highlands fell from 289,711 to 240,631, the percentage of bilingual speakers fell from 4.9 to 2.82 and of monoglot Gaelic speakers from .68 to .15.

Below the Highland line Scotland was being rapidly industrialised. In the eighteenth century at least one-third of the Scottish people made their living from the soil; despite the revolution in technique and the high profits made in the war and after it, the fraction had fallen to less than one-eighth by 1860; and thenceforward the Scottish farmers and stock-breeders were little better able to overcome the competition of imported meat and wool from oversea than their comrades in England and Wales. By 1911 only one-twentieth of the people were left on the land.[14] The following statistics show the fall in the population in the mainly agrarian counties.

	1801	1851	1901	1931
Scotland ..	1,608,240	2,888,742	4,472,000	4,842,000
N.E. Counties[a]	220,712	349,255	467,855	444,228
Southern Counties[b]	184,776	273,119	263,921	250,746
Midland Belt[c] ..	756,016	1,706,175	3,246,790	3,707,393

Those figures reveal the vast growth of industry in the midland belt. Down to 1830 textiles maintained their lead. The old linen industry in the east and the newer cotton industry in the west continued to expand till the nineteenth century was more than half-way through. But the American Civil War (1861-65) cotton as the American Revolution had hit tobacco, and, while certain specialised branches such as Paisley thread continued to prosper, the cotton industry as a whole never recovered from the blow. At the same time the linen industry had begun to suffer seriously from the competition of better situated rivals, and was yielding its place in eastern economy to jute. Between 1858 and 1868 the amount of jute dispatched to Dundee by the wealthy Scottish merchants of Calcutta was more than doubled. The woollen industry, mainly concentrated on the upper Tweed, also began to decline about the middle of the century in face of Yorkshire competition. But long before the sixties metallurgy

[a] Aberdeen, Banff, Kincardine, Moray, Nairn.

[b] Berwick, Dumfries, Kircudbright, Peebles, Roxburgh, Selkirk, Wigtown.

[c] Angus, Ayr, Clackmannan, Dunbarton, Fife, Lanark, Lothian (East, Mid, West), Renfrew, Stirling.

was overtaking textiles. The perfection of Neilson's Hot Blast in 1827 overcame what had hitherto been its heaviest handicap of good coking coal; and between 1826 and 1831 the hitherto somewhat inaccessible coalfield was opened up by railway. Thus aided, heavy industry in Scotland rapidly caught up on the lead which had been previously taken by England and Wales. South of the border its output had been doubled in the first few decades of the century, in Scotland it had risen only by half. But between 1845 and 1865 Scotland produced one-quarter of Britain's pig iron, overhauling South Wales and, for a short time in the sixties, England too. Coal production similarly rose. Without the same facilities for export, it could not rival South Wales, nor share in the ' boom ' which the latter enjoyed at the end of the nineteenth century. It was always, however, a substantial element in Scottish industry, and in 1913 one-seventh of all the coal mined in Britain was Scottish coal. But the most remarkable development was the growth of shipbuilding. When sea-going wooden steamships first took the water in 1818, Leith, Dundee and Aberdeen[a] began to build them as well as Glasgow. But the cradle of the modern steel-cased liner was the Clyde. Its output grew so steadily and fast that by 1910 no less than a third of Britain's steel ships were built there. And the shipping business was linked with ship-building. Samuel Cunard (1787-1865) was born in Halifax, Nova Scotia, but he came back to the land of his fathers and founded his famous company in 1839, mainly with Glasgow capital—the first step in a triumphal progress which has been crowned in our own day by the ' Queens.'

Railways were the necessary complement of the expansion of heavy industry; and in Scotland as in Wales the earliest of them were built to serve the coal mines—such as the Monkland and Kirkintilloch line in 1826. Edinburgh was linked with Glasgow in 1842 and with Berwick in 1846, and Glasgow with Carlisle and Perth in 1848 and with the south-west counties in 1850. Thus

[a] The famous ' clipper ' ships were built at Aberdeen.

at the mid-century the two chief Scottish cities were connected with all South Scotland and with England. Expansion northwards was slower. The West Highland line from Helensburgh to Fort William, extended later to Mallaig, was not opened till 1897.

At the outset of the twentieth century the gross value of the total industrial output of the British Isles was thus divided: England and Wales, £1,483 million, Scotland £208 millions, Ireland £66 millions.

Population grew with the growth of industry, though never so fast as in England. In 1801 the midland belt contained 47 per cent of the Scottish people; in 1901, 72 per cent; in 1931, 76 per cent. And the western section had gained on the eastern. In 1801 Lanarkshire was already the most populous county in Scotland, but it was only some 20,000 ahead of Perth, Midlothian and Aberdeen. In 1901 its population of one and one-third million was twice the size of Midlothian's. Glasgow in 1801 was slightly smaller than Edinburgh with 81,000 people to 82,500; in 1901 it was more than twice as big with 700,000 to 316,000. Thus Lanarkshire and Glasgow held the lead in Scotland as Glamorganshire, Cardiff and Swansea held it in Wales.

Till statistics became available in 1861 it was impossible to say, for Scotland as for Wales, how far the growth of the industrial population was aided by English immigration; but it seems more than probable that fewer English labourers sought work in Glasgow than in Newport, Cardiff, and Swansea, if only because the distance from the border was so much greater. The census of 1861 revealed that 56,000 residents in Scotland had been born in England or Wales. By 1891 the number had risen to 110,000. In 1931 it was 168,000. But during the nineteenth century Anglo-Welsh immigration was far exceeded by Irish. Ulster lies close to the Clyde, and there had long been a seasonal interflow of labour, but the post-war depression in the twenties and, still more, the great famine of the forties brought a far greater number of Irish paupers flowing into Glasgow and spreading over the whole industrial area, not to earn money and go home, but to stay. Aided by the fact that under the Scottish law, unlike the English, these destitute Irishmen were no more subject than Scotsmen to removal,[15] they made homes for themselves, often underground, in the urban slums. There was one material advantage in the influx. In Scotland as in England the best and most numerous workers on the new railways and canals were the Irish navvies. Ireland was relieved and Scotland benefited, wrote Scott to Maria Edgeworth as early as 1829, by the shift of population. ' Our canals, our railroads[a] and our various public works are all wrought by Irish. . . . But most unhappily for all parties they work at far too low a rate. . . . Extreme poverty brings ignorance and vice, and these are the mothers of crime.'[16] Unhappily too, the inflow continued long after all the canals had been cut and most of the railways built. Glasgow suffered worse than Liverpool and Manchester and far worse than Cardiff. In 1871 the number of people born in Ireland and domiciled in Scotland was over 200,000 or 6.18 per cent of the population. In Glasgow the Irish percentage was 14.3, in Renfrew 14.4, in Paisley 9.7, in Edinburgh 4.[b] And to these must be added the children born of Irish immigrants after they had settled in Scotland. It was a substantial ' foreign body,' and for many years it did more harm than good to the country of its adoption. For the miserable conditions of the Irish countryside had not qualified those who fled from it for civilised civic life. Ignorant and filthy, they were largely responsible for the epidemics of dirt-born disease which decimated Scottish town-dwellers till the nineteenth century was far advanced.

Meantime the economic integration imposed by the Industrial

[a] The ' railroads ' in 1822 were tramways along which trucks were pulled by horses.
[b] Irish-born in Monmouth in 1871 were 3.5 per cent, in Glamorgan 2.3 per cent.

Revolution on all Britain was having the same assimilative effect in Scotland as in Wales. The Scottish industrial and financial system became steadily more interwoven with the English. The junction of the railways linked Scottish textiles with Manchester and Scottish steel with Birmingham. The eight Scottish banks in which the lesser ones were ultimatey absorbed were closely associated with the great English banks in London. And, since the difference in distance could be cancelled by a night in the train, the pull of London was scarcely less powerful in Glasgow than in Cardiff. Scottish firms had their branches, many of them their headquarters, in the ' City '; and more and more Scotsmen were appointed to the high command of predominantly English firms. In so far as they had time to think about it, Scottish business men took it for granted that this process of economic association and integration was the natural result of Union. And an exceedingly welcome result. By sharing in the economy of the greatest industrial and commercial country in the world, poor Scotland had become far richer than the authors of the Union could ever have imagined.

III. POLITICAL ASSIMILATION

BECAUSE SCOTLAND possessed a full-scale and efficient system of education when Wales as yet had nothing worth the name, Scottish politics awoke from the slumber of the old régime much sooner than Welsh. Radicalism in the period of privation and unrest after 1815, like the Jacobitism of the preceding generation, was more vigorous and widespread in Scotland than in Wales. So was the demand for Reform. The fact there was no such dramatic Chartist outbreak in Scotland as the Newport fiasco did not mean that Chartism was stronger in Wales; it meant that the Scottish movement was better organised and more wisely led. But it was only in time that the birth of democracy in Scotland differed from its birth in Wales. The case for parliamentary reform, it is true, was stronger in Scotland: its representative system was more grotesquely out of date: a Scottish statesman of a later day described it as 'one monstrous rotten borough.'[a] But otherwise there was nothing distinctive in the Scottish agitation. Radicalism in Scotland was a local reproduction of Radicalism in England. 'Peterloo' in 1819 and the 'Radical War' in 1820 belonged to the same campaign. The election riots at Edinburgh, Ayr, Dunbar in 1831 reflected those at Bristol, Derby, Nottingham. Nor were the Scottish Whigs who routed the Tories at the polls[b] and helped to carry the Reform Bill differentiated from the English or the Welsh Whigs, and their votes were as much at the disposal of their party leaders at Westminster as those of their Tory predecessors in Dundas' 'reign.'

The natural sequel to Parliamentary reform was the drastic municipal reform effected by the Burgh Acts of 1833, but the further output of Whig legislation attracted little interest in Scotland. For just at that time public attention was diverted from the politics of the State to the politics of the Church. Often enough in the past religious issues had taken possession of Scottish minds to the exclusion of almost everything else. The Union itself, as pointed out in an earlier chapter, could not have been achieved if the political and economic settlement had not been accompanied by a religious settlement. It is not surprising, therefore, that secular Scottish politics were completely overshadowed by the religious controversy which began or more strictly was revived on the morrow of the Reform Act and culminated ten years later in the great secession. The 'Disruption' of the Kirk was, next to the Union, the most important event in the history

---

[a] Rosebery in 1871: *Miscellanies Literary and Historical* (London, 1921), ii. 100.
[b] In the election of 1832 Reformers won 44 out of 53 seats in Scotland. Reform was opposed by a majority in England and Wales and carried by a minority of English with the help of the Irish and Scottish votes.

of Scotland since the Reformation. It severed for nearly eighty years the main thread in the texture of Scottish life.

The Scottish Church had been affected, though not so deeply as her English sister, by the spiritual climate of the eighteenth century. The dominant party in the Assembly were the so-called Moderates who were latitudinarian in doctrine and had drifted away in thought and temper from the stern Calvinism of an earlier day. But the old puritan zeal, the old Covenanter spirit, had never died out, and in the later part of the century the same sort of Evangelical revival came about in Scotland as in England. In many ways the two movements differed, but each resulted in a breach in the ranks of the Established Church. It was a wider breach in Scotland, and the dispute which caused it was on an issue which excited little, if any, warmth of feeling in England at that time. It will be remembered that, only five years after the Union, the British Parliament restored the system of lay patronage in the Scottish Church.[a] It was a dishonourable stroke of party politics, but its results were not what its authors had intended. Nor were they wholly injurious. For the Act of 1712 made it possible for a broadminded 'heritor' or patron on occasion to save a parish from the ministrations of the kind of ignorant and bigoted hot-gospeller its inhabitants might have chosen for themselves. Such an argument, however, could scarcely be addressed to Calvinists of the stricter sort, and the grievance continued to rankle. More than once in the course of the eighteenth century a group of conscientious objectors broke away from the Kirk and formed a separate community of their own, and with the coming of the revolutionary Age and the spread of democratic ideas the controversy was re-opened on so wide a scale that for the great majority of Scotsmen it became the paramount question of the time.

The tradition of the Kirk had been anti-erastian from the outset. To many of its members it had always smacked of heresy

[a] See page 138 above.

that, however self-governing it might be, the Kirk was subject to the ultimate authority of a secular State. And after 1832 it could be plausibly contended that, since the law now permitted the Scottish people to choose their own civil representatives in Parliament, the law ought also to permit them to choose their own religious ministers. To trace the controversy in detail would go far beyond the scope of this book:[a] suffice it to say that the legal rights of patronage were confirmed in testing cases by the Court of Sessions and on appeal by the House of Lords, that successive attempts to effect a compromise in Parliament were foiled by the Government's very natural insistence that patronage must continue as long as the Act of 1712 was unrepealed; and that, since a proposal for repeal would certainly have been resisted on both sides of the Commons and rejected in the Lords, an open rupture became inevitable. Led by Thomas Chalmers (1780-1847), the famous preacher, who has been called ' the most illustrious Scottish churchman since John Knox,'[17] the Evangelical party asserted a ' Claim of Right ' which declared that all Acts of Parliament ' passed without the consent of this Church and nation ' and prejudicial to the Church's government as recognised at the Union were, save in their civil implications, ' void and null.'[18] The challenge was worthy of Knox himself and Parliament was bound to rebut it. Whigs and Tories agreed with Peel that the supremacy of the State could not be questioned. Thus the basic principle at issue in the quarrel which had smouldered in the bosom of the Kirk ever since its establishment in the sixteenth century was thrust to the front in all its bare simplicity; and the inexorable result of that, so hard-set were the disputants' opinions, so great the tension, was to break the Kirk in two. On May 18, 1843, a body of nearly 400 ministers, subsequently reinforced till it numbered over one-third of all the clergy of the Kirk, formally seceded from the Established Church, and signed

---

[a] For an authoritative account see W. L. Mathieson, *Church and Reform in Scotland* (Glasgow, 1916).

a Declaration, affirming their allegiance to a separate Free Church of Scotland and renouncing all the emoluments they had hitherto received as beneficed ministers of the Establishment. Since for many of them that meant the loss not only of their churches and their homes but of their sole means of livelihood, this voluntary sacrifice will always be regarded as an outstanding manifestation of the independence and integrity of the Scottish character and the power of religious conviction in Scottish life.

For students of nationalism the Disruption has a special significance. The movement which brought it about may be described as a *national* movement: it was backed by a substantial minority of the whole Scottish people and in some rural areas by a great local majority. But it was not a *nationalist* movement. Only in so far as the seceders grounded their case on the Union settlement, only in repudiating the authority of the Act of 1712, only in denying Parliament the right to legislate in religious matters without the consent of the 'nation' as well as of its national Church, only so far did they urge the claims of nation-hood.[a] And, though they might argue that their conduct was more in keeping with the national tradition than that of their opponents, when it came to the decisive point it was not patriotism that moved them but only conscience. Seldom indeed has a religious movement been so purely religious. Similarly the agitation which developed in due course for the disestablishment of what remained of the Established Church had no nationalist flavour. It was thus wholly different in character from the great campaign for Disestablishment in Wales. For the cause of Disestablishment in Wales, the cause which dominated all Welsh politics till its object was achieved, was an intensely nationalist cause: it was, in fact, the mainspring of the revival of Welsh

[a] Chalmers was a nationalist as that sentence in the 'Claim of Right' is enough by itself to show. But he was also, like Scott, a British patriot. When Napoleon threatened to invade England, 'May I be the first,' he said, 'to ascend the scaffold erected to extinguish the worth and spirit of the country; may my blood mingle with the blood of patriots and may I die at the foot of that altar on which *British* independence is to be the victim.'

nationalism. And the reason for the contrast is plain. The Welsh Nonconformists were at odds with a Church which they regarded as a foreign Church. In Scotland the dispute was purely domestic. One group of Scottish churchmen were fighting another. Apart, indeed, from academic theories of the relationship between Church and State—and these played little part in either country —the two movements had only one thing in common. They were both concerned with the sovereignty of the British Parliament. They both revealed the difficulty of protecting national interests in a unitary multi-national State controlled by a single Parliament.

In the Scottish case the crux became apparent when the Union was in its infancy; but the discussion provoked by the Act of 1712 was not so widespread or protracted as the long and fierce debate which precipitated the Disruption; and it was only then that the most serious defect in the Union settlement was fully understood. It was more obvious now how futile was the Scottish negotiators' attempt on the one hand to restrict the legal sovereignty of the British Parliament and on the other hand to fix fast the government and doctrine of the Kirk in an eternal mould.[a]

As soon as the long religious controversy had ended, Scottish politics were absorbed again in British politics. It was the eve of Peel's surrender to the Anti-Corn Law League, and Free Trade was necessarily a British issue in which Scotland's interest was the same as England's. A few months before the Disruption, as it happened, Cobden and Bright themselves invaded Scotland. They had a great reception. ' Our progress ever since we crossed the border,' wrote Cobden, ' has been gratifying in the extreme. . . . Glasgow, Edinburgh, Kirkcaldy, Dundee, Perth and Stirling have all presented me with the freedom of their burghs.'[19] Bright told a Manchester audience on his return that the Scots were a more intelligent people than the English, and that, if they were to break the Union, they would have a Scottish government ' wholly popular and intelligent to a degree which I believe does not exist in any other country.'[20] One of those intelligent Scotsmen was Duncan McLaren (1800–06) who was soon to be Lord Provost of Edinburgh (1851–54) and later on its representative in Parliament (1865–81); and the triple alliance was presently confirmed by McLaren's marriage with Bright's sister. He soon acquired and retained till his last days, the leadership of the Scottish Liberals.

It was already clear that the Whigs and their Liberal successors were not likely to lose the hold on the Scottish electorate that had been won by the Reform Act. Chartism, as has been observed, was as great a failure in Scotland as in England; and the sequence of elections in 1847, 1852, 1857 and 1865 gave the Whig-Liberals majorities of the Scottish 53 seats, which rose from 32 to 42. At the election of 1868, which made Gladstone Prime Minister for the first time, the Liberals won 53 seats out of 71.[a] Thenceforward, till Labour took the lead, Scotland was almost as impregnable a Liberal stronghold as Wales. Only at one election between 1832 and 1914, only in 1900, did the Tories win a majority of the Scottish seats. And the reasons were much the same. After the Disruption the seceding Free Churchmen, like the earlier and smaller independent sects, were the natural allies of the English Nonconformists and shared their ' conscience '; and the need for its active exercise in the field of social reform was at least as urgent in Scotland as elsewhere. The Glasgow slums were worse than anything in Wales and the drunkenness to be met with in the poorer streets of many Scottish towns was a notorious scandal. But if Liberalism in Scotland stood on much the same platform as in Wales, its footing was not quite so firm. In other than domestic politics, in external or foreign affairs, the Scottish electorate was not so consistently loyal as the Welsh to Liberal ideals. The Crimean War engendered a strong pacifist movement

---

[a] For the increase in the number of Scottish seats, see page 290 below.

n which the Free Trade trio took the lead again in their respective countries; but it was not quite so powerful a cause in Scotland as in Wales. McLaren was not a Scottish ' Apostle of Peace.' There was less interest again in continental nationalism. Maybe because the Scots had never for more than a few short years been robbed of their independence and become a subject nation, they did not feel so warm a sympathy as the Welsh felt for the cause of other small nations. There was little, similarly, of the anti-imperial sentiment that prevailed in Wales. The Scots had played a larger part than the Welsh in the exploration, administration and economic development of the Empire, and they were proud of it. But those differences between Scottish and Welsh nationalism were completely submerged in their common devotion to Gladstone in his prime. Till 1886, in Scotland even more than in Wales, Liberalism was Gladstonianism. He had his great days in Wales—one of them has been recorded above—but they were far transcended by the storm of popular enthusiasm which raged around him during his famous Midlothian campaign (November-December 1879). It was partly, no doubt, as in Wales, a response to the ' call of the blood,' and in this case not only to its Celtic strain. For Gladstone's origin was Lowland as much as Highland; he was the complete Scot; and naturally he made the most of it when he faced those cheering Scottish crowds. He might fairly be regarded as a ' stranger ' in Scotland, he said, at Edinburgh, but he was none the less ' the genuine article,' a full-blooded Scot.[21] ' Not a drop of blood runs in my veins except Scotch blood,' he had said a few years earlier when he received the freedom of Aberdeen, ' and a large share of my heart has belonged and ever will belong to Scotland.'[22] But it was not in fact a very large share. Gladstone was never a Scottish patriot. Though he used to take his holidays in Scotland till he made Hawarden his home and, though he venerated Scott,[a] he was not deeply interested

---

[a] He ranked him as the greatest of Scotsmen and often regretted that he had never met him. Morley, iii. 423, 492.

in Scottish tradition; and though he acknowledged how much
the cause of Liberalism owed to Scotland,[a] he did little himself
to repay the debt. From the time his thoughts and energies became
preoccupied with the claims of Ireland he gave, as will presently
appear, as little attention to Scottish claims as to Welsh. The
greatest Scotsman of his time, in fact, was not in any sense a
Scottish nationalist. It may be said, indeed, that his power in
Scotland as in Wales was the greater because his appeal transcended nationalism. It was a moral appeal, and the response to
it was due, more than to anything else, to the deep religious
feeling nourished by the Kirk in Scotland. That was why
Gladstone was able to persuade most of those stern Presbyterians
to do justice to Catholic Ireland, to make them recognise the
duties of a Christian nation towards suffering Christians in the
Balkans and to recoil from the picture he drew (and somewhat
overdrew) of Disraeli's imperial adventures. This was not
nationalism, it was internationalism; and the key to Gladstone's
triumph in Midlothian was plainly visible when in the peroration
of the last speech of the campaign, he thanked the Scottish people
for giving him the credit of desiring that national policy should
consider ' the wider interests of mankind.' ' There is going on,'
he said, ' a profound mysterious movement that, whether we will
or not, is bringing the nations of the civilised world, as well as
the uncivilised, morally as well as physically nearer to one another
and making them more and more responsible before God for
one another's welfare.'[23]

Great as it was to the end of his life, Gladstone's hold on
Scotland was not so incontestable as his hold on Wales. In the
election of 1885, when he had not yet committed himself to a
definite measure of Irish Home Rule, the Scottish as well as the
Welsh constituencies retained their traditional colour. In Wales
27 Liberals were returned against 3 Conservatives: in Scotland

---

[a] Writing to Sir John Cowan, a Scottish M.P., in 1844, he said that in all the political
conflicts of his time ' Scotland has done battle for the right '; and he repeated the tribute
in his farewell to his Midlothian constituents in 1895. *Ibid.*, iii. 535-6.

62 Liberals against 10 Conservatives. In 1886, on the other hand, when Gladstone had produced his Home Rule plan and thereby split his party, whereas the allegiance of Wales was hardly shaken —23 Liberals were returned against 3 Liberal Unionists and 4 Conservatives—in Scotland there was a serious breakaway. The Liberals were by no means routed as in England: they retained 45 seats; but the Liberal Unionists won 16 and the Conservatives 11. In 1892 and 1895 the Liberals recovered ground, but they lost it again in 1900. And again the contrast with Wales was marked. The issue was the ethics of the Boer War, and, while Wales was as staunchly Liberal as ever, Scotland swung right over to the other side. In Wales 26 Liberals and one Labour candidate were returned against 4 Conservatives: in Scotland 34 Liberals against 38 Conservatives.[a]

The main cause of the difference has been revealed in the preceding chapter. In Wales Liberalism was linked with the nationalism which had been kindled by the fight for Disestablishment. Nothing of that sort happened in Scotland. The first brief nationalist movement, as will presently appear, was a non-party affair; and, while the second and more lasting movement became associated with the Liberal Party, it was never a dominant or even an important factor in its policy. No Scottish demand such as the Welsh demand for Disestablishment was put at the head of its programme. It was always, in fact, a British party and its programme a British programme. And its organisation was British. Its local bodies were grouped in a Scottish Federation but it was no more than a northern branch of the British Liberal Federation. Its 'high command' was in London. And, though party politics were similarly organised in Wales, there was something in Wales but practically nothing in Scotland to check the assimilating, centralising forces which, in politics as in economics, were draw-

---

[a] In 1906 the old balance was restored in Scotland with 59 Liberal seats, 2 Labour, and 11 Conservative.

ing Scotland and England closer and closer together as the Victorian age went by.

The Scottish working class was likewise becoming absorbed in the British economic system. The Scottish Labour movement from Chartist days onwards was no more distinctively national than the Welsh. If anything, it was less so. In Wales, as has been recorded, there developed at certain times and places a sort of primitive economic nationalism; the class-conflict, both agrarian and industrial, took on an anti-English edge. But there was nothing of that in Scotland. Very few English immigrants culti-vated Scottish estates, and the Scottish lairds for the most part were little, if at all, more ' Englishfied ' than their tenants. The Englishmen who obtained high posts in Scottish industry or commerce were likewise a small minority, and the Scottish employers spoke the same language and mostly belonged to the same Church as the men they employed. Nor, if the class-conflict in Scotland had had an anti-English colour, could it have kept it. It would have been washed out, as it was in Wales, by the growing solidarity of the British working class. The career of the famous Scottish Labour pioneer points the moral. Keir Hardie (1856-1915) was born in a Lanarkshire cottage, and he came to the front as the organiser of the Scottish miners and as the chief architect of the Scottish Labour Party which was formed in 1888 with himself as chairman. But the Scottish Unions and Scottish Labour politics were soon merged in British; and when in 1892 Hardie and John Burns (1858-1943) were the first two Labour members to be elected to the House of Commons, the seat the former had won was not in Scotland but in East London. He was the first chairman of the Independent Labour Party formed in 1893 and the first parliamentary leader of the Labour Party in 1906. He thus personified the absorption of the Scottish into the British Labour movement; and it was appropriate that the seat he held for the last fifteen years of his life was Mabon's seat at Merthyr Tydvil.

IV. THE SCOTTISH DIASPORA

AFTER 1843 Scottish affairs, both political and economic, ran in the same groove as English affairs. No distinctively Scottish question came to the front of public life. Nothing happened to compare with the Jacobite troubles of the eighteenth century. Hence it has been said that the disruption of the Kirk was the last event in the history of Scotland. Thenceforward Scottish history was only local history. On the national scale it was merged in British history. And the same applies to most of the individual Scotsmen who 'made history' in the Victorian age. It was British history they made, and they made it outside Scotland. For it was now that able and venturesome Scotsmen took advantage to the fullest possible extent of the opportunities provided by the Union of a wider and richer life than an independent, isolated Scotland could ever have afforded them. The stream of emigration set running by the Union rose to its height, flowing into England, into the British Empire oversea, into almost every corner of the world. And wherever these Scotsmen went and whatever their line of life, there were always some among them of a character and capacity that took them to the highest levels.

For Anglo-Scottish relations the most important result of the outflow was personal. Scotsmen became much more familiar to Englishmen—so familiar, indeed, that the sense of difference was blunted. It became difficult to distinguish a Scotsman in England unless his speech betrayed him, and, even when it did, he seemed much the same as an Englishman from the northern counties. Nor was it only the familiarity of intercourse in work, in business, in public service, in social life: it was familiarity also in the root sense of the word. More and more men of the one nation were marrying women of the other until by the end of the century a

271

high proportion of English families had an infusion of Scottish blood. And this, maybe, like most cross-breeding, was an advantage. Certainly some of the outstanding personalities in Victorian Britain were the offspring of mixed marriages. Some of them, born of Scottish fathers and brought up in Scottish homes, grew up to be more Scottish than English, but Scottish patriots are mistaken when they speak of these children of the Union as if they were Scotsmen *pur sang*. It seems to imply an oddly old-fashioned conception of the status of women for Scotland to claim more than half the credit for an Englishwoman's child. The most curious example is that of A. J. Balfour who was born in East Lothian and has often been called a Scot; for, while his Scottish father's ancestry was not exceptionally distinguished, his mother was Lady Blanche Cecil, a daughter of the most historic family in England.

This process of intermingling would not have been so close and friendly if the eighteenth-century resentment at the Scottish invasion of England had persisted. But there was none of that now. The jealousy fostered by Wilkes and his like had died with them. Englishmen might still grumble at times at the presence of so many Scotsmen in the higher walks of life; they might remark that it was not so easy for an Englishman to get a job in Scotland; and, if they were Tories, they might complain that the Liberal majorities in Parliament could not have been obtained without the help of Scottish as well as Welsh and Irish votes. But there was no talk now of 'locusts.' Englishmen, in fact, had learned to accept the Scots as fellow-Britons and to recognise the value of their share in all the things they were 'doing together' for Britain and the British Empire.

The trite saying that Queen Victoria personified the sentiments of her English subjects is not true of all she said and did; but she certainly reflected the sense of Anglo-Scottish unity and concord that prevailed throughout her reign. She forged a personal link between the British monarchy and Scotland such as none of her predecessors since the Union had even thought of. She created her second son Duke of Edinburgh in 1866—the first royal dukedom with a Scottish title. When her fourth and youngest son was born in 1853, she gave him 'Duncan' for his second Christian name as 'a compliment to dear Scotland,' and created him Duke of Albany in 1881; and the second Duke received at his grandmother's bidding the names 'Charles Edward' in memory of the Young Pretender.[a] These delicacies of nomenclature were not mere trifles; they showed at the least a better frame of mind than the bland indifference to Scottish sentiment—or can it have been sheer ignorance of Scottish history?—which permitted the accession of William III and II and William IV and III to be proclaimed in Scotland without the second numeral. Far more important, however, was the Queen's personal contact with Scotland. On her first visit in 1842 she went by sea to Granton, rode through Edinburgh to Dalkeith and finally stayed at Drummond Castle in Perthshire. On her second visit in 1844 she sailed to Dundee and thence penetrated the Highlands to Blair Atholl. In 1850 she stayed two nights at Holyrood on her way north and in 1855 established a permanent royal residence at Balmoral. The total time she spent in Scotland was about seven years—a sharp contrast to the five weeks she spent in Ireland.

The great part played by Scotsmen of the Diaspora in nineteenth-century British public life may be illustrated by some names and figures. Between 1815 and 1914 four Prime Ministers were Scotsmen—Aberdeen, Gladstone, Rosebery and Campbell-Bannerman—and one a half-Scot, Balfour. There were more than twenty Scottish Cabinet Ministers and two Lord Chancellors —Campbell and Loreburn—and half-Scottish Brougham for a

[a] Queen Victoria's sympathies were frankly Jacobite. She spoke of Mary Queen of Scots as her 'unfortunate ancestress.' What she would have thought of her if she had met her in the flesh may be left to the imagination.

third:[a] three Scottish Viceroys of India—two Elgins and a Minto
—and one half-Scottish, Dalhousie: a dozen Governors-General
of British Colonies and Dominions and numerous Governors of
Indian Provinces, Australian States and non-self-governing
Colonies, while the Scottish quota in the rank and file of the
Indian and Colonial civil services was notoriously high. Scotsmen,
too, were helping to people and develop the young colonies of
settlement which had survived the American Revolution or come
into being after it. The exodus from the Highlands steadily continued and it was not limited to the Highlands. Emigrants from
all parts of Scotland swelled the multitude of English, Welsh and
Irish exiles seeking a new life in the New World. Nor was it only
an unorganised migration of individuals. In 1847, under happier
auspices than those of Darien, a second ' New Edinburgh ' in the
Celtic guise of ' Dunedin ' was founded in New Zealand. It was
a purely Scottish achievement, and it was characteristic of the
earnest Scotsmen who dominated its early life that they regarded
the colony first and foremost as an outpost of the new Free Kirk.[24b]
But the most famous Scottish contribution to the nineteenth-
century history of the British Empire was not in the field of
government or colonisation. None of the great Victorians stands
higher on the roll of honour than David Livingstone, and with
this name will always be linked the name of another Scot, John
Kirk, his close comrade in the Zambesi Expedition and the man
who was mainly responsible for carrying out the task he be-
queathed to the conscience of his country, the abolition of the
Arab slave-trade.[c]

Last but not least, the historic Scottish regiments. For a
century after Waterloo Britain was spared the infliction of another
great war, but in all her lesser wars Scottish soldiers fought as
they had fought on the Heights of Abraham or at Waterloo.

[a] Brougham was born in Edinburgh and his mother, a sister of Robertson the
historian, was Scottish, but his father was of Westmoreland descent.
[b] Compare Welsh 'Wladfa,' pages 213-4 above.
[c] See the author's *Kirk on the Zambesi* (Oxford, 1928), and *The Exploitation of East
Africa* (London, 1939).

Their conduct on three very different occasions seems to have made a particularly strong appeal to British popular sentiment— the charge of the Scots Greys into the heart of the Russian Army at Balaclava (1854), the coming of the Campbells[a] to relieve the siege of the Residency at Lucknow (1857), and the storming of the heights by the Gordon Highlanders at Dargai (1897)

In all this field of public British service, official and unofficial, Scotsmen were doing in the second century of the Union what they had begun to do in the first; and it was the same in much of the cultural field. In science, pure and applied, and in the humanities Scotsmen still stood in the front rank. Only a few outstanding names need be cited to show that the versatility of Scottish genius had outlived the 'golden age'—in surgery and medicine, J. Y. Simpson, William McEwen, Patrick Manson, Ronald Ross; in natural and social science, James Clerk Maxwell, William Ramsay, Geikie, Patrick Geddes, Rutherford, J. G. Frazer; in philosophy, James Mill, Alexander Bain, McTaggart, Caird; in history and scholarship, Carlyle, Finlay, James Murray, Andrew Lang, W. P. Ker. This is an impressive list, and many other distinguished names could be added to it. It was only in literature and the arts that Scottish achievement as a whole declined in quality and scope.

The decline set in early. Save in a few of his best poems James Hogg, the 'Ettrick Shepherd' (1770-1835), would not bear comparison with Burns; and after Hogg there came a host of versifiers who displayed their devotion to Burns by attempting to imitate his language and style and pathos with almost ludicrous results. Yet such was the popular taste in the mid-nineteenth century that, when this 'mass of doggerel and false sentiment,' as a modern Scottish critic calls it,[25] was collected and published in two stout volumes under the title of *Whistle Binkie*, the book had an immense and lasting vogue. After the middle of the

[a] The Argyll and Sutherland Highlanders.

century a gleam of Burns shone for a moment from the work of short-lived David Gray (1838-61) and, later on, from R. L. Stevenson's vernacular poems, and then faded out. The decline of prose was not so swift or steep. For more than a generation, it is true, it seemed as if Scott, too, was to have no successor; but, though Stevenson (1850-94) was not a second Scott, he came near the master's level in *Kidnapped* and, if he had finished *Weir of Hermiston*, might possibly have reached it. But it was now high time for Scottish novelists to break away from a tradition which had become completely detached from modern Scottish life. Scott's Scotland has been wittily called ' Scott-land ';[26] for it belonged so completely to the romantic past as to be virtually a different country from that which in Scott's own day was already being transformed by the Industrial Revolution. And this divorce from the urban industrial society which was now the dominant pattern of Scottish life persisted. The work of the so-called ' kailyard ' school was by no means so contemptible as that embodied in *Whistle Binkie*, especially when it was inspired by the genius of J. M. Barrie (1860-1937). But Barrie's Scotland was scarcely closer to reality than Stevenson's. Scottish writers as a whole, in fact, had turned their backs on the industrial belt. Slums, no doubt, are an unsavoury theme, but they are inhabited, after all, by human beings, and it is strange that no Scottish novelist wanted to write about Glasgow as Dickens wrote about London. The result of this flight from the facts was bad for Scottish literature, because it diverted it from the living Scotland of the day to a country that was dead or dying.

Scottish painting tells a similar tale. Raeburn and Thomson, like Burns and Scott, set a standard their successors could not maintain. On the one hand, there was a school of ' literary painters '—Orchardson (1832-1910) and Pettie (1839-93) are its best-known exponents—who sought, as it were, to illustrate the romantic past. Good as their painting was, it was not essentially Scottish. Scott-land inspired it, not Scotland. On the other hand there were the painters of rustic domestic life. They stemmed from the gifted David Wilkie (1785-1841) who stands in painting where Galt stands in literature. But this school, though it never sank to the depths of *Whistle Binkie*, drifted into the sentimentality which its public wanted: the ' cottage-fireside ' school it is now unkindly called. A third group, McCulloch (1805-67) at its head, painted the Highlands, but not with Thomson's truth. Their patrons, who were mainly the successful business men of the Victorian age, did not want their drawing-room walls to reflect the stern grandeur of the Highland scene. They wanted, as a modern critic puts it, ' " pirlin " burns, heathery hillsides, cloud-shadows, stags, steers, lonely cottages, and occasional bonneted Highlandmen,' a romantic world into which they could escape from the harsh realities of their city life.[27] The result was a ' ben-and-glen ' school of painters closely comparable with the ' kailyard ' school of novelists. In fine, when the nineteenth century entered its last quarter, Scottish painting as a whole had fallen as far below its ' golden age ' as Scottish literature.[a]

Scottish architecture fared no better. It suffered from the blight which covered the whole of Victorian Britain. The growth of Glasgow and the other towns of the industrial belt displayed the same grim materialism as the growth of Birmingham, Leeds and the like. Public buildings clung to the outworn classical tradition. Churches reverted to Gothic without recovering its secret. Chapels were as ugly as in Lancashire or Wales. Broadly speaking, Scottish building only differed from English in the pseudo-romanticism of the country houses in which, as in ' ben-and-glen ' pictures, wealthy business men sought escape from city life. Scott himself set a bad example in Abbotsford; the Prince Consort followed it in helping to design Balmoral; and it is just that the famous memorials in Princes Street and Kensington Gardens should so nearly resemble each other. They were both

[a] There were, of course, exceptions to the general mediocrity: e.g. David Scott (1806-49), J. C. Wintour (1825-82) and J. MacWhirter (1839-1911). See Ian Finlay, *Art in Scotland* (Oxford, 1948), chap. viii.

admired, and it was not till the end of the century that public opinion was awakened to the possibility of a better style of architecture than those which had satisfied the taste of Victorian Britain.

Of this general decline of Scottish culture the fate of Edinburgh was symbolic. By 1837 Edinburgh had already lost its place in the intellectual world. Only the ghost of Scott now haunted the Advocates' Library. The *Edinburgh Review* was no longer in Jeffrey's control, and its two most celebrated contributors, half-Scottish Macaulay and half-Scottish Brougham, lived in London. Southwards, too, had drifted most of the successors to the men who had made Edinburgh the ' modern Athens.' Great Scottish teachers were still to be found there and in other Scottish Universities, but they were now also to be found at English Universities, and an increasing number of students followed their southward lead. Gone were the days when the old Scottish educational system sufficed at all levels for nearly all Scotsmen. Many of them were educated now at ' public schools ' of the English type, and went thence to Oxford or Cambridge; some of the ablest, having taken an honours degree in Scotland, proceeded to take another in England. It was one more proof that Scottish life was being woven with English into a British texture.

Some latter-day Scottish patriots deplore the Diaspora. They regard the dispersion of so many Scotsmen over England and the outer world as having done irreparable damage to the strength and spirit of Scottish nationhood. ' Lost Scots ' they call them: lost because, no longer tied to Scottish soil, they ceased to care about their motherland and its traditions, ceased to be proud of Scotland, ceased at heart to be Scotsmen. But that is scarcely a reasonable complaint. Most of those great Scotsmen would have made names for themselves of a sort, no doubt, wherever they lived; but, even if Scotland had continued to be an independent

State with its own Government and Parliament and official hierarchy, they could not have done all they did within its narrow bounds. To regret the Diaspora, in fact, is to regret the Union. It is no more true, moreover, of Scotsmen than of Welshmen or Irishmen that those who lived in exile forgot their motherland and lost their sense of nationhood. Certainly some of them did, including two of the greatest. Gladstone, as has been seen, became almost wholly anglicised, and Ruskin was more completely 'lost.' He sometimes alluded to his Scottish descent; but, though there were no happier years in his troubled life than those he spent in childhood beside the River Tay, he rarely visited Scotland afterwards. Even the beauty of the Highlands seems to have moved him less than that of the English Lakes. All of his heart, in fact, that he did not give to the art of English Turner, he gave to Switzerland and Italy. Nor was Carlyle a true Scot. His genius was rooted in the Lowlands and their Calvinist tradition; but he spent nearly all his working life in London, and though the Scottish temper is unmistakable in all he wrote, he was not interested in Scotland nor inspired by Scottish life and thought. His philosophy came from Germany. His history was French, Prussian, Cromwellian, anything but Scottish. His place in fact, is more in English than in Scottish literature. It was naturally easier for half-Scots to ' lose ' their Scottish half, and again there are examples among the greatest of them. John Stuart Mill's father was a pure Scot from Forfarshire; his mother was English; and, while he refers to his father's Scottish origin on the second page of his *Autobiography*, he never mentions Scotland again. When in his *Representative Government* he discusses the problem of nationality and propounds his doctrine of the uni-national democratic State,[a] he evidently puts Britain in that category and ignores the fact that the political combination— ' absorption ' he significantly calls it—of one nationality with another need not necessarily involve the extinction of the smaller

[a] See page xxi above.

country's national tradition. Macaulay, too, was half-Scottish. His father, Zachary, was a pure Scot, a 'son of the manse' at Inveraray; but, like Mill, he was born and brought up in England, and he seems to have taken no interest in the Scottish half of his descent. Though he was M.P. for Edinburgh for a time, he did not concern himself closely with contemporary Scotland, and, though he studied and recorded Scottish history, he did it with a quite un-Scottish detachment. 'Read about the Darien affair,' he noted in his journal. 'It will be impossible to tell the truth as to that matter without putting the Scotch into a rage. But the truth must be told.' Often, moreover, he wrote 'England' when in these more careful days he would presumably have written 'Britain.'[a] It might be said, indeed, that the half-Scot in blood was whole-English in spirit. How purely English, for example, was his homesickness in India. 'I feel,' he wrote when his exile was nearing its end, 'as if to exist on English ground and among English people, seeing the old familiar sights and hearing the sound of my mother tongue, would be enough for me.'[28]

But those are exceptions. The vast majority of Scotsmen outside Scotland no more forgot their 'national homeland' than those who lived within its borders. Far more typical than a Gladstone or a Ruskin was Minto, passionately longing to get home from India and spend the 'best years' of his life in retirement in his beloved Elliotdale and tragically dying on the northward road from London.[29] When Livingstone came back from his long ordeal on the Zambesi he visited Ulva island, the ancestral home of his family, and was distressed to find no member of it still living there.[30] But it is needless to argue the point. Everyone knew in the nineteenth century, as everyone knows in the twentieth, that the great multitude of the Scotsmen of the

[a] The author is indebted for these points to Macaulay's grand-nephew, G. M. Trevelyan.

Diaspora can never forget they are Scotsmen. Wherever they are in the world on Burns' birthday or St. Andrew's Day or New Year's Eve, they make it plain enough.

V. THE NATIONALIST MOVEMENT
OF 1853

MODERN SCOTTISH NATIONALISM made its first appearance in 1853, ten years after the Disruption. The date has no particular significance. It is not linked with 1848. There is very little to suggest that Scottish patriots were interested in ' Young Italy ' or ' Young Ireland,' or influenced, like the young Welsh patriots of the next generation, by Mazzini's or Davis' doctrine of the 'national mission.' Nor was the movement prompted in Scotland as it was in Wales by English criticism of her educational system, her language and her morals or by revolt against the privileges of the English Church. Disestablishment, as had been seen, was a domestic affair in Scotland; and, if the Commissioners of 1845-46 had extended their inquiries to Scotland, they could not have raised such a storm as they raised in Wales. They would have found the state of education considerably better in Scotland than it was in England. They would have heard a Celtic language spoken only by a small minority of the Scottish population, only in the Highlands, and they could scarcely have regarded the steadily declining use of ' Broad Scots ' in the Lowlands as a ' disastrous barrier ' to Scottish progress. Nor, surely, would they have been so bold as to impugn the sexual morality of Scottish countryfolk. It was not a Scottish *brâd* that roused the nationalists of 1853. They were agitated only by a dry and practical question —the machinery of government. They contended that the operation of the political system, established by the Union, was unfair and inefficient.

They could make a case on both charges. The Scottish share in Parliament had been determined in 1707 by two considerations.[a] The allocation of 45 seats to Scotland in the Commons as against 486 English and 27 Welsh seats reflected first the fact that the Scottish population was then roughly one-eighth of the population of England and Wales, and secondly the fact that Scotland, being immeasurably poorer, would make a far smaller contribution to the revenues of the United Kingdom. But on both those points the position in 1850 was very different from what it had been in 1707. The population of Scotland had now risen to $2\frac{1}{2}$ millions as against some 14 millions in England and Wales; and though the number of Scottish seats was increased to 53 in 1832, the strict mathematical quota in a House now containing 468 English members, 32 Welsh, and 105 Irish was 89.[b] The change in the balance of wealth was still more marked. In 1850 taxation in Scotland was only one shilling lighter per head than in England; and, whereas till the end of the eighteenth century Scotland had probably got more than she gave, Scottish revenue in 1850 considerably exceeded the cost of Scottish administration, and, while the surplus might fairly be spent on common British services, especially defence, it happened that, till Germany took the place of France as the potential enemy, very little was spent on defence-works or military and naval establishments in Scotland.

But the lack of a few more Scottish seats in the British Parliament was not so serious a matter as the maladministration of Scottish affairs. This was partly due to a weakness at the centre. Since the abolition of the Secretaryship of State for Scotland in 1746,[c] Scottish business had been conducted by the Northern Department till 1782 and thereafter by the Home Office. Normally an Englishman, the Home Secretary was aided and advised

[a] See page 109 above.
[b] Little was now heard of the similar grievance with regard to the House of Lords; for, as time went on, most holders of Scottish titles were also peers of the United Kingdom. Rait and Pryde, *Scotland*, 157-8.
[c] See page 144 above.

by the Lord Advocate for Scotland; but this officer, though necessarily a Scotsman, had little of the power and prestige enjoyed by his predecessors in the eighteenth century. He had long ceased to be a member of the Cabinet; he had no direct responsibility for Scottish affairs outside the legal field, and his duties in that field were heavy enough to occupy most of his time. There was, in fact, no longer a Scotsman in Whitehall who could be called in any genuine sense the Minister for Scotland. And the need for some such person, other than the Home Secretary, to be responsible to Parliament for the supervision and control of Scottish administration, was manifest. The framers of the Union settlement had wisely left the management of domestic Scottish affairs as far as possible to Scotsmen:[a] but the Scotland of 1853 had long outgrown the administrative methods of 1707; and, while the towns had obtained their elected councils in 1834, the local business of the countryside—the supervision of primary schools, roads, police, vagrancy, licences and so forth—were still administered by the Justices of the Peace and the Commissioners of Supply, an antiquated body established in the eighteenth century to assess the land-tax. There were also a number of Boards located at Edinburgh which dealt with such matters as fisheries, prisons, lighthouses and the like. None of those bodies were democratic; most of their members were nominated or even held office by hereditary right; and they were quite incapable of maintaining the higher administrative standards of the nineteenth century or coping with the steady increase of public services and regulations. Clearly a whole-time Scottish minister was needed in Whitehall to promote the reorganisation of this outdated system and control its operation.

It was against this background that Scottish nationalism suddenly came awake, on a very small scale and for a very short time, in 1853. The moving spirit was W. E. Aytoun (1813-65), poet, essayist, and professor of rhetoric and *belles lettres* at Edin-

[a] See page 144 above.

burgh. He belonged to the same old Scottish family as Sir Robert Aytoun (1570-1638) whose bones lie buried in Westminster Abbey, and he had acquired in childhood from his mother a romantic devotion to the Jacobite cause which lasted all his life.[31] But the 'National Association for the Vindication of Scottish Rights' which this high Tory took the lead in founding was a non-party organisation. The published list of the committee was headed with the name of Duncan McLaren, Lord Provost of Edinburgh, the leader of Scottish Liberalism, and one of its warmest adherents was P. E. Dove, a Radical journalist and public speaker whose sympathies were with the working class.[a] But it was probably Aytoun who drafted the pamphlet which, under the watchword of 'Justice for Scotland,' expounded the Association's policy.[b]

It opens with a statement of nationalist doctrine which is remarkable for its moderation. Not a word is said against the Union: its value to Scotland is taken for granted: it is only the manner of its operation that is questioned. Before the Union, it is argued, Scotland's 'national integrity' was never in doubt. 'Scotland, so long as she trusted herself, governed herself, acted for herself and developed her own resources, was a nation full of life and energy and enterprise.' And there was nothing strange in that; for it is only when the affairs of one nation are managed by the men of another or by an unpatriotic clique within itself that it is neglected or misruled. Nor is a nation's natural desire to preserve its national character unjustified. 'Each nation,' the argument continues, and here, perhaps, a faint echo of Mazzini can be heard, 'is only the partial development of a universal humanity. . . . All general advancement consists not in the

[a] Dove's name appears in the list of the members of the Association, but his activities in 1853 seem to have been confined to journalism and the platform. In 1855 he published a tract on *Romanism, Rationalism and Protestantism viewed historically in relation to National Freedom and National Welfare* (Edinburgh), but this was mainly a glorification of Scottish nationalism before the Union. The Union is commended as 'honourable' to both countries, and no reference is made to the grievances of Dove's own day.

[b] A signed article by Aytoun in *Blackwood's* (vol. 74, pages 263-283) closely accords with the pamphlet. Quotations from the article above are marked with an asterisk

eradication of the generic peculiarities of races, but in the wise direction of those peculiarities.' That does not imply a repudiation of the Union. ' The Union neither did nor could denationalise us. It left us in undisturbed possession of our national laws and our national religion.'* And it was only a legislative, not an administrative union: it enabled Scotland to continue to a large extent to govern itself. But there was a flaw in it. No provision was made for adjusting the numerical disproportion between the Scottish and English members of Parliament when it dealt with purely Scottish affairs. It might have provided, for example, that such matters should be handled by a committee composed equally of English and Scottish members. But nothing of that sort was done. 'We allowed our representatives to be swamped,' and there was no means of ensuring that ' the same consideration be shown by Parliament to matters which are purely Scottish as to those which relate exclusively to England.'* The result has now become manifest in a general neglect of Scottish interests which violates the spirit of the treaty on which the Union rests. The time has come for Scotland to make her choice. ' She must either sink the question of her nationality or she must resolve to maintain what legally and justly belongs to her.'

On November 2 the Association held a public meeting at Edinburgh. Over 2,000 people attended, and five resolutions, the second moved by McLaren, were carried with acclaim. The text of the three most important of these resolutions—which constitute the first statement on record of the claims of the new Scottish nationalism—was as follows:

(1) ' That the Treaty of Union ... asserts the individuality and provides for the preservation of the National laws and institutions of Scotland. That any attempt to subvert or place those institutions under English control, and under the pretence of a centralising economy to deprive her of the benefit of local action, is an infraction of the true

spirit of this Treaty, injurious to her welfare, and should be strenuously resisted.'

(2) 'For the better administration of the public business of this part of the United Kingdom, and for securing to Scotland the practical benefits of a united legislative, that the office of Secretary of State be restored.'

(3) 'That the representation of Scotland in Parliament be increased.'

Another meeting was held in Glasgow on December 15. Aytoun called it a 'tremendous' meeting. 'The immense City Hall,' he wrote, 'was crowded from floor to ceiling—I believe not short of 5,000 people . . . all most enthusiastic.'[32] The most notable speech was delivered by Dove, whose allusions to English landlords in Ireland and the Austrian garrison in Italy showed that he at any rate was interested in nationalist movements outside Britain. 'There are two ideas of nationality,' he said, '. . . the first the nationality of race, the second the nationality of reason. . . . The first idea leads only to national antipathy, the second leads to patriotism.' For Scotsmen he identified patriotism mainly with devotion to Scottish institutions, and for their preservation and improvement he wanted more than a Scottish Secretary in London. We want, he said, 'some Scottish assembly for the direction of those matters which are exclusively Scottish,' an administrative, not a legislative body, a sort of 'political synod.'[33]

The enthusiasm Aytoun noted in the City Hall was not so marked outside it. The *Herald* printed a full report of the meeting and was mildly sympathetic, but the business world was apathetic, if not hostile, to a cause which seemed, however faintly, to threaten the economic unity of Britain. A Glasgow merchant, writing to *The Times*, declared that in Glasgow the Association was 'simply laughed to scorn.'[34] And though such backing as it had was mainly in Edinburgh, the *Scotsman*, thinking doubtless more of Aytoun's politics than McLaren's, was positively abusive. 'There has of late sprung up,' said its leader-writer some months before the Edinburgh meeting, ' a small party only describable as the Scottish Repealers.' 'We are proud of being Scotchmen,' he went on, ' but thankful to be Scotchmen living under a British Government' which protects us not only ' from our too bigoted ecclesiasticism and our too narrow nationality,' but also ' from one another—church from church, class from class, even district from district, as the comparatively tolerant and moral East from the bigoted and bibulous West.' Plainly the great Whig journal was still following the anglicising trend of Jeffrey's day. It dismissed the movement as ' this bow-wow agitation ' and its promoters as ' the Scoto-Irish party ' and contemptuously quoted a sympathetic reference in the Dublin *Nation*, the organ of Young Ireland, to the effect that the Scots, after ' wallowing for a century in the obese prosperity of provincialism,' were at last waking up.[35]

With such a lead it is not surprising that *The Times* should have treated the emergence of Scottish nationalism with the same scornful petulance with which it was to treat, a decade later, the first manifestations of Welsh nationalism.[a] 'The separate nationality of Scotland is happily in these days an anachronism.' For a century past the Scotch, unlike the Irish, have ' wisely and successfully applied themselves to the honourable and lucrative pursuits of life, content to become rich and prosperous in their several vocations.' But now a little group of agitators are invoking ' what they call national feeling, but what we call narrow and provincial prejudice. . . . It has been by appealing to this " jargon of nationalities," as it has been aptly called, that half the miseries of Europe have been occasioned.' There may be minor Scottish grievances that need redress; ' but does this constitute a reason for threatening to resolve ourselves once more into the kingdoms of Wessex, Mercia, East Anglia and what not? . . . Surely it is

wiser to leave these matters in the hands of the Scotch member,
than to engage in disgraceful imitation of the worst features of
the Irish character.'[36]

The Press could safely deride the movement, for it made little
stir in Scotland, or in England. Nobody even mentioned it in
Parliament. None of the Scottish M.P.s joined the Association,
only one (Cowan, Member for Edinburgh) attended the Edinburgh meeting, none the Glasgow meeting. And, having no
place in politics, the movement had none in public interest.
Those enthusiastic audiences would seem to have comprised
almost all the Scotsmen who cared about the question. And the
reason for this general indifference seems clear enough. No
Scotsman at that time questioned the necessity of maintaining the
Union; and, though it was an extravagant libel to describe
Aytoun and his collaborators as ' Repealers '—they repeatedly
and quite sincerely proclaimed themselves wholehearted Unionists
—yet it was easy to detect in any proposals to tamper with the
existing machinery of government the taint of separatism. At
that time, too, as the newspapers show, any nationalist movement
in Scotland was bound to be discredited by what was happening
in Ireland. Till Gladstone began his crusade, Scottish Presbyterians
like Welsh Calvinists had no sympathy whatever with the Irish
cause. They were disgusted by the behaviour of the Irish paupers
who kept crowding into their cities. They were shocked by the
black record of agrarian crime in Ireland. If that was what
nationalism meant, no decent Scot could have anything to do
with it. But the chief reason why the movement of 1853 made
such little headway was lack of any widespread discontent with
things as they were. The grievances aired by the Association
might be felt by a few, but not by the public at large. To the
average Scotsman it was obvious that a few more Scottish M.P.s
could not radically affect the English predominance in Parliament
on which the Union had always rested and must always rest; and

his emotions were not deeply stirred by talk of neglected legislation or inefficient local government. Nor, indeed, was Aytoun
thinking only of those practical grievances. His nationalism, like
Scott's, was sentimental. Scottish institutions, he held, must be
preserved or restored, apart from practical considerations, because
they were Scottish. Scotland had not suffered from the removal
of the Scottish mint to London, but he denounced it, correctly
enough, as a breach of the Treaty of Union. He criticised
Scottish administration not so much because it was inefficient as
because, contrary to the intentions of 1707, it was controlled by
an English Minister. He demanded a Scottish Secretaryship not
only because it would remedy that 'injustice,' but also because
it would revive a lost Scottish institution. Those were genuine
sentiments, but something less immaterial, less academic, was
needed to sustain a nationalist movement.

Within a few months of its Glasgow meeting the Association
was already fading into the background; and its brief activities
were soon forgotten in the public excitement at the outbreak of
the Crimean War in 1854 and of the Indian Mutiny in 1857. The
latent Scottish pride in Scottish nationhood had failed to respond
to Aytoun's appeal to the past, but it came to the surface in full
strength when the news arrived of what the Scots Greys had done
at Balaclava and the Campbells at Lucknow and when Livingstone returned from his first journey across Africa and made his
triumphal progress through his native land. As long as Scotsmen
were taking the lead in making British history abroad, their
compatriots were in no mood to nourish minor grievances at
home, and more than a decade passed before Scottish claims were
voiced again. But, when it came, this second nationalist movement had more weight behind it than the first. The grievances
were the same; but, whereas the Association had been avowedly
non-political and had been virtually ignored by the politicians,
it was Scottish M.P.s who now raised the issue. In 1853 the
demand for 'justice' was barely audible beyond the bounds of

Edinburgh and Glasgow. In 1869 it became a topic of debate at Westminster. The scope of the agitation was still narrow, the public response still meagre; but this time it did not flicker out. It is still alive to-day.

VI. THE SECOND NATIONALIST MOVEMENT: THE SECRETARYSHIP

THE TWO chief grievances aired in 1853—the under-representation of Scotland in the House of Commons and the inefficiency of Scottish administration—were remedied to some extent as time went on. In 1863 the number of Scottish M.P.s was raised from 53 to 60 in a House of 658, and in 1885 to 72 in a House of 670. But this in itself, of course, could not safeguard Scottish affairs from the insufficient attention paid to them by Parliament. In 1869, accordingly, a majority of the Scottish M.P.s addressed a letter to Gladstone, then Prime Minister, pointing out that much Scottish business, not being of a legal character, was beyond the Lord Advocate's professional scope and that, particularly in view of the crying need for an improvement in Scottish local government, a second official post should be created to assist in the management of Scottish affairs. To this Gladstone responded by appointing a Royal Commission[a] which recommended precisely what the M.P.s' letter had proposed—the appointment of an additional under-secretary who, as well as the Lord Advocate, would advise the Home Secretary on Scottish matters. But Gladstone took no action, nor did Disraeli who succeeded him in 1874.

Thus, when in the seventies the process of reforming the

[a] Lively evidence was given before this Commission by McLaren. He denounced the 'Edinburgh Boards' which dealt with trade and industry as pure waste of money. Scottish traders could manage their own business better than government departments and Scottish industry had long outgrown the 'kind of nursing' provided by the Board

Scottish administrative system began, there was still no Scottish Secretary in London to take a hand in it. Nor, indeed, was it the result of purely Scottish agitation. It was a British affair. The great reforms of local government were not separate Scottish reforms. Like the new parliamentary system of 1832, the new machinery of local public service was applied to the whole of Britain. The Education Act of 1870 and the growing body of legislation dealing with public health, housing, the regulation of industry and so forth was extended to Scotland in Scottish editions which varied only in minor details from their originals. It was the same with the introduction of County Councils in 1889 and District and Parish Councils in 1894. The general result was a transformation of local government in Scotland at least as radical as in England and Wales. The new legislation enabled Edinburgh and Glasgow, like Manchester and Cardiff, to follow the lead of Birmingham in civic reform; and in the country at large the creation of the new Councils meant that the old complex of ill-composed and irresponsible Boards was replaced at last by democratic elected bodies responsible to their electors. The Boards which survived in Edinburgh were now composed of officials only, appointed by and responsible to the Central Government in London. They might be described as its local branches.

The Scottish grievance, however, was not dispelled by better administration. Its supervision and ultimate control were still exercised in London; and in London, too, rested the sole power of legislation. It was on this latter question that the issue was raised again in 1877, and raised in a manner that revealed that Scottish nationalist thought had moved a long step forward from the ideas of 1853. In the course of a debate in 1877, Sir Graham Campbell, Member for Kirkcaldy, went so far as to say that ultimately some system of federation would have to be devised

of Manufacturers established at the Union. J. B. Mackie, *Life and Work of Duncan McLaren* (Edinburgh, 1888), ii. 128.

for the satisfaction of Scottish claims. At the moment, however, though Scotland was at least as fit as Ireland for Home Rule, most of the Scottish people did not want it. He suggested, therefore, two interim reforms. First, to lower the high cost of promoting private Scottish legislation at Westminster a ' tribunal ' should be set up in Edinburgh to deal with it. Second, public Scottish bills should be submitted to a ' Grand Committee ' of the House mainly composed of Scottish members. If something of this kind were not done to provide for the separate treatment of Scottish business, Scotland would be driven to demand Home Rule. Campbell was followed by McLaren who recalled the resolution he had proposed in 1853 for the revival of the Scottish Secretaryship of State, and complained that the recommendations of the Commission of 1869 had been ignored.[37]

In 1881, nothing having happened in the interval, the issue was raised again by the Earl of Fife. ' Scotsmen feel strongly,' he told the Lords, ' that their business is managed in a second-hand manner.' They did not want a ' complete paraphernalia of government ' such as Ireland possessed. They only asked for a Scottish Secretary, not necessarily a Secretary of State in the Cabinet. Why was this modest plea rejected? ' Why should the law-abiding Scot be penalised?'[38] Argyll and other Scottish peers supported Fife, but the most important speech in the debate was that of the young Earl of Rosebery who was about to take McLaren's place as the leader of Scottish Liberalism. His support of the Scottish claim gave to the nationalist cause an impetus it had never yet obtained. For Rosebery was not only more highly gifted than any other Scottish politician: he was an intimate friend of Gladstone, now for the second time Prime Minister (1880-85).[a]

---

[a] Rosebery acted as Gladstone's host for the Midlothian campaign; and the close friendship continued up to almost the end of Gladstone's life. The panegyric Rosebery delivered when he unveiled the Gladstone statue at Glasgow in 1902 is the more impressive because of the speaker's temperamental moderation. *Miscellanies*, i, 255f.

Descended from the James Primrose who had made his name and fortune in the reign of James VI and I, and owner of great estates in Lothian and Fife, Rosebery had begun to take part in debate in the House of Lords in 1871. He was then only twenty-four, but, once engaged in politics, he had quickly come to the front. He was more deeply interested in foreign and imperial than in domestic affairs, but he was always a Scottish patriot. He was not, as it happens, a pure Scot. His mother was a daughter of the fourth Earl Stanhope. But his family tradition, his home at Dalmeny almost within sight of Edinburgh and his love of the old city, ' the historical, the beautiful, the inspiring,'[34] his interest in the romantic by-paths of Scottish history, his deification of Burns and Scott—it all made him much more a Scot than an Englishman, more so indeed than purely Scottish Gladstone. And certainly there was never any doubt about his Scottishness in Scotland. He was chosen Rector in due course of each of the four Scottish Universities, and on all great ceremonial occasions in his latter days it fell to him by common consent to play the part of public orator for Scotland. Characteristically his appeal to his fellow-countrymen was rational, practical, historical and only rarely emotional; and in that respect as in most others his personality contrasts sharply with that of the man who was soon to become the leader of Welsh nationalism. The Scot a sensitive, self-conscious, intellectual patrician, a democrat in principle but ill at ease with democracy, happy in his library but diffident and nervous in the bustling world outside, an eloquent orator but not at his best in controversy, vulnerable to the shafts of his opponents and mainly for that reason hating politics and always longing to be rid of them: the Welshman a child of the cottage, tough, self-confident, combative, more at home with people than with books, and endowed with all the arts of democratic leadership.

Rosebery's nationalism was never defined in any such programme as the resolutions of 1853; but its general character was made clear enough in his Scottish orations and particularly in the rectorial address on 'The Patriotism of a Scot' which he delivered at Edinburgh University in 1882.[40] Like all previous nationalists, like Scott or Burns, like Chalmers or Aytoun, he stood staunchly by the Union. In all the records of those stirring times, he cried, ' a fairer page will hardly be found than that occupied by the Scottish Union.' Enacted against the people's will—'fortunately plebiscites were not then in fashion'—it proved the salvation of Scotland. But, close as was the conjunction with England, Scottish national sentiment lived on, ' sometimes unexpectedly fierce and sometimes unexpectedly dormant.' Nor could this be anything but welcome to those who believed that, with nations as with individuals in society, uniformity depresses and deadens, variety stimulates and inspires. Would England have gained if Scotsmen had lost their national character? ' They would have made but indifferent Englishmen. . . . Would Scott have been a Wizard in the South? . . .' Nor was it only for the sake of variety that the distinctive Scottish character was worth preserving. It was needed for the proper conduct of Scottish affairs. ' Scotland has been accustomed to be left much to herself,' and with the almost frightening growth of population in the whole of the United Kingdom ' every part of the country will have, it is easy to see, to be left more and more to its own methods and its own devices; for it is impossible that any central Atlas can be found to bear the burden.' . . . But patriotism is not primarily a matter of politics. ' Government is really but a small matter compared with national character and it is the respect for and assertion of national character that constitutes patriotism.' Thus the Scottish patriot's first duty is not concerned with politics, but with morals, with maintaining and improving Scottish virtues. ' The dream of him who loved Scotland best would lie not so much in the direction of antiquarian revival as in the hope that his country might be pointed out as one that in spite of rocks and rigour and poverty could yet teach the world by precept and example, could lead the van and point the moral, where greater nations and fairer states had failed.'[41]

While he put Scottish morals first, Rosebery was by no means unconcerned with Scottish institutions. In that speech in the House of Lords in 1881 he had recited the history of Scottish administration and warmly supported Campbell's plea for a Scottish Minister. He had also repeated Campbell's warning as to the growth of Scottish discontent. 'The words, Home Rule,' he said, 'have begun to be distinctly and loudly mentioned in Scotland.'[42] This time Gladstone's response was immediate. He appointed Rosebery Parliamentary Under-Secretary at the Home Office to deal with Scottish business. But it very soon became apparent that this half-measure was not enough. Rosebery had been barely a year at his post before he felt obliged to tell Gladstone that his position was impossible. His appointment had been taken in Scotland to mean that greater attention would be paid to Scottish business and in fact it had meant nothing of the sort. In particular he had been helpless to speed the discussion of Scottish bills, two of which were suffering at that time from apparently interminable postponement. He did not spare his chief. 'The Prime Minister,' he wrote, 'was returned by a Scottish constituency, backed by an overwhelming majority of Scottish members. From the day of the first meeting of the new Parliament until the present day of its third session . . . not one minute of Government time has been allotted to Scotland or Scottish affairs. Can you be surprised that the people of Scotland complain?' But at a moment when the Phoenix Park murders had just dealt Gladstone the heaviest blow of his life, he could not give his mind to Scotland. He evaded Rosebery as ten years later he was to evade Welsh pressure for Disestablishment. Rosebery wrote again—and again—and at last, at the end of the year, he intimated his intention to resign. He did not value office, he said; it was not a personal matter, but one of principle. 'I serve a country which is the backbone of our party, but which is never recognised.'[43] His persistence was rewarded; for, when a few months later he did resign his useless job, he had already persuaded Gladstone to agree to a genuine full Secretaryship, and in the spring of 1885, having been admitted to the Cabinet as Lord Privy Seal, he introduced a bill which established a separate Scottish Office, headed by a Secretary for Scotland, to take over from the Home Office, the Local Government Board, the Education Department and certain branches of the Board of Trade all business that was concerned with Scotland. Before it could be read a second time in the Commons the Government fell (June 9, 1885); but it was not a party measure, and under Salisbury's Government it was carried into law before Parliament was dissolved.[a]

When Gladstone returned to power early in 1886, Rosebery became Foreign Secretary and thenceforward on to the days of his brief and uneasy tenure of the seat which Gladstone had at last vacated, he was immersed in foreign policy and the new imperialism. His position as a Scottish nationalist was thus comparable with Lloyd George's subsequent position as a Welsh nationalist. He could and did support the cause on occasion, but he could no longer be its leader.

VII. THE SECOND NATIONALIST MOVEMENT: HOME RULE

If HOME RULE, as Rosebery told the House of Lords, was being talked about in Scotland in 1881 it was partly Gladstone's doing. In 1871 he had scouted the notion of Home Rule-all-round, but by 1879 it seems he had come to recognise the need for some effective treatment of the problem of parliamentary congestion, and in the course of his Midlothian campaign he gave an airing,

---

[a] 48 and 49 Vic. cap. 61.

so to speak, to the idea of all-round devolution. He suggested that ' the solution of some national and even imperial difficulties ' might be found in the application of representative government to local affairs. ' We have got an overweighted Parliament . . . and, if we can make arrangements under which Ireland, Scotland, Wales and portions of England can deal with questions of local and special interest to themselves more efficiently than Parliament now can, that, I say, will be the attainmentof great national good.' But he insisted on two conditions. . . . First, the supremacy of the Imperial Parliament must be maintained. Second, nothing should be given to Ireland which was not given equally to Scotland and other parts of Britain.[44] This proposal was well received by Scottish Liberals. McLaren, now in retirement, declared himself in favour of ' a measure of Home Rule which would apply equally to each of the three kingdoms and have a tendency to unite them more and more in one friendly bond of brotherhood.'[45]

Six years later it was a very different story. In 1885 Gladstone had become fully and finally converted to Home Rule; but it was not the kind of Home Rule he had adumbrated in Mid-lothian. It was Home Rule for Ireland at once and by itself, and in a more separatist form than could reasonably be applied to Scotland and Wales. Devolution all round, in fact, as observed in the preceding chapter, was Chamberlain's policy now, not Glad-stone's, and many of the Liberals who had cheered Gladstone in Midlothian abandoned their leader and their party rather than accept his version of Home Rule. Even McLaren forswore his allegiance. ' If I had the health and strength which I possessed in Anti-Corn Law times,' he wrote to Bright a fortnight before he died, ' I would be prepared . . . to do what our ancestors used to call "to testify " against the proposed injustice.' Two days later he resigned the presidency of the Edinburgh Liberal Association.

The effect of this Irish quarrel on Scottish nationalism was profound; for it made it a party question. The nationalist move-ment of 1853 had been non-party: mainly Conservative, it had also been backed by Liberals and Radicals. But from 1885 onwards it was a purely Liberal movement. As soon as battle was joined on Gladstonian Home Rule, the idea of general devolution as an alternative was abandoned by the Conservatives and their new Liberal Unionist allies: they became, as has been said on an earlier page, Unionists-all-round. The Liberal majority, on the other hand, who had kept faith with Gladstone, accepted Home Rule-all-round in principle. If Ireland had it, they said, Scotland was entitled *mutatis mutandis* to have it too—if she needed it. Most of them at that time were not convinced of such a need, but to the nationalist-minded among them Scottish Home Rule seemed the natural sequel to Irish. When a Home Rule Association was founded in Scotland in 1886 on the Manchester model to champion Home Rule for Ireland, its first president was G. P. Clark, M.P. for Caithness, who became, as will presently appear, a leading Scottish Home Ruler. And presently the cause began to spread among the people at large. Aspirants to a political career found it helpful to appeal to the electors as patriots who would like to see the Scottish Parliament restored. Among them were some of those ' leftists' who found the Scottish Labour Party in 1888 but could only win seats at that time if they stood as Liberals. Young Cunninghame Graham, for example, linked the cause of Labour with Home Rule. The demand for the latter in Scotland, he said, sprang from ' the misery of the Scottish poor.'[46]

This trend towards Home Rule was soon reflected in Parliament. The new-won Scottish Secretaryship and Office, it was argued, had already proved incapable of satisfying Scottish needs. Rosebery dryly remarked in 1887 that there had been five Secretaries in sixteen months.[47] What was the use, asked the member for Elgin and Nairn, of a minister who was ' shut up in Whitehall where nobody could approach him?' Scotsmen, he added, now ' cared less for the British Parliament than at any time since the Union ';[48] and in the course of the same debate, R. B.

Haldane, the canny young member for Haddington, admitted that, though he had hitherto hesitated to countenance Home Rule, he was now convinced of the necessity of ' a very large transfer of Scottish business to Scotland.'[49] In 1889 the gathering opinion took formal shape when G. P. Clark, basing his case entirely on the neglect of Scottish interests resulting from the congestion of parliamentary business, moved in the Commons that ' arrangements be made for giving to the people of Scotland, by their representatives in a National Parliament, the management and control of Scottish affairs.'[50] The fate of this first parliamentary resolution for Scottish Home Rule was what might have been expected. The Conservatives, now in power, voted against it to a man, and most of the Liberals followed their leader into the same lobby. While Gladstone had commended the principle of devolution in Midlothian and more recently at Swansea, now and for the rest of his life he went no further. Home Rule for Ireland was his supreme, almost his sole, political objective, and he was determined that his fight for it should not be delayed or weakened by the less urgent claims of Scotland or Wales. Thus, on this occasion, he admitted that Scotland had a genuine and growing grievance and once more suggested devolution as the remedy. ' I hold,' he said, ' that all judicious devolution which hands over to subordinate bodies duties for which they are better qualified by local knowledge and which at the same time sets free the hands of Parliament for the pursuit of its proper business, does not weaken it but strengthen it.'[51] But the specific application of the principle required time and thought, and he refused to support a project ' as yet vague and unformed, in embryo.' The Government, led by half-Scottish A. J. Balfour, firmly opposed the motion and it was defeated by 200 votes to 79. Only 19 of the 72 Scottish members voted for it: 22 voted against it.

A similar resolution was moved in 1890, and again Gladstone made it clear that Scottish Home Rule was not yet an item of the Liberal Party programme. ' The question is not ripe.'[52] The motion was lost be 181 votes to 141—26 of the Scottish members voting for it, 15 against. . . . In 1891 the motion reappeared, but its terms were now extended to cover England, Ireland and Wales. It was proposed by Clark and seconded by a Welshman.[a] But the interest taken in the subject in Parliament had not been augmented by the widening of its scope. The House was counted out.[53] . . . In 1892 a curious scheme was propounded by W. A. Hunter (Aberdeen N.) for evading ' the tyrannical majority of the English members who naturally vote on Scottish questions according to English ideas.' He introduced a Bill providing that the Scottish M.P.s should meet by themselves each autumn and pass legislation for Scotland which would then be submitted straightway for the royal assent without reference either to the Commons or to the Lords.[54] The debate was ill-attended, and before a vote could be taken the House was again counted out. . . . A few weeks later Clark again moved for Home Rule-all-round. This time he appealed to imperialist sentiment. The House had no time, he said, to deal properly with the problems of the Empire. But ' dualistic Home Rule ' as proposed in 1886 was not enough, nor was it right in principle. Not Austria-Hungary or Sweden and Norway should be our model, but the United States, Germany, Switzerland or Canada. In any event ' what you give Ireland we shall claim for Scotland and anything less we will not have.'[55] The motion was lost—74 to 54. Of 24 Scottish votes 10 were ' aye ' and 14 ' no.' . . . In 1893 the Liberals were back in office, and, though they were still not committed to it as a party, the prospects of devolution brightened. When Clark returned to the charge, the adverse majority fell to 18—168 against, 150 for: 22 Scotsmen against and 40 for.[56] . . . In 1894 hopes rose yet higher, for Rosebery was Prime Minister when Sir Henry Dalziel (Kirkcaldy), who had succeeded Clark as chief spokesman of the cause, brought up the hardy annual once more. This time he confined the claim to Scotland—incidentally, though Aytoun

[a] See page 235 above.

ad never dreamed of Home Rule, Dalziel cited his article of 1853
o show how old the Scottish grievance was—and, though he
dvanced no new arguments, he won the day at last. Seconded
by English Birrell and supported by Welsh Lewis and the English
Secretary for Scotland (Sir George Trevelyan), the motion was
carried by 180 votes to 170, Scottish 'ayes' 38, 'noes' 20.[57] . . .
The success was short-lived. In 1895, when the Rosebery
Government was within a few weeks of its fall, Dalziel moved his
all-round motion again. Lloyd-George backed it with a vigorous
speech on Wales' behalf.[a] John Redmond disapproved of linking
the 'vital' needs of Ireland with the somewhat 'academic'
claims of the other nations, but he confessed himself a federalist
and admitted that Irish Home Rule, though it must not be
obstructed by coupling it with Welsh and Scottish, should be
granted in a form which would be subsequently applied to Wales
and Scotland. Trevelyan again supported. Balfour was again the
most damaging opponent. The voting was 128 against and 102
for: the Scottish vote 14 against and 30 for.[58]

To concentrate on the nationalist movement in Parliament and
to recite the resolutions moved in its favour by nationalist
politicians may create a false impression. It may suggest that the
movement was a powerful movement, backed by a great body,
even perhaps a majority, of the Scottish people and exciting the
keenest interest at Westminster. That was not so. Scottish
debates were rarely attended by more than half the Commons.
Twice the House was counted out. And in Scotland ardent
nationalists were a small minority. There was no 'Nationalist
Party.' Scottish candidates might declare themselves nationalists
but none of them put nationalism in the forefront of his programme as Ellis did in Merioneth in 1886. No Scottish orator
pleaded for it with Lloyd George's fire. It might have seemed,
indeed, when the Conservatives returned to power in 1895, as if

---

[a] See page 235 above.

the second nationalist movement was to suffer the same fate as the first. Like the Welsh movement it came to a dead halt. Lloyd George's attempt to rally the defeated Liberals to Home Rule-all-round broke down.[a] On a devolutionist Welsh motion in 1898, warmly supported by R. T. Reid and Campbell-Bannerman, the House was once more counted out.[59] In 1899, when D. V. Pirie returned to the charge with a second Scottish Home Rule Bill, its first reading was its last. The one and only gain achieved throughout the long decade of Conservative rule was a measure on which both parties were agreed—the Scottish Private Legislation Act of 1899.[60] With the coming of the South African War the issue fell into the background, leaving Unionism-all-round in possession of the field.

The Unionist case was simple and straightforward. Except for one or two moderates who continued to believe that devolution was a possible means of escape from the Irish *impasse*,[b] the Conservative majority in England stood firm against any meddling with the solidarity of the United Kingdom. Home Rule anywhere, they said, in Scotland or Wales as much as in Ireland, would quickly lead to the disruption of the British Empire. ' We object to Home Rule,' said Balfour, ' whether it begins with Ireland and ends with Wales or begins with Wales and ends with Ireland. We object to the whole thing.'[61] Unaware that the tide was soon to turn, he maintained (1895) that the trend of international relations was ' to bind together and not to loosen.' ' It appears to be absolute lunacy for this country to pursue alone among the nations of the world an opposite course to that which has built up every other great Empire with which we have to compete.'[62] He did not deny that Parliament was suffering from

---

[a] See page 237 above.

[b] Some Conservatives favoured devolution but only on a demographic or regional, not on a national basis. Sir John Lubbock argued that the existing Anglo-Scottish border was unreal. The character of the Lowlands were virtually identical with that of the northern English counties. The true frontier of nationality was the Highland line. *Hansard*, H. of C., 1894, vol. 23, col. 648.

ongestion of business, but he suggested that other remedies could
e found for it less drastic and dangerous than legislative devolu-
ion; and in any case, he argued, the congestion was mainly due
o the Irish Question which had introduced an unusual period of
stress and storm, in which controversy is long and business
low.' He likened the House of Commons to a ' great steam
ngine' that works badly when it gets too hot.⁶³

Conservative opinion in Scotland followed this uncom-
romising lead. The anti-nationalist sentiment of the business
world, which had been plain enough in 1853, was now more
narked, especially in Glasgow. And now that it was a question
ot merely of a Scottish Secretaryship but of Home Rule, anta-
onism to any weakening of the economic unity of Britain was
narpened by the old jealousy of Edinburgh. 'Glasgow,' said
Ialford Mackinder, the eminent geographer and publicist and
nember for the Camlachie division, ' Glasgow is too great to be
uled by the remainder of Scotland.' Just as industrial Belfast,
apart from the religious issue, refused to be ruled ' by the ignorance
f rural Ireland,' so the Clyde could not surrender the control of
s industrial interests to Edinburgh and the Highlands.⁶⁴ Another
rgument was in tune with the imperialism of the day. Nothing
nust be done, it was said, to lessen Scotland's share in ' the vast
mperial heritage' which Scotsmen had done so much to build
p.⁶⁵

If Scottish nationalism, as these Unionists asserted, had had
o native roots, if it had been only a pale reflection of Irish
ationalism, it would probably have faded away in the course of
nat bleak Conservative decade. As it was, when at last the
iberals came back to power in 1906, it was evident at once that
ne movement, so far from weakening, had grown much stronger
the interval. In the very year of Liberal victory, the Scottish
Iome Rule Association committed itself to Home Rule-all-
und. In 1907 the old request of the Scottish M.P.s for a standing

committee for Scottish legislation was granted. In 1908 th
Scottish Liberal Party nailed devolution to its platform.[a] And i
that same year a third Government of Scotland Bill was intro
duced by D. V. Pirie. It embodied a full-scale plan of ' federal
devolution. While the sovereignty of the Imperial Parliamen
was explicitly reserved, the Scottish Parliament would legislate fo
all Scottish affairs. Only customs and excise duties would b
excluded from the field of its taxing powers. The old Scottis
Privy Council would be revived as a cabinet of ministers to advis
the Crown. Leave to print the Bill was granted by 257 votes t
102; Scottish votes 41 to 9.[66] In 1911 a similar Bill was introduce
by Dalziel who reminded the House that twenty years had passe
since he first asked for the restoration of the Scottish Parliamen
and contended that the threefold case for it—the impossibility o
obtaining under the existing system the legislation desired by th
people of Scotland, the need for Scottish opinion to prevail i
purely Scottish affairs, and the congestion of business in th
Imperial Parliament—had been steadily strengthened since 189
He conceded the Irish claim to priority, but he argued that Hom
Rule for Ireland would be more acceptable to the British publi
if it were linked with Home Rule for Scotland and Wales.[67] Th
Bill was vehemently opposed by Sir Henry Craik (Glasgow an
Aberdeen Universities) who had led the Scottish anti-nationalis
for many years, his Unionism stiffened by his knowledge o
Scottish history. He declared that the ' vast majority ' of h
fellow-countrymen repudiated Home Rule because it woul
weaken a Union which had served Scotland so well and reviv
in England an anti-Scottish prejudice that had long been dea
Do the businessmen of south-western Scotland, he asked, wi

[a] National sentiment was whetted at this time by the conduct of the House of Lor
in holding up two Scottish Land Bills, passed by the Commons, until an English La
Bill had been considered. ' A new Act of Union,' said the Scottish Prime Minist
Campbell-Bannerman, ' was thrust upon us by the Unionist Peers, and the land fro
John o' Groat's to Land's End was to be dealt with on the assumption that milord Lan
downe had dried up the Tweed.' J. A. Spender, *Life of Sir H. Campbell-Bannerm*
(London, 1923), ii. 368.

to break the 'hundred commercial bonds that tie them to England?' Is not Clydeside more closely connected with Manchester than with the Western Hebrides? Does Glasgow, 'with its vast population and great commercial wealth,' wish to be 'made subject to an Edinburgh Parliament?'[68] . . . The introduction of the Bill was approved by 172 to 73; Scottish votes 31 to 4.

The campaign continued. Early in 1912 Dr. Chapple (Stirlingshire) moved that Irish Home Rule, for which the Liberal Government was now drafting its Bill, should be followed by Home Rule-all-round. The motion was supported by the Secretary for Scotland (McKinnon Wood) and carried by 226 to 128, Scots 43 to 6. Bonar Law, Canadian-Ulster-Scot by origin and now Leader of the Opposition, was its chief opponent. 'As far as I am able to judge,' he said, 'there is not the smallest desire for this change in Scotland.'[69] But that was only true of his own party, and a little later it was made manifest how completely the Liberals had been converted to general devolution; for Asquith introduced the third Home Rule Bill for Ireland expressly as the first instalment of Home Rule-all-round. That, he reminded the House, was his attitude to Home Rule in 1893 and the case for it had been strengthened by twenty years' experience.[70] It was a clear official lead and MacCallum Scott (Bridgeton) referred to it when, a few weeks later, he introduced a Government of the United Kingdom Bill which for the first time put fourfold devolution into legislative shape. The Bill repeated the terms of the Irish Bill and extended them with a few modifications to England, Scotland and Wales.[a] The Government, of course, committed as they were to giving Ireland priority, could not accept the Bill and it made no further progress. But the attendance showed how greatly parliamentary interest in devolution had

[a] Ireland was to have a bicameral Parliament, the other Parliaments were to have only one House. Customs and Excise and one or two other 'subjects' conceded to the Irish Parliament were to be reserved for the Imperial Parliament. Wales was to have a Court of Appeal.

increased since the days when the theme had emptied the House. No less than 476 members voted on the first reading—264 in favour, 212 against, Scots 43 to 7.[71]

In 1913 another Scottish Home Rule Bill was introduced by Sir W. H. Cowan (Aberdeenshire, E.) and again supported by McKinnon Wood. Like its predecessor it closely followed the lines of the Irish Bill. One point was of historic interest to Scotsmen—the substitution of the Judicial Committee of the Privy Council for the House of Lords as the final court of appeal from Scottish decisions. Balfour ridiculed as usual ' these shadowy schemes of federalism,' now stressing the instability of a federal system in which one unit was vastly more populous and wealthy than the others; but this time he was not wholly unconstructive. He admitted that devolution might be regarded as a possible, though not the only, method of relieving parliamentary congestion, but it should be on regional, not national lines. The whole of the United Kingdom might be cut up into ' districts ' of a convenient size, each of them possessing ' not a parliament, of course—that is absurd—but something in the nature of a glorified county council.'[72] The second reading was carried by 204 to 159: Scottish votes 45 to 8. . . . In 1914 the fourth and last of the pre-war Scottish Home Rule Bills, virtually a replica of the third, was introduced by I. Macpherson (Ross and Cromarty). It was again supported on the front benches by McKinnon Wood and opposed by Balfour. There were no new arguments. The most interesting speech was Mackinder's, cited above. The debate on the second reading was adjourned, and it had not been resumed when the first World War broke out.[73]

The campaign thus interrupted had made remarkable progress since 1906. Devolution was now an item of the Liberal Party programme and, though Ministers might refuse to embody it in a Bill of their own till Irish Home Rule was on the statute-book, they had accepted the principle, and it seemed only a matter of time before it took legislative shape. And yet, mainly for two reasons, the movement still lacked force and weight. First, it was still, so to speak, amateurish. To disrupt the political unity of Britain was not a simple, easy task, and the formidable difficulties it involved, especially in finance, had not been firmly faced or deeply studied. The critics had ground for their complaint that the speakers who supported Scottish Home Rule Bills talked more about the reasons for promoting them than about their contents. Secondly, the nationalist movement was still a somewhat dry and academic affair. In Parliament the practical aspect of the question was always stressed. Appeals to patriotic sentiment were rare. No Scot complained that the neglect of Scottish affairs was an intolerable insult to Scotland or foretold the extinction of Scottish nationhood if the Union stood unchanged. ' Our national spirit,' said one speaker at any early stage of the campaign, ' has always been able to take care of itself.'[74] Thus national emotion was seldom kindled and there was scarcely a flicker of national antagonism. Historic memories were left asleep. Flodden was on'y mentioned once in all those debates, and then in humorous repartee. Bannockburn was only mentioned once, and then by a cynical Unionist who dubbed it ' the greatest misfortune that ever befel my country.'[75] So Scottish nights at Westminster were quiet nights; and, when in the course of that last debate the Secretary for Scotland commented on ' the good-humoured and passionless manner in which this subject has been argued,'[76] no one in the House could have failed to mark the contrast he implied with the bitterness and turmoil of the Irish debates. It was a significant contrast. The difference was not merely a matter of national temparament. It was a difference in history and circumstance, in the weight of grievance past and present and in the heat of the emotions it had aroused. Compared, indeed, with Irish nationalism Scottish nationalism might well have seemed a cold, imitative, artificial thing. Would any Scotsman, it might have been asked, have wanted Home Rule if

Ireland had not given the lead? The answer may be doubtful, but it is plain enough that, if as many Scotsmen had wanted Home Rule as Irishmen and had fought for it as unitedly and fiercely, they would have got it.

The last Scottish and Welsh Home Rule Bills had hardly made their appearance when the war rang down the curtain on the domestic stage. As a matter of course the claims of Welsh and Scottish—though not, unhappily, of Irish—nationalism were shelved till the combined strength and endurance of the British peoples had saved the British Isles and helped to save all Europe from the onslaught of Prussian militarism. But the national threads which were interwoven in that common strain and sacrifice were always visible. Scottish regiments stood close-knit with English and Welsh regiments at the front, but they never forgot they were ' Scotties.' The high command, too, had a national complexion in the last decisive stages of the war. In Wales was proud that civil and supreme authority lay with Lloyd George, Scotland was proud that the Commander-in-Chief of the British armies in the field was Haig of Bemersyde. And when victory had been won, the Scottish people built on the rock of Edinburgh Castle the noblest war memorial in Britain to honour their own Scottish dead.

[1] Craik, 600.
[2] Lockhart. *Life of Scott* (2nd. ed., Edinburgh, 1839), viii. 264.
[3] *Croker Papers* (London, 1884), i. 318.
[4] Buchan, 325.
[5] *Altavona* (Edinburgh, 1882), 291-4; *The Scottish Highlanders and the Land Law* (London, 1885), *passim*.
[6] J. S. Blackie, *The Language and Literature of the Scottish Highlands* (Edinburgh, 1876), 78.
[7] *Ibid.*, 92-3.
[8] Quoted from A. Carmichael's *Carmina Gadelica* by A. Muir Mackenzie, *Scotland in Modern Times* (Edinburgh, 1947), 234.
[9] J. L. Campbell, *op. cit.*, 66: *The Times*, Jan. 1, 1878; Feb. 28, 1879.
[10] A. and P., 1877, LXVII, 803.
[11] *Report*, A. and P., 1884, XXXIII, page 7.
[12] *The Times*, March 6, 1897.

[13] J. L. Campbell, 72-3.
[14] Sir R. Rait and G. S. Pryde, *Scotland*, (London, 1931), 213-15.
[15] C. R. Fay, *Great Britain from Adam Smith to the Present Day* (London, 1928), 348.
[16] Lockhart, ix. 296.
[17] Rosebery, *Miscellanies*, i. 238.
[18] Mathieson, *Church and Reform in Scotland* (Glasgow, 1916), 357.
[19] J. Morley, *Life of Cobden* (London, 1908), i. 271.
[20] G. M. Trevelyan, *Life of John Bright* (London, 2nd ed., 1925), 84. See also J. B. Mackie, *Life and Work of Duncan McLaren* (Edinburgh, 1888).
[21] *The Times*, Nov. 26, 1879.
[22] *The Times*, Sept. 27, 1871.
[23] Morley, ii. 596.
[24] A. H. McLintock, *History of Otago* (Dunedin, 1949), chaps. iv-v.
[25] J. M. Reid, *Modern Scottish Literature* (Saltire Pamphlets, No. 5, Edinburgh, 1945), 10.
[26] *Ibid.*, 12.
[27] Ian Finlay, *Art in Scotland* (Oxford, 1948), 118-19.
[28] Sir G. O. Trevelyan, *Life and Letters of Lord Macaulay* (London, ed. 1911), 330.
[29] Lady Minto, *Lord Minto in India* (London, 1880), chap. xv.
[30] W. G. Blaikie, *Life of David Livingstone* (6th ed. London, 1925), 288.
[31] T. Martin, *Memoir of W. E. Aytoun* (Edinburgh, 1867), 72-3.
[32] *Ibid.*, 141.
[33] *Glasgow Herald*, Dec. 16, 1853.
[34] *The Times*, Oct. 26, 1853.
[35] *Scotsman*, July 6, Nov. 5 and 19, 1853.
[36] *The Times*, July 7 and Nov. 5, 1853.
[37] *Hansard*, 1879, vol. 232, col. 929-35.
[38] *Hansard*, 1881, vol, 262, col. 308-25.
[39] *Miscellanies*, ii. 194.
[40] *Miscellanies*, ii. 106f.
[41] *Ibid.*, 98, 94-5, 110, 114-116, 120, 131.
[42] *Hansard*, 1881, vol. 262, col. 315-21.
[43] Earl of Crewe, *Lord Rosebery* (London, 1931), i. 154-60.
[44] *The Times*, Nov. 27, 1879.
[45] Rait and Pryde, 124-5.
[46] *Hansard*, H. of C., 1889, vol. 335, col. 97.
[47] *Ibid.*, H. of L., 1887, vol. 318, col. 692.
[48] *Ibid.*, 1888, vol. 331, col. 1782, 1790-91.
[49] *Ibid.*, col. 1805.
[50] *Ibid.*, 1889, vol. 335, col. 74.
[51] *Ibid.*, col. 103-6.
[52] *Ibid.*, 1890, vol. 341, col. 717.
[53] *Ibid.*, 1891, vol. 351, col. 440ff.
[54] *Ibid.*, 1892, vol. 3, col. 1450-2.
[55] *Ibid.*, col. 1686-90.
[56] *Ibid.*, 1893, vol. 13, col. 1828ff.
[57] *Ibid.*, 1894, vol. 22, col. 1116ff.
[58] *Ibid.*, 1895, vol. 32, col. 523ff.
[59] *Ibid.*, 1898, vol. 54, col. 168ff.
[60] *Ibid.*, 62 and 63 vict., c. 47.
[61] *Ibid.*, 1898, vol. 54, col. 1732.
[62] *Ibid.*, 1895, vol. 32, col. 560.
[63] *Ibid.*, 1898, vol. 54, col. 1733-4.
[64] *Ibid.*, 1914, vol. 62, col. 1491-2.
[65] e.g. Sir G. Young, among others. *Ibid.*, 1913, vol. 53, col. 511.
[66] *Ibid.*, 1908, vol. 189, col. 968ff.
[67] *Ibid.*, 1911, vol. 29, col. 1929-31.

[68] *Ibid.*, 1932-4.
[69] *Ibid.*, 1912, vol. 34, col. 1489-90.
[70] *Ibid.*, vol. 36 col. 1403.
[71] *Ibid.*, 1912, vol. 40, col. 1158-62.
[72] *Ibid.*, 1913, vol. 53, col. 529-41.
[73] *Ibid.*, 1914, vol. 62, 1467-1549.
[74] *Ibid.*, 1889, vol. 335, col. 94.
[75] *Ibid.*, 1893, vol. 13, col. 1840.
[76] *Ibid.*, 1914, vol. 62, col. 1542.

PART SEVEN

English Interlude

I. THE DEBATES OF 1919

THE STIMULUS given to national sentiment in the British Isles as elsewhere by the ideology of the war was most marked in Ireland, but it was also apparent in Scotland and Wales. Already in the autumn of 1917 the Scottish Trades Union Congress had sent a deputation to seek the Prime Minister's support for Home Rule in Scotland, and Lloyd George had told them that he was 'in complete agreement with the principle of devolution.'[1] Six months later the Scottish 'National Committee'—a group of Liberal and Labour M.P.s who had backed the Scottish Home Rule Bill of 1913[a]—decided to press for the expansion of Irish Home Rule into 'a complete federal system for the United Kingdom.'[2] Wales, too, was stirred, and more vigorously. Already before the end of the war the discussion of Home Rule, in which Mr. David (later Lord) Davies, an ardent patriot and one of Lloyd George's intimate friends, took the lead, was keener and more widespread than in the pre-war years, and it was hoped in nationalist circles that the Welshman who had acquired such immense prestige as the champion of small nations in the war might now recover his youthful ardour for self-government in little Wales. How strong, for the moment at any rate, the

[a] See page 306 above.

311

movement had become was made evident when at Whitsuntide, 1918, a national conference at Llandrindod carried with only one dissenting vote a resolution in favour of 'a comprehensive measure of autonomy for Wales, including a Welsh Parliament upon which shall be conferred all the functions of government which are not by common consent Imperial concerns.' This move was warmly welcomed by public opinion throughout the Principality. North and South were for once united. No less than eleven of the seventeen County and County Borough Councils supported the resolution. Only those in Flintshire and Newport dissented.[3] It was mostly Liberals who had gathered at Llandrindod, but Labour took the same line. A special conference of the South Wales Labour Federation declared that the sequel to Irish Home Rule ought to be Home Rule-all-round.[4] Never, in fact, since it was first ventilated in the eighteen-eighties had the idea of Home Rule for Wales roused so much interest or obtained so much support. But before action could be taken on the resolution, the Welsh movement found itself caught up in a wider agitation. The deputation which waited on the Prime Minister at the end of June to state the case for devolution was not composed of Welshmen only. It was an all-British deputation, headed by Lord Brassey and including representatives of all three countries as well as all three parties. The significance of this was plain. Before the war the pressure for Home Rule-all-round had come mainly from Wales and Scotland. Now England had taken the lead.

That change was also an outcome of the war. Victory had made democracy safe from Prussian militarism—or so it was assumed in 1918—but to serious students of politics democracy now seemed to need saving from itself. British parliamentary government, in particular, it was thought, no longer commanded the unqualified respect and confidence it had once enjoyed. It had survived, it was true, the strain of war; but it was even more obvious in 1918 than it had been in 1914 that British Government would soon cease to be parliamentary in the old meaning of the word unless the canker of congestion were removed. And this was a vital issue when the efficiency of democratic procedure was on all sides being challenged by the revolutionary spirit nourished by the war. Nor, it was clear, had any effective remedy for congestion been discovered. A Select Parliamentary Committee had been appointed in 1914, but devolution was not within its terms of reference, and its main recommendation was that the system of Standing Committees already in operation for Scottish and Welsh affairs should be extended to English and Irish. But to this there were serious objections. It did not do away with congestion. It only shifted the burden from the House as a whole on to its individual members, many of whom, it was said, would be unable to do their duty without being in two or three places at once. The plan, moreover, seemed, in the light of French and American experience, to involve a risk of interference with ministerial responsibility for administration. Even Balfour confessed in evidence before the Committee that, much as he disliked devolution, he would prefer it to the system now proposed.[5]

This new growth of English interest in the ' federalist ' movement at once affected its whole character. For the English attitude to the question was different from the Welsh and Scottish. The evils of congestion were felt in Wales and Scotland at least as much as in England; but for Welshmen and Scotsmen Home Rule was more than a question of efficient government; it was, to a greater or less degree, a matter of national sentiment. To Englishmen, on the other hand, this sentimental aspect of Home Rule meant nothing or almost nothing. Some of them might grumble when an English minority in Parliament secured a majority on an English issue with the help of non-English votes or complain that it was easier for a Scotsman to obtain a coveted post in England than *vice versa*. But such minor manifestations of English nationalism could not compare with the strength, active or latent, of Welsh or Scottish feeling, rooted as it was in the disparity between the associated nations and the history it had bred. The senior partners in the United Kingdom firm had no need to assert their nationhood or take heed for its protection or preservation.

This attitude of mind was shared by all three English parties, whatever their differences might be on devolution. If Liberals and Labour[a] favoured Home Rule in Wales and Scotland, it was partly because it accorded in principle with the Irish policy to which Gladstone had committed them and partly because many of their Welsh and Scottish supporters desired it, but not at all because they wanted Home Rule in England. Most Conservatives, as has been seen, had hitherto been Unionists-all-round on principle, and those of them who had been won over to 'federalism' before the war were mainly concerned with the chance which it offered of restricting the scope of Irish Home Rule. As the war drew to an end, that was still the main reason for their interest in devolution, but it was no longer their only reason. In the spring of 1918 a group of Conservatives wrote to *The Times* urging a prompt settlement of the Irish controversy on 'federal' lines. But 'apart altogether from the urgency of Ireland,' they said, ' we are deeply impressed by the need of a far reaching system of Federal Devolution for the United Kingdom. We cannot see how otherwise the problems which are awaiting solution after the war can possibly be dealt with, or how, without it, we can escape from the most dangerous congestion.' They asked, accordingly, for the appointment of a Speaker's Conference on devolution.[6] Two days later letters appeared from F. S. Oliver and L. S. Amery, the one pointing out that federalism provided the best constitutional check on the operation of democracy, the other calling for the early introduction of a Bill

---

[a] The annual Labour Party Conference in the summer of 1918 carried a resolution submitted by the Executive in favour of a federal system for the United Kingdom and for the British Commonwealth as well. Chiao, 261.

to establish national governments in Britain as well as Ireland.

Thus the new interest in ' federalism ' in England at the end
of the war was purely practical. English ' federalists,' irrespective
of party, were almost wholly devoid of national sentiment, almost
exclusively concerned with the question of good government.
And the difference between this English attitude to devolution
and the Welsh and Scottish attitude was of great political importance. It might be hard enough to persuade the majority of
Welshmen and Scotsman to favour Home Rule; but it would be
harder still to win over a majority of Englishmen to a cause which
for them, unlike those others, had no emotional appeal. Yet,
without English approval or at least acquiescence, it was plainly a
hopeless cause.

That crucial point was duly stressed in Lloyd George's sympathetic reply to Lord Brassey's deputation. He avowed that he
had ' always been a strong federalist,' and he recalled that Mr.
Chamberlain had said in 1886 ' that the only rational solution of
the Home Rule problem was on federal lines.' Among other
anomalies of the existing system he pointed out that no less than
some three-quarters of Parliament's time was occupied with
business that concerned only one part of the United Kingdom,
and that, while only Scottish M.P.s listened to Scottish debates,
English and Welsh M.P.s could share in the decisions. But so
great a change as the ' federalisation ' of Britain could not be
made without the backing of a substantial majority in all three
countries. It was apparently forthcoming in Wales and Scotland,
but what of England? The English electorate must make up its
mind.[7]

The next moves were made in Parliament. In March 1919,
Lord Brassey proposed a resolution in the Lords declaring that
' the establishment of local legislatures throughout the United
Kingdom is an urgent necessity.' Most of his speech was on

familiar lines, but he made two new points: (1) the desirability of dividing England, Scotland and Ireland, but not Wales, into two provinces each; (2) the possibility that Ulster might accept this version of Home Rule.[8] The resolution was seconded by Lord Selborne, one of the Conservative peers who had taken a ' die-hard ' line in the pre-war controversies. His experience as a member of the War Government had taught him, he said, that the Cabinet was as much overworked as Parliament and that no ' tinkering ' with procedure would avail to prevent the break-down of a system based on Cabinet responsibility to Parliament.[9] When Lord Birkenhead spoke from the ' Woolsack,' he was evidently in one of his masterful moods and seemingly quite indifferent to the opinion of his own Prime Minister. He de-nounced the resolution as ill-considered and inopportune. De-volution, he said, had not been put to the people at the last election, and he was sure that no Englishman wanted it and questioned whether it was wanted by Scotsmen or Welshmen either. His main objection was that a federal system necessitated the abandonment of our well-tried ' flexible ' constitution in favour of a ' rigid ' one requiring interpretation in the Courts. ' Does anyone really suppose that at this period of time, after muddling on tolerably well for ten centuries on centripetal lines,' we are suddenly to adopt the contrary policy and in a form ' which for the first time makes the Law Courts the masters of Parliament '[10]? Lord Bryce's opposition was more temperate and scholarly. He admitted the existence of a body of public opinion in favour of devolution, and he deplored the evils of congestion. But, speaking with the authority of an expert on American federalism, he strongly disapproved of the application of the federal principle to the United Kingdom, mainly on three grounds. It would raise the very difficult problem of the division of powers: it would involve a costly multiplication of executive governments: and the preponderance of England would make the system virtually unworkable.[11] It is curious that Bryce should have supposed that Brassey was advocating federalism in the strict sense of the word, and it was easy for Lord Charnwood, who was also well acquainted with the American constitution, to deal with his chief objection, which was also Birkenhead's. It was not proposed, he pointed out, to create ' anything in the nature of a strict federation like that of the United States.' There could be no conflict over powers because the provincial legislatures would be subordinate to the United Kingdom Parliament. And what would it matter in practice if one legislature were in charge of a larger area and population than another? Illinois was far bigger than Rhode Island.[12] . . . There was no division, the motion was withdrawn, but in weight of argument the ' federalists ' had clearly won.

The same theme was discussed in the Commons a few months later when Major Edward Wood (M.P. for Ripon, now Lord Halifax), moved a resolution

That with a view to enabling the Imperial Parliament to devote more attention to the general interests of the United Kingdom, and, in collaboration with the other governments of the Empire, to matters of common Imperial concern, this House is of opinion that the time has come for the creation of subordinate legislatures within the United Kingdom, and that, to this end, the Government, without prejudice to the proposals it may have to make with regard to Ireland, should forthwith appoint a parliamentary body to consider and report (1) upon a measure of Federal Devolution applicable to England, Scotland and Ireland, defined in its general outlines or existing differences in law and administration between the three countries; (2) upon the extent to which these differences are applicable to Welsh conditions and requirements; (3) upon the financial aspects and requirements of the measure.[13]

Major Wood began his opening speech by remarking on the sharp divergence between the views expressed by the Lord Chancellor in the recent debate in the Lords and the well-known opinions of the Prime Minister and some of his other colleagues, and the tone of his speech contrasted no less sharply with Birkenhead's dogmatic optimism. He gravely warned the House that the British people were beginning to lose faith in parliamentary government and that some of them were coming to believe that their grievances could only be redressed by ' direct action.' ' I do not think it is too much to say that, in the times immediately in front of us, what may tilt the scale between civilisation and disruption may be the confidence that our people may have in their institutions.' That depended on the efficiency with which those institutions did their work, and it was as foolish to suppose that the inefficiency resulting from congestion could be remedied by ' tinkering ' with procedure as to suppose ' that you can make a horse pull more than a certain load by merely refitting the harness in which he pulls it. It is not the way he is pulling that is wrong, it is the load you are asking him to pull.'[14] The motion was seconded by Mr. Murray Macdonald (Stirling) who expounded with his usual clarity the evils of congestion ' which had been slowly and almost insensibly accumulating upon us for at least eighty years.'[15] . . . In the course of the debate an English supporter of the motion, Sir Ryland Adkins (Lancaster, etc.) complained that the control of the House of Commons over the administrative departments was steadily dwindling and declared that Home Rule for England was the only way of stopping the silent conversion of the Government of England into a bureaucracy.[16] . . . The difference between this English speech and that of Scottish and Welsh supporters of the motion was an interesting illustration of the theme discussed above. Major Mackenzie Wood (Aberdeen, etc.), for example, dealt first with the practical issues. The electorate in Northern Scotland, he pointed out, was utterly out of touch with Westminster; and he maintained that many able Scotsmen whose business made it impossible for them to sit in Parliament in London would be able to sit at Edinburgh. But he went on to assert that 'the spirit of nationalism' had roused in Scotsmen 'the desire to develop along their own peculiar national lines.'[17] Mr. T. A. Lewis (Pontypridd), like other Welsh speakers, repudiated the suggestion implicit in the terms of the motion that Wales had a weaker claim to Home Rule than Scotland or could be given an inferior status in any 'federal' scheme, and he boldly maintained that the question 'of expediency and of procedure' was quite a secondary question in Wales. What mattered most was the opportunity which devolution offered for the development of Welsh national life.[18] ... Another interesting contrast was afforded by Sir Edward Carson's speech. His earlier intransigence evidently softened by his experience in the war, he accepted the principle of devolution, but on one condition: it must not be based on nationality. The reference to Ulster was plain. It would be difficult, he said, to treat England as one province, and difficult, he quietly added, to treat Ireland as one province.[19] This plea for regional rather than national devolution—which accorded with Brassey's motion in the Lords—was backed by Sir H. Mackinder as a means of resolving the conflict between East and West Scotland.[20] ... Mr. Walter Long, then First Lord of the Admiralty, was leading the House, and he began his speech by explaining that the Government was not committed on the issue and had left Ministers and their supporters free to take what line they chose. His own line was not the Lord Chancellor's. He declared himself a strong 'federalist,' and he echoed Wood's warning. 'You must give the people the feeling of confidence that, when they come here, their just and legitimate demands can be met without undue delay, or you will have them saying, as they are beginning to say now, that Parliament is of no use and they have lost their respect for it. Can you do this unless you are prepared to set up subordinate Parliaments and to devolve some part of your work upon them?' But his ' federalism,' he made it clear, was of the pre-war Unionist brand. He would have nothing to do with a ' federal ' system which treated Ireland separately and differently from other parts of the United Kingdom; and, while he favoured the motion in principle, he objected to its wording in so far as it implied such a separate treatment of Ireland.[21] . . . Of the few speakers who opposed the motion the most vigorous and uncompromising was the veteran Scottish Unionist, Sir Henry Craik.[22] . . . On a division the motion was carried by 187 votes to 34.[a]

This two-day debate deserves attention because it marked the highest point yet reached by the ' federalist ' movement. Not that it drew a large audience. Twice on the first evening the House was very nearly counted out, and considerably less than half its members mustered for the division. But the character of the debate was more significant than the attendance. Pre-war discussion of ' federal ' devolution had arisen either from the introduction of Bills which had no chance of enactment or from the moving of resolutions which were statements of opinion only, not requests for action. But the motion in this debate asked for a parliamentary inquiry, and if the outcome of that inquiry should be a favourable report—and there seemed at the time at least a chance of that—then devolution would at last become a matter of practical politics. Still more important was the ' international ' character of the debate. Before the war the parliamentary advocates of Scottish and Welsh Home Rule had been almost always Scotsmen and Welshmen, but on this occasion the weightiest speeches were made by Englishmen. If, moreover, the request for an inquiry was granted as it was almost bound to be, the English quota chosen to take part in it would necessarily be larger than the Welsh or Scottish. England, in fact, was keeping the lead.

[a] Among others who spoke and voted for the motion were Major Ormsby-Gore (now Lord Harlech), Sir Donald Maclean who, after the break-up of the Coalition, became the leader of the Liberal Party, and Mr. Clynes who was Minister of Food in the second Coalition Government.

II. THE SPEAKER'S CONFERENCE

IN OCTOBER 1919, in accordance with the motion carried in the Commons, the Government appointed a parliamentary 'Conference on Devolution' presided over by the Speaker, Mr. T. W. Lowther. Of the sixteen members of the House of Lords who sat on it[a] nine were English, two Scots and two North Irish. The only Welshman was Lord Aberdare.[b] The other two were of mixed blood, but more or less thoroughly anglicised. Of the sixteen Commoners, five were English, six Scottish, two Welsh and three North Irish, and eight were Conservatives, three Coalition-Liberals, two Liberals, and three Labour. The Conference held thirty-two meetings and reported to the Prime Minister in April 1920.[23]

At the outset of this Report the Speaker made two preliminary points. (1) The terms of reference had been taken to mean that the Conference was 'not required to pronounce for or against the principle of devolution, but only to consider what, if devolution is accepted, is the most practicable way of putting it into operation.' (2) In view of the introduction of the Irish Home Rule Bill the Conference had felt justified in restricting its inquiry to Great Britain.

On most of the questions discussed, the Report went on, the members of the Conference had found themselves in substantial agreement. (1) They were agreed that the territorial basis of devolution should be national, not regional. England was the

---

[a] The peers were the Duke of Buccleuch, the Marquis of Dufferin, Viscounts Gladstone, Hambleden and Harcourt, and Lords Aberdare, Brassey, Inchcape, Charnwood, Denman, Emmott, Faringdon, Gorell, Oranmore and Browne, Southborough and Stuart of Wortley. In the course of the Conference Lord Brassey died and Lords Inchcape, Hambleden, Harcourt and Dufferin resigned. The places of the first four were taken by Lords Strafford, Chalmers, Elgin and Selborne. Lord Dufferin resigned so late in the proceedings that his place was left unfilled.

[b] Lord Aberdare's mother was an Englishwoman, but the close association of his family with Welsh life entitles him to be regarded for most purposes as fully Welsh.

only doubtful case, and ' it was generally felt that the subdivision of England presented such formidable administrative difficulties that, while it might possibly be grafted on to a system of devolution already in operation, it ought not to form a feature of such a system in its initial stage.' (2) They were agreed on the subordination of the 'Provincial' legislatures to the 'Central' Parliament, on the distribution of powers between them, and on the allotment of ' residual ' powers to the ' Centre.'[a] (3) They were agreed on most of the recommendations of Lord Chalmers' Committee: viz., that for an initial period of five years (after which the financial settlement should be reviewed) certain Licence and other duties should be assigned to the ' Provincial ' legislatures.[b] The Committee recommended that the estimated deficiency should be met by grants-in-aid; but the Conference as a whole preferred that the ' Provinces ' should receive such a share of the yield of Income Tax (excluding super tax) as would balance the account.[c] (4) They agreed in adopting the Report of Lord Stuart of Wortley's Judiciary Committee which recommended (a) that the definition and punishment of major crimes and the regulation of procedure in the trial thereof should be reserved to the United Kingdom Parliament; (b) that the Scottish judicial system should remain unchanged and a change should be made in Wales only if and when the Welsh legislature asked for it; (c) that Monmouthshire should be transferred from the Oxford to the South Wales circuit.

This wide measure of agreement was remarkable. Now that

[a] 'Residual' powers are powers not specified in any of the lists which may come in to existence as the result of future developments in government. The allotment of ' residual ' powers is one of the tests of the ' tightness ' or ' looseness ' of a federal system.

[b] Liquor Licences (dealers and retailers, but not producers), Establishment Licences, Entertainments Duty, Inhabited House Duty, and Land Values Duty.

[c] The Committee's calculations were based on very rough Treasury estimates of the expenditure on the services now to be ' Provincial ' which had been incurred in England, Scotland and Wales respectively in 1919-20, and on a similar division of the yield of the allocated Licence Duties, etc., in that year. The Committee pointed out that it was much easier to frame estimates for Scotland which was already separated from England in finance and administration, than for Wales which had hitherto been treated as a single unit with England. *Conference on Devolution*: A. & P., 1920, xiii, pp. 19-21.

for the first time the practical problems of devolution had been closely examined by an authoritative non-party body, it appeared not only that most of them were soluble but also that the method of solving them could be settled without sharp dispute. Those problems, however, for all their intrinsic importance, were minor problems. The major problem, ' the fundamental point ' as the Speaker called it, was the character and composition of the subordinate legislatures. And on this there was no agreement, nor any approach to it. On the primary principle at stake the Conference split in two. The Speaker, therefore, finding compromise impossible, appended to his letter the two conflicting schemes, one drafted by himself, the other by Mr. Murray Macdonald, which had been adopted by the opposing sections of the Conference.

The main points of the Speaker's scheme, which was described as ' transitional,' were as follows: (1) the subordinate legislatures for England, Scotland and Wales[a] shall be styled' Grand Councils ' and shall consist of a ' Council of Commons ' containing all the members elected to the House of Commons in England, Scotland and Wales respectively, and a ' Council of Peers,' containing half as many members as the Council of Commons, selected from among the members of the House of Lords by a Committee of that House. (2) The Grand Councils will normally sit in the autumn, in London or elsewhere as each may choose. (3) The powers devolved on the Grand Councils shall be the same for all of them. As to the validity of their exercise in legislation, the Home Secretary shall be entitled to refer a bill or an act to the Judicial Committee of the Privy Council. (4) ' The United Kingdom Parliament will not be debarred from legislating on developed subjects and may pass an Act overriding a Grand Council Act,' and ' the Royal Assent may, on the advice of the

[a] Throughout this Report and in most other official documents Monmouthshire appears in brackets after Wales. In the text the inclusion of Monmouthshire in Wales is taken for granted.

United Kingdom Cabinet, be withheld from a Grand Council Act—on the ground not only of invalidity but also of general policy.' (5) Each Grand Council will appoint a Chairman who will select heads of departments to form with him an Executive Committee responsible to the Council for administration. (6) The Executive Committee will communicate with the United Kingdom Government through the Home Secretary. (7) At the end of five years the Grand Councils will be required to submit to Parliament proposals, which need not be uniform, as to their future constitution.

This scheme was supported by the Speaker and twelve other members of the Conference, five of whom were English, three Scottish, and four Ulster.[a]

Mr. Murray Macdonald's scheme was submitted as ' the only possible scheme of devolution ' which would relieve parliamentary congestion, maintain popular control of legislation and administration, and prevent confusion in the conduct of ' local ' and ' central ' affairs. Its main provisions were as follows: (1) Subordinate legislatures shall be established for England, Scotland and Wales, each having an elected chamber, containing the same number of members as now represent those counties in Parliament and elected by the same constituencies. In the lack of adequate knowledge of local wishes, the question of second chambers is left to the decision of the United Kingdom Government. (2) The provisions for determining the validity of ' provincial ' legislation and for overriding it are practically identical with those summarised above as point 3 of the Speaker's scheme. (3) Each legislature will have an Executive Committee ' appointed by His Majesty the King in accordance with the existing constitutional practice.'

This scheme was supported by thirteen members of the

---

[a] Lords Chalmers, Elgin, Faringdon, Southborough, Strafford, Stuart of Wortley and Oranmore and Browne, and Messrs. Craig, Hogge, Macmaster, McNeill and Moles.

Conference, ten of whom were English, two Scottish, and one Irish.[a]

Thus twenty-six of the thirty-one members were evenly divided between the two schemes, and the division went deep. Though they were to exercise the same powers, the character and status of the two kinds of legislature would be utterly different. In the first scheme the United Kingdom Parliament would continue to be the only Parliament. The Grand Councils would be no more than sections of it sitting apart for certain purposes. They would have no independent life. Their party politics would be an automatic small-scale reproduction of party politics in Parliament, and, whatever crisis might occur, they could not overcome it by a dissolution: for they could only be dissolved when Parliament was dissolved. The scheme, in fact, was no more than an extension of the system of Standing Committees. It had nothing whatever to do with federation. The second scheme, on the other hand, was frankly federal. Save only in the subordination of the local legislatures to the ' Centre,' it followed the lines of existing Federations. The legislatures might not be called ' parliaments,' but they were comparable with the Legislative Assemblies in Canadian Provinces or Australian States, separate bodies, separately elected by the people of their respective areas. Their executive organs, whatever their names, would in fact be Cabinets and the chiefs thereof Prime Ministers, appointed by the King.

The schemes, indeed, were so far apart that, though the first was called ' transitional,' it is hard to suppose that any of its supporters expected or intended it to be a stepping-stone to the

[a] Lords Charnwood, Denman, Emmott, Gladstone and Selborne, Sir R. Adkins and Sir F. Young and Messrs. Murray Macdonald, Forestier-Walker, Goulding, Graham and Murray. Lord Gladstone, though Scots-Welsh in blood, may be reckoned in this context as an Englishman. It should be observed that Lord Selborne as Governor-General of South Africa had taken the lead in bringing about the Union of South Africa under a constitution which provided for subordinate Provincial Governments and that Lord Gladstone had been the first Governor-General of the Union when it came into force.

second. One of them evidently did not. In one of the three memoranda appended to the Report Lord Southborough made it clear that he was opposed in principle to any 'federal' form of devolution. He attacked Mr. Macdonald's scheme mainly on the following grounds. (1) ' The change in our parliamentary system, which is the gradual growth of centuries of evolution, would be very abrupt '; and, whereas all federal systems have been created by the combination of existing smaller units in a greater, the present proposal would reverse the process by an unprecedented devolution of power from an old-established sovereign body to a number of quite new ones. (2) There are few, if any, signs that England wants so great a change. (3) The cost of new buildings, staff and a second series of elections would be very great. (4) If an independently elected legislature and its executive, particularly such powerful ones as the English, should come into conflict with the United Kingdom Parliament and Government, the friction between the two might develop into ' an extremely dangerous situation.' (5) If the issues which the people at large care most about are dealt with by the ' Provincial ' legislatures, the United Kingdom Parliament will be in danger of sinking ' into comparative insignificance or even contempt.' . . . Plainly these opinions ruled a ' federal solution ' out of court.

Even firmer, if possible, was the anti-federalist attitude of the three Irish members of the Conference—Mr. Ronald McNeill, an Ulsterman by origin who sat as a Unionist for a Scottish constituency, and Messrs. Craig and Moles who held Ulster seats. Since the Irish Nationalists had turned their backs on Westminster in 1918, these Ulstermen were the only Irish members of the Conference; and, though it had been decided at the outset that, since an Irish Home Rule Bill was now before Parliament, the Conference would not discuss the application of devolution to Ireland, the Ulster members, staunch citizens of the United Kingdom, were doubtless entitled to express their opinions on devolution for England, Scotland and Wales. But those opinions were necessarily coloured by their Irish politics. They were anti-nationalist and anti-federalist in Britain because they were anti-nationalist and anti-federalist in Ireland. Thus, while they repeated in more vigorous terms some of Lord Southborough's objections to Mr. Macdonald's scheme,[a] they went far beyond that. They complained, in effect, that the scope of the discussion had exceeded its proper limits. The Conference had been instructed to consider devolution only as a means of relieving parliamentary congestion. Nothing was said about satisfying national sentiment. Yet this second reason for devolution had not only been discussed; it had on certain vital points prevailed over the first. If the relief of congestion had been the sole purpose of the Conference's recommendations, it might well have been proposed to divide all Britain into several regional units, and to devolve on them the minimum of powers needed for relief. But that policy, in the Ulstermen's view the right policy, had hardly been given a hearing. Deference to national sentiment had smothered it. And in the event the views of both the main sections of the Conference, though of one much more than the other, had acquired a nationalist complexion. In both schemes the units of devolution were to be undivided national units; and in both the powers to be devolved were not minimal but maximal, i.e., all the powers which were not of necessity reserved to the United Kingdom Parliament. The Ulstermen, therefore, disliked both schemes, but they subscribed to the Speaker's because it was ' avowedly tentative and could be tested at an infinitely smaller cost and risk.' . . . A well-argued forensic case, but not very sensible. For it was obviously impossible to discuss devolution without any regard for Welsh and Scottish sentiment. And, as it happened, the near future was to provide an ironical comment on such unbending unionism. The Report of the Conference was presented on April 27, 1920. On May 3, 1921, the people of

[a] More mindful, perhaps, of Irish than of English history they contemplated the possibility of Britain being paralysed on the outbreak of a war by a dispute between the English and United Kingdom Parliaments.

Ulster began to operate a quasi-federal system of devolution in Northern Ireland based on ' Ulster Nationality ' and to operate it so well as time went on that Welsh and Scottish ' federalists ' found themselves furnished with a new and powerful argument for the adoption of a similar system in Scotland and Wales.

The original signatories of one or other of the two schemes were Englishmen, Scotsmen and Ulstermen. The three Welsh members of the Conference[a] took a line of their own. Together with one Englishman and one Scotsman[b] they subscribed their names as a separate group to *both* the schemes. They backed Mr. Macdonald's scheme, they said, because of its ' fundamental principle '; but they also backed the Speaker's scheme because, unlike some and probably most, if not all, of its original supporters, they held that, while providing an immediate measure of devolution on national lines, ' it paves the way for the larger scheme of subordinate Parliaments *which in our opinion can alone satisfy the national aspirations of both Scotland and Wales.*'[c] That is an interesting sentence: for it is the only sentence in the whole Report which directly asserts the claims of nationhood. Those claims had been discussed, against the wishes of the Ulstermen, in the Conference, but they did not figure in the schemes. Nor did Lord Southborough mention them in his memorandum. If the Ulstermen referred to them, it was only to deplore their being raised at all. Mr. Macdonald might have been expected to urge them in support of his ' federal ' plan; but from the outset of his long campaign Mr. Macdonald had always treated devolution as primarily a question of efficient government—there was little, indeed, in his speeches and writings to show he was a Scot—and the note with which he prefaced his scheme defined its purpose as no more than the relief of congestion, the strengthening of responsible government, and the removal of the confusion

[a] Lord Aberdare and Messrs. C. Edwards and J. H. Edwards.
[b] Mr. W. T. Wilson and Sir Henry Cowan.
[c] Author's italics.

between local and central interests. In his memorandum, similarly, there was not a word about nationality. It confined itself to demonstrating that the Speaker's scheme, so far from relieving congestion, would create worse evils than those it sought to cure. No doubt this neglect by the ' federalists ' of one of their strongest arguments was due to the terms of reference. They respected them more strictly in the Report than they had in the discussions; but for that very reason the Report was lacking in the kind of realism which the discussions would have lacked if the Ulstermen had had their way. It may be argued, therefore, that the Welsh group were justified in defying the terms of reference and ensuring that in a report on devolution the factor of national sentiment was not completely ignored.

In retrospect, however, it seems that they were ill advised to subscribe to both the schemes. They could have asserted their nationalism by backing the Macdonald scheme only. By backing the Speaker's also, despite their explanation, they kept the balance even and so helped to convey to the public which never reads official documents the impression that the Conference was evenly divided on the principles of devolution. And that, of course, was not the case. On the ' fundamental principle ' eighteen members stood on one side and thirteen at most on the other. Excluding the Ulster votes and reckoning British votes only, the balance was eighteen to ten or less.[a]

III. SEQUEL

THE PUBLICATION of the Report (May 12, 1920) made no great stir. *The Times* leader on it was allotted not the first but the third place on the page. And the tone was cold and cautious. ' Much

---

[a] As pointed out above, it cannot be assumed that *all* the supporters of the Speaker's scheme were anti-federalist.

to be said for and against both schemes.' On the whole the Speaker's scheme was preferable ' if only on the grounds that in so radical a departure from the constitutional practice of the Kingdom it is well to look before we leap.'[24] The *Scotsman* followed suit. The Speaker's scheme was the more attractive because ' it made the least possible change in the constitution.'[25] The *Western Mail* likewise commended ' the attitude of caution which proposes an experimental plan '; but its dislike of the federal alternative, despite its Welsh supporters on the Committee, was more outspoken. The separation of Wales from England would be like a ' surgical amputation.' There was no such ' clarity of public and expert opinion on the subject as would justify the early enactment of a definitive Home Rule scheme.'[26]

While the newspapers favoured the less ambitious scheme, they made it clear that they did not regard the question as of great, still less of vital importance; and this apathy truly reflected the attitude of the politically-minded public. For them the Report had acted as a catalytic. Previous discussions of it had been more concerned with principles than facts. Now for the first time the idea of devolution had taken concrete shape. What it meant in practice was set down in black and white—in constitutional schemes, in financial calculations, in lists of powers to be reserved or transferred. And viewed thus in factual detail, the proposed change seemed, as indeed it was, a revolutionary change. At once the English temperament recoiled. Clearly a far more urgent and more cogent case would have to be made for ' federalism ' if England were to be induced to contemplate the abandonment of her ancient institutions and the adoption of such a complicated, unfamiliar, un-English form of government. The threat to Parliament, in particular, the proposal to break it, as it were, in two, provoked an almost instinctive opposition; for round Parliament was woven one of the main threads of the English political tradition. It may be said, in fact, that the cause of

' federalism ' in England was dead as soon as Englishmen understood what it meant.

The ' federalists ' in Parliament made one last effort to revive the corpse. On July 6 Sir R. Adkins, Mr. Murray Macdonald, Mr. Edward Wood and others convened a meeting of their followers. It was well attended, and by English M.P.s as well as Welsh and Scottish. Mr. Walter Long presided and restated the case for a drastic treatment of the problem of parliamentary congestion. Sir Austen Chamberlain, whose loyalty to Lloyd George had not impaired his high repute among all parties, did not attend the meeting, but he had authorised Mr. Macdonald to declare his 'keen sympathy' with the federalist cause. There was little discussion, no difference of opinion, and a spirited resolution was adopted asking the Government to frame a Bill for administrative and legislative devolution for England, Scotland and Wales and to introduce it in the next session.[27] *The Times*, meanwhile, had been won round from its neutrality. In the course of the week in which the meeting was held it published no less than six articles by Mr. Murray Macdonald, fully expounding the ' federalist ' case;[28] and in an introductory leader it not only stressed the importance of the issue, but for the first time admitted that ' new factors of national sentiment ' were involved. ' It is time,' it said, ' that the mind of the public should turn to the question of Devolution . . . as a vital issue in which every citizen is profoundly concerned '; and it called on the Government to obtain without delay the information needed for full discussion and final decision of the question.[29]

On that bold note the curtain fell. Not another word was said in Parliament or the Press about Devolution. The public mind was preoccupied with what seemed to be more urgent matters—the settlement of post-war Europe, the last stage of the ' civil war ' in Ireland, the growth of labour unrest at home. There was only one chance at that time, it has been said, of keeping the ' federal ' cause alive. If Lloyd George had now done for Home

Rule in Britain what Gladstone had done for Home Rule in Ireland, if he had put it above the claims of party and the interests of his own career, if he had set himself to fan the spirit of nationalism in Wales and Scotland, he might conceivably, at any rate before his war-prestige was dimmed, have won England's acquiescence. But that is a dubious speculation. The Irish and the British cases are hardly comparable. The grievances of Irish nationalism were far greater, the need for dealing with them far more urgent, the situation they had engendered far more dangerous; and, while Home Rule in Ireland was fiercely demanded by the great majority of the Irish people, the agitation for Home Rule in Wales and Scotland was confined to a small and by no means militant minority. Gladstone's decision in 1885 could scarcely be regarded, therefore, as a precedent for Lloyd George in 1920. And, in any case, Lloyd George was not a second Gladstone.

In the course of the next few years any chance of reviving the short-lived 'federalist' movement in England was destroyed by the impact of two events. In 1921 the 'Irish Problem' was settled at last, and seemingly for good. That meant that those few Unionists in England who had still clung to Home Rule-all-round as a means of restricting its scope in Ireland were now finally disillusioned, while those more numerous Unionists who had long despaired of Ireland were furnished with a new argument for maintaining the unity of Britain. Would not Scotland or Wales, once given a taste of Home Rule, seek sooner or later to attain the full self-government which the Irish Free State had acquired? There was only one feature of the Irish settlement which favoured the 'federalists.' It provided, as was noted above, a working model of a bilateral quasi-federal system under which the field of government was divided between a subordinate Parliament in Northern Ireland and the United Kingdom Parliament at Westminster. But that interesting development was almost unnoticed in Britain. As soon as the quarrel which had tormented and distorted British politics for generations past had been composed, the British people behaved like sleepers awakened from a long bad dream. They heaved a sigh of relief and forgot about Ireland, Free State and Ulster together, as soon as they could. It is remarkable and not very creditable how completely, for a long time after the Treaty, Irish affairs were blacked out from parliamentary discussion, from the news columns of the Press, and even from private conversation.

The second event was the General Strike in 1926. That it occurred at all—that the great Trade Unions, whose natural sympathy with the Russian Revolution had not yet been estranged by its results, should have decided to back the miners in an attempt to coerce the State by ' direct action '—might well have seemed to justify the fears expressed by Major Wood and his supporters at the end of the war. It was an open challenge to parliamentary government. But in the event the fears proved groundless. The British people did not want a revolution. The Government obtained all the volunteers needed to run the essential services. Food never ran short. And on the strikers' side it was soon evident from the marked restraint of their more experienced and trusted leaders and from the orderly conduct of the rank and file that the whole affair was more like a monster demonstration than a serious attempt to seize power. There was little real bitterness in it, hardly any ugly incidents, nothing at all resembling the spirit of the ' barricades '; and its collapse at the end of nine days was one more proof, not unobserved by an anxious Europe, of the strength of the British political tradition.

The result of the General Strike completed the process which the Irish Treaty had begun. It wiped out of the public mind the second reason for a serious consideration of the framework of the constitution. The historic tradition of parliamentary government had been assailed by organised Labour, but the challenge had been half-hearted and quickly and easily repulsed. Illogically, but not unnaturally, this seemed to the average Englishman to prove that there was nothing much wrong with Parliament. Its critics were discredited. Its easy victory over the revolutionary forces—if those somewhat timid and reluctant Unions could be so described—obscured the fact that a silent revolution was going on within its walls, that congestion was fast robbing it of its old character. So, well before the onset of the great Depression diverted the public mind from politics to economics, Devolution had resumed the back seat it had occupied before the war. And there it stayed right on to the Second War and after it. Year by year, as will be recorded in the next two chapters, the tedious pre-war story was repeated. Welsh and Scottish nationalists continued to move their academic resolutions and introduce their still-born Bills. And now, as before, few Englishmen were found to back them. Lord Birkenhead, it seemed, had been right. His countrymen were not prepared to break the habit of centuries: they meant to go on ' muddling on tolerably well.'

[1] Chiao, *Devolution in Great Britain* (New York, 1926), 260.
[2] *Ibid.*
[3] E. L. Chappell, *Wake up, Wales!* (London, 1943), 75-6.
[4] Chiao, 261.
[5] *Report of Select Committee on Procedure* (1914), 88.
[6] *The Times*, April 16, 1918, quoted by Chiao, 258.
[7] *The Times*, July 1, 1918.
[8] *Hansard*, H. of L., 1919, v. 33, c. 501-509.
[9] *Ibid.*, c. 514-517.
[10] *Ibid.*, c. 521-530.
[11] *Ibid.*, c. 538-540.
[12] *Ibid.*, c. 541-547.
[13] *Hansard*, H. of C., 1919, v. 116, c. 1873.
[14] *Ibid.*, c. 1873-8.
[15] *Ibid.*, c. 1885.
[16] *Ibid.*, c. 1932-3.
[17] *Ibid.*, c. 1916-19.
[18] *Ibid.*, c. 2080-5.
[19] *Ibid.*, c. 1897.
[20] *Ibid.*, c. 1920.
[21] *Ibid.*, c. 1905-10.
[22] *Ibid.*, c. 1903-4.
[23] *Conference on Devolution: Letter from Mr. Speaker to the Prime Minister*, 1920, reprinted 1924. [Cmd. 692.]

²⁴ *The Times*, May 13, 1920.
²⁵ *Scotsman*, May 13, 1920.
²⁶ *Western Mail*, May 15, 1920.
²⁷ *The Times*, July 7, 1920.
²⁸ *Ibid.*, July 5 to 9 and 12, 1920.
²⁹ *Ibid.*, July 9.

PART EIGHT

Wales, 1918-1945

I. THE DARK YEARS

IT IS a chastening exercise to recall to-day the sanguine expectations cherished by the victorious nations of the Western World on the morrow of the First World War; and, nowhere in the British Isles, as it happened, was the process of disillusionment so harsh and painful as in Wales. The Welsh people emerged from the war with a heightened sense of national self-consciousness and pride. They had played their full part with Englishmen and Scotsmen in maintaining the British tradition of resistance to the power that strove to dominate Europe and the world. And the freedom they had helped to save was especially the freedom of the little nations. Belgium had been liberated, Poland reconstituted, Czechoslovakia and Jugoslavia created from the wreck of the Austro-Hungarian Empire. The map of Europe had been redrawn, far beyond what was possible in Mazzini's day, along the lines of nationality. Thus, all over the world, in Asia as in Europe, the national self-consciousness stimulated by the war was strengthened by the peace; and in Wales as elsewhere a new impetus was given to nationalist ideas and aspirations. All the more violent, therefore, was the reaction to the great depression.

The boom created by the war both in industry and agriculture began to collapse in 1923, and the subsequent depression was enhanced by an outbreak of industrial unrest which particularly affected the coal-fields. Then came the great world-wide slump of 1929 to 1934. Coal and the heavy industries it fostered were hit hardest by the shrinkage of world trade; and, while there were other black areas of depression in Britain—in Scotland and North-East England—the blackest was in Wales. For Welsh production was more completely confined to a few major industries—coal, iron, steel, tin-plate—and, when all of these wilted under the slump, when firm after firm closed down, when exports dwindled and the docks were emptied of shipping, there were few lighter industries to soften the impact of unemployment on the heavier. And, whereas there were areas of relative prosperity in England and Scotland, there was no such area in Wales. The people on the land were little better off than those in industry. The fall in agricultural prices, the impoverishment of urban markets, the lapse of land from cultivation, the swing over from corn to milk, and the persistent low wages swelled the current of farm labourers seeking but not finding work in the towns. From 1927 to 1931 the amount of unemployment in Wales was ten per cent and from 1931 to 1936, sixteen per cent above the level for the United Kingdom as a whole.[1] At its peak in 1932 no less than 245,000 Welsh people were unemployed out of a total population of about 2,500,000. And the psychological effect of years of enforced idleness was not the only injury done to Wales. Tens of thousands of Welshmen were driven to seek employment beyond the border. It has been reckoned that no less than 300,000 people or more than thirteen per cent of the population left Wales between 1923 and 1936.[2] Despite the high rate of Welsh fertility the population at the census of 1931 was 62,000 less than at the census of 1921.

Those dark years will never be forgotten by the Welshmen who lived through them, and in some of them their fate engendered a distrust and dislike of England such as they had felt before only faintly if at all. Would Wales have suffered so much, it was asked, if her industrial development had not been so tightly linked with that of England? Decaying organisms suffer first at their extremities, and it was natural that shrinking British firms centred in London should close their distant Welsh and Scottish branches before their English ones. But to angry Welshmen it seemed a deliberate sacrifice of Welsh to English interests. Even to-day a sober Welsh patriot can talk about the exile enforced on so many Welshmen by unemployment in the same sort of language as Irish patriots used about emigration at the time of the Great Famine.[3]

The belated recognition of the German menace and the process of rearmament transformed the economic situation. The heavy industries recovered their strength. The spectre of unemployment faded out. From the eve of the last war till to-day Welsh working men have been far more fully and regularly employed and for far better wages than ever before. And with economic recovery went a revival of the sense of unity with the rest of Britain. Once more the British nations stood together to defend the freedom of all Britain, and this time they were more fully and firmly united than at any previous crisis. For the war was now ' total ' war: the whole of the adult population was engaged: children died with their mothers in the *blitz* at Cardiff as at Liverpool and Glasgow. And the sense of comradeship was quickened by the gravity of the common danger. In the previous war there had been no serious risk of invasion, but in 1940 it seemed possible that England would suffer the fate of France. And, of course, not England only. All three nations were fighting for their lives, and the smaller ones could not have hoped—nor indeed could they have wished—to survive the conquest of England. The decisive battle was fought over South-East England, but it was rightly called the Battle of Britain.

The *blitz* was more or less confined to the southern industrial belt, but there was another hardship inflicted by ' total ' war which affected rural more than urban Wales. Under the conscription and direction of labour thousands of Welshwomen were taken from their homes and compelled to work in the war factories of the English Midlands. Such rough handling of the population was unavoidable if the war was to be won, and it was not, of course, confined to Wales. But it was a greater hardship for Welshwomen, especially those who lived in the less anglicised districts of Wales, to be transplanted to English industrial towns than for Englishwomen to be moved from one part of England to another; and, since it was inflicted by order of a predominantly English Government, it was regarded by some Welshmen as one more proof of English selfishness.

The depression and the war were the outstanding events in Welsh history between 1918 and 1945, but Welsh life was also deeply affected by two other factors, one political, the other cultural. Like the depression they were shared by all Britain, but their effect in Wales, like that of the depression, was somewhat greater than in Scotland and much greater than in England. The first was the rise of the Labour Party, the second the decline of religion.

When the Liberal Party split, the Welsh electorate did no more than the English and Scottish to resist the eclipse of Lloyd George; and the leftward swing of the working class was more marked in Wales than in England or Scotland. The Liberal stronghold in Wales was rapidly converted into a Labour stronghold. Between 1918 and 1945 the share of the Welsh seats won by Labour rose from 11 to 25.

The decline of religion, like the swing to the left in politics, had begun before the First World War, but the momentum of both was accelerated in the years of disillusionment and depression that followed it. There is a touch of irony in the fact that, when in 1920 Welsh Dissent at last attained the objective for which it had fought so long and fiercely—the disestablishment of the Church of Wales—it was already losing its hold on its own flock. To-day no serious Welshman questions that Wales is failing to maintain its great religious tradition. The Nonconformist ministers are no longer the unquestioned leaders of the people. Their sermons are no longer the events they once were in Welshmen's lives. The older generation preserves its puritan outlook and still goes to chapel and Sunday School; but the younger folk have drifted away from their fathers' moorings, often away from Christianity itself. When one of Wales' ' elder statesmen ' returned to his native country in 1945 after twenty-five years of public work in London which had carried him to the highest level of administrative service, he put the loss of faith among the young first and foremost among all the changes that had taken place since last he had lived in Wales; and he quoted a striking passage from a broadcast by Principal Gwilym Edwards. ' Religion is not attacked, nor is it fiercely dismissed, but it is subjected to something worse—it is ignored as something irrelevant, something that makes no difference either way.'[4] To the patriots who led the national renaissance in the nineteenth century, such an attitude of mind in Wales would have seemed wellnigh inconceivable. If it hardens and spreads, who can say how much and in what way it will affect the spirit of a nationalism which from the time of its birth till yesterday has been so closely associated with religion ?

II. THE CULTURAL CAMPAIGN

THE NATIONAL spirit of Wales was dimmed but not extinguished by the great depression. On its political side, it is true, Welsh nationalism is still relatively weak; but the cultural campaign, the movement started in the later nineteenth century to make Welshmen more conscious of their nationhood, more aware of their national heritage and more determined to preserve it, has steadily grown stronger.

Its mainspring has been the University of Wales. More and more young Welshmen and Welshwomen have been able to obtain in Wales the higher education which was only available beyond the border before the University was founded. Between 1939 and 1949 the number of students at the four constituent Colleges and the National School of Medicine rose from 2,779 to 5,147. And for all these students the University, aided by the National Library at Aberystwyth and the National Museum at Cardiff,[a] has afforded the opportunity, if they choose to take it, of acquiring a thorough knowledge of the Welsh historical and cultural tradition. At each of the four Colleges there is a chair of Welsh language and literature, and at three of the four a chair of Welsh history.[b] All these chairs are held by Welshmen, and by their teaching of undergraduates and promotion of post-graduate research and by their own writings, largely in Welsh, they have deeply affected, within little more than one generation, the intellectual life of Wales. The dream of the nineteenth-century pioneers has come true.

The pursuit of historical and literary research and the publication of its results have been greatly assisted by two ancillary bodies, the University Board of Celtic Studies and the University Press Board. The former[c] was established in 1920 ' for the purpose of encouraging the study of, and research concerning, the history, language, literature, laws, customs, archaeology, art and institutions of the Celtic peoples.' The major tasks on which the Board is now engaged are the preparation of a ' shorter standard dictionary ' of Welsh in two or three volumes and a gazetteer

[a] The building of most of the Library, which is one of the five British libraries of ' national deposit,' and of half the Museum was completed before the last war.

[b] These subjects are provided for in the examination for the United Kingdom administrative Civil Service by the inclusion of an ' option ' called ' Welsh Civilisation.' It covers a wide field of Welsh political, social and literary history and requires that some of the answers should be written in Welsh.

[c] The Board consists of representatives of the University Colleges, the National Library and the National Museum, Jesus College (Oxford), the Cymmrodorion Society and the Cambrian Archaeological Association. It functions through three committees: (1) History and Law; (2) Language and Literature; (3) Archaeology and Art. *Statutes of the University of Wales,* xxvii.

341

of Welsh place-names. The Board issues a *Bulletin* in two parts annually and has recently begun the publication of a new Welsh periodical dealing with the history of Welsh literature. It also publishes learned works, historical and literary, from time to time, including transcriptions of medieval documents,ᵃ and promotes and assists the excavation of ancient sites.[5] The University Press Board, established in 1922, is responsible for the publications of the Celtic Board and publishes a wide range of books, mostly in Welsh, on its own account. In particular it copes, as best it can, with the increasing demand for Welsh text books in the schools and colleges.

Another function of the University and the Library has been to encourage and assist the research work which has long been fostered by the two leading Welsh Societies. The Cambrian Archaeological Association continues to devote itself mainly to the study of the distant past. Most of the articles in its learned journal in recent years have dealt with such archaeological topics as Bronze-Age barrows, the early Iron Age in Anglesey, or the old copper mines on Great Orme's Head. The scope of the Cymmrodorion is wider and less antiquarian. Besides its *Transactions* it publishes an annual volume called *Y Cymmrodor* which used to be a learned magazine but is now confined to a single work. To this series have recently been added *inter alia* a study of the Welsh house, a translation of fifty poems of Dafydd ap Gwilym, and a collection of Morris Letters. The Society is also engaged on compiling a Dictionary of Welsh National Biography.

Adult Education is another means by which interest in Welsh culture is being kindled. The founders of the University were well aware of the service it could render to the Welsh people by organising adult education outside its walls; but for several years

ᵃ Among recent publications are edited transcripts of *A Survey of the Duchy of Lancaster Lordships in Wales* and *Records of the Court of Augmentation, The Early Christian Monuments of Wales* and a *Glossary of Early Welsh Poetry*.

the Colleges were too much occupied with the difficult task of building up the University to give to extra-mural work the time and care it needed. Its first ' tutorial class ' was held in 1910-11;[a] but it was not till the establishment of the University Extension Board in 1919 that, in close co-operation with the North and South Wales branches of the Workers Educational Association,[b] a full-scale system of tutorial and other classes was gradually developed. It would now be true to say that there is no locality in Wales which cannot obtain this kind of adult education if it wants it. In 1947-48, 391 classes of varying length, attended by 6,498 students, were conducted by the four Colleges of the University in their respective regions, and 292 classes by the two branches of the W.E.A. There is also Coleg Harlech, a residential College for adult students, founded in 1927. In 1947-48, 27 students were in residence for a year, 18 for more than one term, 15 for one term or less. The College also conducted three summer schools in its own quarters, and 19 elsewhere.

Like the University itself, this extra-mural system of education is essentially Welsh and, like the University, it is a natural vehicle of Welsh culture. In the long and varied list of subjects chosen for the classes conducted by the University in 1948-49 the lead was taken by the language, literature and history of Wales (66), well in front of international relations (42) and economics and political science (32). In 103 of the 356 classes the language used was Welsh.[c]

Another illustration of the cultural revival is the new interest taken in the traditional Welsh folk-songs and folk-crafts—the natural products of a national life which, till the coming of the Industrial Revolution, was mainly rural life. In Wales as in other countries the folk-songs would have faded out of memory if they had not been saved by a few enthusiastic recorders, and happily

[a] This first class was conducted by (Sir) J. F. Rees at Blaenau Ffestiniog.
[b] Classes are also organised by the Y.M.C.A. and the Council of Music.

343

John Lloyd Williams did for Wales what Cecil Sharp did for England.[7] Knowledge of the old Welsh folk-crafts might similarly have dwindled and died out if the National Museum had not been built. It houses to-day a superb collection of furniture, metal work, agricultural implements, and the products and tools of the small or cottage industries that flourished before the days of mass-production. As a supplement to the National Museum a Welsh Folk Museum was established at St. Fagans, a few miles west of Cardiff.[a] The Elizabethan castle was furnished from kitchen to roof to illustrate the life of the landed gentry in the seventeenth and eighteenth centuries; while the life of the countryfolk was displayed by the acquisition of characteristic farmhouses, cottages, workshops and so forth and this re-erection in the spacious castle grounds. When this project was completed in 1948 it could bear comparison with anything of the kind in Europe.

This keen and varied interest in the culture of the past has naturally stimulated the creative spirit in the present. Before 1914 the influence of a new generation of Welsh graduates on current Welsh literature was already manifest; and, if the harsh experience of the subsequent years tended to darken the tone of poetry and prose in Wales as in England, it did not check its outflow nor lower its quality. T. Gwyn Jones and W. J. Gruffydd retained their lead in poetry. Some of the best work of R. Williams Parry and T. H. Parry-Williams was written during the first war. It was between the wars that Saunders Lewis came to the front not only as a political nationalist (of which more anon), but also as a dramatic poet and the best Welsh literary critic. The outstanding achievements in the prose of scholarship have been T. Parry's *Hanes llenyddiaeth Gymraeg* (*History of Welsh Literature*), G. J. Williams' *Traddodiad llenyddol Morgannwg* (*The Literary Tradition of Glamorgan*), and the writings of Sir H. I. Bell, once

[a] Through the generosity of the Earl of Plymouth.

President of the British Academy, whose *Development of Welsh Poetry* has been a priceless boon to Englishmen whose interest in Welsh culture is not stifled by their ignorance of Welsh. There has also been a marked increase in the range and quality of essay-work—a field in which the delightful essays of T. H. Parry-Williams, R. T. Jenkins, T. J. Morgan and I. C. Peate may be ranked with Saunders Lewis' criticism. The Welsh novel, on the other hand, has been slow to come into its own. It was not till 1943 that *From Hand to Hand* revealed a first-rate novelist in Rowland Hughes. On the whole the Welsh short story, of which Kate Roberts has been the most gifted writer since her first book appeared in 1926, has done better than the novel. 'Indeed the short story,' says Bell, ' is probably the branch of prose literature in which contemporary Wales has been most successful.'[8] Drama has been backward and not unnaturally, since it was not till the latter part of the nineteenth century that the curse which puritanism laid upon the theatre began to lose its force. But the tradition of amateur play-acting has never died out, and there are now numerous dramatic societies in all parts of Wales. The main obstacle to the growth of Welsh drama is the paucity of theatres; and, partly for that reason perhaps, play-writing, though encouraged by the Eisteddfod, has not yet produced the genius ' who will do for Wales what Ibsen did for Norway and Capek for Czechoslovakia.'[9] [a] It is the same with painting. Augustus John is a Welshman, but he belongs to London and his inspiration is not distinctively Welsh. As yet there is no Welsh ' school of painting,' no Welsh ' style.' Sir William Goscombe John is also a Welshman. He has shown more interest in Wales than his namesake, and the National Museum contains some of his finest sculpture; but again it is not distinctively Welsh work. And the same may be said of Sir Parry Thomas who has thrice been chosen

[a] The London stage is indebted to several Welsh actors of whom the best known are Ivor Novello (Davies) and Emlyn Williams. Some of the leading ' film stars' are also Welsh: so is the popular ' crooner' Donald Peers who, despite his name, is a bilingual Welshman.

President of the Royal Institute of British Architects.[a] But musical Wales has produced two great makers of music much of whose work is indubitably Welsh in inspiration. Walford Davies was born at Oswestry, not far from the Welsh border, and lived for many years at Aberystwyth. Vaughan Williams was born in Gloucestershire and lives in Surrey, but his Welsh origin is manifest in his work.

Of the institutions and associations which have fostered the growth of cultural nationalism in Wales the most important is the National Eisteddfod. Organised for many months before-hand and at considerable cost, it is now recognised by every Welshman as the one great national celebration of that year, the occasion on which Wales, so to speak, proclaims her nationhood. Held alternatively in North Wales and South, it draws its crowds from both and manifests the unity of national consciousness which underlies the differences between them. The Eisteddfod, it has been well said, provides for a week the national capital which Wales has never had. And it reveals more directly and clearly than anything else the distinctive character of Welsh culture. ' However numerous their faults and shortcomings,' writes Wyn Griffith, ' let it always be remembered of the Welsh that the most widely popular event of the year in Wales is a Festival devoted to the Arts, and that in it the highest form of tribute is reserved for poets. There is nothing quite like it anywhere else in the world.'[10]

Every student of nationalism must be interested in this unique institution, and it may not be out of place for one such student to put on record here his personal impressions of the Eisteddfod of 1949. It was held that summer at Dolgelley, a little country town in Merioneth where the Mawddach flows seawards beneath the noble crest of Cader Idris. Normally this lovely valley is wrapt in rustic peace, but during that August week it was invaded by crowds of Welsh folk from all parts of Wales. Most days some

[a] No one else has held this office more than once.

346

fifteen thousand people streamed up the road to the meadow, about half a mile above the town, where the great pavilion had been erected. It held about ten thousand, and for all the more important items of the programme every seat was occupied. It was a week of music and poetry and ceremonial. The outstanding feature, as one would expect, was the choral singing. There were fine performances of the *Hymn of Praise* and Bach's *St. Matthew Passion*. But for a stranger it was even more moving to hear those ten thousand Welsh men and women singing, in four-part harmony, their national anthem, *Hen Wlad Fy Nhadau* (The Land of My Fathers). No less impressive and significant was the ceremonial climax of the festival when the names of the two victorious poets were announced and, rising from their seats, they advanced through the acclamations of the multitude to the great stage where the members of the Gorsedd sat tier above tier in robes of white and blue and green according to their rank, and were duly chaired and crowned. And, since chairing and crowning are traditional ways of doing honour not peculiar to Wales, there seemed little in this to vex the conscience of the scholar who knew that the druidic ritual which most of the ceremonial purported to represent was in fact one of Iolo Morganwg's ingenious fabrications. Is it, nevertheless, pure pedantry to wish that some of the pseudo-druidism might be pruned away and the need for historical pageantry—and it is a real need—supplied by true history? The heroes of Wales are not creatures of the prehistoric twilight, and Hywel and Llewellyn and Glendower are more inspiring figures than a whole battalion of arch-druids. To one visitor, at any rate, some of the romantic play-acting, competent and colourful though it was, seemed a little out of harmony with the utterly genuine sentiment of the festival as a whole, a little beneath the dignity of a great national demonstration.

But it was none of these things, not even the singing, that made the deepest impression on the stranger from beyond the border: it was the popular and the national character of the whole affair. The men and women who filled the pavilion and thronged the meadow were not the sort of middle-class intellectuals who attend the musical festivals in England. The intellectuals were there, of course, but the vast majority were drawn from the common people and, since Merioneth is a rural county, mainly from the countryfolk. Nor could any ' highbrows ' have listened more intently and silently to the proceedings or expressed more confidently their private judgements on the various competitions by the measure of their applause. It was a notable demonstration of the fact that Welsh culture is the culture of the people.[a] And it was not only a popular festival, it was also, from first to last and out and out, a national festival. The president of the assembly was not the chairman of the day: it was the Red Dragon of Wales rampant above the great platform. Not a word of English was spoken to the microphones. The announcements, the ceremonial, the reading of the judges' awards of Crown and Chair— it was all in Welsh. Only one or two choral classics were sung in English: even the words of the *Hymn of Praise* had been translated into Welsh. It is a literal fact that whether sitting in the pavilion or strolling in the meadow, the writer heard hardly one word of English spoken except in conversation with his friends. And the effect was curious. I felt I was in a foreign country, friendly but foreign. It might have been the Bernese Oberland or Czechoslovakia in its happier days.

The national festival, in fact, was true to its name. It was completely and intensely Welsh. Consciousness of Welsh nationhood, pride in Wales, were implicit in all that happened. Verbal expression of it was not needed. There were no emotional appeals to patriotism. Only once, indeed, apart from the frequent singing

[a] I was staying at Coleg Harlech, and, when I was returning thither late one night from Dolgelley, a railway porter got into my compartment going home from his day's work. He at once began to talk in Welsh to my Welsh companion, and, when presently they changed over to English (out of courtesy to me, no doubt), I found that they were having a lively argument about the technique of choral singing. Does that sort of thing happen in English railway carriages?

of the national anthem, was the strength of national sentiment
openly expressed, and that was when the Welsh ' exiles ' who
happened to be on a visit to their mother country and attended
the Eisteddfod, were given a ' welcome home,' There were some
four hundred of them this year and they came from all over the
world—a selection, as it were, from the Welsh diaspora. The
largest quota belonged to the United States, next came Canada
and the other nations of the British Commonwealth, and there
were smaller groups or individuals from Belgium, Holland,
Patagonia, West Africa, India, China, Singapore. As they moved
in slow procession down the length of the pavilion to take their
places, group by group and tier above tier, on the platform, the
audience rose to their feet and sang with them *Unwaith Eto
Nghymru Annwyl* (*Once Again in Dear Wales*).

Interesting, too, though less realistic and less moving, was
the welcome given to a little group of Celts from other Celtic
lands—from Eire, Brittany, Cornwall—who responded in a few
words of Celtic in its local forms.[a]

One last comment, and not the least important for our
student. This Eisteddfod—and the same is true, no doubt, of all
of them—was purely cultural. Only at the tent in the meadow,
where *Plaid Cymru*, the Welsh Nationalist Party, flew its own Red
Dragon and displayed its propagandist literature, was there any
sign or suggestion of politics. And only one thing happened all
that week which might, if one took it seriously, be called a
political incident.' The Eisteddfod was widely reported in the
English Press—in a very different tone, it hardly needs saying, from
that of Matthew Arnold's day—and the correspondent of one
London daily, describing the surroundings of the festival, mentioned in all innocence the Union Jack which flew from the tower
of Dolgelley church. It can scarcely have been pure coincidence
that in the course of the following night some youngsters of the

---

[a] In the spring of 1950 some twenty-five members of the Welsh Gorsedd went to
Brittany to attend the first revival of the Breton Gorsedd since the war. See *Western Mail*,
April 10 to 15.

Nationalist Party climbed the tower, hauled down the flag and hoisted the Red Dragon in its place.[a] But except for the one ten that one bit of skylarking politics were out of the picture. It may be doubted whether one in a hundred of the Welshmen at the Eisteddfod was thinking about Home Rule, and certainly still fewer were sharpening their patriotism with any separatist o anti-English feeling.

Wales, since the ' Apostle's ' day, has always championed the cause of international goodwill; the first Professorship of International Politics in the British Isles was founded at Aberystwyth in 1919; and it was natural that an attempt should be made to awaken in Welsh cultural nationalism the sense of an international ' mission.' If Wales claimed to lead the world in choral singing should she not invite the world to share in it? In 1947, accordingly a younger sister of the National Eisteddfod was brought to birth the Llangollen International Musical Eisteddfod. Llangollen, little riverside town in Denbighshire, was chosen as its permanen seat, and thither most of the countries of Europe were invited to send choirs for an international competition. At subsequen annual meetings the list of competitors was widened to include solo-singing, pianoforte and violin playing, children's choirs, folk songs and folk dances. All the four meetings have been highly successful. In 1949 some 60,000 people attended, and choirs cam to compete from Austria, Belgium, Czechoslovakia, England France, Germany, Italy, the Netherlands, Norway, Portugal Scotland, Spain, Sweden, and the United States of America. ' Blessed is the world that sings,' is the first phrase of the motto composed for the Llangollen Eisteddfod by Gwyn Jones; an certainly the happy atmosphere of the festivals and the friendl

[a] Questioned by journalists the vicar explained that the Union Jack had been hoiste ' because we had no other flag and we felt we must honour the Eisteddfod.' The Unio Jack was re-hoisted by some of the church bell-ringers who were ex-service me *Liverpool Daily Post*, August 5 and 6, 1949.

[b] Eire, Poland and Switzerland were represented in the folk-song and folk-danc competitions.

intermingling of foreigners and Welshmen have confirmed the belief that, since music speaks a universal language which every lover of it understands wherever his national home may be, to share in making and hearing music is one of the easiest ways of fostering good fellowship among the peoples of the world.

The Eisteddfod is the most spectacular manifestation of the effort to maintain the Welsh tradition and the best known outside Wales; but there are three other organisations concerned to foster the spirit and preserve the Welshness of Wales. One is *Plaid Cymru* whose cultural activities will be dealt with when its politics are discussed later on. Another is *Undeb Cymru Fydd* (New Wales Union). The third is *Urdd Gobaith Cymru* (Welsh League of Youth).

Undeb Cymru Fydd was formed in 1941 by the fusion of two kindred bodies, the National Union of Welsh Societies, founded in 1913, and the Committee of the National Conference held at the end of 1939 ' for safeguarding Welsh culture.' Its declared objectives are (1) To safeguard Welsh interests and traditions; (2) to obtain the recognition of Welsh as the official language of Wales; (3) to make sure that Welsh education is founded on the Welsh way of life; (4) to energise and co-ordinate the Welsh societies, and (5) to keep the Welshmen of the ' dispersion ' in touch with their homeland. The *Undeb* has been active in all those fields. It has prompted and supported the Welsh M.P.s on Welsh issues in Parliament It has collaborated with the Churches in pressing on the Government the special needs of the many Welshwomen who were uprooted from their homes and sent to factory work in the English Midlands during the war. It took a leading part in rousing public opinion against the continued occupation of Welsh land by the Defence Ministries and in organising the conferences and deputations which brought about a great reduction of the occupied area. It has promoted the publication of Welsh books and the making of Welsh gramophone records. It has urged the claims of the language on the educational authorities, and it has taken a hand in the recent movement for establishing Welsh schools. As regards the ' exiles,' it has made contact with Welsh societies abroad, and during the war it distributed 25,000 copies of a monthly news-letter in Welsh, *Cofion Cymru*, among Welshmen and Welshwomen in the forces. Yet active as it is, in the social and cultural field, the new *Cymru Fydd* has not yet acquired the national status of the one which Ellis and Lloyd George headed sixty odd years ago.[a] It has branches all over Wales and several Welsh societies are affiliated to it, but its own membership is relatively small. The old *Cymru Fydd*, moreover, adopted from the outset a political objective: its chief aim and purpose was to obtain Home Rule for Wales; whereas it was only after ten years of its life that the new *Cymru Fydd* has stepped out into the political arena.

The *Urdd Gobaith Cymru* was founded in 1922 by Sir Ifan ab Owen Edwards, son of ' O.M.' It was one of the ' youth movements ' which were set on foot in several countries after the First World War. Manifestations of the new strength which nationalism had acquired all over the world, they soon proved their power for evil as well as for good. But the *Urdd* can claim to have avoided from the outset the arrogant, militarist nationalism which so hideously perverted the corresponding movements in Nazi Germany and Fascist Italy. Its spirit has been Mazzini's, not Hitler's. It was ' an intense love for Wales ' that prompted its foundation, but its members are pledged to a threefold allegiance —' to Wales, to follow man and to Christ.' It welcomes foreign visitors to its holiday camps and conferences and it organises tours in foreign countries for its own members. Before the Second World War, for example, it ran sea cruises to North Europe and the Mediterranean.

[a] The present Secretary is T. I. Ellis, son of T. Ellis. He lives at Aberystwyth and has recently published a biography (in Welsh) of his father.

The League is enlisted from the youth of Wales, male and female, between the ages of 15 and 25. To-day its membership totals over 107,000. It operates through a network of local clubs, of which there are now 656 *Adrannau* or Junior clubs (under 15) and 411 *Aelwydydd* or Young Wales clubs (15 to 25). A chain of centres is being built up for courses and conferences and camps: the most important is the fine camp at Llangrannog on the Cardiganshire coast. There are two annual festivals—the Urdd National Eisteddfod, at which some sixty local youth eisteddfodau are represented, and the *Mabolgampau* or Youth Games. Both festivals have proved in their way as successful as the National Eisteddfod itself.

The *Urdd* is far more truly national than the *Undeb*—it operates as widely in South Wales as in North—and it is a far more powerful force in the life of Wales to-day. Nor is its nationalist ardour weaker because it is more widely spread. In Glamorgan as much as in Caernarvon it preaches devotion to Wales and the Welsh tradition. It has been committed from its birth to the duty of upholding the Welsh language—one of its services to that cause is the selling of Welsh books in rural areas where there are no bookshops—but its branches in monoglot English areas in the South accept without demur the necessity of speaking English. 'The *Urdd* believes,' says the official booklet, 'that all Welshmen, whether Welsh-speaking or not, can grow to full stature only by having their roots in their own historical tradition and inheriting that wonderfully rich culture of the democracy that is Wales.'[11] The *Urdd*, indeed, is doing more than anything else to make the Welsh a united nation. It bridges not only the gulf between North and South but also the minor clefts that impair the solidarity of Wales. It knows neither party nor sect. Assured as it is of the requisite financial support,[a] it is

[a] The *Urdd* is aided by the State and local authorities and the Jubilee and Carnegie Trusts, but more than half its revenue comes from Welsh subscriptions.

creating a Young Wales of patriots who know that ' patriotism is not enough.'

Lastly, the schools. The cultural campaign cannot succeed unless the educational system is in tune with it. Even the *Urdd* would find its task too hard if the youth it enlisted knew nothing about their country. The destiny of Welsh culture, in fact, will be determined in the schools; and, aware of that, the leaders of the cultural campaign have made it their first objective to make the schools a nursery of nationhood. Their aims and methods are clearly set forth in two notable documents. The first is the report of a departmental committee appointed by the President of the Board of Education ' to inquire into the position of the Welsh language and to advise as to its promotion in the educational system of Wales.' Published in 1927 in Welsh and English editions, under the title of *Welsh in Education and Life*,[12] it did far more for the national cause than can have been imagined when the committee was set up. Its authors did what was required of them. They examined and explained the decline in the use of Welsh. They discussed its place in the schools and colleges and the methods which were and should be used for teaching it. But they did more than that. They wrote a remarkable book—a comprehensive and very readable history of Welsh culture as embodied in the language and of the growth from its beginnings of Welsh education. No such book had hitherto been written, and it was widely read, not only by educationalists but by the general public. It has been out of print now for some time, but it is still the most valuable literary weapon in the armoury of the cultural campaign. The second document is the report, published in 1949, of the Central Advisory Council for Education in Wales on the future of a Welsh secondary education. It is much shorter than its predecessor, and it deals not only with language but with the whole curriculum. Yet it is a kind of sequel to *Welsh in Education and Life*. It is inspired by the same philosophy. It preaches the same patriotic doctrine. It maintains that Welsh children must learn in their schools to understand what it means to be Welsh. The longest chapter is entitled ' The Secondary School in Wales in relation to the Social and Cultural Background,'[13] and its theme is the application of the doctrine to the teaching not of the Welsh language only but of every literary subject that is taught. History and geography should start their march across the world at the child's home. Economics should begin at the village shop. A synopsis is provided of a model ' course on the Wales of to-day which will give pupils a picture of the society into which they have been born.'[14] ' The simple facts about the country itself— its position, size, relief and climate, the distribution of its population and the different occupations of its people; the story of the Welsh language and the crises through which it has passed, the numbers and distribution of those who now speak it; the main landmarks of its literary history with reference to and emphasis on some modern men of letters; the milestones of its chequered history; the structure of its religious life, its educational system and its administrative machinery; an outline of its architecture, its arts and crafts, its music and its folk-life; and a sketch of its social and cultural institutions—all this will help the pupils not merely to take a pride in the Wales of yesterday but to understand the Wales of to-day.'

This is only a programme for schools, but it is, in elementary shape, the programme of the whole cultural campaign. And its significance for students of the latter lies in its scope and its solidity. It reveals the extent to which Welsh cultural nationalism has widened its range and defined its meaning since the nineteenth-century revival. The nationalism preached by the Aberdare Committee in 1880[a] was expressed in general terms. It spoke of maintaining the national life of preserving the traditional sentiments and national characteristics of the Welsh people. But few Welshmen of that day had translated this vague language into

[a] See page 201 above.

355

specific terms or considered exactly what it was they wanted to preserve. The nationalism of the twentieth century has done that and done it thoroughly. It has defined the Welsh ' way of life.' It has singled out the distinctive features of the Welsh cultural tradition. It knows, clearly enough now, what it wants to preserve and it is fighting to preserve it.

It is, of course, a fight. While the cultural campaign has been gaining strength, the forces that oppose it have grown stronger too. Few Englishmen nowadays want to anglicise Wales; but the pressure exerted by the mighty neighbour to absorb the Welsh into the English way of life is no less powerful because it is unconscious. The age-long English invasion never ceases. More and more English tourists are haunting the mountains and the coasts of Wales. Aided now by the motor-car they penetrate to those districts of wild natural beauty where Welsh life has hitherto been least affected by English contact. More and more the holiday crowds of Lancashire overflow into the North Welsh coastal towns; and all over England the railway stations placard in glowing colours the charms of the inland as well as the seaside Welsh resorts. And the invaders are not only holidaymakers. The inflow of Englishmen seeking work, professional, clerical, industrial, continues. In the course of the last few years whole companies of English workmen have been planted in the heart of Wales to carry out afforestation and other development schemes promoted by the Government. But the increase of English immigration is not the most formidable threat to the Welshness of Wales. For many years now, as explained in Part Five above, the gravest menace to Welsh nationhood has been the integration of British life brought about by the Industrial Revolution and parliamentary democracy, reinforced in recent years by Socialism. Can it possibly be withstood? it is sometimes asked. Is not the fight to save Welsh culture a desperate rearguard action which sooner or later must be overborne?

It is too soon, perhaps, to attempt an answer to such questions; for the cultural campaign has only recently acquired its full force. But there are one or two forecasts that can be hazarded with some assurance. The study of Wales and its traditions will remain firmly planted in the Welsh educational system—in the University, in adult aducation, in the schools. In that field the campaigners have already done something that will not be undone. Nor will the Welsh people fail to maintain their best-known cultural tradition. The Welsh will still be as famous for their choral singing as they were in the days of Giraldus Cambrensis. But what of the other and even finer cultural tradition? It is not so easy to feel sure about the future of Welsh poetry and prose; for that, it is plain, depends on the future of the Welsh language. And who can tell what that will be? The nineteenth-century paradox persists in the twentieth. While the revival of national culture waxes, the use of the national language wanes.

The censuses of 1921 and 1931 revealed that the decline in the number of Welsh-speakers had steadily continued since the census of 1911.

		1911	1921	1931
Population (over 3)	..	2,247,927	2,486,740	2,472,378
Welsh monoglots ..	..	190,292	156,995	97,932
Bilingual	..	787,074	772,188	811,329
English monoglots	..	1,208,282	1,477,741	1,563,117

Thus between 1911 and 1931 the number of people who spoke Welsh (alone or together with English) fell from 43 per cent to 37 per cent of the population, while the number who spoke English only rose from 54 per cent to 63 per cent. Nobody in Wales has any doubt that the census of 1951 will reveal that the use of Welsh is still decreasing and at a faster pace.

Some of the reasons why more Welshmen now speak English

and fewer Welsh are old and some are new. The old ' materialist ' argument has lost none of its force. Still, as always since Tudor days, the fact that English is the language of material and social advancement is the main reason for the decline of Welsh. But there are other reasons which have only begun to operate since the latter part of the nineteenth century. One of the most potent of them is the decline in religious faith or at least in its traditional observance. Since the services, the sermons, the Sunday Schools no longer play the part they once played in the life of every Nonconformist family in Wales, they cannot do the work they once did for the preservation of the Welsh language. The chapels are finding it increasingly more difficult, especially in South Wales, to carry on their worship, preaching and teaching in Welsh. The Church in Wales, which has shown a far better understanding of the national spirit than its predecessor, finds a corresponding difficulty in maintaining both Welsh and English services in bilingual areas, and in recruiting a sufficient number of Welsh-speaking clergy.[a]

Another reason for the decline of Welsh has been the relatively recent growth in the power and scope of English publicity. The strongest and most far-reaching instruments of the English invasion now are the Press, the radio and the cinema. There is no Welsh daily newspaper. The *Western Mail* in the South and the *Liverpool Daily Post* in the North provide the only news available till the early editions of the London papers arrive. There is still a rich variety of Welsh weeklies and other periodicals, but their number is gradually decreasing.[b] Gee's *Faner* still flies

[a] Part II of the *Report of the Nation and Prayer Book Commission* of the Church in Wales illustrates the Church's present attitude to Welsh nationhood.

[b] There are two Welsh weeklies which are read throughout Wales, *Y Cymru* (about 24,000 circulation) and *Y Faner*, and a third, *Y Herald Gymraeg a'r Genedl*, which circulates in North Wales, particularly in Caernarvonshire. There are several local Welsh papers with small circulations. The best-known denominational weeklies are *Y Goleuad* (Calvinist Methodist), *Seren Cymru* (Baptist), *Y Tyst* (Congregational), *Y Slan* (Church in Wales)—Of the more important Welsh journals *Y Llenor* is the chief literary review, *Llen Cymru*, is the organ of Welsh and Celtic scholarship, and *Efrydiau Athronyddol* of philosophy. The leading theological journals are *Y Traethodydd*, which is more than a century old, *Yr Efrydydd* which deals with current affairs and literature as well as theology,

bravely, but it is flying now ' against the wind.' . . . As to broadcasting, before the recent efforts to ensure that Welsh life and the
Welsh language should be adequately represented in the programmes of the B.B.C., every Welshman who wanted and could
afford to ' listen' was always or almost always listening to
English. English, in fact, was being spoken within the walls of
isolated cottages among the hills where it had never been spoken
before. And even now, with Welsh programmes available, there
are many ' features' of interest to every Welshman which cannot
be rendered in Welsh—the Queen's Christmas message, for
example, or a speech by Mr. Churchill or Mr. Attlee or President
Truman or Pandit Nehru. . . . Broadcasting affects the older more
than the younger folk, but it is the young who suffer most
from the cinema—that perilous school in which, perhaps, they
hear good English spoken or, more probably, the *argot* of Holly-
wood, but certainly never a word of Welsh.

And in the background of all this organised English publicity,
the English language continues to spread through countless
channels of every kind as it has done since the process of anglicisation began in the distant past. The English tourist, for example,
makes Welshmen use his language wherever he goes. Hospitality
to strangers is an ancient Welsh tradition, and Welshmen welcome
the tourist not only because, as in Defoe's day,[a] they take pride
in his admiration of the beauties of their homeland but also
because of the money he spends; and, since no Englishman learns
Welsh for a visit to Wales, his hosts and guides—the hotel-
keeper, the small tradesman, the taxi-driver, the vendor of
picture postcards—must perforce acquire a little English. Hence
the wistful saying that the beauty spots of Wales, even the most
remote, have become or are fast becoming ' outposts of Saxon-
dom.'[15]

For all these reasons the linguistic assault on Wales steadily

and *Seren Gomer,* which first appeared as a weekly in 1814, became a monthly in 1820,
a quarterly in 1880, since 1888 has appeared bi-monthly.

[a] See page 60 above.

continues, and its end is as certain as that of the territorial invasion in the Middle Ages. In the industrial belt of South Wales the conquest is already virtually complete. The conquest of the rest of the country is only a matter of time. Sooner or later every Welshman will be able to speak English.

That is not only inevitable: it is also plainly right. For no one would deny to Welshmen the material advantages of knowing English or the moral and intellectual gain of being able to read English literature. But there has been a change, a supremely important change, in intelligent opinion as to what that admission implies. A century ago championship of English meant hostility to Welsh. The Commissioners of 1846 regarded the Welsh language as an 'evil' to be rooted out because it obstructed the spread of English. And for years afterwards this harsh judgment was coarsely echoed in the English Press. Even a critic so sensitive as Matthew Arnold and so much in sympathy with the Welsh spirit was no friend of the Welsh language. He did not vilify it, of course; but, doubtless because his knowledge of Welsh literature was confined to a much smaller stock of translations than is now available, he did not fully appreciate the value of the language and believed it would die out. 'For all serious purposes in modern literature,' he said, ' the language of a Welshman must be English.' Welsh literature should be more widely and carefully studied, but it was waste of effort, a defiance of destiny, to write it. Unaware of the hold that the doctrine of nationality was soon to win on European thought, he believed in the inevitable ' fusion of all the inhabitants of these islands into one homogeneous English-speaking whole.'[16]

Those sentiments sound strange to-day. The official attitude has been transformed. The creation of the Welsh Department of the Board of Education in 1907 was an implicit repudiation of the ideas of 1846, and, a generation later, it was made explicit when the President of the Board did what he could to make public expiation for the blunder of the *brâd*. ' I regard as obscurantist,' said Mr. R. A. Butler in the House of Commons in 1942, ' the attitude of the Commission of Inquiry a hundred years ago which went to Wales and took the view that to keep alive a knowledge of this beautiful tongue was tantamount to crippling Welsh initiative and penalising Welsh endeavour. I wish now to make amends for that attitude.'[17] And the same change has taken place in literary circles. No leading English man of letters would take Arnold's line to-day. T. S. Eliot, for example, does not want a homogeneous Britain. He values the variety of national cultures and for the preservation and transmission of a culture he looks on language as the indispensable instrument. And to serve that purpose, he maintains, ' it must continue to be a literary language.' ' If it is no longer cultivated, the people to whom it belongs will tend to lose their racial character. The Welsh will be less Welsh; and their poets will cease to have any contribution to make to English literature beyond their individual genius.'[18]

Welcome as English sympathy may be, the Welsh defenders of their language are well aware that its fate will be decided in Wales. What, then, is their policy? They are not, of course, opposed to the spread of English. They know it is inevitable. They admit it is desirable. But they hold—and it is the cardinal point in the change of thought on the linguistic issue—that, if all Welshmen should speak English, it does not necessarily follow that no Welshman should speak Welsh. In other words their aim is to make Wales a bilingual country. They realise that it is a difficult, a very difficult task, but they realise too, that it is the only way of saving Welsh.

The approach is necessarily one-sided: for, as has been seen, no propaganda is required to induce the hundred thousand Welsh folk, who speak Welsh only, to learn English. That is happening, so to speak, of itself. What is needed is first to induce those

Welshmen who acquire English not to drop their Welsh and second to induce the million and a half who speak English only to learn Welsh.

To those ends the first aim of the bilingualists has been to make the average Welshman understand what the Welsh language means to Wales. Much has been written to expound its distinctive character and quality, its beauty, its flexibility, its capacity to move and grow with the times. Despite its venerable age, it is pointed out, it is very much alive, adapting itself without effort to all the linguistic demands of our modern scientific world. The language ' which discusses the atom bomb or a problem of bacteriology remains the language of the eleventh-century *Mabinogon*.'[19] And it is not only valuable in itself, the argument runs on, it is an indispensable element in the national life of Wales. Since the misty days when the Welsh began to be a nation, it has been the hall-mark of their nationhood and the mainspring of their culture. Welsh nationality, in fact, is rooted in the language and, if the root withers away, the plant will die.

This teaching has begun to take effect. One notable example is the support given by bilingual parents to the movement for establishing elementary schools in which Welsh is the vehicle of instruction. Another example is the growing acceptance by public opinion, especially in the dominantly Welsh-speaking areas, of the principle that anyone who takes a leading part in Welsh life should be able to speak Welsh. This is having an increasing effect on the choice of personnel in local government. All, however, that bilingualism achieves in other fields will ultimately be of no avail unless it is successful in the schools. It is not too much to say that, with rare exceptions, a child who only speaks one language in his home and does not learn to speak the other when he goes to school will never speak it. It is in the schools, therefore, that the decisive battle is being fought, and it is a long way yet from victory. For the hopes that were cherished by the champions of the Welsh language when the schools were brought under local Welsh control have not yet been realised. The efforts of the Welsh Department of the Ministry of Education to sustain the claims of Welsh have been wholehearted and persistent. It has done all it could do by way of advice and appeal. But the County Councils as a whole are not yet in line with Whitehall. While several of them accept the bilingualist doctrine and act accordingly, others are indifferent and passive. The bilingual policy assumes that ' every child in Wales should receive an education which will fit him to earn a livelihood in any part of the country and enable him to feel at home in whatever part of Wales he visits.' Its programme may be summarised as follows:[a] (1) In primary schools both in Welsh-speaking and in English-speaking areas the children should be thoroughly taught their home-language or mother-tongue. (2) They should also be given a practical working knowledge of the second language, English or Welsh as the case may be. (3) As far and as long as possible the language of instruction should be the mother-tongue. (4) In ' mixed ' areas, i.e. where Welsh is spoken in some homes and English in others, the children should be classified accordingly and taught separately, as far as need be, on the lines laid down above. (5) Secondary schools should continue the policy of the primary schools which feed them: the children should be similarly divided in accordance with their mother-tongue unless their parents desire otherwise or unless they have by some means become more proficient in the other language.

The crux of this policy lies in the ' mixed ' areas. The linguistic classification and division it requires are plainly undesirable in themselves and must involve an increase of staff and cost. Yet without some such scheme—and what other scheme can be devised?—it is hard to see how Welsh can hold its own. And, if it loses its foothold in the ' mixed ' areas, it has small chance of winning a foothold in the English-speaking areas where, as things

[a] For a full account, see *Language Teaching in Primary Schools*, pamphlet No. 1, published by the Welsh Department of the Ministry of Education (1945), and the report on *The Future of Secondary Education in Wales* mentioned above.

are, French is taken as the second language in several schools and Welsh not taught at all.

The prospects of this broad-fronted battle for Welsh are necessarily more favourable in North Wales than in South: for it is an easier task to persuade the tens of thousands of Welsh monoglots who learn English not to drop their Welsh than to persuade the hundreds of thousands of English monoglots to acquire the other language. Yet that second task must somehow be accomplished if the cause of bilingualism is to prevail. It needs more than a partial or local victory. The future of Welsh can only be safe if all Wales becomes bilingual. And the reason is plain. As long as a substantial number of Welshmen speak English only, the pressure on them to learn Welsh for the practical purposes of life will be weakened by convenience and courtesy. It has often been observed that on any collective occasion—at a public meeting or conference or social function or on the playing-field—a unilingual minority will get its language spoken, however large the bilingual majority may be. If fifty Welshmen meet for a common purpose and five of them know English only, those five can take no part in the proceedings, they had better not be there, unless in deference to them the forty-five who know both languages abstain from speaking Welsh. And that is what usually happens. Pessimists, indeed, have argued that in the long run an incomplete bilingualism will prove to be only a stage in the process of converting all Welshmen into English monoglots.

Conceivably that might be so if the salvation of Welsh depended on purely practical considerations. But the campaigners maintain that it does not. It depends, they say, on patriotism, on whether anglicised Welshmen, especially in the industrial area, can be brought to recognise that the Welsh language is a vital element in Welsh nationhood.

It would be a gross mistake to suppose that the South is less patriotic than the North. Anglicised Welshmen are no less aware

than anglicised Scotsmen of their distinctive nationality and no
less proud of it. It would be unwise for an Englishman who did
not possess unusual physical strength to put the question to the
test by telling a miner in the Rhondda valley that he was really
an Englishman. But he need not run that risk. He can join the
crowd at an international football match at Cardiff or Swansea
when Wales is playing England. He can read in the newspapers
that St. David's Day is celebrated everywhere. He can visit
Cardiff and sense the national pride which claims that the city
should rank not with Birmingham or Liverpool, but with
Edinburgh. And at Cardiff he would see the National War
Memorial in Cathays Park and note that a Welsh inscription runs
round the edifice meaning 'To the Sons of Wales who gave their
lives for their country'[a] and that over the three portals are
inscribed quotations from well-known Welsh poems. . . . *Of
course* the South is Welsh and proud of it.

In this patriotism and in nothing else lies the hope of making
South Wales bilingual. Even if it be assumed—and it is a bold
assumption—that the policy of adjusting education in the schools
to a background of Welsh life and tradition is generally adopted
in English-speaking areas, it will still take time for a generation
to emerge which understands that the language is a vital part of the
national heritage. But, while this is happening, the bilingualists
will doubtless try to convince the existing adult population of
industrial South Wales that a patriotism which would let the
language die is an unintelligent and short-sighted patriotism. It
is unintelligent, they will argue, because it fails to realise that in the
Welsh language and Welsh literature, more than anywhere else,
is to be found the distinctive Welsh contribution to the common
treasury of Western civilisation and for which, more than anything
else, she is held in honour among other nations. And it is short-
sighted, they will say, because, if the language dies, Wales

---

[a] Inside there is an English inscription: 'Remember here in peace those who in
tumult of war by sea, on land, in air, for us and for our victory endured unto death.'

will lose her strongest rampart against the cultural invasion; that, if the language goes, the process of anglicisation will one day be so complete that Welsh nationhood will have disappeared; and that, therefore, the Welshman who is content to speak English only is yielding unawares and without a fight to English conquest.

III. POLITICAL NATIONALISM

WHILE CULTURAL nationalism was steadily gaining strength in Wales between the wars, political nationalism was declining. On the eve of the Speaker's Conference the public interest in Home Rule seemed as keen as in the early days of Cymru Fydd; but with the inconclusive ending of the Conference the interest died away as quickly as it had arisen. When the Welsh M.P.s resumed their sterile agitation in the Commons, it made no more stir in Wales than it had done before the war.

In 1921 the claim to a Welsh Secretaryship, of which little had been heard since 1891-92,[a] was revived. A Bill was introduced in the Commons by Mr. D. Matthews (Swansea) providing for the transfer to a Secretary for Wales of ' such powers and duties as relate to Wales ' and had hitherto been exercised by various departments in Whitehall.[20] It was read a first time and no more. Early in 1922, at the prompting of Lloyd George who advised a Welsh deputation to drop the Secretaryship and ' go for the big thing,'[21] a Welsh Home Rule Bill, based on Mr. Murray Macdonald's scheme, was introduced by Sir Robert Thomas (Wrexham) backed by four other Welsh M.P.s. There was ' a very strong desire in Wales,' said Sir Robert in the debate on the second reading, that the country should be treated as ' a separate entity ' and not merely as a number of English counties.[22] ' All the Welsh

[a] See pages 229-30 above.

constituencies,' said Mr. Hugh Edwards (Neath), supported the Bill in principle.[23] But those assumptions were questioned. A conference of Welsh local authorities, it was said, which had been held at Shrewsbury to consider the Bill, had been attended by only fifty persons; Glamorgan, the predominant county, had not sent a single representative; and the conference had spent most of its time on the old wrangle between North and South as to the basis of representation in a Welsh legislature.[24] The contrast with the ardour and unity of the Llandrindod Conference four years earlier was striking. To all appearance the national sentiment, so warm in 1918, was now again as cool as it had been before the war. To the fate of the Bill—it attained a second reading but no more—all save a handful of parliamentarians seemed quite indifferent.

The breakdown of the Coalition Government followed, and those Welshmen who had still believed that there was always a chance of Home Rule as long as Lloyd George was in power began to despair of their cause. The Conservatives now dominated Parliament and Government and, though they might welcome the alliance of those few members of the other Parties who still clung to the idea of coalition, though at one time they might even install a minority Labour Government, they continued to dominate till the coming of another war. And the Conservatives as a whole had always been Unionists, always anti-federalists. Even those few of them who had flirted with devolution for a year or two had now fallen back into line. As to the Labour Party, it is true that the Labour candidates who won 18 of the 36 Welsh seats at the elections of 1922 all professed themselves in favour of Home Rule for Wales; but none of them could pretend that it was a real live issue in the campaign. Still less significant was the action of the two Welsh Labour members who at the outset of the new Parliament tabled an amendment to the Address, regretting the absence of Home Rule from the ministerial programme. It was no more than a gesture, the first of the many that were to be made from time to time right on through the years of the Depression to the next war and after it.

In the spring of 1924 Ramsay MacDonald declared his readiness to appoint a committee of inquiry into the question of Home Rule-all-round. A month later he announced that, since the co-operation of all Parties in the inquiry had proved unobtainable, no further action could be taken for the time being.[25] ... In 1928 Baldwin, answering the same question on three separate occasions, declined to consider the creation of a Secretaryship of State for Wales.[26] ... In 1930 Baldwin not only twice again repudiated the Secretaryship;[27] he refused to contemplate a separate legislative assembly for Wales or even the provision of facilities, such as Scotland had long enjoyed, for the passage of Welsh legislation;[28] nor would he consider the extension to Wales of the Scottish system of administrative devolution. The present time, he said, was inopportune for radical changes in Welsh administration.[29] ...In 1933 and 1934 Ramsay MacDonald repeated these negations. He was not aware, he said, of any widespread desire in Wales for either administrative or legislative devolution.[30] ... Apart from asking the questions which received these dusty answers, the only move made by the Welsh M.P.s before the Second World War was the presentation of one more Secretary of State for Wales Bill in 1937.[31] It was introduced by Clement Davies (Montgomery) and backed by four Liberal, three Conservative and three Labour members for Welsh constituencies. No more was heard of it. ...
In the early years of the war Scottish nationalists continued from time to time to raise the issue of Home Rule, but the Welsh M.P.s were silent till 1943 when the claim for equal treatment with Scotland was urged again in questions and debate. The Government's attitude was unchanged. ' I prefer,' said Mr. Churchill, ' to be a little backward in that matter.'[32] ... But when at last the end of the war was in sight, a concession was made to Welsh sentiment. One day in each session of the Commons was reserved for the discussion of Scottish affairs, and in 1944

Wales, 1918-1945

a corresponding 'Welsh day' was inaugurated on October 17. Led by Lloyd George's daughter, the Welsh members warmly thanked the Government for this concession. It was the first day, said Miss Megan Lloyd George (Anglesey), for 400 years that Parliament had given to the affairs of Wales.[33] But the subsequent debate was not very interesting or very useful. Political issues being ruled out, only one or two speakers referred in passing to the claim for a Welsh Secretaryship. Nothing else was said about devolution except for Mr. James Griffiths' (Llanelly) brief and bold assertion that it was 'essential for the proper working of democracy.'[34] Almost all the speakers, naturally enough, were Welshmen, who, no less naturally, took occasion to plead the economic needs of their constituencies; and almost all the listeners were likewise Welshmen. The average attendance, said one speaker late in the day, had been no more than twenty.[35] But the general dullness of the proceedings was relieved by three significant speeches. The first was Mr. H. Richards' (Wrexham) brief breakaway from economics. 'Wales,' he said, 'is a nation and a community which in its tradition, history, language and literature is quite distinct from England. There are many people in Wales who are more concerned about the future of Welsh culture than about the economic life of Wales.'[36] More startling was the intervention, late in the debate, of Mr. Aneurin Bevan (Ebbw Vale) who had made his mark in the House by his unbridled criticism of the Government's conduct of the war. Alone of the Welsh members, he denounced the 'day.' It was a 'farce,' he said. Wales needed no such separate treatment. 'My colleagues, all of them members of the Miners' Federation of Great Britain, have no special solution for the Welsh coal industry which is not a solution for the whole of the mining industry of Great Britain. There is no Welsh problem.' And so with other economic questions. How did sheep in the Welsh mountains differ from sheep in the Scottish Highlands?[37] The challenge to national sentiment could not have been more direct. It was a frank avowal that Socialist ' planning ' for the whole of Britain would take no account of national differences; and it was confirmed by Dr. H. Dalton (Bishop Auckland) when he wound up the debate. He swept aside the pleas which two or three speakers had made for the construction of a North-South road to promote the unity of Wales. It is ' much more important,' he said, ' to tie up the South Wales industrial community with the great Midland industrial community.'[38]

While Welsh M.P.s were repeating from time to time their ineffective demand for a Welsh Secretaryship, a more ambitious project of administrative devolution was being canvassed outside Parliament. As early as 1906 a member of Welsh educationalists, well aware of the part played by education in the national revival in the nineteenth century, had proposed that a National Council of Education should be established to assume control of the Welsh educational system as a whole. This plan had made no headway before the First World War mainly owing to disagreement between the various educational authorities concerned and the conflict of opinion between North and South.[a] When it was taken up again in 1917, it had obtained the backing of a large majority at a national educational conference, but again it had proved impossible to bring the authorities into line. In 1921 the project was revived and this time it was not only adopted by two successive national conferences, but sufficient agreement was subsequently forthcoming to make possible a formal approach to Government. Partly, however, owing to the distraction of two general elections, no action was taken till 1927 when a joint deputation of the Central Board, the Federation of Local Authorities and the University Court submitted the case for a National Council to the Minister of Education. Lord Eustace Percy did not favour the proposal, but he was willing to consider ' the possibility of appointing a purely advisory Council to which

[a] See page 198, above.

he could turn for advice on matters of national importance to Welsh education.'[39] Nothing came of this suggestion: attempts to obtain agreement on an advisory basis broke down; and in 1930 another national conference reverted to the National Council plan. Then came the great depression, pushing all other issues into the background, and it was not till 1935 that the Council plan was taken up again, and again referred to the various educational authorities, and blocked again by disagreement. When the Second World War broke out, the question of setting up some representative Welsh body for dealing with Welsh education was still unsettled. It would be dealt with, it was thought, as part of the Government's policy of post-war reconstruction.

This agitation for a Secretaryship and a Council of Education —the two projects were sometimes combined—was not wholly fruitless. It made more Welshmen aware of the practical realities of devolution. In the first place it was now recognised that the Welsh claim for a Secretaryship differed from the Scottish. In Scotland the appointment of a Secretary was the restoration of something the Scots had lost. In Wales it was a novelty. Secondly, a political difficulty became apparent which was also felt in Scotland but not so acutely. Since the mid-nineteenth century Welsh party politics had been one-sided—more so than Scottish. Up to 1923 the Liberals, and after that Labour, had held the majority of the Welsh seats. If this one-sidedness should become—and it seemed not unlikely—a permanent feature of Welsh politics, what would happen to the Secretaryship if another party won a British general election? The Conservatives, say, would have won most of the seats outside Wales, but they would have to choose the Welsh Secretary from among two or three Conservative Welsh M.P.s, none of whom might be well-qualified for the post, or from among the Welshmen in the House of Lords. In neither case could he be regarded as a representative of the Welsh people. Thirdly, it appeared that the Secretaryship might not prove to be as useful as its advocates assumed. It was forcibly

argued that Welsh interests would be better served if Welsh
M.P.s and public bodies could still state their case to the Minister
directly concerned rather than to a Welsh Secretary, and that the
most effective reform would be the creation in all domestic
Ministries of Welsh Departments like those which already existed
in the Ministries of Education, Health, Labour and Agriculture.[a]
Lastly, the constitutional realities which lay behind the projects
of the Secretaryship and the Council of Education were now
better understood. The appointment of a Welsh Secretary, it
became clear, would not be a concession of national self-government. He could watch over Welsh interests at Westminster and
in Whitehall. He could inform and influence his colleagues in the
Government on Welsh affairs. But that was all. The people of
Wales might profit from having, so to speak, 'a friend at court'
in London, but they would have no more governing *power* than
they had had before. And it was because the scheme for a Council
of Education contemplated the transfer of *power* that it was quite
impracticable. For the Council was to assume control of the
Welsh educational system and so become responsible for the
expenditure of the public funds supplied for its maintenance.
Responsible to whom? To the Local Government authorities
which it was mainly (but not solely) to represent? But revenue
from local rates would not nearly suffice to meet the full cost of
education: a substantial grant from the Treasury would still be
indispensable; and, since the funds at the disposal of the Treasury
are provided by English and Scottish taxpayers as well as Welsh,
responsibility for their expenditure could be vested only in a
Minister accountable to English and Scottish as well as Welsh
members of the House of Commons.

Such argumentation made it clear at last that 'administrative
devolution' was a *cul-de-sac*: that it did not and could not lead
to national self-government: that it was no more than ' delega-

[a] For the best statement of this case, see Sir P. E. Watkins, *A Welshman Remembers*
(Cardiff, 1944), 221-8. The author was in charge of the Welsh Department at the
Board of Education from 1925 to 1933.

tion' unless accompanied by legislative devolution. There could, in fact, be no self-government for Wales without a legislature empowered to raise Welsh taxes, to make Welsh laws and to hold Welsh ministers responsible for their administration.

To these discussions and their barren outcome Welsh public opinion as a whole was seemingly quite indifferent. But there was an exception to this general apathy. To a little group of intellectuals the off-hand treatment accorded in Parliament after the war even to so mild a claim as that for a Welsh Secretaryship seemed an intolerable affront to Welsh nationhood; and their sense of humiliation was enhanced when they saw Ireland attaining self-government, part of it as a province, most of it as much more than that, as an independent national State enjoying a 'Dominion Status' which in 1926 was defined as a status of complete equality with that of the United Kingdom. Like T. E. Ellis in his day, these young nationalists were students of Irish nationalism. They had read the works of Thomas Davis and had followed the stormy history of the Irish Party. And the lesson was unmistakable. Home Rule for Wales would remain a dream as long as Welsh politics were regarded as a section of British politics, as long as Welshmen in Parliament were members of British parties. The only hope was to revive the project of a Welsh Nationalist Party which Ellis and Lloyd George had adopted for a moment and then dropped. It would prove, no doubt, a long and arduous task to convince the Welsh electorate that loyalty to a British party was inconsistent with loyalty to Wales; that the promises made by Liberal or Labour candidates at Welsh elections were waste of breath unless they accorded with the policy of their party leaders and the orders of their party whips; that only when the Welshmen in the House of Commons formed a separate party on the Irish model and mobilised the Welsh electorate behind it, only then would the claims of Wales be taken seriously. Such was the challenge thrown out to the old-established parties when, at a little public meeting in a chapel at Pwllheli in the course of Eisteddfod week in 1925, *Plaid Cymru*, the Welsh Nationalist Party, was born.

The outstanding personality in the little company of 'highbrows'—professors, school teachers, preachers, students, mostly from North Wales—who attended the Party's birth was John Saunders Lewis.[a] Born in a Liverpool suburb in 1893, son of a Calvinistic Methodist minister, he spent his childhood in a thoroughly Welsh atmosphere. Welsh was the language of the home. The Nonconformist tradition, the battle for Disestablishment, the rise of Ellis and Lloyd George, the fortunes of Cymru Fydd—such was the normal stuff of conversation. But young Lewis had not become deeply interested in Welsh nationalism when he went to Liverpool University and, before he had finished his course there, was caught up in the First World War. His reaction, he said later on, was that of an 'English patriot.' He obtained a commission in the South Wales Borderers and fought on the Western Front. Not long after the death of his only brother in Flanders he was wounded at Bourlon Wood. The end of the war found him in the British Army Intelligence service in Athens. On demobilisation he returned to Liverpool to finish his work for the M.A. degree, and there he fell in love with a fellow-student, Margaret Gilchrist, an Irishwoman, once a Wesleyan but converted to Catholicism. When a few years later they were married, Lewis adopted his wife's religion; and it was now that the pattern of his life took shape. On the one hand by his contributions to the newspapers in South Wales—he had obtained a librarianship under the Glamorgan County Council—and by the production of a short play, *The Eve of St. John*, he began to make his reputation as a man of letters. On the other hand, he became a passionate Welsh patriot. He threw himself with enthusiasm into the cultural campaign for the preservation of the Welsh language,

[a] For what follows the author is mainly indebted to a remarkable study of Lewis published anonymously in *The Welsh Review* in 1946 (vol. v. no. 4) when Gwyn Jones was editor.

the Welsh tradition, the Welsh way of life. But, unlike most of his fellow-campaigners, he went far beyond that. In hot reaction against industrialism as he saw it in South Wales, he preached a social revolution. And, since he regarded industrialism as an evil which England had forced on Wales, he proclaimed what might now be called a ' cold war ' against England. ' We must release Wales,' ran the manifesto of the *Plaid* of which from the first he was the undisputed master, ' from the grip of the English. We can aim at nothing less than *to do away with the English language in Wales.* . . . We must blot it out of our land. Delenda est Carthago.' And freedom from England must be political as well as cultural. ' We demand Dominion Status for Wales and let no one offer us any other.' So and only so would the way be opened to the social and economic revolution. ' For the sake of the moral and physical health of its people South Wales must be de-industrialised ' and the country as a whole revert to agriculture as the basis of its civilisation.[40]

In the course of the next few years, Lewis, who was appointed Lecturer in Welsh at the newly founded University College at Swansea, came to the front of the literary world in Wales. He wrote profusely, and all his writing was suffused with his nationalism. Thus the keynote of his criticism of contemporary Welsh literature was his belief that the Welsh genius lost its genuine inspiration when Tudor England broke the threads which had linked medieval Wales with the Catholic tradition of continental Europe, and that only by throwing off the narrow materialistic influence of English Protestantism and reverting to the old philosophy and the old faith would Welsh writers be able to sound once more the ' authentic note.' There was another strain in Lewis's doctrine. Pacifism, as has been seen, had long been a hallmark of Welsh political thought, and in Lewis's case the hatred of war was doubtless hardened by his own experience. But it was in a sense a militant pacifism. For the enemy of peace, it seemed, was England, and the worst humiliation inflicted on subject Wales was her enforced entanglement in England's 'imperialistic' policy.

Such uncompromising doctrine may well have frightened the more moderate members of Lewis's little party, and it was altogether unacceptable to the great majority of Welshmen. In the general election of 1929 the *Plaid* determined to try its fortunes at the polls. The Rev. L. Valentine stood for Caernarvonshire, asserting in the Irish manner that, if he were elected, he would not take his seat. He obtained 609 votes against 38,043 cast for his Liberal, Labour and Conservative opponents together. In the elections of 1931 members of the *Plaid* contested three seats, two of them under the label of 'Independents.' Their total vote was 2,516, that of their opponents 76,239. Lewis himself stood for the Welsh Universities and obtained 914 votes against 2,229 given to the Liberal candidate, Professor W. J. Gruffydd. In 1935 only Caernarvonshire was contested and the *Plaid*'s candidate was again defeated, obtaining 2,534 votes against his two opponents' 34,397.

In 1930 and in 1936 Lewis was involved in personal 'incidents' which made some stir in the Welsh Press. In the winter of 1930 he was asked by the B.B.C. to broadcast on 'Welsh Nationalism,' but, when he submitted his script, the 'talk' was banned. Thereupon Lewis published the text as a pamphlet, explaining in a foreword that 'an official of the Corporation defended the official action by saying that " the talk was calculated to inflame Welsh national sympathies." ' 'The author fervently hopes,' Lewis added, ' that its publication now as a pamphlet may have that effect.'[41] Readers of it must have been puzzled as to what the B.B.C. expected Lewis to say when they asked him to talk. For its tone is studiously moderate. It claims that a genuine nationalism must be political nationalism and that the objective of the party is Dominion Status. But there is nothing more inflammatory than that. There is no attack on England. It is not suggested that the economic depression, then at its peak in Wales, was England's fault. It is admitted that parts of England are in the same plight. It is argued that England will benefit, too, if Wales overcomes her difficulties by the united efforts which only a 'national revival' can inspire.

The second incident was more dramatic. In 1936 the Air Ministry decided to lay out R.A.F. aerodromes in three sparsely-peopled localities—at Abbotsbury in Dorset, at Holy Island off the Northumbrian coast, and at Penrhos in South Caernarvon-shire. The first two projects were withdrawn in face of local protests, backed in the case of Abbotsbury by English ornitho-logists. But the Welsh protest was ignored; and in due course the land was cleared at Penrhos and buildings erected for what was expected to be a bombing school. On the night of September 8, Lewis, together with the Rev. L. Valentine and Mr. D. J. Williams, set fire to several of the hutments and surrendered themselves forthwith to the local police. Charged at Caernarvon with inflicting damage estimated at over £2,000 on public property, the accused did not deny what they had done. They had done it, said Lewis, 'to call the attention of Wales and England' to their protest against the bombing school.[42] The jury disagreeing, the case was set down for the next assizes and later, because of the local feeling it had excited, transferred to the Central Criminal Court.[a] On January 19 the trial was held at the Old Bailey. Lewis and his associates admitted the charge and offered no evidence in their defence. They were sentenced to nine months' imprisonment in the second division. There were many Welshmen in the court, and outside a crowd collected and sang " Land of our Fathers " in Welsh.[43] Ten days later R. Richards, M.P. for Wrexham, asked the Home Secretary to review the sentence on the ground that the case was political. Sir John Simon refused.[44]

When Lewis came out of prison, he found himself dismissed

[a] The transfer was contested by counsel for the defendants, but upheld by the Lord Chief Justice and two other judges. *The Times*, Dec. 8, 1936.

from his Swansea lectureship. But that was not the judgment of those Welsh patriots who felt that, fanatical as it might seem, Lewis's gesture had been a sincere and not wholly illegitimate demonstration against the high-handed conduct of the British Government; and for many of the younger folk he had become a national hero. There was an opportunity, it seemed, for a vigorous nationalist campaign with England's ex-prisoner at its head. But Lewis abstained from public agitation. Withdrawing to ' the cloistered backwaters of a Cardiganshire village and the class-rooms of a Roman Catholic seminary,' he quietly continued his literary work, apparently heedless of the thunder-clouds gathering in Europe. Study and meditation, however, did not soften the bitterness in his heart. When the storm broke the *Plaid*'s voice—and it was still his voice—was raised in protest against the involvement of Wales in a ' foreign ' war, an ' English imperialistic ' war. Wales, it said, should follow Eire's lead and be neutral like Holland and Belgium and Denmark. That was highly unpopular doctrine, especially when Welsh regiments were under fire and Welsh towns bombed. If Lewis supposed that a victorious Hitler would reward the little neutral nations by acknowledging and respecting their independence, the vast majority of his fellow-Welshmen did not share that illusion. So the *Plaid* made small progress in the war. In 1942 the ' Independent ' candidate at a South Wales by-election obtained 975 votes: his Conservative and Labour opponents over 19,000 and 13,000 respectively. In 1943 Lewis himself emerged from seclusion to confront his old opponent at a by-election for the Welsh Universities. He did better than before, polling 1,330 votes; but Gruffydd's poll was 3,098. In the spring of 1945 by-elections were pending for Caernarvon Boroughs and Neath, and Lewis published four articles in *Y Faner*, afterwards reprinted as a lengthy pamphlet, in which he pleaded that Wales must be saved from the materialism and militarism of English post-war reconstruction and that only a Welsh party in Parliament could do it. ' An independent party like that of Parnell, standing from day to day in Parliament for the rights of country and nation, creates a will and a determination in that land that will in the long run prove stronger than the Parliament of England.'[45] But the electors were stone-deaf. At Caernarvon they gave the Liberal candidate 20,754 votes and the Nationalist 6,844; at Neath they gave the Labour candidate 30,847 and the Nationalist 6,290.

It was thus evident that the *Plaid* was not much stronger at the end of the war than at its beginning. The number of voters that backed its candidates at the series of by-elections had risen, but nowhere above a negligible level. No Welsh Nationalist had yet won or come near to winning a seat. The hold of the British parties on the constituencies, in North Wales as in South, was unshaken.

[1] M. P. Fogarty, *Prospects of the Industrial Areas of Great Britain* (London, 1945), 87.
[2] *Ibid.*, 89.
[3] Wyn Griffith, *The Welsh* (Pelican Books, 1950), 161.
[4] Thomas Jones, C. H., *The Native Never Returns* (Aberystwyth, 1946), 13-17.
[5] *Board of Celtic Studies*, Annual Report 1948-49, pars. 3-5.
[6] *Survey of Adult Education in Wales* (University of Wales, 1940; *Twenty-Eighth Annual Report of the University Extension Board* (Cardiff, 1949); *Twenty-Fourth Annual Report of the W.E.A., North Wales District* (Bangor, 1949); *Forty-Second Annual Report of the W.E.A., South Wales District* (Cardiff, 1949).
[7] Wyn Griffith, 130.
[8] *Welsh Literature in the Twentieth Century* in *English*, vol. vii. No. 41, 1949.
[9] *The Future of Secondary Education in Wales*, Report of the Central Advisory Council for Education (Wales), 1949, page 41. See also Wyn Griffith, 133-5.
[10] *The Welsh*, 136.
[11] *The Urdd* (Aberystwyth, 1947), 2.
[12] H.M. Stationery Office, 1927.
[13] H.M. Stationery Office, 1949.
[14] *Ibid.*, 45-6.
[15] *Welsh in Education and Life*, pages 173-4.
[16] *Celtic Literature*, 10-12.
[17] *Hansard*, H. of C., 1946, v. 380, c. 1411.
[18] T. S. Eliot, *Notes towards the Definition of Culture* (London, 1948), 57.
[19] *The Future of Secondary Education in Wales*, 37.
[20] *Hansard*, H. of C., 1921, v. 138, c. 441.
[21] Chappell, 84.
[22] *Hansard*, H. of C., 1922, v. 153, c. 929.
[23] *Ibid.*, c. 937-8.
[24] *Ibid.*, c. 993-4.
[25] *Ibid.*, 1924, v. 173, c. 1340, 2189; v. 174, c. 2119.
[26] *Ibid.*, 1928, v. 218, c. 628-9; v. 222, c. 1723-4.

[27] *Ibid.*, 1930, v. 234, c. 203.
[28] *Ibid.*, v. 234, c. 842-3.
[29] *Ibid.*, v. 241, c. 2395; v. 242, c. 270.
[30] *Ibid.*, 1933, v. 281, c. 761; 1934, v. 295, c. 670.
[31] *Ibid.*, 1937, v. 328, c. 417-18.
[32] *Ibid.*, v. 390, c. 845; 1928-9, v. 395, c. 296-7.
[33] *Hansard*, 1944, v. 403, c. 2237.
[34] *Ibid.*, c. 2314.
[35] *Ibid.*, c. 2311.
[36] *Ibid.*, c. 2285.
[37] *Ibid.*, c. 2311-14.
[38] *Ibid.*, c. 2325.
[39] Chappell, 46.
[40] *Welsh Review*, vol. v. no. 4, 260. Author's italics.
[41] S. Lewis, *The Banned Wireless Talk on Welsh Nationalism*, published by Swyddfa'r Blaid Genedlaethol, Caernarvon.
[42] *The Times*, Oct. 14, 1936.
[43] *Ibid.*, Jan. 20, 1937.
[44] *Ibid.*, Jan. 29, 1937.
[45] S. Lewis, *Save Wales by Political Action* (published by the Welsh Party, Swyddfa'r Blaid, Caernarvon).

PART NINE

Scotland, 1918-1945

I. SCOTLAND BETWEEN THE WARS

THE FATE of Scotland between 1918 and 1939 was broadly the same as the fate of Wales. In both countries the pride in what they had done in the war and the dreams of what they would make of the peace were soon overshadowed by the onset of the great Depression. The average level of unemployment in Scotland was two per cent higher than that of Britain as a whole between 1927 and 1931 and six per cent higher between 1931 and 1936. But Scotland suffered less than Wales where the corresponding figures were ten and sixteen per cent. The Depression, moreover, was more localised in Scotland. Un-employment was spread all over Wales; but in Scotland it was concentrated in the western and northern counties. In most of the East and South the level was not above—in some parts it was below—the British average; and in Perth, Edinburgh and parts of the Lothians it was as low as in the relatively prosperous English Midlands.[1] The volume of emigration, similarly, was high—on balance Scotland lost between 40,000 and 50,000 people a year between 1921 and 1931[2]—but it was not so high as in Wales; and, when the Second World War came, there was much less forced migration of Scottish workers into England. Social conditions, on the other hand, apart from unemployment were worse at this time in Scotland than in Wales. The census of 1931 revealed that the poorer urban areas were shockingly over-crowded. No less than 44 per cent of the total population were living in one or two rooms. The report of the Committee on Scottish Health Services in 1936 was equally sombre. It disclosed not only the high rate of infant mortality and of malnutrition and disease among the young, but also the physical unfitness of a large proportion of Scotsmen who were not yet middle-aged. ' The vital statistics of Scotland are disquietingly less favourable than those of England and Wales and several other European countries.'[3]

Scottish nationalists were not slow to draw the moral, as they saw it, from these dark facts. They admitted, of course, that England was also suffering from the Depression, but why, they asked, was Scotland suffering more? And what was the use of airing Scottish grievances at Westminster? Nobody listened. Nothing was done. But such attacks on the Union had seemingly made little impression on the public mind when re-armament revived the basic Scottish industries and the outbreak of the Second World War and the common effort and danger and suffering it involved revivified the consciousness of British solidarity. When it came to the issue of life or death, of freedom or slavery, national distinctions seemed irrelevant. Scotland and England had to stand or fall together.

The common experience of Scotland and Wales between 1918 and 1945 was not confined to the Depression and the war. The two most significant changes in the pattern of Scottish and Welsh life were the same. In Scotland as in Wales, though not so steadily nor to the same extent, the Labour Party strengthened its hold on the electorate. In Scotland as in Wales, though not so fast and far, the influence of religion on the younger generation weakened.

The number of the 71 Scottish seats won by the Labour Party at successive elections was as follows:

1918	*1922*	*1923*	*1924*	*1929*	*1931*	*1935*	*1945*
8	29	35	26	37	7	24	40

The decline of religion cannot be measured so exactly, but in the later years of the peace it was stated in the General Assembly that about two-fifths of the young people (between 15 and 19) and roughly one million of the total population were not openly associated with any Church.[4] It has been argued that in the cultural field, at any rate, the national spirit in Scotland as in Wales will be more vigorous and creative in so far as it is freed from what remains of the old Puritan tradition. It is not for the present writer to discuss that issue, still less to predict what the ultimate result will be. It is enough to stress the importance of the matter for the student of Scottish nationalism as of Welsh. Whatever may happen in the future, it is the Kirk and the Chapel which have done most in the past to mould the national character of their countries and direct their way of life.

II. THE SCOTTISH RENAISSANCE

MEANTIME IN Scotland as in Wales the silent process of assimilation has steadily continued. It has become harder every year for an Englishman on his way to Scotland to be aware that he has crossed the border. Edinburgh forces the fact on him, but only by means of its historic buildings and monuments, not by its life. The hotels, the cafés, the shops, the chain-stores—is there any difference, save in scale, from York? The same 'stars' look down from the cinema hoardings; the same cheap fiction litters the bookstalls. And, without Castle or Holyrood or Princes Street, Glasgow or Dundee may well seem to the hasty visitor to be much the same as Manchester or Newcastle. It is only when he reaches the Highlands and the Western Isles that he finds a country differing more in speech and custom from the South than

383

the Lowlands differ from Lancashire; and even there, he will be told, the difference is steadily diminishing. His own presence there abets the process. The procession of motor-coaches which wind along the roads day after day throughout the season and night after night disgorge their passengers into crowded local inns is one of the things that is making the Highlands less Scottish as it is making ' Wild Wales ' less Welsh. There also, as in Wales, the old native language is in retreat. Only along the western coastlands and in the islands is Gaelic still in common use; and a growing proportion of those few who speak it speak English too.

The assimilating power of the English Press is not so great in Scotland as in Wales. For Scotland possesses two great daily papers of its own. Both the *Scotsman* and the *Glasgow Herald* are independent Scottish journals owned by Scotsmen and their influence is as great as their standards are high. Associated with the *Herald* is the little *Bulletin* which has been described as ' easily the most readable and reliable popular daily on sale in Scotland.'[5] The other ' dailies '—and ' weeklies ' too—are mostly confined to a local circulation; and many of them have now been absorbed by the Kemsley combine, inevitably losing something of their Scottish colour and independence in the process.[6] But a much greater menace to the national character of the Scottish Press is the invasion of two popular English papers, the *Daily Mail* and the *Daily Express*, especially the latter. Both have long been established in Manchester but, while the *Mail* has only recently begun to produce a Scottish edition at Edinburgh, the *Express* has done it at Glasgow since 1928. And with immense success. More Scotsmen read it than any other paper;[7] and, though it affects a Scottish air, it is essentially an English paper, getting most of its news and its policy from London, seeking to impose as much on the Scottish as on the English public the opinions of its galvanic master who, though his father was a minister of the Kirk, has not yet betrayed an interest in Scottish nationalism.[a] There are

[a] Lord Beaverbrook.

384

other less formidable invaders. The *Daily Herald* and the *News Chronicle*, which have also their half-way houses in Manchester, are expected soon to follow the *Express* to Glasgow.

Broadcasting in Scotland is on the same footing as in Wales. Since 1932 Scotland has been a ' Region,' administered by a regional staff at Edinburgh which, with the aid of an Advisory Council, is responsible for linking specifically Scottish programmes with the services intended for all Britain and the outer world. Public events—visits by Royalty, meetings of the General Assembly, annual conferences of the political parties and the Scottish T.U.C. and so forth—are fully recorded; and, if the cultural fare provided—such as dramatic adaptations of Scott or Stevenson, talks on the Scottish country and Scottish institutions, debates on Scottish affairs—seems somewhat less substantial than the corresponding output in Wales, it may be due, in part at least, to the linguistic difference: neither Gaelic nor ' Scots ' can be allotted as much time as Welsh.[a] But, whatever may be said in its defence, the champions of Scottish culture are at least as much dissatisfied with the existing organisation as their comrades in Wales.[b] They denounce the rigid control, in policy no less than in finance, exercised by the B.B.C. in London. They claim that broadcasting in Scotland should be on a national not a regional basis: i.e. that it should be administered by a Scottish Board of Governors living in Scotland.[c] And they cite the high authority of the late Sir Frederick Ogilvie who was Director General of the B.B.C. from 1938 to 1942 and publicly upheld the principle of national autonomy both in Welsh and Scottish broadcasting.

As to the cinema, the position seems again to be much the

[a] A section of the annual report presented to Parliament by the B.B.C. (1948-49; Cmd. 7779) is devoted to ' Regional Broadcasting.' the Regions being North, West and Midland England, Scotland, Wales and Northern Ireland.

[b] See page 359 above.

[c] The case is fully stated in the pamphlets on broadcasting published by the Saltire Society (see page 391 below) in 1944 and 1946 and in the evidence it submitted to the Broadcasting Committee in 1949.

same as in Wales. One or two first-rate Scottish films have been made in the last few years, *Whisky Galore*, for example, but not by Scottish companies in Scottish studios.

It may be said, in fine, that, with the partial exception of the Press, none of the three great instruments of publicity have availed to stem the tide of cultural assimilation. But no more in Scotland than in Wales has the ultimate issue been decided. Since the outset of the century a movement for the salvation of Scottish culture has been steadily gaining strength.

In Wales, as has been seen, the reaction against assimilation came first in the field of education. It was the construction of a Welsh educational system, crowned by a new Welsh university, that did most to promote the campaign for the preservation of the Welsh way of life. Nothing of that kind could happen in Scotland. The Scottish Universities are not new—they were flourishing for centuries before the Union—and it is only recently that the rising standards of the English schools have challenged the lead long held by the Scottish schools. Among Scottish educationalists, therefore, there could be no such sense of a national crusade as that which inspired the Welsh movement in the later nineteenth century. The so-called Scottish Renaissance[a] was not the outcome of a deliberate policy planned in academic circles. It came into being casually and without premeditation, first in an artist's studio, next on an architect's drawing-board, and then at a novelist's desk.

The painters of the celebrated 'Glasgow School' were not conscious nationalists; and, when their admirers on the Continent called them 'Scottish' they were only giving a local name to a group of artists who shared in the European revolt against traditionalism. And certainly W. Y. Macgregor (1855-1923) and the 'boys' who gathered in his studio were deeply influenced by the French Impressionists and their Dutch disciples and by

[a] This term was first used by a French critic, and only with regard to literature.

Japanese art. Nevertheless, wherever their main source of inspiration lay, they were a brotherhood of Scotsmen living and working
and arguing together in Scotland, completely detached from their
fellow-painters in England. There were distinctive features in
their work, moreover, particularly their love of sunlight and
bright colours, which seemed to reflect, like tartan and tweed, the
spirit of the Celt.[a] And the same has been said of at least one
other contemporary Scottish painter. William McTaggart (1835-
1910) was born of a Gaelic-speaking crofter's family in Argyll-
shire. Though in later life he made his home near Edinburgh, his
heart was always in Kintyre; and in the work of his maturity,
especially in his great pictures of the wind-driven ocean breaking
on the western coast, there is an ecstasy of light and motion that
seems to derive as naturally as Gaelic poetry from the Celtic
world.

Overlapping with the Glasgow School and coming to its
prime between the two world wars was another remarkable
group of Scottish painters known as the ' Scottish Colourists '—
first S. J. Peploe (1871-1935) and then G. L. Hunter (1879-1936),
J. D. Fergusson and F. C. B. Cadell (1883-1937). These men were
more deeply influenced by Paris than the Glasgow School. They
lived for long periods in France. Their work has been described
as a renewal of the ' auld alliance ' in the realm of art. But they
remained Scottish. Peploe, indeed, the greatest of them, has been
called ' the most typically Scottish of painters,' betraying again a
Celtic heritage in his delight in colour and in his attitude to
nature.[8]

The renaissance was not confined to painting. On the heels
of the Glasgow artists came two great Scottish architects, Sir
Robert Lorimer (1864-1929) is best known for his National War
Memorial in Edinburgh Castle,[b] but his most characteristic work
was in the country houses in which he adapted the vernacular

[a] These paragraphs are mainly based on Ian Finlay's delightful *Art in Scotland* (Oxford,
1948), chaps. ix, x.

[b] See page 308 above.

tradition of the sixteenth and seventeenth centuries to the domestic needs of modern life. C. R. Mackintosh (1868-1928) was a prophet who was little honoured in the Scotland of his day, and a generation which admired the Tower Bridge in London scoffed at the contemporary School of Art at Glasgow. But he was widely acclaimed in continental Europe as a pioneer of the modern functional school; and, for all its seeming novelty, his work was at once national and traditional; it was as firmly rooted as Lorimer's in Scottish history.

The renaissance in literature came a little later than in art and architecture. Its forerunner in prose was G. D. Brown (1869-1902), an Ayrshire man whose Scottish temper was not softened by his southward drift to Oxford and London. The sombre realism of his one famous novel, *The House with the Green Shutters*, gave a salutary shock to those English and American readers who had looked at Scotland with the eyes of the ' kailyard ' sentimentalists. But for several years after Brown's early death it seemed as if his rebellion was to have no sequel; and it was not till after the First World War that the challenge to popular taste was repeated by Leslie Mitchell, better known as Lewis Grassic Gibbon (died 1935), whose trilogy, *A Scots Quair*, depicted the decline of Scottish country life from the early nineteenth century onwards in colours that were no less true than Brown's because they were not so wholly dark. Nor were these novels Scottish only in theme and spirit. They were written in a ' peculiar rhythmic prose, Braid Scots in idiom and intonation but not in spelling.'[9] There was another Scottish writer of the time who was, perhaps, too British to be accorded a share in the Scottish Renaissance. Indeed John Buchan (1865-1946), who started life as a ' son of the manse ' and died as Lord Tweedsmuir and Governor-General of Canada, would be regarded by some Scottish patriots as a typical ' lost Scot.' Yet, he spent most of the holidays he snatched from an unusually busy and many-sided life in the

Highlands; nothing gave him greater pride than his tenure of the High Commissionership at Holyrood; and the best of his many books are his admirable biographies of Montrose and Scott. Of living novelists Neil Gunn is indubitably a Scot and a Celt; and there are others, Compton Mackenzie and Eric Linklater at their head, who, though their work so far has not been intrinsically Scottish, have shared in the re-awakening of the national spirit. 'James Bridie,' too, the playwright, was less British and more Scottish than Barrie. He wrote, like Barrie, for the London stage. Most of his themes, like Barrie's, were not Scottish. But it is significant that, while Barrie would not have felt at home anywhere away from London, Bridie lived in Glasgow.

It is in poetry more than in prose that the literary renaissance has shown its strength: in poetry which is Scottish not only in theme and sentiment but also in language. It began with Violet Jacob (1865-1946) who in the best of her Scots poems stands to Burns on the same sort of footing as Stevenson to Scott; and it reached its climax in our own day in the genius of Christopher Murray Grieve or 'Hugh McDiarmid.' He was born in 1892, the son of a rural postman at Langholm near the English border of Dumfries. In due course he made his way to Glasgow University, but before he could settle down to make his living he was caught up in the First World War. He served in the R.A.M.C. at Salonika and in France. Back at Glasgow he soon made his name as a writer both of prose and poetry. The mainsprings of his work were his passionate devotion to Scotland—'the little white rose that smells sharp and sweet, and breaks the heart'—and his contempt of sham and syrup. When he published his two books of lyrics in 1925 and 1926 it seemed to many of those who read them as if Scotland had at last produced another great Scottish poet. But he failed to reach the heights which seemed at that time to be within his grasp. Was it the Depression and the shadow of the Second World War? Whatever the reason, it was as if politics had taken control of his poetry. And his politics were astringent. He had acquired—it is hard to say why or when— a hatred of England as bitter as that which infected Lewis, his contemporary and fellow-nationalist in Wales.[a] 'Since the Union,' he wrote in the strange autobiographical hotch-potch he published in 1943, ' Scotland's has simply been the role of cater-pillar-grub stung into immobility by devouring wasp.'[10] And his antipathy had a personal edge which is happily not often to be found in Welsh or Scottish or even Irish nationalism. ' I could never have married an Englishwoman,' he says, seemingly in all seriousness; and in fact his first wife was of Highland stock and his second a Cornishwoman. Stranger still—in a poet indeed astonishing—is his reaction to the English cultural tradition. ' I look forward eagerly and confidently to the United States sup-planting England in the leadership of the English-speaking world, and the speech and literature of " the old country " dwindling in relation to the whole to a place of no greater importance or interest than the quaint surviving traces of the Elizabethan English in Dublin.'[11] But that dream of America's destiny did not survive the end of the war and the rise of Soviet Russia. Already, on a later page of the same book, Grieve was looking East, not West. Like Lewis, he desired to turn back the pages of history; but, while Lewis wanted only to undo the Reformation and repair the links it broke between Wales and Western Europe, Grieve wanted to undo the Renaissance! It was necessary, he wrote, to get back ' behind that Greek national whitewashing of all other European countries which has prevented them getting down to their own Urmotives and realising themselves in turn as Greece itself had done.'[12] Was it cause or effect that associated this startling repudiation of the European heritage with a growing sympathy with Lenin's Russia ? ' Lenin, like myself,' he wrote, '—the Slav and the Celt—lies outside Europe.'[13] In later years he drifted into a sort of revolutionary pessimism which has frozen

[a] See pages 374-8 above.

the springs of poetry he drank from in his younger days. But the
work he did then will endure, not only in what he wrote but
in the influence he exerted on other writers, an influence so great
that the question has been asked whether any real literary renaissance would have come about without him.[14] And certainly
the young national-minded poets of to-day—George Bruce,
Maurice Lindsay, S. G. Smith and Douglas Young—admit
without reserve the greatness of the debt they owe to Grieve.

Such, in bald summary, is the literary side of the renaissance.
Prose and poetry alike, it is inspired by ' the wish to be Scots.'
It has already done much for Scottish literature: for it has broken
beyond repair the pseudo-Scottish nineteenth-century tradition.
But its future is uncertain because the future of the Scottish
nationalist movement as a whole is uncertain. 'It depends,' says
a sympathetic critic, ' not so much on the authors—who so
plainly wish to give all that they can to Scotland—as on the mass
of intelligent Scots who alone can provide them with an understanding public. . . . Is Scotland prepared to deserve a literature
of her own? '[15]

A significant outcome of the Renaissance was the foundation
of the Saltire Society (1936) ' by a group of people who cared for
the culture of Scotland and who wished to see not a mere revival
of the arts of the past but a renewal of the life which made them.'
The first of the Society's purposes as defined in its constitution
is ' to foster the Scottish way of life; Scottish literature, music,
arts and crafts, past and present; the study of Scottish history
and geography; and the study (speaking, writing and reading)
of Gaelic and Lowland Scots.' With its headquarters at Gladstone's Land in the Lawnmarket at Edinburgh, a house which
dates back to the sixteenth century,[a] and with branches in
Glasgow, Ayr, the Border country, Perth, Inverness and London,

---

[a] The story of this noble house, which was saved and restored under the auspices
of the National Trust for Scotland, is told in *Gladstone's Land* by Robert Hurd, published
jointly by the Trust and the Saltire Society.

the Society has already acquired a status comparable with that of the old Welsh Societies. Its activities are many-sided. It organises lectures and discussions on Scottish cultural and social questions, recitals of Scottish poetry, concerts of Scottish music and it has published a wide range of literature—reprints of Scottish classics; illustrated booklets on the Scottish tradition in poetry, silver, burgh architecture, printed books; pamphlets on Scottish arts and institutions; Christmastide chapbooks of Scottish hymns and lullabies and children's stories, and so forth. . . . Among other bodies actively concerned with Scottish culture are the Scottish Texts Society, the Gaelic Texts Society, *An Commun Gaidhealach*, the Burns Federation, the Community Drama Association and the Scottish Country Dance Association.

Not first as in Wales but last, cultural nationalism has begun to win a footing in the Scottish educational world. For some time past Scottish education has seemed to be losing something of its distinctive national character. It is partly, no doubt, because science has wrested so much ground from the humanities: for the study of the humanities in Scotland has usually possessed, so to speak, a Scottish flavour while there can be nothing Scottish in machinery or chemicals or atomic energy. Linked with this, perhaps, has been the growing proportion of Englishmen on the University staffs. But if, as is often said, the Scottish Universities have been steadily becoming more like their English sisters, that does not mean that there is no Scottish element in the curriculum. There are Chairs of Scottish History at Edinburgh and Glasgow, both with a distinguished record, and a lectureship at St. Andrews. There are no separate Chairs of Scottish literature. Glasgow has a lectureship attached to a ' Scottish Department ' which also deals with history. But at the other Universities Scottish literature is taught under the head of English Literature. The contrast with Wales[a] is striking; yet, as regards literature at any rate, it is not

[a] See page 341 above.

unnatural. For the study of Welsh literature is inseparable from the study of the Welsh language, and there is no such nexus in Scotland. More surprising is the relative neglect of Scottish history. At none of the Universities is the subject required for an ' honours ' degree: it is purely optional, and the students who take the option are comparatively few. For that reason, it is said, Scottish history has been badly taught in the schools. But there are signs of a change. Edinburgh has recently decided to enforce attendance at a Scottish History class for all students seeking ' honours ' in History; and at Edinburgh also a scheme is now being considered for a ' School of Scottish Studies ' to provide advanced study and research in all branches of Scottish culture— archaeology, history, geography, languages, literature and art.

The schools, too, have lost something of their Scottish character. State education has provided a more efficient but also a more uniform school-system; and Scottish schools have become at once more like one another and more like English schools. Though they are controlled by the local Scottish authorities and the Scottish department of education in Edinburgh, the examinations and the curriculum they dictate have been much the same as in England. There has been nothing so far comparable with the Welsh attempt to impress a national character on the schools, to use them to preserve and strengthen the cultural tradition. But in this field, too, there are signs of an awakening. Under the Act of 1945 an Advisory Council on Education was established in Scotland as in Wales, and its Report on primary education, published in 1946,[16] contains a remarkable chapter on ' Scottish Traditions ' which closely resembles the chapter on ' The Social and Cultural Background ' in the Welsh Council's report on secondary education.[a] There is one great difference. The Scottish educationalists are not concerned to save the life of a national language. For Gaelic cannot be in Scotland what Welsh is in Wales; and, while the authors of the Report plead not only for

[a] See page 355 above.

393

more Gaelic-speaking teachers and more Gaelic school-books in Gaelic-speaking areas but also for more study of Gaelic life and legends and traditions in all Scottish schools, they maintain that for centuries past the native language of Scotland south and east of the Highlands has been English and that it is ' the first duty of every school to give every child its rightful heritage of good English speech.'[17 a] But it does not follow, they go on to say, that the old Scots variant of English should be ignored. If it is primarily English literature that the children must study, they should be ' reminded that, while they share this literature with English-speaking people all over the world, they have something which is peculiarly their own.' The reading of good Scots prose and verse should be encouraged; but more should be made of ' our unique ballad literature '; and the older children should be ' at least as familiar with Dunbar, Henryson and Gavin Douglas as they are with Chaucer.' Nor should the legacy of homelier Scots be over-looked—its characteristic words and phrases and particularly the pithy proverbs which so ' vividly reflect the character and condi-tions of life of old Scotland.'[18] There can be no comparison in this with the campaign for a bilingual Wales, but in all other respects there is little to distinguish the Scottish Report from its Welsh counterpart. It preaches the same cultural nationalism in much the same terms. The distinctive traditions and characteristics of Scotsmen—their national pride, their love of liberty, their democratic record especially in local self-government, their freedom from class-consciousness—this is the patrimony of an ' ancient race ' of which its youngest members must be made aware. Scottish history must no longer be taught as if it came to an end in 1603 or 1745. ' Modern Scotland is the land which the children of to-day and to-morrow have to live in and should therefore know and understand.' They should be better acquainted, too, with their ' great heritage of folk song ': they

---

[1] The Report (page 75) cites a statement by Robert Bridges that standard English as spoken by educated people in Scotland is ' a firmer and cleaner form than the Southern English of to-day.'

should learn to sing both in and out of school the best of their own traditional airs. The recent revival of traditional folk-dancing, likewise, should be encouraged and extended.[19]

It appears, then, that the Scottish educationalists are as whole-hearted champions of cultural nationalism as the Welsh; and there is one last important point of agreement. Nationalism in each case is tempered by internationalism. The Scotsmen go at least as far as the Welshmen in insisting on their nation's duty towards other nations. 'It is infinitely more significant,' they say, 'that a child is born into the *world* than that he is born in Scotland.'[20]

In one educational or quasi-educational field nationalism has not yet begun to operate in Scotland as it does in Wales. There is no purely Scottish youth movement, nothing corresponding to the *Urdd Gobaith Cymru*. The Scottish Scouts and Rovers are brigaded with the English in one British organisation. It is a small but not insignificant point that not long ago they sought and obtained the permission of their British 'high command' to distinguish themselves at international gatherings by wearing kilts and 'balmorals.' Their normal dress is the same as that of their English comrades.

One striking difference between Welsh and Scottish cultural nationalism is the lack of anything in Scotland corresponding to the Eisteddfod. The Edinburgh Festival, which in only a few years of life has won an almost world-wide reputation, is nothing like the Eisteddfod. It is a manifestation of culture in Scotland but not of Scottish culture. The Eisteddfod is national and popular. The Festival is cosmopolitan, and, apart from one or two ceremonial displays, it caters only for a cultivated minority of Scotsmen. But the most significant distinction is linguistic. Only Welsh is spoken as a rule at the Eisteddfod, only English at the Festival.

The more ardent Scottish nationalists deplore the fact that a separate Scottish language is not spoken and written in Scotland at least as widely as Welsh in Wales. The lack of it, they hold, forbids the full fruition of the national renaissance. They differ from those who maintain that English is as much a native language in South-West Scotland as in England. English in their view is an alien intruder in Scotland as in Wales; it is the natural language only of English immigrants. To reawaken, therefore, the true spirit of Scottish nationhood Scotsmen must learn to speak again an authentic Scottish tongue. The logical choice is Gaelic, for Gaelic is the only language once spoken by all Scotsmen; and its champions plead that to teach all Scottish children about Gaelic life is not enough; they should be taught the language too. But is that possible? It is a hard enough task for Welsh nationalists to persuade all Welshmen to speak Welsh; yet in 1931 more than 900,000 of them or 37 per cent of the population did so, whereas in Scotland less than 140,000 or 2 per cent of the population were Gaelic-speaking, and it is taken for granted that the census of 1951 will register a further drop. Can it reasonably be doubted that Gaelic as a spoken language is doomed in course of time to die out?

There is an alternative to Gaelic. Though every Scotsman outside the shrinking Gaelic fringe now speaks English, a variety of local dialects, commonly classed together as ' Scots,' are still in vigorous use, and Grieve has attempted in his writing to weld them into one language and to enrich the mixture with words that were current in the age of the Makars and after and have since become obsolete. He claims ' that only through this medium can the real feelings of the Scots people to-day be got at and that tremendous new forces will flow into Scots culture as a result.'[21] Among Grieve's disciples the most vigorous advocate of this ' Synthetic Scots ' or ' Plastic Scots ' or ' Lallans '[a] as it is variously called, has been Douglas Young, who not only preaches and

---

[a] This name is taken from Burns' *Epistle to William Simpson*: 'They speak their thochts in plain braid Lallans, like you and me.'

practises the use of it in poetry,[a] but also pleads for the development of its potentialities in prose 'as an independent literary medium as distinct from English as it is from German or Norwegian.'[22] It is hard to quarrel with this genuine literary idealism, and yet, to an outsider at any rate, it seems a desperate cause. It cannot be compared with the campaign for Welsh in Wales. There was a time, it is true, when Welsh was in danger of succumbing to English conquest and losing itself in a medley of rude local dialects; but that danger was overcome in the course of the national revival in the eighteenth century.[b] For two centuries now Welsh has been spoken as a single, living, growing language, needing no artificial injections from the past, and the writing of Welsh poetry and prose, however its quality may have varied from time to time, has never ceased. Yet, Welsh is now battling for survival and no one can be sure of the result. What chance, then, has Lallans? Can it be more than the literary language of a zealous *coterie*?

III. POLITICAL NATIONALISM

WITH THE collapse of the short-lived federalist movement of 1918–21 the cause of Scottish nationalism in Parliament fell back —or so for a time it seemed—into the old pre-war slough of still-born Bills and sterile speeches. In February 1922 yet another Government of Scotland Bill was presented by Mr. John Wallace (Dunfermline), backed by five other Scottish members.[23] It provided for a single-chamber Scottish Parliament to exercise similar powers to those conferred on the Irish Parliament by the Home Rule Bill of 1914.[c] 'We demand a Scottish Parliament,'

[a] e.g. in *Auntran Blads* and *A Braid o' Thristles.*
[b] See Part Four above.
[c] The chief differences were that the Scottish Parliament would not deal with the Post Office or Tariffs, but would control the administration of Old Age Pensions, National Insurance and Labour Exchanges.

said Mr. Wallace in the debate on the second reading, ' firstly on national grounds and secondly on grounds of legislative efficiency. . . . I can assure the House that behind the Scottish Home Rule movement there is a rising tide of well-informed and resolute Scottish opinion.'[24] Sir Donald Maclean agreed that there was 'a general feeling in Scotland' for Scottish work being done 'by Scotsmen in the Parliament House of Edinburgh.'[25] So also said Mr. Tom Johnston, Labour M.P. for Renfrew, who had taken an active part in Scottish local government and was now beginning to make his mark in the House of Commons. If you disregard moderate opinion, he said, ' you will play into the hands of the extremists' and teach people ' to emulate the example of the people of the sister isle.'[26] But that, said Sir Henry Craik, his old antagonism unsoftened by the interval of war, is what any agitation, however moderate, will bring about. ' You will arouse in Scotland some of that dread, pernicious, fatal feeling which Home Rule has aroused in Ireland.'[27] There was little other opposition. The motion was quietly talked out and nothing more was heard of it. . . . In the same session Mr. Murray Macdonald's joint Bill to establish subordinate Scottish and Welsh Parliaments appeared and disappeared.

At the outset of 1924 the prospects of Home Rule for Scotland and consequentially for Wales suddenly brightened. Ramsay MacDonald was now Prime Minister, head of the first Labour Government, and Ramsay MacDonald, like Lloyd George, had always professed himself a nationalist. Early in the new session, as it happened, a Government of Scotland Bill was introduced once more. Drafted on the same lines as the Bill of 1914, it was backed by all the thirty-two Scottish Labour members, and its introducer, Mr. Buchanan (Glasgow, Gorbals) claimed that twenty-three Scottish Liberal members and one Conservative had accepted it in principle—a total backing of no less than fifty-six out of the seventy-four Scottish members.[28] Opening the debate on the second reading, Mr. Buchanan grounded his case mainly on the old evil of congestion and the delay and expense imposed on Scottish local authorities, by their having to go to London to press for the minor legislation they required. He told his English fellow members to remember Ireland. ' Unless they concede the mild meagre measure for which we are now asking, forces at work that neither we nor anyone can stop will soon demand not this measure but a bold and bigger measure.'[29] Mr. Macpherson (Ross and Cromarty) also stressed the moderation of the Bill. There was ' no suggestion of secession or separation.' Scotland was asking only for what Ulster had got.[30] Mr. Tom Johnston's speech went deeper; for he raised the basic problem of international relations and upheld a doctrine which was not so familiar twenty-six years ago as it is to-day. ' We may believe,' he said, ' very earnestly in internationalism, but you cannot have internationalism without nations. The word " international " means " between nations," and any political party in this House that seeks to destroy their national characteristics and diversities is doing something that is for the ill-being of the British Empire. . . . The British Empire—and, whatever view we take of it, it is a big thing in the world—cannot last but will fall . . . as other great Empires of the past fell, unless you give to each component part of it the right to express its own individuality in its own way —not dragoon them by a central bureaucracy sitting many miles away. . . .'[31] A few days after this debate MacDonald stated that the Government was prepared to appoint a committee to inquire into the question of Home Rule for Scotland, Wales and England.[32] But the Government was a minority Government, backed by only 192 Labour members of the House and confronted by 257 Conservatives and 157 Liberals; and Home Rule-all-round was an issue on which party agreement had never been attainable. The Liberals had always favoured it, but the Conservatives were still Unionists-all-round. So in due course it was announced that, as the Government had failed to secure the co-operation of all parties, it must abandon the proposed inquiry that session;[33] and, before the next session opened, another election was fought and the Conservatives were back in power with a decisive majority of 413 against 151 Labour and 40 Liberals. Thus the door was shut once more on Home Rule anywhere. Baldwin, however, was willing to make one harmless concession to Scottish sentiment. At the end of 1925 he yielded to the long-standing claim that the Secretary for Scotland should become a Secretary of State,[34] and a Bill to that effect was duly enacted in 1926.[a]

In the course of the next three years three more Government of Scotland Bills were introduced by the Rev. James Barr, Labour M.P. for Motherwell, backed by some dozen other Scottish Labour members. Their importance lies only in the fact that, while outside the House the Scottish Nationalist Party was beginning (as will be seen) to agitate for Dominion Status, this was the first occasion on which something more than legislative devolution on federal lines was proposed in Parliament. There was only one debate—on the second reading of the second Bill in 1927—and the short time allotted to it was mainly taken up by Mr. Barr who, in a speech embellished with lavish quotation from Burns, declared that his Bill proceeded ' on the principle of self-determination . . . on the basis of Scotland being a sovereign state.'[35]

In 1929 the fading light of Ramsay MacDonald's nationalism flickered up for a moment and went out. The occasion was a discussion of the Scottish Local Government Act in the debate on the address. MacDonald, Prime Minister for the second time and now leader of the strongest party in the House but not of a clear majority, suggested that at the end of a year an inquiry should be held into the working of the Act, an inquiry which he hoped would cover the question of Scottish self-government. ' It will not be my fault if the terms of reference are so narrow that the larger questions of Scottish self-respect and the recogni-

[a] 16 and 17 Geo. V, cap. 18.

tion of Scottish historical authority are excluded.'[36] The Scottish Nationalists made the most of this opening. Interpreting Mac-Donald's somewhat casual and cloudy language as a pledge to promote Home Rule, they plied him with questions about it. But his Government, though stronger than in 1924, was again a minority Government, and for the rest of that session and in the next he told his questioners that he had nothing more to say.[37]

When a National Government was formed in 1931 to meet the financial crisis, MacDonald was still Prime Minister and so remained till failing health compelled his resignation in 1935. But he was now a leader with only a handful of followers, and, though he secured the adoption of his own foreign policy, he could not take an independent line in domestic affairs. It was left to Baldwin to deal with the renewal of Scottish agitation, and in Scotland as in Wales Baldwin's unionism was unshakable. The Government, he declared early in 1932, did not intend to introduce a Bill for Scottish Home Rule.[38] A few months later he declined to summon a round-table conference of Scottish representatives to discuss the re-establishment of a Scottish Parliament. There is no evidence, he said, ' that the creation of small units makes for the prosperity of the world.'[39] But by the time the new session opened in November it had become clear that the question of Home Rule could no longer be stalled off. The approach of winter, the persistence of the Depression and the use which Scottish Nationalists were making of it to strengthen their cause, made it desirable that the issue should once more be fully ventilated in the Commons. Accordingly, the whole of the third day of the debate on the address was devoted to it,[a] and the result was the most thoughtful and practical discussion it had as yet obtained. The opening speech was made by Sir Robert Horne. Born (1871), like so many other eminent Scotsmen in the past, ' a son of the manse,' and educated at Edinburgh and Glasgow,

---

[a] This was in order because the King's Speech had contained a proposal for the reform of Scottish private bill procedure.

Horne made his way to the front of the British business world, and he was one of those men of affairs whom Lloyd George chose to strengthen his Coalition Government. He was Minister of Labour in 1919, President of the Board of Trade in 1920-21, and Chancellor of the Exchequer in 1921-22. In 1921 he was elected Lord Rector of Aberdeen University. Like most of his colleagues he never held office again after Lloyd George's fall, but he retained the seat for the Hillhead division of Glasgow which he had held since 1918, and his lucid, moderate, well-informed speeches always commanded the ear of the House. His speech on this occasion went straight to the root of the matter. 'I am not one of those,' he said, 'who deride the Scottish Home Rule movement, nor am I disposed to treat it lightly.' It was the natural outcome of the sense of defeatism and humiliation engendered by the Depression. But the notion that the high rate of unemployment in Scotland was due to neglect of Scottish interests at Westminster was wholly false. There was more unemployment in Durham than in Lanarkshire. And what more could a Scottish Parliament do than the British Parliament to deal with a disease which was afflicting parliamentary countries all the world over? It was the same with the southward drift of industry. That, too, was not confined to Scotland—it was happening in the north of England—and a Scottish Parliament would not prevent Scottish industrialists doing what they thought was needed to keep their hold on the English market. Dealing briefly with finance, Horne pointed out that, to judge from such figures as were available, Scotland for several years past had been receiving a larger share of British expenditure on social services than, on a population-basis, was her due. 'That, I think, is perfectly fair. It is obvious that Scotland is not so wealthy a country as England, and so long as she is part of the same system with England she is entitled to the full benefits derivable from that union. If she chooses to be independent and run her own finances, then, of course, she must take the consequences.' And, since no reasonable Nationalist proposed to disrupt the fiscal unity of Britain, the money needed to maintain the social services at their previous level could not be found by raising the tariff but only by direct taxation. As to the scope of a Scottish Parliament's authority, Horne made two points: first, economic common sense required that communications—not only post, telegrams and telephones but also railways—must be under British control; second, since the Trade Unions were organised on a British basis, difficulties would arise if the two Parliaments should differ in their party composition and enact discordant measures for the regulation of industry. And what would happen, he asked, if, say, a Conservative Parliament in England and a Socialist Parliament in Scotland were confronted with another General Strike. 'Imagine the appalling confusion. . . . I entirely disagree with the Socialist view of policy; but I would rather have the United Kingdom governed by a body which was Socialist than I would have different political legislatures in the two ends of the Island.' . . . Horne closed his speech with one or two suggestions for the improvement of Scottish administration: a second Scottish Under-Secretary of State should be appointed and the Scottish departments at Edinburgh should be concentrated in a single building.[40]

One other important speech was made in this debate.[41] John Buchan had succeeded Sir Henry Craik as one of the members for the Scottish Universities.[a] His interest in Scottish culture, particularly in Scots poetry, had long been manifest,[b] and he took this occasion to explain how far his cultural nationalism was also political. 'I believe,' he said, ' that every Scotsman should be a Scottish Nationalist. If it could be proved that a separate Scottish Parliament were desirable—that is to say that the merits were greater than the disadvantages and dangers—Scotsmen should support it. I would go further. Even if it were not proved to be desirable, if it could be proved to be desired by any sub-

[a] Craik died in 1927.
[b] See page 389 above.

stantial majority of the Scottish people, then Scotland should be allowed to make the experiment, and I do not believe that England would desire for one moment to stand in the way.' What, he went on, had caused the recent growth of political agitation? It was the spread of a belief that Scotland was losing 'its historic individuality. . . . It seems to many that we are in danger very soon of reaching the point when Scotland will have nothing distinctive to show to the world.' What, then, could be done, apart from the restoration of the Scottish Parliament, 'to intensify that consciousness of individuality and idiom which is what is meant by national spirit?' The existing machinery should be improved—private bill procedure eased, 'tacking' abolished, the salaries of Scottish Civil Servants raised from a provincial to a national scale. But the chief need was 'a visible proof of our nationhood,' and for that he recommended one of Horne's proposals. 'If we created in one building or in one area a dignified and worthy centre of Scottish administration, we should do a great deal to enlist Scotland's interest in her own administration. Glorify Edinburgh as against Whitehall.'

The proposal backed by Horne and Buchan in this debate for the appeasement of Scottish nationalism was adopted by the Government. In 1939 St. Andrew's House was opened at Edinburgh to provide a common home for the local departments of the Scottish Office in London, of which agriculture, education and health were the most important. The system of administrative devolution was thereby improved, but that was all. Edinburgh was no more independent than Cardiff, for the control of finance was still vested in Whitehall; and Scottish nationalism, thought it had fared better than Welsh—it had obtained, for example, in 1926 the Secretaryship of State denied to Wales— was no more content than Welsh with administrative devolution. And it was better organised. A 'National Party of Scotland' had been founded, mainly by Mr. John McCormick, a Glasgow lawyer, in 1927, and a more moderate 'Scottish Party,' led by the Duke of Montrose, in 1932. In 1934 these were fused into a single 'Scottish National Party,' which advocated a Scottish Parliament of the 'federal' type. Like *Y Plaid* in Wales and for much the same reasons, it fared badly at successive General Elections; and it fell into the background with the advent of war;[a] and in 1942 it was finally eclipsed by the foundation, mainly again by Mr. McCormick, of the 'Scottish Convention,' a non-party organisation whose chief aim was to obtain Scottish self-government on a 'federal' basis. Only a handful of extreme nationalists, under the quixotic leadership of the poet, Douglas Young, continued to demand the rupture of the Union and the revival of an independent Scottish state.[b] One final feature of the war years must be mentioned—the strenuous championship of Scottish interests in London by Mr. Tom Johnston who was Secretary of State for Scotland from 1939 to 1945.

[a] Its unexpected victory at Motherwell in 1944 was due to local circumstances and reversed in 1945.

[b] Young denied the right of the U.K. Government to conscript him for military service and suffered two terms of imprisonment for refusing medical examination.

[1] Fogarty, 131.
[2] *Ibid.*
[3] Ian Finlay, *Scotland* (Oxford, 1945), 67-9.
[4] *Acts, Proceedings and Debates of the General Assembly*, 1936, page 213; 1937, page 306.
[5] D. Ferguson, *The Scottish Newspaper Press* (Saltire Pamphlet, Edinburgh, 1946), 17.
[6] *Ibid.*, 21.
[7] *Ibid.*, 23.
[8] Finlay, *op. cit.*, 151-2.
[9] Reid, *op. cit.*, 22.
[10] C. M. Grieve, *Lucky Poet* (London, 1943), xv.
[11] *Ibid.*, 11.
[12] *Ibid.*, 375.
[13] *Ibid.*
[14] Reid, *op. cit.*, 19.
[15] *Ibid.*, 25.
[16] *Primary Education, a Report of the Advisory Council on Education in Scotland*, 1946. Cmd. 6973.
[17] *Ibid.*, 41-2, 75-6.
[18] *Ibid.*, 75-6.
[19] *Ibid.*, 77-8.
[20] *Report on Primary Education*, cited above.
[21] Ian Finlay, *Scotland* (Oxford, 1945), 123-4.

[22] *The Use of Scots for Prose* (John Galt Lecture, 1949; Greenock Philosophical Society), 17. See also '*Plastic Scots*' *and the Scottish Literary Tradition* (W. Maclellan, Glasgow, 1947).

[23] *Hansard*, H. of C., 1922, v. 150, c. 471. Text: *ibid.* c. 472.

[24] *Ibid.* v. 154, c. 1609-11.

[25] *Ibid.*, c. 1628-33.

[26] *Ibid.*, c. 1645.

[27] *Ibid.*, c. 1621-8.

[28] *Ibid.*, 1924, v. 173, c. 789.

[29] *Ibid.*, c. 790-6.

[30] *Ibid.*, c. 808.

[31] *Ibid.*, c. 800-1.

[32] *Ibid.*, c. 810.

[33] *Ibid.*, cc. 1340, 2189; v. 174, c. 2119.

[34] *Ibid.*, 1925, v. 189, c. 1612.

[35] *Ibid.*, 1926, v. 198, c. 2214; 1927, v. 202, c. 443, v. 206, c. 865-878; 1928, v. 215, c. 996-9.

[36] *Ibid.*, 1929, v. 229, c. 334.

[37] *Ibid.*, v. 230, c. 212; v. 231, c. 2206; v. 242, c. 694.

[38] *Ibid.*, 1932, v. 262, c. 773.

[39] *Ibid.*, v. 265, c. 1107-8.

[40] *Ibid.*, 1932-33, v. 272, c. 235-253.

[41] *Ibid.*, c. 259-267.

PART TEN

Post-War Postscript

IT SEEMED desirable to close the record of this book at the end of the last war; but, since the story is by no means finished— it is coming, indeed, to a climax at this moment of writing— it may be useful to summarise briefly the course of events since 1945.

Both in Wales and in Scotland public interest was absorbed for a time by the vast task of reconstruction and re-adjustment not only in Britain but in Europe and the overseas world. The nationalist agitation which had followed the First World War was not at once repeated. But it was not dead: it was only delayed; and, when presently it revived, it displayed in both countries a much greater strength and evoked a much wider response than it had before the war.

There were several reasons for this—in Scotland the alleged favouring of England in the reconstruction of devastated areas, in the siting of new factories, in the southward shifting of the terminals of transatlantic transport by air and sea and so forth: in Wales the adoption of hydro-electric schemes in aid of English as well as local industry to the detriment, it was held, of the natural beauty of mountain, lake and forest. But the chief grievance was the continuance of the war-time control exercised by the Government in London over Welsh and Scottish life. It was easy to ignore its necessity for the recovery of all Britain and easy to resent the interference it involved with personal freedoms and the host of minor officials it required for its administration; and the grievance was intensified when it appeared that one of the two main British parties wanted the control to be perpetuated as a cardinal feature of the ' welfare state.'

The remedy proposed by the more moderate Scottish nationalists was not new. It was the ' federal ' solution which had been so often advocated and rejected before the war. At the third annual assembly of Scottish Convention at Edinburgh in the autumn of 1949, a declaration, with the historic title of ' Scottish Covenant,' was published pledging the Scottish people, ' in all loyalty to the Crown and within the framework of the United Kingdom, to do everything in our power to secure for Scotland a Parliament with adequate legislative authority in Scottish affairs '—which meant, it was explained, a subordinate legislature on the model of Northern Ireland. Before long the Covenant obtained no less than 2,000 signatories, some of whom, no doubt, were ignorant or irresponsible, but others certainly were men of sense and standing. Naturally the movement appealed to the younger generation and in the autumn of 1950 the students of Glasgow University chose Mr. Robert McCormick, Chairman of Scottish Convention, for their Rector.

At the end of the year three of those students committed an act of wild misconduct which shocked public opinion in Britain and was widely reported elsewhere. On Christmas night they broke into Westminster Abbey, removed the so-called ' Stone of Destiny ' which had formed the seat of the Coronation Throne ever since it was carried away from Scone by Edward I as booty of war in 1296, and took it away by car to Scotland. For some time the secret of its whereabouts was kept; but in April the culprits were identified by the police and the Stone restored to Westminster. No legal proceedings were taken and the discussion in the newspapers on Scotland's right to recover the Stone soon died away.

Meantime the Scottish Covenanters continued their crusade for a Scottish Parliament, and they were supported up to a point by Scotsmen outside their ranks. In 1950 both the Assembly of the Scottish Kirk and the Convention of Scottish Burghs asked for a Royal Commission to examine the possibilities of Scottish self-government. In Wales, too, there was a marked revival of agitation. The Nationalists made contact with the Covenanters and began to campaign for a Welsh Covenant of the Scottish type.

As before the war and for the same reasons, the Nationalists could do little or nothing to affect the results of a General Election; but none of the Parties at Westminster could afford to ignore the movement altogether. Only the Liberals, however, were prepared to concede the Nationalist demand for a Parliament and at the end of 1949, they reinserted in their programme, after an interval of fifty years, the policy of Home Rule-all-round which they had adopted in 1901. Neither the Conservatives nor Labour were willing to go to that length. Mr. Churchill declared at Edinburgh in 1950 that his party had ' no intention of separating the link of parliamentary union which since 1707 has joined Scotland to Great Britain.' 'I feel sure,' he said, ' that with patience and firmness of character we can solve our difficulties together far better than if we sprawled apart.'[1] Mr. Attlee was known to share this opinion, and the Scottish T.U.C., while they asked for an inquiry into the possibilities of further administrative devolution, stood firmly by the legislative union.[2]

Anxious to conciliate nationalist opinion but unwilling to concede the drastic action it demanded, the post-war Labour Government attempted to appease it by a number of minor concessions. In 1948 the Standing Committee on Scottish Bills was authorised to discuss bills on second reading as well as at the Committee stage and also to discuss the Scottish estimates for six days instead of two; and a Scottish Economic Committee was appointed to confer with representatives of industry at Edinburgh. Later that year a bolder step was taken in Wales by Mr.

Herbert Morrison, Home Secretary. He created a ' Council of Wales and Monmouthshire' consisting of twenty-seven representatives of industrial, agricultural, educational and other cultural organisations. Its purpose, he explained, was ' to secure that the Government are adequately informed of the impact of Government activities on the general life of the people.' The Council was authorised only to discuss and report: it had no other powers; and its meetings were to be held *in camera*.[3] Naturally Welsh M.P.s resented this intrusion into a field they regarded as their own preserve; and, since the Council's proceedings could not be reported except by hearsay, the public soon lost interest in them. . . . In 1950 another concession was made to the Scottish Nationalists. A Committee was appointed with Lord Catto at its head to consider whether a separate estimate could be made of Government revenue and expenditure in Scotland as distinct from the United Kingdom as a whole. Could this be intended, it was asked, to prepare the ground for a discussion of ' federal ' devolution? . . . Lastly, in 1951, not long before the fall of the Labour Government, Mr. Chuter Ede, Home Secretary, manifested his sympathy with cultural nationalism in Wales. Learning that the champions of the Welsh language were greatly handicapped by the lack of sufficient books, especially school books, in Welsh, he set up a committee to consider the question. In the autumn of 1952 it recommended the establishment of a ' Welsh Books Foundation.' It should be provided for the first five years with an annual income of £40,000, derived partly from local and partly from central Government sources. Its function would be mainly to increase the supply of Welsh school books, but also to check the decline in the publication of general Welsh books. The proposed expenditure would be a small price to pay for ' the stimulation of Welsh authorship, publishing and reading, and thereby the preservation and development of the national character and life.'[4]

When Mr. Churchill took office he showed at once that he

was as mindful of Welsh opinion as his predecessors. He did not concede the separate Secretaryship of State for Wales which the Nationalists had long demanded, but he provided a sort of substitute for it. The Home Secretary, Sir D. Maxwell Fyfe (West Derby, Liverpool) was to act as ' Minister for Welsh Affairs.'

In Scotland Mr. Churchill made a different move. When the Catto Committee reported in July that it was possible to prepare a separate return of Government revenue and expenditure in Scotland, he at once announced the appointment of a Royal Commission ' to review, with reference to the financial, economic, administrative and other considerations involved, the arrangements for exercising the functions of His Majesty's Government in Scotland.' These were not the terms of reference which Scottish Nationalists had wanted. There was a significant omission, and Mr. J. Wheatley (Edinburgh E.) asked if the terms were ' designed to exclude consideration of legislative devolution.' ' Legislative devolution,' replied the Secretary of State for Scotland (Mr. J. Stuart, Moray and Nairn), ' is considered to be a matter for Parliament.' When Mr. Clement Davies asked if the same privilege would be extended to Wales, Mr. Churchill said he would await the verdict of the Scottish Commission.[5]

---

[1] *Scotsman*, May 20, 1950.
[2] *Ibid.*, April 22, 1950.
[3] *The Times*, Nov. 25, 1948–.
[4] Cmd. 8661. *The Times*, Oct. 9, 1952.
[5] *Hansard*, H. of C., 1952; v. 503, c. 771-5.

Conclusion

WE CAN now at last return to the questions raised at the outset of this book and weigh them in the light of the facts recorded in it. Does the spirit of a nation require a political body in order to maintain its life and vigour? 'If so, must it be a state? Need it ever be a sovereign state?' So far our answer to both questions has been No. Save for one brief period of virtual independence in the days of the Llywelyns Wales has never been a state, and Scotland ceased to be a state two centuries and a half ago. Yet the Welsh and Scottish nations are still vigorously alive. *A fortiori* a nation need not be embodied in a sovereign state, if indeed any such thing now exists in the western world.

But, if that has been sure enough till yesterday, it is not so sure to-day. For, while the Welsh and the Scots have so far succeeded in preserving their national identity, a second process has been steadily at work. Long association has made most Welshmen and Scotsmen feel that they are not only Welsh and Scots but also Britons and that ever since the Elizabethan age they have shared with the English in a great common tradition—the defence and development of liberty at home and its extension overseas. And since the three nations have not only done ' great things together ' but live in the same island, speak (with relatively slight exceptions) the same language, and are fast acquiring a similar way of life, it might fairly be said that the British state has come to incorporate a composite British nation. So far, so good. In this ' age of violence ' the supra-national unity of Britain, the combination of its three nations for their common defence, is still what it has been for centuries past, the main safe-guard of liberty in Europe. But this process of integration may

412

be too complete. Strategy only requires political and economic unity: it is not concerned with culture; yet, as has been shown in the preceding chapters of this book, political and economic unity has tended to promote cultural uniformity. And since England is so predominant a partner, does not this integration mean that in the long run Wales and Scotland will lose their distinctive cultural character and, save only in their Celtic blood and their memories of the past, will differ from England no more than Yorkshire differs from Devon? If so, the long process of anglicisation will have reached its climax. Wales will have been reconquered, Scotland conquered at last.

Anyone who welcomes this conclusion fails to distinguish between uniformity and unity. Unity is the safeguard of freedom. Uniformity is one of its most dangerous foes, clinching the stranglehold of mass production, mass thinking, mass emotion, on modern life, and reaching its logical end in a totalitarian society. It negates and crushes out that diversity in habit, thought and art by which the spirit of man is nourished and enlightened. Hence the need of combating uniformity with all our strength: hence the value to all Britain of the efforts described in this book to preserve distinctive national ways of life in Wales and Scotland.

One final question must now be faced. Would it reinforce these efforts if the Welsh and Scottish nations were incorporated in some kind of state? Hitherto, as has just been said, it has not been needed, but may it not be needed now that the forces of centralisation and assimilation have become so powerful? It could only be, of course, a subordinate ' federal ' kind of state. Strategic necessity and economic integration rule out Dominion Status, still more the visionary independence which the more headstrong nationalists demand. But might not the possibility of local parliaments and governments as contemplated by the now long-forgotten Speaker's Conference[a] be reconsidered?

[a] See page 321 above.

A strong case can be made against a ' federal' reconstruction of Britain.

(1) It would greatly increase the cost of government both in money and in man-power.

(2) In so far as purely local affairs may require varying treatment they can be handled by local governments, but national affairs are broadly the same for all three nations. Why triple the legislative and administrative machinery needed to deal with them?

(3) Scottish legislation is already practically determined by Scottish members of Parliament; and administrative devolution in Scotland, if not in Wales, has already gone far enough to complicate and embarrass the work of central government.

(4) A primary function of the national governments would be the maintenance of the social services. Could they maintain them at their present level from their own resources? They would still have to bear their share of British taxation for such essential common purposes as defence. Would the residue suffice? If not, either the standard of the services must fall or the national governments must be aided by grants from the British Treasury, and that would mean that the power of spending public money would be divorced from the responsibility for raising it.[a]

Welsh and Scottish Nationalists would contest these arguments.

(1) Administrative devolution, they would say, however far it is carried is not self-government. In fact and in law the government of Wales and Scotland is under the control of a Parliament in which their representatives are a small minority.

(2) Only Welsh and Scottish governments controlling their national ways of life can avail to check the English cultural ' conquest' and the disastrous uniformity it threatens to impose.

(3) Only a ' federal' reconstruction of Britain can lighten the

[a] That this a common practice in local government is no excuse for its application to a much wider field. For further arguments, see Sir Robert Horne's speech (page 402 above), and the anti-federalist opinions expressed at the Speaker's Conference (pages 326-7 above).

burden borne by Parliament[a] and prevent the final conversion of parliamentary government as we have known it into parliamentary bureaucracy.

(4) A 'federal' reconstruction, similarly, would check the process of increasing the power of the central authority at the expense of the local self-government in which British liberty is historically rooted.

(5) The higher cost could be borne at need, and more than once in our time the British people have shown that there is no limit to the sacrifices they are willing to endure when their freedom is at stake.

The issue is plain. On its decision the future of Welsh and Scottish nationalism depends.

[a] See the warning given by Major Wood (now Lord Halifax) in 1918 (page 318 above) and by Lord Rosebery in 1882 (page 295 above).

THE END

INDEX